FOURTH EDITION

Global Marketing *and* Advertising

FOURTH EDITION

Global Marketing *and* Advertising

Understanding Cultural Paradoxes

Marieke de Mooij

Los Angeles | London | New Delhi
Singapore | Washington DC

Los Angeles | London | New Delhi
Singapore | Washington DC

FOR INFORMATION:

SAGE Publications, Inc.
2455 Teller Road
Thousand Oaks, California 91320
E-mail: order@sagepub.com

SAGE Publications Ltd.
1 Oliver's Yard
55 City Road
London EC1Y 1SP
United Kingdom

SAGE Publications India Pvt. Ltd.
B 1/I 1 Mohan Cooperative Industrial Area
Mathura Road, New Delhi 110 044
India

SAGE Publications Asia-Pacific Pte. Ltd.
3 Church Street
#10-04 Samsung Hub
Singapore 049483

Printed in the United States of America

Library of Congress Cataloging-in-Publication Data

Mooij, Marieke K. de, 1943–

Global marketing and advertising : understanding cultural paradoxes / Marieke de Mooij. — Fourth Edition.

pages cm
Includes bibliographical references and index.

ISBN 978-1-4522-5717-4

1. Target marketing—Cross-cultural studies.
2. Advertising—Cross-cultural studies. 3. Consumer behavior—Cross-cultural studies. I. Title.

HF5415.127.M66 2013
658.8'02—dc23   2013016276

Acquisitions Editor: Patricia Quinlin
Editorial Assistant: Katie Guarino
Assistant Editor: Megan Koraly
Production Editor: Jane Haenel
Copy Editor: Patrice Sutton
Typesetter: C&M Digitals (P) Ltd.
Proofreader: Rae-Ann Goodwin
Indexer: Terri Corry
Cover Designer: Bryan Fishman
Marketing Manager: Liz Thornton

This book is printed on acid-free paper.

13 14 15 16 17 10 9 8 7 6 5 4 3 2 1

COVENTRY UNIVERSITY LONDON CAMPUS

Brief Contents

Detailed Contents

Foreword

A naive set of assumptions, quite common in both business and academia up till the present day, is that people's rationality as a producer differs from their rationality as a consumer. Producers' rationality is supposed to mean maximizing income; consumers' rationality is something for marketing people to discover.

Fundamentally, there is not such a thing as a universal rationality—a discovery which economists applying "rational choice" models have yet to make. What is rational or irrational to a person depends on that person's value system, which in turn is part of the culture this person has acquired early in her or his lifetime. What people around the world value varies enormously: It includes poverty next to maximizing income, togetherness next to individuality, cooperation next to competition, modesty next to assertiveness, saving next to spending, chastity next to sexual fulfilment, self-effacement next to self-actualization. Downsizing personnel in order to maximize a company's profits may be rational in one society—say, the United States—but not in another—say, Japan—in which employees' commitment is the company's main capital.

Marketing and advertising are basically about consumers, not about producers. Marketing and advertising theories based on producers' logic but missing consumers' logic are useless. Market research agencies try to bridge the gap between the two kinds of logic, and their excellence depends on their ability to make the producer think in consumers' terms. Even within one country, this is not easy; it becomes extremely difficult if consumers are children of other countries' cultures.

In the broader area of management, ethnocentric approaches over the past thirty years have gradually lost support, if only because they proved ineffective, even fatal. International or comparative management has become a recognized subdiscipline of management education; no current management text- or handbook can do without it, even if the treatment of the subject often betrays hidden ethnocentrism.

It is a paradox that in the areas of marketing and advertising theories, ethnocentrism has survived longer than in (general) management. A paradox, because if there is one aspect of the business that is culture-dependent, it is consumer behavior. As Marieke de Mooij argues, there may be global products, but there are no global people. The success of a business in the end depends on how well its products reach customers whose behavior is affected by values that may vary in unexpected ways from those of the business managers.

Marieke de Mooij is a world pioneer in the field of culture and marketing. She brought along a thorough experience base in advertising, extensive teaching and consulting experience in different parts of the world, and the ability to empathize with people in other countries. The evolution of this book—four editions since 1998, each new version thoroughly re-worked, reflects her leadership in the field. The book is now adopted at universities worldwide, equally in the various world regions.

In the first edition, she linked her insights into marketing and advertising practice in different parts of the world to state-of-the-art outcomes of culture research. The second, 2005 edition, integrated new information about differences in consumer behavior and their development over time. The third, 2010 edition, kept up with the dynamics of electronic media including the cultural role of websites and with the cultural component in product and packaging design. This fourth edition, with more world regions covered and based on more comparative data than ever, confirms the stability of value differences over time. It shows how the usage of modern media reflects basic differences in human communication. Age-old philosophies like Buddhism and Hinduism are still at the root of Eastern communication, just like Western communication has built its theories on Aristotle's *Rhetoric*.

This foreword is written at a time of ongoing global business crisis, in which cultural factors are playing a crucial role. Success in cross-cultural marketing asks for a new style of marketing leadership. Not, at least as the stereotype goes, oriented to quick judgment and action according to trusted principles. The successful cross-cultural marketing manager is more reflective, open to alternatives, with a broad interest in other societies and what makes people in them tick. This book is for those aspiring to be or become that kind of person.

Geert Hofstede
Velp, The Netherlands, March 2013

Preface to the Fourth Edition

Interest in understanding culture's influence on marketing and advertising is growing worldwide. New digital developments in the global marketplace also reinforce the need to understand how communication works across cultures, as the digital media are hybrid forms of interpersonal and mass communication. This is an important addition to the text.

Next to updates throughout the book, other changes are a result of comments from users. I changed Chapter 4 substantially, covering the three major dimensional models and explaining why the Hofstede model still is the most useful one for application to marketing and advertising. Both practitioners and students should be able to understand the basics of how they operate and be able to compare them to make a choice. I extended this comparative analysis to Chapter 6 and made it into a chapter for researchers, for analyzing the different models for application in research, moving the value structure map to Chapter 11 on strategy.

Chapter 5 on culture and consumer behavior was substantially updated and a few topics were added. Chapter 7 now includes sections on human communication across cultures and explains how different age-old philosophies of each world region are at the basis of human communication. I moved Public Relations, product- and packaging design as well as retail to the final chapter on strategy. To that chapter, I added a summary of market entry strategies and the marketing mix. Some users would expect this at the beginning of the book, however, as this book focuses on the influence of culture, and culture must be explained first, I deal with most strategic aspects in the final chapter.

Chapter 8 on media includes information on culture's influence on the traditional media and the electronic media, in particular the Internet and mobile phone. It is important to understand how people use the ubiquitous social media and why the design of these media varies. Many data are now available on usage differences.

Chapters 9 and 10 have remained more or less the same. Some of the illustrations and charts were updated or replaced by new ones, some have been added, but many are still valid examples, so these were not changed. I have been able to cover more and different countries in the various world regions, but not all areas have a similar amount of data available.

Instructor Resource Site

The password-protected Instructor Site at www.sagepub.com/demooij4e gives instructors access to a full complement of resources to support and enhance their courses. The following assets are available on the instructor site:

- Editable, chapter-specific Microsoft® PowerPoint® slides offer you complete flexibility in easily creating a multimedia presentation for your course. Highlight essential content, features, and artwork from the book.
- Chapter-specific questions, key points, and activities help launch discussion and learning by prompting students to engage with the material and by reinforcing important content.
- In-text images are available for instructors to download and include in handouts, lecture slides, and teaching visuals.
- A wide array of international commercial videos and add images are provided for instructors to support the text and chapter content.

Acknowledgments

For this fourth edition, I acknowledge the input by the reviewers Deborah DeLong, Maria Kniazeva, Peter Magnussen, Patrice Prusko Torcivia, Paolo Sigismondi, Maria Elena Villar, and Christine M. Von Der Haar; all those who have helped me with the three previous editions; Marlies van Oudheusden of Ipsos Synovate in Amsterdam for providing the data of EMS 2012; and Susanna Lam of Ipsos in Hong Kong for providing data of the Young Asians Survey.

Marieke de Mooij
www.mariekedemooij.com

Summary of the Book

This book describes the various problems and opportunities of culture in global marketing and advertising. It argues that the main dispute in global marketing and advertising should not be about the efficiency of standardization but about the effectiveness of cultural segmentation. Knowledge of cultural specifics or the value paradoxes is the basis of effective marketing communication strategies.

Chapter 1 introduces the concept of the value paradox and the paradoxes in globalization and in global marketing theory. It discusses the global-local dilemma and a few of the myths of global marketing: the assumed existence of global communities and convergence of consumer behavior. It summarizes the standardization-adaptation debate in global marketing.

Chapter 2 describes the brand concept, branding models, and various aspects of global branding: what makes a successful global brand, how global brands are perceived by consumers, and the role of global brand communication. It defines the brand as an association network in the minds of consumers.

Chapter 3 introduces the value concept and defines culture. It describes various aspects of culture, such as language, signs and symbols, imagery and music, and global culture.

Chapter 4 describes various classifications of culture, such as concepts of time and high and low context. The three major dimensional models of national culture, by Hofstede, Schwartz, and GLOBE are described and compared for application to marketing and advertising.

Chapter 5 provides an overview of the influence of culture of various consumer behavior theories. Four aspects of consumer behavior are covered: consumer attributes (the self and personality), social processes (needs, motivation, emotion, and group processes), mental processes (perception, information processing, and decision making), and consumer behavior domains (product ownership and usage, brand loyalty and diffusion of innovations).

Chapter 6 deals with the various problems of value research across cultures. Examples of country-specific values are given. It explains how to compare different dimensional models and specifics for applying the Hofstede model to advertising. It provides some information about commercial value and lifestyle studies.

Chapter 7 deals with communication and culture. How we communicate is related to culture, which is reflected in interpersonal communication and in how we use the new electronic means of communication, that are hybrid forms of personal and mass communication. It demonstrates how the age-old philosophies of the major world regions explain current communication behavior. Culture explains differences in advertising styles, and these differences are also reflected in website design. The creation of advertising follows assumptions of how advertising works that are based on U.S. studies of how consumers process information.

Chapter 8 describes how media usage is influenced by culture: both usage of the traditional media, television, radio, and press and the new electronic media. It also points at other media that may be effective in reaching consumers in emerging markets. The differences of various activities on the Internet, such as e-commerce, social networks, and blogging, are described and how culture can explain these. Several forms of advertising on the Internet have emerged. Internet marketing and advertising are described including social media marketing, viral marketing, and mobile marketing and advertising.

Chapter 9 describes the value paradoxes in advertising appeals and explains how appeals in advertising reflect culture. It also shows examples of advertising ideas and concepts that can or cannot travel.

Chapter 10 describes seven basic advertising forms and the degree to which they are culture-related, with many examples.

Chapter 11 deals with aspects of strategy. At corporate level, entry modes of international markets are summarized, and the mission statement, corporate identity, and international public relations are discussed. At marketing level, the global marketing mix is discussed including product/market development across cultures, product and packaging design, and retail. An important part is brand positioning across cultures or the matching of identity and image which across cultures is even more difficult than within cultures. Finally, several marketing communication strategies are reviewed and the different strategies to be used at different stages of market development.

Appendix A provides a list of countries with scores for the Hofstede dimensions and income per capita of 2011. The data can be used by students for cultural analysis of consumption data or for making culture maps for products or brands.

Appendix B reviews the various databases used for the cross-cultural analysis presented in this book.

CHAPTER 1

The Paradoxes in Global Marketing Communications

I n a meeting between the Duke of Wellington and Napoleon after the battle of Waterloo, Wellington is said to have reproached Napoleon with the words "You fight for power, we fight for honor," and Napoleon is said to have answered, "Yes, one always fights for what one does not have."

The two had fought with different approaches to the battlefield. Wellington was a military leader and saw himself as an agent of the British government. Napoleon's perspective was that of a head of state in pursuit of glory.[1] To some, honor comes with the function, and one doesn't have to fight for it, and true honor is public esteem or glory. For others, honor is faithful performance of duty. Again, for others, honor is inner integrity. There are as many different kinds of honor as social groups.[2]

What seems paradoxical is that in some nations, one has to fight for something that in other nations is inherent in the function or the person. Skills that come automatically in one part of the world have to be learned in another part of the world. Leadership is a concept that comes automatically to the French: You have it or you don't. There is no proper word for leadership in either the French or the Spanish languages. In the United States, leadership is an integral part of primary education; children in elementary schools take turns being class leader for the day and may be publicly honored for their efforts. U.S. leaders are the heroes of capitalism; they are admired, whether they succeed or fail. Japanese leaders are faceless.

Advertising often appeals to what is lacking in society. The happy family is more often depicted in advertising in nations where family coherence is lacking. In countries where family is part of one's identity, advertising focuses less on family values. Family is like air: You don't have to pay attention to it.

In global marketing, "think global, act local" is a paradox. Thinking and behavior are equally influenced by culture. Someone who thinks globally is still a product of his or her own culture. Watching young people worldwide drinking Coca-Cola or wearing jeans may lead some to conclude that they are becoming the same, but there is ample evidence that to consumers, the local is more meaningful than the global. Global marketers suggest a global youth segment with homogeneous desires. However, when global youth cultural styles are readily available, a localized version of youth culture emerges.[3]

The Internet is the ultimate example of global communication. In particular, the Internet is assumed to cross cultural barriers.[4] Yet, in the short time of its existence, it has become very local as people in different countries use it in different ways and in different languages. The technology needed for computers to communicate with other computers was invented by the American defense research agency. The Internet as we use it now was invented by a British computer scientist and developed in the English language world, but in 2008, most weblogs were not in English but in the Japanese language.[5] Already in 2005, a relatively high level of localization of websites for global brands of U.S. origin was reported.[6]

Globalization has not produced globally uniform consumers. Although there is a worldwide convergence of technology, media, and financial systems, desires and behaviors of consumers are not converging.

These are examples of paradoxical aspects that marketing and advertising managers have to understand when they enter the global marketplace.

This chapter introduces the concept of the value paradox, discusses a few global marketing paradoxes, and summarizes assumed effects of globalization, such as convergence of consumer behavior. Finally, because of the continuing debate on standardizing or adapting global marketing, branding, and advertising strategy, a short history of that dialogue is provided discussing the various aspects of standardization-adaptation decisions.

The Value Paradox

Skills that come automatically in one part of the world have to be learned in another part of the world. Although teamwork training is big business in the United States, there is hardly a market for it in Japan. Individualistic behavior comes spontaneously to Americans, but the Japanese have to learn it. The Japanese, for whom group values are so important, have to learn to be self-reliant and to take greater responsibility for their own actions.

Chaos is said to be a key ingredient of Silicon Valley's success. But chaos management has not been accepted as a management style in all of corporate America because it conflicts with the desire for control. It is paradoxical to suggest that the Germans would benefit by a bit more chaos instead of rules. The Germans cannot thrive on chaos. On the contrary, German life is highly structured.

Tradition and modernity are seen as contradictions in the West; in Japan, they go side by side. The Japanese can be conservative and at the same time attracted by new ways. Whereas in the West, the old must be discarded and the new must be embraced, in much of Asia, the traditional is exploited, recycled into modern ways of life.

Paradoxical values are found within cultures and between cultures. Every culture has its opposing values. Equality is an American core value, yet in the United States, there is a wide gap between rich and poor. What is confusing in the global marketplace is that certain opposing values of one culture also exist in other cultures but in reverse. An example is the individual freedom-belonging paradox. Individualism is a strong element of American society, and so is the need to belong. It seems paradoxical that both freedom and belonging are strong values of a single culture. The explanation is that in an individualistic society where people want to "do things their own way" and "go it alone," people tend to become lonely if they don't make an effort to belong. The reverse is found in Japan, where belonging is an integral part of society, and it takes an effort to behave in an individualistic way. According to the American Society of Association Executives in Washington, D.C., in 1995, there were some 100,000 associations and clubs in the United States. Seven of every 10 Americans belong to at least one club.[7] There is no such phenomenon in Japan. It is said that social media like Facebook facilitate making friends. However, according to Dr. John Cacioppo, in the United States, Facebook increases feelings of loneliness. In other parts of the world, for example, in Asia and Africa, social media reinforce community feelings.[8]

These are examples of what I call the *value paradox*. Paradoxes are statements that seem contradictory but are actually true. Understanding these paradoxes is basic to understanding the consequences of culture for global communications, branding, and advertising. More about the value paradox can be found in Chapter 3.

The Global-Local Paradox

The way people think and perceive is guided by the framework of their own culture. People are inclined to see similarities from the framework of their own culture. These similarities are often pseudo-similarities. They are based on what people want to see, not on what is actually there. Perception of the phenomenon of Japanese individuality as a sign of Westernization of the Japanese is an example of such a misperception.

The global-local paradox is that the more people know about other countries and cultures, the more they become aware of their own cultural or national identity. Along with unification of the different European nations, when citizens of the various nations learned more about each other, symbols and appeals in advertising became more nationally oriented.[9]

Along with globalization, people increasingly prefer local music. At the beginning of the 21st century in the United States, 93% of music sold was by local artists. In Japan, it was 74% and across Europe more than 50%.[10] In 2008, most young people said their favorite singers were local. In China, the most popular singer was Jay Chou; in India, it was Himesh Reshammiya; in Australia, it was Fall Out Boy; and in Taiwan, it was Jolin Tsai.[11] Marketing knowledge has spread across the world, but its use has supported localization of products and services rather than standardization.[12]

The Technology Paradox

Technological development is increasingly global, but the argument that technological development makes us global and leads toward similar needs for similar products is not correct. There is great variety in the adoption of technological innovations and usage of technological products. In economically developed countries, one would expect a similar penetration of personal computers and Internet usage, but the percentages of people who have a PC at home still vary considerably, also across equally wealthy countries. Examples in Asia are 65% in Japan versus 92% in South Korea, and in Europe 98% for Finland versus 56% in Italy.[13] The Netherlands and Belgium are neighboring countries and economically similar. Yet it took the Belgians a much longer time to accept the Internet than the Dutch. Although in the developed countries most people now have access to the Internet, the way people use the Internet still varies considerably, and these differences are not related to national wealth. For example, the frequency of usage, what people do on the Internet, and the place where people access the internet vary across nations. With converging economic development, only cultural values can explain such differences. That is what this book is all about.

Statistical analysis of ownership and usage of technological products confirms that convergence of technology is not the same as convergence of people's values and habits. Instead, technology reinforces the differences and together with increased wealth leads to divergent behavior instead of convergence. People will embrace new technology to do the things they are used to doing, but in a nicer or more efficient way.

The Media Paradox

The growing number of satellites and global TV channels is supposed to create a global village in which anybody can receive any TV channel. This is theory. In reality, there is no viewer freedom. Increasingly, media companies decide what viewers in a country can access: usually only national or local channels and a limited number of mostly non-commercial channels from other countries. A variety of techniques and coding systems across countries makes it virtually impossible to receive everything that is available on satellite. In some ways, in the less technologically advanced, non-commercialized Europe of the past when the airwaves were government controlled, there was more freedom to receive television programs from other countries than there is with the new technology. Inhabitants of the Netherlands, for example, do not have access to commercial TV channels in their neighboring country, Belgium. The Internet, still viewed as the ultimate global medium, already has become local as it instantly recognizes a computer's local IP address and adapts its content accordingly.

Paradoxes in Global Marketing Theory

The concept of marketing and many of the theories of consumer behavior with respect to consumption, buying, and communication originated in the United States and have been copied and used by teachers in many other countries. There is little evidence of meaningful adaptations of these theories to other cultures. As a result, numerous students of marketing and advertising have learned marketing and consumer behavior theory that is relevant for marketing to U.S. consumers and that may not always fit consumer behavior in their own countries. This has led to paradoxical concepts.

Local Markets Are People, Global Markets Are Products

A much discussed topic in global marketing and advertising is the choice between global and local, reaping the economic benefits of standardized production or accommodating local consumer needs and habits for greater effectiveness. The paradoxical aspect is that all marketers have learned that markets are people, which should translate into a local approach, but when companies go global, they are production driven. They talk about products, brands, and markets, not about people. There may be global products, but there are no global people. There may be global brands, but there are no global motivations for buying those brands.

The Sony Walkman is often used as an example of a global product, developed for global consumers with global needs, who would use it with similar motives. That is not true: There are two distinctly different motives for using that product. In the Western world, the motive is to enjoy music without being disturbed by others. This was not the motive for Masaru Ibuka—cofounder with Akio Morita of the Sony Corporation—for inventing the Walkman. He wanted to listen to music without disturbing others.[14]

Advertisers take great pains to try to understand certain subcultures, such as youth culture, knowing that they can appeal to the young only if they address them in the right way. When it comes to addressing adult women or men of different national cultures with very different value systems, many advertisers suddenly think one standard message is sufficient. This is paradoxical behavior.

The decision to standardize has more to do with corporate culture than with the culture of markets and nations. Many global advertisers are not market oriented; they are product oriented. They search for that one universal great idea to sell their one standard product to assumed universal, global consumers. This is demonstrated by the fact that cost saving is most often mentioned as argument for standardization. In reality, the cost of developing one standard idea that truly crosses borders is very high. To get consensus about a "great idea," product managers, marketing managers, country managers, advertising managers, account supervisors, account directors, and creative directors of advertising agencies and the like in various countries have to get together, organizing meetings and travel. Then, in the end, it appears that many adaptations are needed. Voice-overs or subtitles have to be made, pack shots must be changed, and texts have to be translated, adapted, or rewritten. Slogans developed for global use have to be translated, and in the end, some translations appear to include subtle changes of meaning influenced by culture.

People of different countries speak different languages, and those languages represent different worldviews. Translations do not uncover the different worldviews, different ways of thinking, and different intellectual styles. International advertising consultant Simon Anholt[15] says, "Translating advertising copy is like painting the tip of an iceberg and hoping the whole thing will turn red." Advertising is more than words; it is made of culture.

Focus on a Unique Individual

Theories of buying behavior, decision making, and communication behavior generally describe individuals of Western societies, who are defined as unique personalities. When the influence of groups on individual buying behavior is considered from the sociological perspective, the individual is implicitly unique, as in Western societies. The group dynamics of Eastern societies are ignored.

The concepts of self and personality that are the basis of Western consumer behavior theories are drawn from Anglo-Saxon psychological research and include the hypothesis that people will buy products that are compatible with their self-concept or that will enhance their ideal self-image. Culture plays an important role in the construal of self and in the perception of ideal images. An example is the ideal woman's figure. The fashion industry tends to present the ideal woman's figure as slim: The figure of the Barbie doll has become a white adolescent ideal. But even within the United States, the degree to which this is perceived as ideal varies: Contrary to white teens, black teens connect a full figure, rather than a slim one, with health and fertility.[16] More about this is included in Chapter 5.

Modern branding theory was developed in the United States and the United Kingdom and uses concepts from Western psychology. Metaphors such as brand identity and brand personality are used and exported to countries in which words for *identity* or *personality* do not exist in the local language. Asking people about "brand personality" in Asia will result in irrelevant answers. Yet many global marketers, because of their need for consistency, wish to communicate one uniform global brand personality.

Globalization

Globalization in the broadest sense is defined by Robertson as "the concrete structuration of the world as a whole"[17] The term *globalization* is used to cover the global flow of capital, technology, and media, as well as changes in human behavior that are expected to result from globalization forces. The level of world trade is much higher than ever before and involves a much wider range of goods and services than it used to in the past. The biggest change, however, is in the level of finance and capital flows.[18]

Global communication refers to the flow of information, communication, communication products, media, and technology worldwide. Next to the term *global*, the term *international* is used that strictly taken refers to communication between nations and between members of nations. There are many assumptions about the effects of global communications that rarely have been substantiated. Global media and advertising are expected to mould consumers into one global consumer culture. The Internet is viewed as the ultimate globalization tool, but defining the Internet as global in its usage is dangerous. Increasingly, all sorts of software are localized. Some social networks may be global services, but they are mostly used to connect to people already known in local communities.

The globalization discourse in marketing is dominated by Anglo-Saxon authors. As a result, many of the most visible expressions mentioned as examples are Coca-Cola, McDonald's, or Starbuck's. Especially in the 1980s when the globalization discussion started, the U.S. penetration of global markets was particularly aggressive and visible, writes Harvard professor John Quelch.[19] As a result, some view globalization as Americanization.

The success of global brands has led some writers to predict an inevitable colonization of world cultures by international corporate brands that would lead to the demise of local cultures. However, there also is evidence that social relationships and values in local cultures are relatively resistant to the assumed erosive effects of globalization. Ethnographic studies of mobile phone use in South Korea and of MTV in East Asia found that proliferation of global products and services in East Asia, instead of destroying local cultures, reinforced and reinvented moral values in local communities.[20] This is the paradoxical aspect of globalization at which Giddens[21] points, when he defines globalization as "a complex set of processes that operate in a contradictory or oppositional fashion." On the one hand, globalization is expected to destroy local cultures; on the other hand, it is the reason for the revival of local cultural identities in different parts of the world.

Convergence and Divergence of Consumer Behavior

Industrialization, modernization, wealth, and technology are supposed to bring a universal civilization, including universal values and consumption patterns. This is a distinctive product of Western thinking.[22] As U.S. advertising professor John Philip Jones[23] states, "Logic points to similar patterns emerging in other countries when their per capita income levels approach that of the United States." The concept of a rational consumer plays an important role in convergence theory. Economic convergence is assumed to lead to better educated consumers, resulting in rational choice behavior.

The consumption symbols of the assumed universal civilization are mainly Western or American. As a result, global cultural homogeneity is also called "Westernization," "Americanization," or "cultural imperialism," suggesting that Western companies with their global brands force Western lifestyles on consumers in other parts of the world. The idea is not new, and, not specifically American. Already in 1958, the Italian Stefano Bakonyi[24] wrote about divergence and convergence in culture and communication and stated that the vigorous expansion on the part of Western culture had carried Western emotional values and concepts to the far corners of the globe and had also made them a common treasury of non-Western cultural communities. But he also warned that the process would not go on without inducing a counter-expansion of non-Western values and concepts, in particular those of the potent sleeping cultures of India and China. This is indeed happening in the 21st century, now that China and India have become important players in world markets.

In the developed world, countries have economically converged to the extent that the majority of people have enough to eat and have additional income to invest in new technology and other durable goods. Countries may be similar with respect to penetration of such goods, but not with respect to what people do with them or the motives for buying them. Technology has not brought a global village in which global consumers behave in the same way.

When the Canadian media philosopher Marshall McLuhan[25] coined the concept of the global village, he was referring to Plato's definition of the proper size for a city—the number of people who could hear the voice of the public speaker. By the global village, McLuhan meant that the new electric media of his time, such as telephone and television, abolished the spatial dimension. By means of electricity, people everywhere could resume person-to-person relations, as if on the smallest village scale. Thus, McLuhan viewed the electronic media as extensions of human beings. They enhance people's activities; they do not change people. If you assume people are the same everywhere, global media extend homogeneity. If you realize that people are different, extensions reinforce the differences. McLuhan did not include cultural convergence in the concept of the global village. In fact, he said the opposite—that uniqueness and diversity could be fostered under electronic conditions as never before.

This is exactly what new technology has accomplished. People have embraced it to enhance current activities. In the cold climates where people used to preserve food in the snow, they have embraced deep-freeze technology most intensely. The colder the climate, the more deep freezers. Initially, the mobile phone penetrated fastest in countries that already had advanced fixed telecommunications infrastructures, but after that initial stage, it penetrated most intensely in cultures where interpersonal communication is more important than written communication. The World Bank publishes data from the International Telecommunication Union (ITU)[26] that show that the numbers of mobile subscribers per 100 population vary strongly, from 93 in the United States to 215 in Hong Kong. In Japan, school children on long commutes to school would read *manga* (Japanese cartoons) books to pass the time. Now they play video games on Nintendo's Game Boy or on their mobile phones.[27] Contrary to expectations, people have embraced the Internet and other new technology mostly to enhance their current activities; it mainly has reinforced existing habits. Where people like to talk, the mobile phone allows them to talk more; where people like to write, the Internet has facilitated writing. The Internet has not changed people. It has reinforced existing habits, which instead of converging tend to diverge.

Whatever convergence takes place is at a *macro level,* such as convergence of demographic phenomena like national wealth or graying populations. If consumption converges, it also is mainly at the macro level, and it follows economic development (i.e., household penetration of products, such as dishwashers or color television sets). Empirical evidence of convergence tends to be based on macro data, such as the numbers of telephones, television sets, or passenger cars per 1,000 population.

There is increasing evidence that at *micro level,* there is little convergence. U.S. sociologist Alex Inkeles[28] finds that macro-level data often mask diversity at micro level. Convergence at a macro level—for example, convergence of Gross National Income (GNI) per capita (the new term for Gross National Product [GNP] per capita)—does not necessarily imply convergence of consumer choice. Countries similar economically are not necessarily similar in their consumption behavior, media usage, and availability patterns. There is no support for the argument that increased global mobility for business and vacations will cause people to homogenize. People do not travel to an extent that they are frequently confronted with other cultures. Even if all people were to have enough money to travel abroad, they would not all travel to the same extent. In 2007, only 27% of the inhabitants of 25 European countries said they had traveled abroad three times in the previous 3 years.[29] Only 9% had a job that involved contact with organizations or people in other countries. Annually, only 0.4% of Europeans (1.5 million) worked in another European Union member state; 2.4% of Americans work in a state other than the one where they grew up. In 2004, the percentage of people who *lived and worked* in another country in Europe than the one where they grew up is even lower: 0.1%, or 225,000 people.[30] In 2011 in Europe, 44% of young people aged 15 to 35 years old were not willing to work in another country. These percentages varied between 20% in Sweden, 41% in the United Kingdom, and 55% in Italy.[31]

The proportion of people around the world who watch international television programs regularly is small. Global television channels, such as CNN and MTV, were envisaged as global standard channels but have localized content and language. For some time, it was assumed that watching North-American television soaps would lead to cultural homogenization or that watching television programs from other cultures would change basic values, but this was based on the assumption of a homogeneous media audience, consisting of members who will process programs in similar ways. When in their study of *Dallas* across cultures Liebes and Katz[32] asked for the meaning derived from this soap opera, respondents from other cultures derived all sorts of different meanings from the soap than intended by the producers, and these meanings were related to their own culture (see also Chapter 11). Whatever effects were found were very weak, mainly that exposure to foreign TV might increase purchase of foreign products.[33]

Also, young people do not travel to an extent that induces them to adopt different habits and values. Of the young Europeans who visit other European countries, the majority do so while on vacation.[34] White[35] adds that people on vacation are not in a mood that has much to do with their domestic purchasing behavior, so the relevance of any advertising they see is limited.

Differences in consumer behavior across countries are persistent. As people around the globe become well educated and more affluent, their tastes actually diverge. With increased wealth, people accord greater relevance to their civilizational identity.[36] At a certain level of economic development, in what I have called "postscarcity"[37] societies—when people's stomachs are filled, when most people can afford proper housing and durable products, such as cars and television sets— people reach a higher level of unsatisfied needs. That is the moment when cultural values become manifest, and these are reflected in the different choices of products and brands. At that level, countries tend to diverge. What people do with their incremental income, the extra money they have after they have bought the necessary durables to live a comfortable life, varies increasingly. If, for example, we look at ownership of digital cameras in 2011,[38] national wealth explained differences across countries worldwide, but the influence was weaker when we compared 28 countries worldwide with GNI per capita over US$19,000. Then the main explaining variable was cultural. The phenomenon is strongest in Europe, where countries have converged most in terms of GNI per capita. With respect to cultural values, Europe is not a homogeneous area at all.

Here are a few specific examples of macro convergence and micro divergence: Countries in Europe have converged for the total number of passenger cars per 1,000 population, but the distribution across populations, numbers owned per household, or type of car owned have diverged. Ownership of television sets converged until 1997 and diverged after that year. With respect to daily TV viewing minutes, countries converged between 1991 and 1993 and diverged after 1993. Since then, the differences have remained stable. Newspaper readership in Europe has diverged.[39] Also, Nowak and Kochkova[40] found examples of divergence across 25 European countries, such as spending on communications.

In regions other than Europe, the trend is also toward divergence. Initially, with increased wealth, standards of living appear to converge, but a closer look makes clear that there are large differences. In Latin America, because of the large differences between rich and poor, the rich in each country have more in common with the rich across borders than with their poorer compatriots, but middle-income people differ from one country to another in the use of their discretionary income. All Latin Americans use toothpaste and shampoo each day, but there are varying brand preferences. Although 25% of Latin Americans eat cold cereal for breakfast, the national figures vary from 48% in Central America to 11% in the Southern Cone.[41] Japan was the country that developed earliest and fastest of all Asian countries, and it was expected that development patterns of other countries in Asia would follow the pattern of Japan. This has not happened. The economies of Malaysia and Indonesia are developing in different ways. The values gap of American and European elites has widened, according to studies conducted in 2002.[42]

Next to convergence or divergence, in many cases, differences between countries are stable in time. The Belgians drink 10 times as much mineral water as the British and 6 times as much as the Dutch, their neighbors. Although the quality of tap water has improved all over Europe, consumption of mineral water has increased in some areas and remained the same in others, and differences have remained similar since 1970 or have become larger. These differences cannot be explained by differences in national wealth, only by culture. Figure 1.1 illustrates the differences in mineral water consumption across Europe between 1970 and 2003. Data of 1970 and 1991 represent the percentages of people who answered "agree" to the question "I drink mineral water every day." Data of 1992, 1997, and 2003 are liters per capita consumed, of which 2003 data are for bottled water.

The wealthier countries become, the more manifest is the influence of culture on consumption and consumer behavior. This phenomenon is reflected in many changes of the past decades, such as increased interest in local music and TV programs, which in turn resulted in localization of most of the international media, such as MTV and CNN. More discretionary income gives people more freedom to express themselves, and that expression will be based in part on their national value system. Wealth brings choice. It enables people to choose leisure time or buy status products or devote free time to charitable work or to self-education.[43]

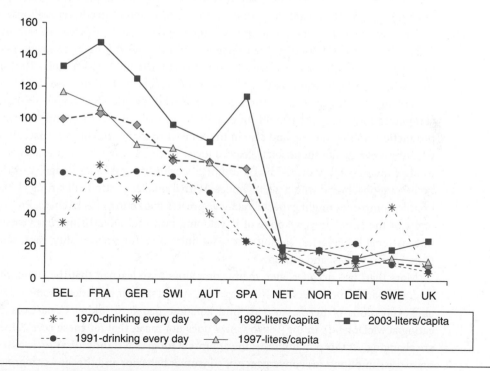

Figure 1.1   Mineral Water Consumption 1970–2003

SOURCES: Reader's Digest Surveys 1970 and 1991; Food for Thought/Unilever 1992 and 1997; Beverage Marketing Corporation 2003 (www.beveragemarketing.com).

Often, economic similarity of the member countries of the European Union is confused with cultural similarity, although differences in consumer behavior are recognized across Europe.[44] The member countries of the European Union are culturally very different, and these cultural differences cause differences in consumer needs. Understanding culture is the first step to take by global companies when deciding on the type of strategy for their global brands.

The Global-Local Dilemma in Global Marketing

The core dilemma in global marketing is whether to sell an identical product (a global brand) throughout the company's sales area or to make whatever modifications are needed to account for local differences. A global brand can be a mass brand looking to satisfy a common product need in all countries, or it can be a niche brand targeted at common niche segments in every country. Conversely, a global product, via its advertising, can be loaded with local values to add local significance. In both global branding and global advertising, the choice has to be made between standardization and adaptation or some variation in between, called the contingency approach.

The ultimate form of standardization means offering identical products worldwide at identical prices via identical distribution channels supported by identical sales and promotion programs. Assumed homogenization of needs across borders is the most frequently mentioned reason for standardization. Harvard Professor Ted Levitt,[45] in his 1983 article, "The Globalization of Markets," mentioned successful examples of fully standardized brands like McDonald's, Coca-Cola, Revlon cosmetics, Sony television, and Levi's jeans—products that Levitt said could be bought in an identical design throughout the whole world. By standardization, companies could reap the benefits of economies of scale in procurement, logistics, production, and marketing and also in the transfer of management expertise, all of which was eventually supposed to lead to lower prices. Standardization is also said to offer the possibility of building a uniform worldwide corporate image, a world brand or global brand with a global image. With a smaller portfolio of strong global brands, companies might expect to achieve greater marketing effectiveness. Proponents of the Levitt theory spoke of developing powerful advertising that crosses international boundaries, cutting across all lines of culture, nationality, race, religion, mores, values, and customs.

More than two decades later, many companies have learned that the standardized approach is not effective. Needs may be universal, but attitudes, motivations, and expressions of needs vary. To find Japanese people drinking Coca-Cola or eating at McDonald's in the Tokyo Ginza does not mean that Japanese core values are changing. At this point in time, the argument for global standardization is based on two assumptions: (a) convergence of consumer behavior and (b) the existence of globally uniform segments, or global communities with similar lifestyles across borders. In the previous section, it was shown that there is no evidence of converging consumer behavior. The existence of groups of people across borders with homogeneous values, wants, and needs is also increasingly in doubt.

Global Communities

One of the preconditions of standardization is the existence of homogeneous global segments across borders with similar values. Focus on similarities or marketing universals rather than differences has led international marketers to search across countries for market segments of people with similar lifestyles and values, which they call "global communities" or "global tribes." The assumption is that an 18-year-old in Denmark has more in common with an 18-year-old in France than he has with his elders, or that a young Japanese woman shopping in the Ginza has more in common with a young American woman strolling a Manhattan street than she has with her own parents. Business travelers and teenagers are most often cited as examples of such homogeneous groups. In the eyes of many U.S. marketing managers, the European youth market is considered to be homogeneous because these youngsters were reared on the same movies and global brands, such as Coca-Cola and Levi's,[46] and watched MTV, all of which has supposedly encouraged the development of a global teenager with common norms and values. Assumed uniform consumption habits of young people worldwide, their clothing styles, music tastes, and media habits, are viewed as evidence of a homogenized group of consumers.

Increasingly, this has been found to be a myth created by the marketing industry. It is a direct product of marketers' own ideologically framed cultural constructions via advertising, practitioner-oriented literature, and various other forms of cultural production.[47] Several value studies show that across countries, young people vary as much as adults. General evidence is the fact that cross-cultural psychologists who study value differences across cultures tend to use students as subjects. Also, studies among parents and students in the United States, Japan, New Zealand, France, Germany, and Denmark demonstrate the strong influence of culture on the values of both parents and students. The values of parents and students *within* a culture are relatively similar, with the greatest similarity between Japanese students and parents.[48]

Youths from Stockholm to Seville may use the same type of mobile phone or computer, but they may have bought it for different reasons. A survey by the advertising agency Euro RSCG showed that attitudes toward technology vary enormously among youth in large European cities. For example, 16% of respondents in Amsterdam said entertainment was their primary reason for using technology, compared with 9% in Helsinki and London and only 4% in Milan.[49] Across European countries, young people's leisure time activities vary, with 45% of Portuguese youngsters watching TV as a leisure activity as compared with 8% of German youngsters.[50]

Western magazines suggest that Asian teens, in the way they behave and dress and express themselves, increasingly resemble American and European teens, but this behavior is not driven by Western values. Moreover, there is no single teenage culture in Asia; there is enormous diversity among Asian teenage lifestyles.[51] Young Japanese or Chinese may be typically Western on the surface, but they retain traditional values like hard work in addition to aspiring to make and spend money and display success via branded goods.[52] Typical Indian teenagers in Bombay, Delhi, or Calcutta may be wearing a Lacoste shirt or Nike shoes, but they are very much

Indian in their values. They respect their parents, live together in a family, and remove their Nike shoes before entering a place of religion. Bond and King[53] found that most Hong Kong Chinese believed that modernization involved technology, behavior, or material progress, whereas Westernization involved values, thinking, or Western cultural traditions. Almost two thirds of respondents believed that modernization could proceed in Hong Kong without cultural implications. About half of them claimed that they managed to preserve their Chineseness by holding onto basic Chinese moral values, such as filial piety and respect for teachers. Wang[54] states, "One should not analyze what is emerging in China by taking a European model as a starting point. . . . 'Cool' music and 'alternative' youth in China hardly signal the same thing as their counterparts in Euro-America."

A common misperception is that everywhere exist the young rebel against their elders as a universal aspect of adolescence. However, the way the young develop their identity, the way they relate to their elders, and the way they behave in school vary enormously across cultures because of the values with which they are raised. Indian adolescents show much less conflict than U.S. adolescents, who are involved in self-creation and integrating an identity. In traditional Indian society, adolescence is not the separate psychological state that it is in U.S. culture.[55] A study by ACNielsen found that Indonesian youth increasingly like to use traditional Indonesian products, prefer advertisements that use Indonesian models, and when sick would rather use Indonesian medicine than Western medicine.[56] Among Hong Kong Chinese, although the younger generation values autonomy more than the older generation does, teenagers give lower priority to early autonomy than do their Western counterparts.[57] Westerners make a mistake when they think Japanese values are changing because students between 18 and 25 years old act in an extreme and revolutionary way. They have to realize that these years are the only free years a Japanese person has in his or her entire life. With the advent of work comes conformance to the typical Japanese behavior. Also, Chinese punk cannot be equated with a carefree spirit.[58]

Global homogeneous markets, such as businesspeople, youth, or rich people, exist mainly in the minds of Western marketing managers and advertising people. Even people with similar lifestyles do not behave as a consistent group of purchasers. Yes, across countries, there are young people and yuppies (young urban professionals), rich people, and graying populations that have economic and demographic aspects in common, but marketing communications cannot use similar motives and arguments because these groups do not have the same values across cultures. This is demonstrated by ownership of luxury products as measured by the European Media and Marketing Survey (EMS). The high-income European target, consisting of people who read international media, is not one homogeneous, cross-border target group for high-touch and high-tech luxury articles. Expenditures on expensive luxury articles by this high-income group in Europe vary enormously. In 2007, 17.2% of Portuguese respondents said they had bought an expensive watch in the past year as compared with 8.5% of the Finns. Expensive fragrances were bought by 43.4% of the French respondents and only 12.8% of Swedish respondents.

Businesspeople are generally considered to be a "culture-free group" because of assumed rational decision making as compared with consumer decision making, but decision making by businesspeople is also culture bound as are many business habits. In 1999, a sample of businesspeople were asked where, outside of the office, they would most like to discuss business with their most valuable customer; 49% of Spaniards opted for lunch at a restaurant or hotel, something favored by only 8% of Italians, who preferred a breakfast or dinner meeting. The favorite of Germans was a meeting at an airport or conference center. Asked about the use of new technology, 94% of British managers said they used e-mail, whereas only 53% of French managers did so.[59]

Global or Local? The Standardization-Adaptation Debate

During the past five decades, academics have studied the behavior of firms in foreign markets to understand the factors that influence the choice between standardizing operations and adapting to local environments. The focus of these studies has varied from individual elements of the marketing mix (mostly product or advertising) to the entire marketing mix or a firm's entire business strategy.[60] The majority of these studies were conducted by U.S. academics, studying global strategies of U.S. firms. The debate is ongoing. On the one hand, standardizing processes and products across markets can yield economies of scale in marketing, production, and research and development (R&D). On the other hand, firms need to appreciate the differences among foreign markets and adapt their practices and offerings to suit consumers' needs and wants. The question is where along this continuum lies the level of adaptation that delivers the maximum economic payoff.

Review of a 50-Year Debate

The wish to standardize marketing and advertising lies in export practice. In 1966, one of the early U.S. advertising professors, Watson Dunn,[61] stated,

> One of the first questions that an international marketing executive has to answer when he enters a foreign market is "How much of our advertising can we use in this particular country?" On one hand, he will be told that everything from American hair spray to tourism can be sold throughout the world with the same illustrations, copy and advertising approach. On the other hand, he will be told that every foreign market is different and he will run into a variety of problems including cultural taboos if he tries to use the American approach abroad.

This quotation covers the dilemmas of U.S. companies when selling their products outside the United States: standardize for greater efficiency or adapt for greater effectiveness. Most papers published since Dunn's article have focused on opinions, attitudes, and practices of the manufacturer with respect to this choice. Many of these were conceptual and based on assumptions without empirical evidence.[62] The standardization discussion basically is a sales discussion and not grounded in marketing philosophy as the wants and needs of consumers are not considered. Proponents of standardization rely on a strong belief in the universality of fundamental human needs as well as the assumption that advertising purposes are universal; thus, advertising can be the same everywhere. The idea was that a strong concept or buying proposal crosses borders; only the execution must be adapted.

Frequently quoted authors proposing a standardization strategy are Erik Elinder[63] and Theodore Levitt.[64] Elinder, then chairman of the board of the Swedish Sales Institute, believed that convergence of standards of living and improving technical means were facilitating standardization of advertising would justify identical advertising messages for all European countries. He believed in the emergence of one-language (English) television, in all-European media, and in increased travel that would lead to European consumers with similar habits. His criteria for convergence were mainly economical. According to Levitt, the driving forces for convergence of needs and desires are technology and modernity.

> A powerful force drives the world toward a converging commonality, and that force is technology. It has proletarianized communication, transport, and travel. It has made isolated places and impoverished peoples eager for modernity's allurements. . . . Even people who adhere to ancient religions and attitudes are in favor of modernity: the Ibos in Biafra are seen drinking Coca-Cola and in isolated Siberia people want digital watches. . . . The world's needs and desires have irrevocably homogenized.

Levitt's argument was that standardization enables a company to compete on the basis of appropriate value—the best combinations of price, quality, reliability, and delivery for products that are globally identical with respect to design, function, and even fashion. Many of the U.S. products and brands Levitt mentioned as examples were unique at the time. To foreign consumers, they had American flavor and status value; they were the type of products and/or brands preferred by a large part of the developing world. Twenty years later, there is much more competition, and most of the examples have adapted to different environments, tastes, and habits. Levi's saw its sales plummet as consumers turned to homegrown brands, such as Italy's Diesel and Spain's Zara. Coca-Cola changed its strategy to "think local, act local." With their centralized decision making and standardized marketing, they had lost touch with the new global marketplace.[65]

Increasingly, Levitt's statements of 1983 have been challenged. Later authors point at the lack of empirical evidence behind the arguments for standardization.

> Although anecdotal support for convergence and standardization was plentiful, empirical evidence was in short supply. . . . What Levitt may have witnessed

was an increase in global branding rather than a big increase in global products. But even this may not be as extensive as it seems. The point has been made often; the same names, such as Coca-Cola and McDonald's, that were originally cited are still cited today. Very few new ones have been added to the list. . . . Levitt may have taken the extensive diffusion of a few brands as representative of the wide diffusion of many.[66]

In the 1990s, the statements on universality became more modified. Standardization would only apply to some specific segments or to some marketing mix elements, such as packaging and advertising.[67] The conditions under which standardization is appropriate were specified. It was possible for some types of consumers, similar segments; for some product attributes, such as novelty, international image, stage of life cycle; for industrial goods and for some consumer products.[68]

Agrawal[69] reviewed the debate in international advertising from the perspective of the (U.S.) practitioner and academician. He distinguished three schools of thought regarding international advertising: *standardization, adaptation,* and the *contingency perspective.* The latter approach is based on the idea that the most effective advertising strategy varies, depending on the situation.

Over time, a variety of studies were conducted. An analysis of five decades of advertising standardization research including 56 studies has shown that focus has shifted from international to regional level. Regions most covered are Western Europe, (Chinese) Asia and the Middle East or Arab world. The study showed that in Europe, full standardization of advertising is rare. The study also analyzed the different measurement approaches of advertising standardization. Of the 56 studies, 27 were based on surveys among managers and 21 on analysis of advertising.[70] There are four types of studies that can be distinguished.

1. Conceptual papers that present models or conceptual frameworks. Such papers tend to review the assumptions and/or research findings of the past or add to that by categorizing them into new frameworks to be used as tools for marketing managers. An example is a paper by Merz et al. who apply Western categorization theory to the global consumer culture debate.[71]

2. Surveys among managers. Such papers do not always present reality. In particular, those who believe in convergence are more likely to standardize their strategies.[72] Several authors point at the phenomenon that when marketing and advertising practices are investigated in surveys among practitioners, what managers say about what they do often tends to be different from actual practice. In particular, executives at U.S. headquarters believe that there is more standardization than actually exists. What people say does not always reflect reality. So-called multinational campaigns are never quite as standardized as many executives think.[73]

3. Complex studies that include environmental variables, measures of adaptation standardization, and performance measures. These studies try to find the degree of adaptation that optimizes the export performance of the firm.[74]

4. Content analysis of advertising. Such papers present research findings based on the manifestations of actual practice and not on perceptions of managers. An example is a content analysis study of advertising for luxury brands in the categories of cosmetics, perfumes, and fashion, which found various forms of standardization across regions (Europe and the Middle East).[75] As the product category is an important adaptation variable, such studies have to be conducted for various product categories to get a representative impression of standardization-adaptation practices.

Increasingly studies are focusing on the effects of standardization-adaptation on profitability and analysis of the variables that influence this effect.

Variables Influencing the Standardization-Adaptation Decision

Numerous variables influence the decision to standardize or adapt. Various strategic aspects can be analyzed, of which we mention the most used:

- The product, including product category and product life cycle
- The company, its organizational culture, the culture of the country of origin of the company, and its export dependence
- The business environment: the competition, economic development of markets, marketing infrastructure, environmental factors such as laws and government regulations, and media infrastructure
- The consumer: spending power, and cultural and social variables including local tastes, habits, and conditions of use (often included in the catchall of environmental variables)

The Product Category and Product Life Cycle

A few product categories seem to be successful if they follow a standardized marketing approach. Examples are whiskey and perfume, for which a standardized country-of-origin concept can be used (perfume from Paris). French perfume comes from France, Scotch whiskey from Scotland. In global media, such as the magazine *Cosmopolitan*, beauty products are more likely to use standardized approaches than other products such as cars, food, and household goods.[76] Logic points at technology products for having the greatest chance of successful standardization. Annual surveys by Reader's Digest[77] show that a number of more or less standard global brands that are equally highly trusted in a large number of countries are in the technology area (Sony, Nokia, Canon, IBM). These brands have remained strong by offering consistently high quality.

The phase of the product in the product life cycle defines the possibility of standardization. New products or brands and marketing communications for these products are easier to standardize than mature products (see also Chapter 11). Yet by selling one single product worldwide and not adapting to usage and attitude differences that become apparent some time after introduction, manufacturers run the risk of finding a mass market in one culture and a niche market in another. In different phases of a product's life cycle, different advertising approaches are needed. Established brands in different markets may have different brand images, making it difficult to move the product to a global approach.

A Company's Organization, Type of Company, International Experience, and Corporate Culture

The culture of a company's country of origin strongly influences the vision of its managers, and the vision of a company's management influences the degree of standardization. Across countries, managers have different worldviews. In particular, U.S. companies have universalistic philosophies about people's values and focus more on laws and regulation than on culture. With the European Union, U.S. firms expected Europe to become one cohesive market. Similarly, U.S. companies used to expect similarities across the ex-Communist countries of central Europe, but there are marked differences in responses to advertising across these countries.[78]

Whereas European and Japanese managers think marketing and advertising should be adapted to local customs, North American managers believe in the strategic advantages of standardization. A 2001 survey among 680 U.S. corporate executives showed that the majority of firms do not seem to incorporate cultural factors when deciding whether to standardize their brand names or adapt them to the environmental conditions of the host countries.[79] A 2006 survey among U.S and Japanese managers about standardization across Europe showed that managers of U.S. firms are more inclined to standardize advertising and to create a uniform brand image and appeal than Japanese managers. Japanese headquarters allow a greater degree of localization than U.S. headquarters.[80]

There is a dividing line between the Latin and Anglo-Saxon countries. German and British brand managers claim more frequently to be aiming at standardization of their brand's marketing mix than French and Italian managers.[81] In 1992, 43% of executives working for international advertising agencies in the United Kingdom had positive attitudes toward standardized advertising.[82]

The degree of export dependence of a firm influences the degree of standardization-adaptation. Firms with high export dependence tend to have a more aggressive product adaptation strategy than firms with lower export dependence, where export delivers only some additional revenue. So companies that highly depend on sales in foreign markets know that adaptation leads to better performance. The costs to adapt products are recouped through improved export performance.[83] This may explain why so many U.S. firms standardize. Exporting has been less critical for them because of a large domestic market. When companies export, they tend to select easy-to-satisfy foreign markets where significant product adaptation is not necessary. So export dependence may be an important antecedent of product adaptation strategy. So-called born-global firms, those which at their founding intend to sell a substantial share of their product offerings in international markets, appear to focus on their foreign customers and thus adapt.[84]

The Business Environment

The business environment includes differences in infrastructure, level of competition, laws and regulations, and media infrastructure. An often heard argument for standardization is the existence of international media. The availability and growing penetration of international media have led to high expectations, but increased availability of cross-border television has not resulted in more cross-border campaigns. Different cultures demand different television programming, reflecting national tastes, so the scope of pan-regional television programming is limited to a few types of programs, such as sports.[85] Even these programs tend to be in the local language. There are very few truly international consumer magazines: Magazines such as *Elle* and *Cosmopolitan,* which used to be "exported" to other countries in the original format, have turned to local editions in most countries where they are sold.

The Consumer

Consumer factors (also called environmental factors) include customer similarity (lifestyles, preferences, tastes) and differences (culture, climate, language), along with spending power.

Although traditional thinking in international marketing has primarily focused on the similarities of market segments, increasingly, it is recognized that the critical factor is differences. The more marketers understand the differences in consumer behavior across countries, the more effective international marketing and advertising will be.[86] As Kenichie Ohmae already stated in 1989,

> When it comes to product strategy, managing in a borderless world doesn't mean managing by averages. The lure of a universal product is a false allure. . . . When it comes to questions of taste and, especially, aesthetic preference, consumers do not like averages.[87]

Effect on Performance

The most important question to ask with respect to standardization is whether it is effective and improves company performance, but few studies have tested the effect on performance. Statements on effectiveness tend to be based on beliefs that a uniform brand image can make strong brands. Zou and Cavusgil[88] state that the lack of empirical evidence for the effect of standardization on performance is a serious issue because if the effect cannot be substantiated, much of the knowledge in global marketing could be called into question.

Increasingly, studies have included performance, and the results vary. The relationship of standardization and performance varies across target markets.[89] A study among U.S. and Japanese multinationals in five countries in Europe reported that standardized advertising is effective across the European Union.[90] Several other studies have found that adaptation leads to better performance. One study discovered that managers were underadapting their offerings in foreign markets and that more adaptation might make them more profitable.[91] Brand repositioning, or the adaptation of the total representation of a domestic brand to one that is relevant to the minds of its foreign customers, contributes to greater performance.[92] A three-nation study of the international marketing practices of manufacturing firms in the United States, Japan, and South Korea found that product adaptation strategy is positively associated with export performance in all three countries.[93]

Those who find a positive relationship between adaptation and performance note that scholars underscore the need to understand the factors that transform market-oriented behavior into superior performance. Superior performance means marketing competence in handling product adaptation, the marketing planning process, control of marketing activities, and insight about how to differentiate the product, as well as conducting highly effective pricing, advertising, and distribution strategies.[94] These positive relationships between performance and adaptation seem to indicate that standardization is not good business practice.

The well-known advertising research company Millward Brown has studied the effects of advertising for a long time and concluded that few advertisements can transcend cultural boundaries. While using the same advertising campaign across borders may offer cost efficiencies, the savings may not outweigh the benefit of local engagement.[95]

Summary

The theoretical foundations of global marketing theory center on the perception of consumer homogeneity and/or the movement toward homogeneity as a result of various globalization forces. There is little empirical evidence to support this. On the contrary, evidence shows that the future doesn't hold one global culture. Several aspects of global marketing theory are paradoxical.

The global-local paradigm is a paradox: One cannot think globally; every human being thinks according to his or her own culturally defined thinking pattern. One can act globally, and that is what global companies do. When they globalize, they produce and distribute globally, which demands many strategic decisions. An important decision is whether to standardize global operations or adapt to local requirements. The academic debate about this decision has been ongoing for the past 50 years, without clear-cut solutions. Studies of the relationship between adaptation and performance seem to show that adaptation leads to better results. Studies described in this chapter have focused on various marketing mix instruments. The following chapters of this book will focus on branding and advertising.

In global marketing communications, companies use the systems of one culture to develop advertising for other cultures. There is no adequate global language for reaching global consumers. Some find pseudo-similarities and think they are real and universal. Many companies use one culture's motives to try to move people of other cultures. What is needed is a new language to understand what moves people of different cultures and systems that understand the differences and find the real similarities, which are few and far between. As a start, marketers have to learn to see the value paradoxes in the global marketplace and to understand them. This chapter has presented only a few examples. The rest of this book will focus on the value paradoxes used in marketing, branding, and communications; and tools will be presented for understanding the paradoxes for developing effective global brands and advertising.

Notes

1. Roberts, A. (2001). *Napoleon and Wellington: The battle of Waterloo and the great commanders who fought it.* New York: Simon & Schuster.

2. Sudermann, H. (1912). *Die Ehre* (Honor/What money cannot buy). Stuttgart und Berlin: J. G. Cotta'sche.

3. Kjeldgaard, D., & Askegaard, S. (2006). The glocalization of youth culture: The global youth segment as structures of common difference. *Journal of Consumer Research, 33,* 231–247.

4. Cheon, H. J., Cho, C.-H., & Sutherland, J. (2007). A meta-analysis of studies on the determinants of standardization and localization of international marketing and advertising strategies. *Journal of International Consumer Marketing, 19*(4), 109–145.

5. Sifry, D. (2006, May 1). State of the blogosphere, April 2006, Part 2: On language and tagging. Retrieved April 29, 2013, from http://www.sifry.com/alerts/archives/000433.html

6. Okazaki, S. (2005). Searching the web for global brands: How American brands standardize their websites in Europe. *European Journal of Marketing, 39*(1/2), 87–109.

7. America's strange clubs: Brotherhoods of oddballs. (1995, December 23). *Economist,* p. 63.

8. Vaszily, B. (2010). "How Facebook makes lonely people even lonelier" Revealed by distinguished University of Chicago professor in interview with Brian Vaszily on IntenseExperiences.com. *PRWeb,* June 5, 2010. Retrieved September 13, 2012, from http://www.prweb.com/releases/loneliness/help/prweb4088414.htm

9. Snyder, L. B., Willenborg, B., & Watt, J. (1991). Advertising and cross-cultural convergence in Europe, 1953–89. *European Journal of Communication, 6,* 441–468.

10. Pepper, T. (2004, August 2). Building a bigger star. *Newsweek,* p. 52.

11. Synovate. (2008). *Young Asians survey. Tapping into the hearts and minds of 8–24 year olds across Asia.*

12. Baker, M., Sterenberg, G., & Taylor, E. (2003, December). *Managing global brands to meet customer expectations.* Miami, FL: Global Cross-Industry Forum.

13. *2011 TGI Product Book.* (2011). Retrieved from http://www.wpp.com/wpp/marketing/consumerinsights/the-2011-tgi-product-book/

14. Morita, A., & Reingold, E. M. (1987). *Made in Japan.* Glasgow, Scotland: William Collins.

15. Anholt, S. (2000). *Another one bites the grass: Making sense of international advertising.* New York: Wiley, p. 5.

16. Springer, K., & Samuels, A. (1995, April 24). The body of the beholder. *Newsweek,* pp. 50–51.

17. Robertson, R. (1990). Mapping the global condition. In M. Featherstone (Ed.), *Global culture: Nationalism, globalization, and modernity* (pp. 15–30). London, UK: Sage.

18. Giddens, A. (2000). *Runaway world.* New York: Routledge, p. 27.

19. Quelch, J. (2003, August). The return of the global brand. *Harvard Business Review, 81*(8), 22–23.

20. Ho-Ying Fu, J., & Chiu, C.-Y. (2007). Local culture's responses to globalization. *Journal of Cross-Cultural Psychology, 38*(5), 636–653.

21. Giddens, 2000, p. 31.

22. Huntington, S. P. (1996). *The clash of civilizations and the remaking of world order.* New York: Simon & Schuster, p. 58.

23. Jones, J. P. (2000). Introduction: The vicissitudes of international advertising. In J. P. Jones (Ed.), *International advertising: Realities and myths* (p. 5). Thousand Oaks, CA: Sage.

24. Bakonyi, S. (1958). Divergence and convergence in culture and communication. *The Journal of Communication, 8*(1), 24–30.

25. McLuhan, M. (1964). *Understanding media: The extensions of man.* New York: McGraw-Hill, pp. 225, 268, 276.

26. International Telecommunications Union (ITU). Data. (2010). Published by the World Bank, Retrieved from http://www.itu.int/en/Pages/default.aspx or http://data.world-bank.org/indicator/IT.CEL.SETS.P2

27. Belsen, K., & Bremmer, B. (2004). *Hello Kitty: The remarkable story of Sanrio and the billion dollar feline phenomenon.* Hoboken, NJ: Wiley, p. 127.

28. Inkeles, A. (1998). *One world emerging? Convergence and divergence in industrial societies.* Boulder, CO: Westview, pp. 20–23.

29. *European cultural values.* (2007). Eurobarometer Report (EBS 278). Retrieved from http://ec.europa.eu/public_opinion/index_en.htm (or see Appendix B)

30. Theil, S. (2004, November 1). Not made for walking. *Newsweek,* pp. 36–37.

31. *Youth on the move* (2011). Flash Eurobarometer Report (319). Retrieved from http://ec.europa.eu/public_opinion/index_en.htm (or see Appendix B)

32. Liebes, T., & Katz, E. (1993). *The export of meaning. Cross-cultural readings of Dallas.* Cambridge, MA: Polity Press.

33. Elasmar, M. G., & Hunter, J. E. (2003). A meta-analysis of cross-border effect studies. In M. Elasmar (Ed.), *The impact of international television. A paradigm shift.* Mahwah, NJ: Lawrence Erlbaum.

34. *Young Europeans in 2001.* (2001). Eurobarometer Report (151). (See Appendix B.)

35. White, R. (1998). International advertising: How far can it fly? In J. P. Jones (Ed.), *International advertising.* Thousand Oaks, CA: Sage, p. 34.

36. Huntington, S. P. (1996). The goals of development. In A. Inkeles & M. Sasaki (Eds.), *Comparing nations and cultures.* Englewood Cliffs, NJ: Prentice Hall.

37. De Mooij, M. (2011). *Consumer behavior and culture: Consequences for global marketing and advertising* (2nd ed.). Thousand Oaks, CA: Sage, p. 7.

38. *2011 TGI Product Book,* 2011.

39. An explanation of the calculations can be found in De Mooij (2011), *Consumer behavior and culture: Consequences for global marketing and advertising* (2nd ed.). Thousand Oaks, CA: Sage, pp. 57–88.

40. Nowak, J., & Kochkova, O. (2011). Income, culture, and household consumption expenditure patterns in the European Union: Convergence or divergence? *Journal of International Consumer Marketing, 23,* 260–275.

41. Allman, J. (1997, January). Variety is the spice of Latin life. *M&M Europe,* pp. 49–50.

42. Living with a superpower. (2003, January 4). *Economist,* pp. 18–20.

43. Madsen, H. (2001). The world in 2001. *Economist,* p. 150.

44. Viswanathan, N. K., & Dickson, P. R. (2007). The fundamentals of standardizing global marketing strategy. *International Marketing Review, 24*(1), 46–63.

45. Levitt, T. (1983). The globalization of markets. *Harvard Business Review 83*(3), 92–102.

46. Berger, P. L. (2002). Introduction: The cultural dynamics of globalization. In P. L. Berger & S. P. Huntington (Eds.), *Many globalizations: Cultural diversity in the contemporary world.* Oxford, UK: Oxford University Press.

47. Kjeldgaard & Askegaard, 2006.

48. Rose, G. M. (1997). Cross-cultural values research: Implications for international advertising. In L. R. Kahle & L. Chiagouris (Eds.), *Values, lifestyles, and psychographics.* Mahwah, NJ: Lawrence Erlbaum, p. 395.

49. Galloni, A. (2002, February). Marketers face divergent tech targets. *Marketing & Media,* p. 26.

50. *Young Europeans.* (2007). Flash Eurobarometer Report (202). (See Appendix B.)

51. Lau, S. (2001, March). I want my MTV, but in Mandarin, please. *Admap, 36*(3), 34.

52. Cooper, P. (1997, October). Western at the weekends. *Admap, 32,* 18–21.

53. Bond, M. H., & King, A. Y. C. (1985). Coping with the threat of Westernization in Hong Kong. *International Journal of Intercultural Relations, 9,* 351–364.

54. Wang, J. (2008). *Brand New China. Advertising, media and commercial culture.* Cambridge, MA: Harvard University Press, p. 201.

55. Roland, A. (1988). *In search of self in India and Japan.* Princeton, NJ: Princeton University Press, p. 236.

56. ACNielsen Insights. (1998, November), p. 8 [Company newsletter].

57. Fu & Chiu, 2007.

58. Wang, 2008.

59. There was a German, a Belgian, and a Spaniard. (1999, January 23). *Economist,* p. 68.

60. Dow, D. (2005). Adaptation and performance in foreign markets: Evidence of systematic under-adaptation. *Journal of International Business Studies, 37,* 212–226.

61. Dunn, S. W. (1966, February). The case study approach in cross-cultural research. *Journal of Marketing Research, 3,* 26–31.

62. Zinkhan, G. M. (1994). International advertising: A research agenda. *Journal of Advertising, 23,* 11–15.

63. Elinder, E. (1965). How international can European advertising be? *Journal of Marketing, 29,* 7–11.

64. Levitt, 1983.

65. Quelch, 2003.

66. Whitelock, J., & Pimblett, C. (1997). The standardization debate in international marketing. *Journal of Global Marketing, 10*(3), 45–66.

67. Banerjee, A. (1994). Transnational advertising development and management: An account planning approach and a process framework. *International Journal of Advertising, 13,* 124. See also Domzal, T. J., & Kernan, J. B. (1993). Mirror, mirror: Some postmodern reflections on global advertising. *Journal of Advertising, 22*(4), 1–20.

68. Snyder, L. B., Willenborg, B., & Watt, J. (1991). Advertising and cross-cultural convergence in Europe, 1953–89. *European Journal of Communication, 6*(4), 441–468.

69. Agrawal, M. (1995). Review of a 40-year debate in international advertising. *International Marketing Review, 12*(1), 26–48.

70. Fastoso, F., & Whitelock, J. (2010). Regionalization vs. globalization in advertising research: Insights from five decades of academic study. *Journal of International Management, 16,* 32–42.

71. Merz, M. A., He, Y., & Alden, D. L. (2008). A categorization approach to analyzing the global consumer culture debate. *International Marketing Review, 25*(2), 166–182.

72. Okazaki, S., Taylor, C. R., & Doh, J. P. (2007). Market convergence and advertising standardization in the European Union. *Journal of World Business, 42,* 384–400.

73. Whitelock, J., & Chung, D. (1989). Cross-cultural advertising. An empirical study. *International Journal of Advertising, 8,* 291–310.

74. Dow, 2005.

75. Harris, G., & Attour, S. (2003). The international advertising practices of multinational companies: A content analysis study. *European Journal of Marketing, 37*(1/2), 154–168.

76. Nelson, M. R., & Paek, H.-J. (2007). A content analysis of advertising in a global magazine across seven countries. *International Marketing Review, 24,* (1), 64–86.

77. Reader's Digest Trusted Brands. (2012). Retrieved September 21, 2012, from www .rdtrustedbrands.com

78. Orth, U. R., Koenig, H. F., & Firbasova, Z. (2007). Cross-national differences in consumer response to the framing of advertising messages. An exploratory comparison from Central Europe. *European Journal of Marketing, 41,* (3/4), 327–348.

79. Alashban, A. A., Hayes, L. A., Zinkhan, G. M., & Balazs, A. L. (2001). International brand-name standardization/adaptation: Antecedents and consequences. *Journal of International Marketing, 10*(3), 22–48.

80. Taylor, C. R., & Okazaki, S. (2006). Who standardizes advertising more frequently, and why do they do so? A comparison of U.S. and Japanese subsidiaries' advertising practices in the European Union. *Journal of International Marketing, 14*(1), 98–120.

81. Kapferer, J.-N. (1993). The challenge of European branding: Facing inter-country differences. *Journal of Brand Management, 1*(1).

82. Cheon et al., 2007.

83. Calantone, R. J., Kim, D., Schmidt, J. B., & Cavusgil, S. T. (2006). The influence of internal and external firm factors on international product adaptation strategy and export performance: A three-country comparison. *Journal of Business Research, 59,* 176–185.

84. Knight, G., Madsen, T. K., & Servais, P. (2004). An inquiry into born-global firms in Europe and the USA. *International Marketing Review, 21*(6), 645–665.

85. Dibb, S., Simkin, L., & Yuen, R. (1994). Pan-European advertising: Think Europe— Act local. *International Journal of Advertising, 13,* 125–135.

86. Samli, A. C. (1995). *International consumer behavior.* Westport, CT: Quorum Books.

87. Ohmae, K. (1989, May/June). Managing in a borderless world. *Harvard Business Review, 67*(3), 152–161.

88. Zou, S., & Cavusgil, S. T (2002, October). The GMS: A broad conceptualization of global marketing strategy and its effect on firm performance. *Journal of Marketing, 66,* 40–56.

89. Cheon et al., 2007.

90. Okazaki, S., Taylor, C. R., & Zou, S. (2006). Advertising standardization's positive impact on the bottom line. *Journal of Advertising, 35*(3), 17–33.

91. Dow, 2005.

92. Wong, H. Y., & Merrilees, B. (2007). Multiple roles for branding in international marketing. *International Marketing Review, 24*(4), 384–408.

93. Calantone et al., 2006.

94. Knight et al., 2004.

95. Hollis, N. (2009, May). Culture clash: Globalization does not imply homogenization. *Millward Brown's POV*. Retrieved from http://www.milwardbrown.com

CHAPTER 2

Global Branding

Marketing was invented as a response to the industrial age that was product driven, with a rational view of the consumer. Product categories were narrowly defined in terms of product functions that were supposed to solve problems, not in terms of consumer perceptions or experiences. The answer has been a shift from traditional marketing to a communication-centered branding approach. Brands have become forms of communication and entertainment. Marketing is also increasingly driven by information technology, both locally and globally, and images can be available instantly and globally.[1] Thus, branding is an essential aspect of global marketing and advertising.

The practice of branding, attaching a trademark to a product, is very old. Originally, a branded item signaled to the consumer the origin of the product, provided assurances about the place and methods of production, and certified that the brand-owning corporate entity stood solidly behind the brand. Later, the brand was viewed as a site to produce perceived uniqueness of products and services, to differentiate against the competition, and to build intangible value in the form of customer goodwill, trust, and loyalty. Emotional benefits or values are added to give products their distinct identity. Brands create emotional connections with consumers, provide experiences, and are portrayed as platforms for creating consumer communities; they are viewed as storytellers and vehicles for reinforcing myths.

Global commerce has brought global brands. The ubiquity of global brands has become one of the features of modern life and one of the core subjects of global marketing. Along with the increased number of global brands, there has been an increase in the number of firms ready to advise companies on taking a brand to the global marketplace, as well as the variety of strategic brand models. There is no single blueprint companies can follow when taking a brand global, nor a single definition of a global brand. Strategic brand models tend to be developed locally and cannot be applied globally without modification. The more focus on emotional benefits, values, or myths, the greater the need to localize, to be culture-specific.

The ultimate global brand is uniform, accompanied by uniform global advertising. Yet companies increasingly listen to local consumer demand. Coca-Cola tends to be presented as the ultimate example of a global brand, yet the company is also increasingly localizing.

Because throughout this book the consequences of culture for global branding are discussed, this chapter reviews the theoretical background of branding and discusses the various aspects of the global brand, branding models, branding strategies, and the role of communication in global branding. Because in this book many general terms and concepts of branding will be used, the first sections summarize some aspects of branding in general.

Branding

In most categories, today's companies do not compete with products but with brands, augmented products that are differentiated and positioned versus other brands in the category. A brand is something made to appear unique. A brand is trust. A brand is not merely a product: It's the feeling a product evokes. A brand is why people will pay more for a product. A brand is the proprietary visual, emotional, rational image that people associate with a company or a product. The fact that you remember the brand name and have positive associations with that brand makes your product selection easier and enhances the value and satisfaction you get from the product. Although Brand X cola may win blind taste tests over Coca-Cola, the fact is that more people buy Coke than any other cola, and most important, they enjoy the experience of buying and drinking Coca-Cola. Memories of people, places, and occasions associated with a drink are often more important than a little bit better cola taste. This emotional relationship with brands is what makes them so powerful. Brand strength is due to the meaning that a brand creates.[2] It is made up by consumer experience over time, including what they have felt, seen, and heard. Consumer experiences have intensified in a world that is saturated with communication, where everything is branded. Consumers have more choice about where they receive brand messages, and they are increasingly in control.[3]

Brands have become intangible assets that produce added benefits for the business. The value created by brand management is the cash flow resulting from consumers' willingness to buy one brand more than its competitors, even when another brand is cheaper. Consumers do this because of the beliefs and bonds that are created over time in their minds through the marketing of the brand. This is consumer equity. Brands have financial value because they have created assets in the minds of consumers. These assets are brand awareness, beliefs of exclusivity, and superiority of some valued benefits, as well as emotional bonding.[4]

The Brand Concept and Branding Models

Branding is not rooted in theory. There seem to be as many branding models or descriptions of what the brand is or should be as there are brand consultants. On the one hand, brands are constructs created by marketing companies and their agencies to label items on supermarket shelves in the real world; on the other hand, brands are ideas that exist in consumers' imaginations. Successful brands are viewed as human personalities, ideologies, belief systems, stories, icons, or myths. These views reflect how consultants, researchers, or academics analyze the function of brands in the consumer's mind and in society.

One way of conceptualizing brands is viewing the brand as an *association network* in the mind of the consumer, a perceptual map of positive and negative associations, a symbolic language. Associations are the brand name, visual images, user associations, product attributes, benefits, and values, as well as places and occasions of usage. A brand's values must fit the mental mapping of people. The positive perceptions of the brand in the mind of the consumer create *mindshare*. At its most precise, mindshare measures how often consumers think about a particular brand as a percentage of all the times they think about all the brands in its category. Mindshare is brought about by multiple brand encounters. At the end of this chapter, the association network will be discussed in more detail. A conceptual tool that uses elements of the brand association network is the *means-end chain model*.[5] A means-end chain is a conceptual structure, linking a product (defined as a bundle of attributes) and a consumer (regarded as a holder of values). Attributes of products are assumed to lead to various consequences or benefits of product use, which in turn satisfy consumers' values. Such connections can be identified using the laddering technique, a method that helps explain consumer choices through the identification of the network of links among product attributes, the consequences or benefits of these attributes, and consumers' values. The means-end chain model will be discussed in more detail in Chapter 6. Viewing the brand as an association network leads to understanding the variety of consumer perceptions linked with a brand in different cultures, and the means-end chain helps marketers decide which attributes can be linked with which different concrete or abstract benefits and/or values of various cultures.

The *brand personality* model defines the brand as a human personality. Marketers attribute human personality traits (e.g., seriousness, warmth, imagination, sincerity) to a brand as a way to achieve differentiation. Personal characteristics of brands are created by transferring personality features of the typical brand consumer to the brand itself. In addition, the brand may take on the characteristic features of the marketers who create the brand.[6] Brand personality is a central component of *brand identity,* the expression of the brand, including its name and visual appearance. The brand identity is the input by marketers, what they want consumers to "take out"; this can be the brand's uniqueness, meaning, and values and how the brand aims to be positioned in the marketplace. The *brand image* is the consumer's *out-take* from the brand, the picture of the brand in the minds of consumers. It reflects how the brand signals are decoded by users, nonusers, and stakeholders. For users, brand image is based on practical experience of the product or service concerned (informed impressions) and how well it meets expectations; for nonusers, it is based almost entirely on impressions, attitudes, and beliefs. In a market that is culturally homogeneous, the likeliness that a brand personality created by a company is recognized by consumers is quite high because people share cultural meanings. Across cultures, a brand's personality may not be perceived in a manner consistent with how a firm has designed it to be because cultural differences influence the meaning consumers in different markets assign to the brand. The choice of what human characteristics to associate with a brand is made by marketing managers. It is quite possible that the brand personality created may resonate only in the market that has a similar culture as the marketing manager or that people do not connect personal characteristics to brands anyway. In Asia, the term *brand identity* is rarely used and generally not understood.[7] Brands are linked to real life entertainers or (sports) celebrities and thus to their identities. Also, the aim of providing brands with identities is to get people to see them as unique, and uniqueness is a concept that doesn't fit Asian cultures well (see also Chapter 5).

The *cultural branding model* was proposed by Douglas Holt,[8] who defines powerful brands as *iconic brands* or *myth brands*. Examples are Marlboro, Nike, Coca-Cola, and Mountain Dew. According to Holt, "myth brands derive their value from how well they respond to tensions in the national culture. They have to respond, adapt to cultural shifts."[9] An example is Coca-Cola's famous campaign, "I'd like to teach the world . . . ," so often used as the ultimate example of the start of global advertising, yet it was not targeted at the world but at Americans. The myth was intended to symbolically heal acute racial tensions tearing at U.S. society. "Sipping a Coke with a friend or stranger was a symbolic act of healing racial, political, and gender divides. Americans responded. The ad was first aired in Europe, where it received only a tepid response." In Peru, Inca Kola, introduced in 1935 and unique in its association with the glory of the Inca Empire, will be more of an iconic brand than Coca-Cola. To Americans, Oreo cookies may be an iconic brand, tying into childhood memories, but in other countries where people don't have such memories, the brand cannot be such an icon.[10] If we follow Holt's descriptions, the iconic or mythical brand cannot be global, as most myths are national. Experiences, history of use, and brand associations, all are usually at a national level. So brands that are icons in their own country are not necessarily the same icons in other countries—if they are iconic at all. Global brands have different histories in different countries. For example, for Indians, Lux—often presented as the ultimate global brand—is the prototype of an iconic brand with a history in India since 1895. The Chinese brand Haier may be an icon in China with a story that is typical of Chinese production history, as its owner smashed faulty refrigerators to pledge his commitment to quality.[11] But it doesn't have that history in Europe or the United States.

The *viral branding,* or *tribal branding,* model is rooted in the idea that the public has influence as a result of *brand communities,* or *brand tribes,* discussing the brand. Taste leaders set trends and create the brand's must-have desirability when they use it and talk about it, according to this view or model. In particular, the Internet advanced the idea that brands can create consumer communities revolving around websites. These communities are groups of people who possess a common interest in a specific brand and create a parallel subculture rife with its own myths, values, rituals, and vocabulary.[12] The model suggests that marketers don't influence the brand anymore, as consumers take the lead. However, communities of this sort are too diffuse to develop the resources that would allow them to influence a company's strategy. In particular, brand communities around global brands have limited interactions. Although a brand community in one country can be strong, it will not automatically lead to genuine brand communities in other countries, although there are examples where behavior in one country has been copied in others. When the first Apple iPhone was introduced in the United States, Apple fans lined up in front of stores. In Poland, this outcome was not anticipated, so for publicity reasons, Orange Poland, the service provider, hired actors to create fake queues in front of 20 stores around the country.[13] After this first happening, Apple has been very clever in creating consumer experiences by publishing this lining up for the introduction of each new iPhone version. In 2012 in many large cities in the world, people lined up in front of Apple stores at the introduction of the iPhone 5. These lines had become events, experiences of hanging out with other Apple fans. The lines were not an indication of demand as the phone could be preordered online.[14]

Brand Equity

Brands are recognized as corporate assets to be audited and managed in ways similar to the company's more traditional, tangible revenue generators. The world's most famous brands have values that can be measured in tens of billions of dollars. Brand valuation draws together a financial analysis, brand analysis, and brand strength score to arrive at a financial brand value. There are several agencies that calculate brand value, or brand strength, and they do this in different ways. Examples are Interbrand and Millward Brown. Interbrand[15] is an agency that has developed a brand valuation method that has gained global acceptance. Its calculations include consumers' purchasing behavior by market sector, the value contributed by the brand as part of the company's value, the position of the brand in the minds of customers, and the strength of the brand compared with its competitors. The resulting value is important, but understanding the themes or forces behind this value is what really drives the brand's performance. Effective brand management means orchestrating these forces.[16] Millward Brown calculates Global Brand Power scores and publishes these scores in a BrandZ Top 100 Ranking list. They calculate the present value of future earnings, showing how strong brands create value in three ways: (1) The total dollar value created by the brand, (2) the impact of brand equity on the customer purchase decision, and (3) the brand's future growth potential. This measurement shows that the world's most valuable brands are not necessarily global brands but also that the most valuable brands are corporate brands, not consumer brands. Such brands that historically have built strong relationships with consumers are mostly individual or product brands that don't create enough total value to be counted in the BrandZ top ranking.[17]

The basis of brand equity is the existence of the brand in the mind of the consumer (mindshare) and the influence on buying behavior (consumer equity). Consequently, consumer equity influences the brand's financial performance (brand value). Elements of consumer equity are brand awareness, brand associations, brand symbols, perceived quality, and brand loyalty. Many of these elements are abstract. Since the way consumers respond to abstract brand associations varies across nations, it is difficult to measure and compare brand equity across nations.[18]

Managers in Asia have reservations about investing in intangible assets such as brands. Not uncommonly, branding is perceived as part of marketing communications and thus a cost in the marketing budget.[19] For Asians, the brand concept is too abstract (see Chapter 5, Personality and Identity in Marketing subsection, this book).

Brand Architecture

The term *brand architecture* is used for how an organization structures and names brands as part of their brand portfolio strategy. The three main types of brand architecture systems are the following:

1. *Corporate branding,* where the corporate name is used on all products and services offered by the company. Only the mother brand is used, and all products carry this name. Examples of corporate brands are Benetton (clothes, perfume), Mitsubishi (banks, cars, domestic appliances), Philips (hi-fi, television, light bulbs, electric razors), Braun (razors, coffee machines, kitchen machines), Sony (television, audio, video), Canon (cameras, photocopiers, office equipment), and major Chinese brands, such as Haier (household appliances) and Wahaha (food and beverages).

2. *Endorsement branding,* where all subbrands are linked to the corporate brand by means of either a verbal or visual endorsement. The mother brand is tied to product brands. Endorsed brands benefit from the standing of their mother brand and thus save a company some marketing expense by promoting all the linked brands whenever the mother brand is advertised. Nestlé's name on the package of Nescafé, Maggi, or Dairy Crunch means it endorses the quality. GM endorses Pontiac, Buick, Oldsmobile, Cadillac, and Chevrolet. The L'Oréal company has a full range of personal care products under the corporate L'Oréal umbrella. When one brand name is used for several related products, this is referred to as *family branding.* One brand name serves as an *umbrella brand,* and different products or brands are marketed under one name. Examples are Nivea (Beiersdorf) soap, facial products, body milk, deodorant; Knorr (Unilever Bestfoods) soups and sauces; and Sanex (Sara Lee) personal care products.

3. *Product branding,* where the corporate brand operates merely as a holding company, and each product or service is individually branded for its target market. In product brand architecture, the company supports many different product brands, each having its own name and style of expression, but the company itself remains invisible to consumers. Procter & Gamble (P&G), considered by many to have created product branding, is a choice example with its many unrelated consumer brands, such as Tide, Pampers, Ivory, and Pantene. Product branding is a resource-intensive strategy because each brand must be commercially promoted and legally protected. The vast majority of existing brands were developed as single-product brands that were built to position products within national boundaries.[20]

When a company uses the brand equity associated with an existing brand name to introduce a new product or product line, this is referred to as *brand leveraging*. The new products are *line extensions* (if they are of the same category, e.g., Cherry Coke) or *brand extensions* (if the extension is of a different category from the main brand, e.g., Marlboro clothes). Another term is *range brand* or *line brand*. A group of products is ranged under one name, under one promise or positioning. The purpose is to give a product a place in a range of other products. An advantage of range brands is that products can share brand awareness and meaning. Examples are Schweppes (tonic, bitter lemon, soda water, ginger ale), Budweiser (light, dark), and Mercedes (C240, E500, S600). In the West, a line or brand extension should fit product class and values of the parent brand (*brand extension fit*). Consumers from Asian countries also perceive brand extension fit for extensions that are far from those associated with the main brand.[21] The Indian Tata brand, originally a steel mill, now stands for steel, cars, salt, tea, and watches. The corporate brand is trusted, so the various products under its umbrella are trusted as well.[22]

When large retailers put their own brand name on products, this is called a *private label, store brand*, or *distributors own brand (DOB)*. Generally, consumers view supermarkets' own brands as good value for money, but consumers in Europe, Canada, and Australia agree more with this statement than consumers in Thailand and Japan. Consumers in Taiwan, Malaysia, Indonesia, and the Philippines view private label goods as suitable for those who cannot afford the "best" brands.[23]

The Global Brand

In professional literature, global branding appears to apply to the whole complex of decisions involved in the development of a global brand. Definitions of a global brand vary from "brands that are available across multiple geographies"[24] to "brands with the same strategy in all target markets" or brands "that consumers can find under the same name in multiple countries with generally similar and centrally coordinated marketing activities." This begs the question of whether global brands are merely those that are distributed worldwide or whether "globalness" itself is an element of their existence or success.

Academic literature on global or international branding is sparse, although branding policy is understood to be a major issue within a firm's overall marketing strategy. A great majority of the work produced in the international branding field stems from researchers working for U.S. institutions (75%). This is followed by the United Kingdom, with 20% of the academic articles, which shows the predominance of research from Anglo-Saxon institutions in the international branding field.[25] In Anglo-Saxon literature, the global brand ideally is a standard, one-size-fits-all brand, and the rationale for developing global brands uses arguments and assumptions similar to those supporting standardization of global marketing and advertising, such as cost savings and homogeneous consumer motives.

A summary of academic descriptions of what constitutes a global brand is the following:

A global brand is one that is available in most countries in the world and shares the same strategic principles, positioning, and marketing in every market throughout the world, although the marketing mix can vary. It has a substantial market share in all countries (dominates markets) and comparable brand loyalty (brand franchise). It carries the same brand name or logo.

With respect to *availability*, a brand that fits this definition is McDonald's, which in 2012 offered its services via approximately 33,000 distribution points in 118 countries. Coca-Cola is sold in more than 200 countries.

To dominate, a global brand must have a *substantial market share* and be a *leadership brand* in all important markets in the world. Several brand consultants have compiled annual lists of the most powerful brands worldwide, and Coca-Cola has repeatedly been number one. In 2011, it topped the Interbrand list of global brands with the highest brand value, and it had been at the top of that list for a long time.[26]

With regard to sharing the *same strategic principles and marketing,* the facets of the brands referred to are usually the formal brand identity (logo, symbol, trademark, brand name, colors, shapes), its positioning, its marketing mix, product mix, distribution, and advertising. The classic examples of global brands are rarely fully globally standardized. If a global brand is defined as one in which all elements are standardized (identical brand name, package, and advertising worldwide), there are hardly any global brands—even Coca-Cola is not fully standardized.

An example of *similar positioning* is a premium-priced brand that is premium priced around the world. If it is positioned vis-à-vis an age segment of the market, the positioning must be similar in every market. This is an ideal that cannot always be implemented, as the competitive environment of markets may vary, causing the need for adaptations in positioning; cultural habits also vary. In Japan, the Japanese brand Hello Kitty attracts not only little girls but also adult women. In Western countries, it is only for kids.

For most global brands, the *product mix* will vary to meet local consumer needs and competitive requirements. For example, both Coca-Cola and Pepsi-Cola increased the sweetness of their drinks in the Middle East, where consumers prefer a sweeter drink. McDonald's has standard specifications for its technology, client service, hygiene, and operational systems, but much else is localized, such as its products and most of its communications. Through the logo and color combination, it is recognized worldwide (see Illustration 2.1). Perhaps one of the causes of McDonald's success in foreign markets is the fact that, next to maintaining a strong brand image and consistent service standards around the world, its advertising is mostly local, its product offerings have a local touch, and the restaurant design is adapted to local preferences. Examples of products are the Kiwi Burger in

**Illustration 2.1
McDonald's in Tokyo,
Japan**

New Zealand, the Maharaja Mac in India, the Prosperity Burger in Malaysia, the Teriyaki Burger and the Ebi Filet-O (a shrimp burger) in Japan, the McKroket in the Netherlands, the McLaks (a grilled salmon burger) in Norway, and the Croque McDo in France, a name that refers to the popular French "croque monsieur," a hot ham and cheese sandwich. Although the burger is the core product, in India, the company offers various vegetarian options, such as the McAloo Tikki burger or the McSpicy Paneer. Advertising by McDonald's has tied into local habits and symbols. For example, advertising for McDonald's in France was linked to "Astérix and Obélisk," the most famous historical cartoon of the nation. Around the world, consumers don't use McDonald's in the same way. In some countries, McDonald's is the place to go for children's birthday parties, whereas in others, it is the typical family restaurant (as it is announced in India, Illustration 2.2). In China, McDonald's is the place to go for a date because the typical Chinese restaurant with large-group tables doesn't provide the privacy couples may want. With its tables for two, McDonald's does. In Taiwan, McDonald's added VIP rooms for family dinners or parties because in Taiwan, as in many countries in Asia, families want private space.[27]

McDonald's has increasingly adapted to local consumer wishes. In Europe, they changed fixed plastic seating to more comfortable upholstered furniture. McDonald's design studio developed 11 designs that franchise holders could choose from, and restaurants retained local customs. This resulted in a higher sales growth than McDonald's in the United States.[28]

A global brand can carry *one name* or *logo* and thus be recognized worldwide, but the product may not be standard at all. An example is Knorr soups and sauces. The package with brand name and logo, found in supermarkets around the world, provides the global brand image, yet the contents follow local tastes. Examples are goulash soup in Hungary, and chicken noodle soup in Singapore. The logo and packages are similar worldwide, however, and can be recognized easily among competitive brands everywhere.

Illustration 2.2
McDonald's in Mumbai, India

Brands may have all the characteristics of a global brand without carrying the same brand name everywhere. Sometimes, the brand identity is global, but the names or symbols vary from one country to another, often for historical reasons. Examples are the different brand names of Unilever ice cream, many of which are the names of the original companies Unilever acquired, yet the combination with the same logo makes them recognizable worldwide. Examples of names are Ola in the Netherlands; Olá in Portugal; Frigo in Spain; Langnese in Germany and Russia; Eskimo in Hungary; Algida in Poland, Greece, and Bulgaria; Eldorado in Italy; Good Humor in the United States; Wall's in the United Kingdom, Singapore, and Malaysia; and Streets in Australia. Illustration 2.3 shows examples from Poland, Germany, the Netherlands, Finland, Spain, and Denmark.

Names of Unilever's detergent brands are Surf and Wisk in the United States, Omo in the Netherlands and France, Skip in Spain, Persil in the United Kingdom, and Pollena in Poland. Reasons for using different names in different

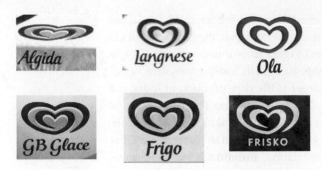

Illustration 2.3 Ice Cream Logos, Poland, Germany, the Netherlands, Finland, Spain, Denmark

countries or regions may be legal, political, historical, or cultural, or they may be due to language differences. The most important reason may well be to keep and leverage the brand names of an acquired company after having acquired it for its well-known local brand names. Companies buy other companies because of the brand name in which that company has invested for years, building an association network in the minds of consumers. Change would include loss of investment in the consumers' minds.

The branding literature suggests that managers should be consistent in branding decisions. This consistency is increasingly difficult to sustain in managing global brands. When brands are introduced to new cultural contexts, brand meanings are reinterpreted and changed. Brands can make emotional connections to consumers, and these can vary in different social and cultural contexts. Consumers may derive different meaning from brands than those intended in the home market, putting organizations in a dilemma. Managers have to cope with the development of "local" meanings that may diverge from those in the originating market.[29] As the influence of culture increases, marketers will need to apply more local understanding. Nigel Hollis of the global market research agency Millward Brown says, "Companies that have moved too far in the direction of global brand consistency may be ill-equipped to do this."[30] Even if a common buying motive for a brand is found, a different communication approach may be needed. Different authors tell different stories about the success of global brand consistency, often from different perspectives. The view on effectiveness may differ between the view of the consultant and that of the researcher. An example is the "Dirt is good" concept for the detergent brand Omo/Persil. This "Dirt is good" concept was based on the idea that children can better develop if parents leave them free to get dirty. Omo is there to clean. So child development is the ultimate benefit the brand offers. From the organizational perspective, it has been described as a successful, consistent inspirational positioning.[31] From the communication perspective, this brand promise cannot be consistent. In Asia, the Omo brand delivers the "Dirt is good" message in a different way than the Persil brand does in the United Kingdom, because attitudes to dirt differ.[32]

Perception of Global Brands by Consumers

A brand may be sold worldwide and show all the characteristics of a global brand, but that does not necessarily make it a brand that is perceived as global by consumers in all countries. A global brand usually has originated in a particular country. In some cases, in spite of being global, it is associated with that nation. This can be beneficial if the image of the country remains constant. In case of change, both upgrading (Japan from "shoddy" to "high quality") and downgrading (e.g., political activities by the country of origin) may influence the brand's image and acceptance. Yet such influences do not necessarily influence perceptions in the long term. In 2012, a territorial dispute about islands in the East China Sea between China and Japan caused a boycott of Japanese goods, and sales of Japanese cars decreased substantially, but it was doubted if that could seriously influence the perception of high quality of many Japanese brands.[33] In a similar sense, "American values" may temporarily have become ambiguous; for some, they are positive, for others, negative. However, in spite of accusations of American cultural imperialism, there is little evidence of broad-scale rejection of American brands. Most global consumers appear to separate the United States, including American values, from American brands. A key reason is the fact that many brands have transcended their "American-ness."[34] Consumers may know that Coca-Cola is American, but they attach their own values to the brand, in the context of their own consumption styles. Similarly, episodes of American Francophobia have had no impact on brands of French origin. Americans may lack knowledge of France or may not be willing to visit the country, but they will buy themselves a real Chanel purse because it carries a desirable cachet.[35]

There is a relationship between consumer equity and country image, but it is category-specific for the product. Cars, for example, are more sensitive to country image impact than television sets.[36] Attitudes are related to the combination of the product category and country of origin. A positive product-country match exists when a country is perceived as very strong in an area (e.g., design or technology), which is also an important feature for a product category (e.g., furniture, cars). The role of the country image acts differently in different target countries.[37] For quite a few global brands, a positive image of the country of origin has impact on brand equity.[38]

Few brands are perceived as global by the consumer, and the importance of a global image ("globalness") varies by culture. Successful global brands can be perceived as local in certain countries: for example, Nivea, a brand of Beiersdorf in Germany, or Colgate, which originated in the United States. In the Chinese market, the Olay brand is not connected with its American heritage.[39] Many successful global brands, of all brand types, are very old. If a brand has been used in families for generations, it has become ingrained in people's lives. It may well be that part of the success of a global brand is its integration into the local culture. Coca-Cola has existed since 1886, the German Nivea brand, now a global brand, has existed since 1911, and Japanese sauce brand Kikkoman since 1917. Adidas is from 1924. Lux toilet soap was introduced in the United States in 1895, in the United Kingdom in 1899, and in India in 1929. Coco Chanel opened her millinery shop in 1912. The house of Gucci was founded in 1921. Rolex was founded in 1908. The origin of L'Oréal lies in a company founded in 1907. The Bata shoe brand originated in 1894 in Czechoslovakia (now the Czech Republic) and now has retail presence in more than 50 countries. The Colgate Company began in 1806. Such heritage brands have made an early impact and remain in the memory of consumers. In India, brands like Surf and Colgate are still remembered by the initially used jingles or spokespersons.[40]

Consumers have good memories, even for brands that have not been advertised for some time. Once a brand is known to consumers, it cannot easily be erased from consumers' minds.[41] An interesting example is the German cigarette brand Ernte 23, which had become very weak in West Germany from the 1980s onward. After the Berlin Wall came down, the brand became very strong in Saxony in former East Germany. People remembered the "good old days," which were expected to return after reunification.[42] The shampoo brand Pantene Pro V, for which Procter & Gamble launched pan-European campaigns in the early 1990s, was still remembered by older people who knew it as the Swiss brand Pantene. Many strong brands, even if they are distributed worldwide, still have a strong national base and an unequal market position in other countries. Danone, for example, is a prominent leader in France but a challenger in Germany and the United Kingdom. In addition, many global brands do not have a global image in the home country. Heineken is a local brand in the Netherlands, but outside, it is a prestigious international brand.

The local environment plays a strong role in the perception of global brands and the values consumers attach to these brands. When the Berlin Wall fell in 1989, the first things Eastern Europeans wanted were Western brands. But in 1995, local brands returned as a result of growing nationalism. Lower prices, improved quality, and nostalgia have made Eastern European consumers return to their "good old" local brands. This is a slow but steady shift in consumer behavior. For a short time, values attached to a foreign or global brand may have a strong appeal, but as time goes by, people return to their own values. Whereas for years, rich Chinese have been buying Western brands such as Chanel and Cartier, they are increasingly buying expensive luxury fashion brands that are homegrown, such as Ports 1961 and Passerby or Yue Sai cosmetics.[43] In Asia, managers build brands that have local or regional appeal by using contemporary Asian symbolism, embracing consumer trends that emerge in Asia. Younger Asians, particularly Asian females, consider Japan and Korea to be more fashionable countries than France or the United States.[44]

Consumers tend to have a stronger preference not only for products that originate in their home countries but also for those originating in the same geographic region.[45] Since 2000, the *Reader's Digest* has conducted its Trusted Brands study,[46] asking respondents which brand they trusted most for several product categories. Although some global brands are among the most trusted in all countries (examples are Nokia, both in Europe and Asia, and Nivea in Europe), in several product categories, the most trusted brands are local, originating in a person's home country or close by. In the shampoo category in Austria and Germany, the originally Austrian brand Schwarzkopf is most trusted. In France, the car brand Renault is most trusted; in Germany, Switzerland, and Austria, it is Volkswagen; and in the Czech Republic, it is Skoda. The most trusted car brand in India is the Indian brand Maruti. Most trusted soft drink brands in Asian countries are mostly local. In India, it is Frooty, owned by the Indian company Parle Agro, and in Thailand, Malee, owned by the Malee Sampran Public Company Ltd., the leading Thai canned fruit and fruit juice processor.

People increasingly prefer brands rooted in their own history, which can be national or regional. In Italy, there is no such thing as an Italian restaurant. Rather, restaurants focus on the regional cuisines of Tuscany, Venice, Sardinia, or Umbria.

The fragmentation of the German beer market has to do with historical and cultural issues, not with differences in consumer tastes.[47] In China, domestic brands like Bird and Lenovo have been attacking global brands like Motorola.[48] In Peru, Inca Kola outsells Coca-Cola.[49]

A study of 12 product categories in the food sector in the United Kingdom, Germany, France, and Italy showed that (1) among consumers, the awareness level of local brands is significantly higher than that of international brands; (2) the perception of quality is as high for local brands as it is for international brands; (3) the image of trust is significantly stronger for local brands; (4) value is perceived as higher for local brands; (5) local brands are perceived as more "down to earth" than international brands; and (6) local brands are viewed as more reliable than international brands. Whereas international brands score higher ratings in usage intention, local brands score higher ratings in usage.[50] The BrandZ database of Millward Brown shows that on average, local brands are stronger than global ones. Brands distributed across multiple countries tend to have weaker overall relationships with consumers than local brands. For most brands, their strength comes from their original home market. Global brands may be mentioned first in surveys but are purchased less often.[51]

Global Brand Strategies

Global brands develop in several ways. Companies can use basically six strategies for internationalizing their brands:

1. *Cultivate established local brands.* Develop a national brand into an international brand, transporting brand value and strategy to more countries. Coca-Cola is the best example of an originally local brand that became global. Timotei shampoo, which originated in Scandinavia, is another example: Its formula as well as its nature-based imagery seems to appeal to Asians.

2. *Global concept, local adaptations.* Develop one formula, a concept for the world that can carry local products with local values. This strategy is followed by McDonald's.

3. *Create new global brands*, also called *"born global" brands*. Recognize a global need or want and develop a new product for it. There are few successful examples of truly global needs and wants, so this is a very risky strategy. Several technology brands can serve as an example: Apple, Nokia, Google, and the Nintendo Gameboy. Another example is the Spanish clothing retailer Zara which from the start went global, providing fashion trends rapidly to consumers.[52]

4. *Purchase local brands and internationalize.* This is a strategy used by such major packaged-food companies as Unilever, Danone, Kraft, and Nestlé. The purpose of most mergers and acquisitions has been to become owners of a company's brands in order to thrive on local brands first, then, add

international brand names or harmonize local brands with international brand portfolios. When a company has acquired a brand and doesn't want to lose brand equity of the name, it retains the original brand name combined with the umbrella name. One example is the various ice cream brand names used by Unilever, which were the names of the original local brands. Another example is the many biscuit brand names under the umbrella brand name Lu (Kraft). Names like Pim's (United States), L'Ecolier (in France and Belgium, but called Little Schoolboy in the United States), Petit Beurre and Digestive were the original brand names when bought.

5. *Develop brand extensions.* Extend a brand name to other related categories. Besides razors, Gillette offers shaving foam, aftershave, and deodorants. L'Oréal started in 1907 with hair care and expanded its corporate brand name to cosmetics, skin care, sun care, and bath and shower products. The German company Beiersdorf started with an all-purpose cream called Nivea in 1911 and extended the Nivea brand across a wide range of personal care products. Since 1913, Clorox has extended from a liquid bleach product into household cleaning products, disinfectant wipes, laundry care, and toilet care. Gerber extended its baby care product line to the categories of personal care, food, beverages, confectionary, and health care. The Cartier watchmaker extended its brand into the wider luxury goods market with leather goods, pens, and perfume. An advantage of brand extension is reaping the benefits of global promotion programs. The investment in global sports or event sponsorship is so enormous that trying to catch more products as extensions of one name is an appealing strategy.

6. *Employ a multilocal strategy.* Different strategies are developed for different countries for local recognition. The company name is often used as endorsement for quality guarantee ("Nestlé, the best of Australia").

A company's international brand architecture reflects how the company has grown. A company that has expanded through acquisitions will have a different brand architecture than a company that has expanded through organic growth.[53]

The Global Company's Brand Portfolio

At the beginning of the 21st century, some global companies owned large portfolios with a mix of global and local brands that were not all profitable. The 10 largest L'Oréal brands accounted for 90% of turnover. For Nestlé, one large brand represented 40% of turnover. The five largest Unilever brands, however, accounted for only 5% of turnover; 90% of turnover was represented by 400 brands. As a result, companies like Unilever started to change diverse multinational portfolios into a limited number of global brands. This process is called *brand rationalization.* Procter & Gamble had advanced in the process. In 10 years, they reduced their portfolio to one third of the product variations. Unilever's target was to reduce

1,600 brands to 400 brands. In 2012, twelve of these 400 brands generated a turnover of one billion euros annually. Examples of such brands are Knorr, Lipton, Becel, Dove, and Axe. Such large companies are continuously restructuring their brand portfolios. In October 2012, Unilever put the North American peanut butter brand Skippy up for sale, a brand they had acquired 12 years earlier when they bought the Bestfood company.

The risk in deleting local brands is that it leaves holes in the market for new entrants. It also means destroying capital investment of the past, as many of these brands were bought at a high price because of their strong local brand franchise.

Rationalizing brand portfolios often implies harmonizing brand names. Early examples of harmonizing brand names were the change of the Marathon candy bar to the Snickers bar and Treets and Bonitos being replaced by M&Ms. Brand names for the household product Cif used to be Jif and Vim. When brand names are changed, it too often confuses consumers and retailers and leads to waste.

The countermovement to brand rationalization is developing mixed brand portfolios of both global and local brands, a strategy followed by the Coca-Cola Company, which at the turn of the century changed its strategy to "think locally and act locally." The Coca-Cola Company now owns many successful local brands in addition to a few successful global brands, such as Coke, Diet Coke, Sprite, and Fanta. Schuiling and Kapferer[54] argue that a brand portfolio with strong local and strong international brands is in a better position to manage risk on a worldwide basis than an international brand portfolio of mostly international and global brands. Added to international brands, local brands can offer a company strategic advantages. They provide firms greater strategic flexibility in many marketing areas because they can respond to the specific needs of local consumers, in contrast to international brands that must deliver a standardized product to satisfy the largest possible number of consumers. L'Oréal has discovered that local brands have the power to retain clients. In globalizing the U.S. Maybelline brand, L'Oréal has pursued a double-branding strategy in which Maybelline is the host brand and another name is the local brand, for example, the company markets Gemey-Maybelline in France and Jade-Maybelline in Germany.

Although the development of global brands offers opportunities for capitalizing on economies of scale, matching the characteristics of specific markets can also be profitable. Adapting a domestic brand to one that is relevant to foreign customers is found to contribute to greater performance.[55]

Global Brand Communications

Global communications play an important role in building global images and brand experiences for global brands, but it is not only the global image that makes a global brand strong. Product performance also remains important. As a result of economic globalization in particular, many global brands have become detached from their origins and the process of production and have become signs, each valuable in itself. Because of the focus on added value, at times, product performance has almost been ignored. Marketers tend to view it as essential but not exciting.[56] However, the willingness to pay a premium price for a global brand is declining. At the end of the 20th century, Sony charged 44% more for its DVD players than the average manufacturer. Five years later, Sony DVD players cost just 16% more than the average.[57]

A renewed focus on the product side may be needed because great brand relationships with consumers begin with powerful product experiences. The quality signal of the global brand is still viewed as important by global consumers. A quantitative study among consumers worldwide shows that 44% view global brands as a signal of quality and innovation. Consumers say they like global brands because they usually offer more quality and better guarantees than other products. Global brands are viewed as very dynamic, always getting upgraded, the owners coming up with new products all the time.[58] Some global brand managers may have lost interest in the product, although the founders of many strong global brands were specialists, obsessed with the product: chemists, milliners, watchmakers, or athletic runners. Some of these originally local brands have managed to become successful global brands because the owners have continuously been innovative, using new technology and research. Nike is continuously innovating. So is Nokia. So is L'Oréal.

Illustration 2.4   Coca-Cola Distribution in the United States

Illustration 2.5   Coca-Cola Distribution in India

Also, many brands have become global because of successful distribution. Nivea was already sold worldwide before the existence of television advertising. The cause of Coca-Cola's success was the formula and intensive distribution. The company controlled the bottlers and was able to claim that Coke was available always, everywhere, when people are thirsty. This product benefit has been the core of the Coca-Cola concept. The company's intensive distribution system also makes the brand visible everywhere. (Illustrations 2.4 and 2.5 show Coca-Cola delivery vans in the United States and in India.)

Coca-Cola has always been one of the first to penetrate developing markets and to create strong positions in these markets. Early in the 21st century, the company was the largest investor in the Ukraine, a country Coca-Cola entered right after it opened up to Western companies. Illustration 2.6 shows outdoor advertising for Coca-Cola in 1996.

So on the one hand, quality, product performance, and distribution have remained important for building and sustaining strong global brands; on the other hand, branding is viewed as a communication tool in the new world of digital communication, and companies increasingly concentrate on corporate or umbrella brands. The cost of launching and developing new brands is so enormous that many international companies prefer endorsement strategies. In particular, Asian companies have invested more in building corporate brands, extending product lines under the umbrella of the corporate brand. A likely reason is that in Asia, the role of brands is different from that in the Western world. When evaluating products, a corporate brand image has greater influence on Japanese consumers than on U.S. consumers.[59] With growing Asian markets, global companies of Western origin are inclined to adapt their strategies worldwide.

Illustration 2.6   Coca-Cola Outdoor Advertising in the Ukraine

The Importance of Culture for Global Communications

Global standardized communication is assumed to be necessary because of its ability to create a uniform brand image.[60] Companies want consistent brand images, but the same brand may be perceived in totally different ways by consumers around the globe. Much of the standardization debate has concerned itself with the issue of standardizing the advertising stimulus, the message. Yet it is the response that counts. People process advertising messages in social and cultural contexts and then respond. Jeremy Bullmore,[61] with 33 years of experience at the advertising agency J. Walter Thompson, writes,

> Do not believe the old saying that good advertising speaks for itself. Good advertising speaks for itself only to those for whom it is intended. Much good advertising speaks quite deliberately in code, or uses a secret language, and excludes the rest of us. That's one of the reasons why it's good.

Even when products or brands are accepted in more than one culture, communication will have to be culture relevant, and that means more than translating a central message. Differences among languages go far beyond mere translation problems. Some concepts are not translatable because they do not exist in other cultures. The values included in advertising must match consumers' values to make advertising effective.

Kentucky Fried Chicken (KFC), for example, has been more successful in China than McDonald's because of a different approach. McDonald's extended its central theme of happiness to family life, but KFC went further and adopted traditional Chinese themes like Peking Opera in addition to depicting harmonious family life.[62]

The Internet has opened new ways to communicate with consumers worldwide. Even more than in classical advertising, this demands that marketers understand cultural differences (see Chapters 5 and 8).

Advertising styles of countries vary. Why do the British use so much humor in advertising? Why does comparative advertising work well in the United States when it is not accepted in Japan? Why do people prefer different types of promotions? Taking into account cultural differences doesn't mean that all advertising must be local to be effective. Countries can be clustered according to similar values that are relevant for a product category in order to reach consumers in each cluster with relevant values. This will be described in Chapters 7, 9, and 10. A useful tool for understanding how to relate values to product attributes and benefits across cultures is viewing the brand as an association network, which is described in the next section.

The Brand as an Association Network

The previous sections have shown that a brand is more than a product with a name, a trademark, or a promise of performance. A brand is a network of associations in the mind of the consumer. When we talk about brand knowledge, it includes more than facts; it is all the thoughts, feelings, perceptions, images, and experiences that become linked in the mind of consumers.[63] The association network notion of a brand is crucial for understanding advertising's role in developing global brands because it so clearly shows the link between consumers and brands as a result of advertising. The associations (meanings) that people attach to the objects of the material world influence their purchasing and decision processes.[64] Advertising tries to attach meanings to brands, and these meanings are interpreted in the light of the target's motivations and aspirations. Association networks may vary across target groups, and the ultimate goal of advertisers will be to develop strong association networks for brands that fit the target's values and motivations. The associations in the consumer's mind will relate to a number of aspects of the brand (see Figure 2.1):

- The brand name and the brand's visual images: the package, logo, brand properties, and other recognizable aspects
- The product or products linked with the name (one product is a monobrand; a number of products or extensions represent a range brand)
- Product attributes: what the product is or has (characteristics, formula)
- Benefits or consequences: rewards for the buyer or user—what the product does for the buyer
- Places, occasions, moments, moods when using the product
- Users: users themselves or aspiration groups
- Values: corporate or product values

Associations are structured in the human mind: Attributes and benefits will be linked with users and may be specific for the product category or for the brand. The essence of the brand is the strength of associations between the product or service, its attributes, benefits, values, and user imagery.

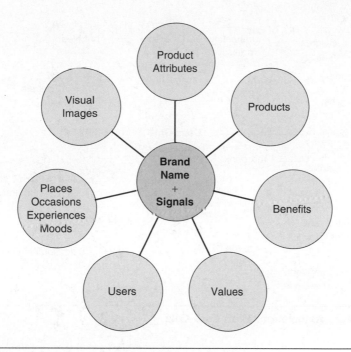

Figure 2.1   Elements in a Brand Association Network

SOURCE: Franzen, G. (1994). *Advertising effectiveness*. Henley-on-Thames, Oxfordshire, UK: NTC.

An example is a simple association network or perceptual map for Coca-Cola (Figure 2.2) that I developed by conducting a number of interviews in my own environment in 1995. This association network is not representative for the Dutch and is meant to serve only as an example. Association networks for Coca-Cola in other countries are likely to be quite different.

An important finding from a simple exercise like the one with Coca-Cola is the fact that associations included advertising properties of both Coca-Cola (Coca-Cola light break) and Pepsi-Cola (Michael Jackson). An explanation is that both Coca-Cola and Pepsi-Cola used music marketing in the past. For the people I interviewed, the attribute "American" was indiscriminately linked with both Michael Jackson and Coca-Cola's advertising. New cola drink brands such as Virgin Cola or the Islamic brand Mecca-Cola could easily attack the positions of both Coca-Cola and Pepsi-Cola, not only by price differentiation but also because of the undifferentiated values of both market leaders. Coca-Cola and Pepsi-Cola have the following attributes in common: soft drink, sweet tasting, thirst quenching, cola drink, and being "an American drink."

In a world of abundant brands and communications, differentiating a brand by its attributes or benefits is very difficult. It will work only if a product has unique attributes that distinguish it from the competition. Such distinctions usually do not last long, as they are copied quickly by the competition. Only a few strong global brands of large multinational companies have managed to

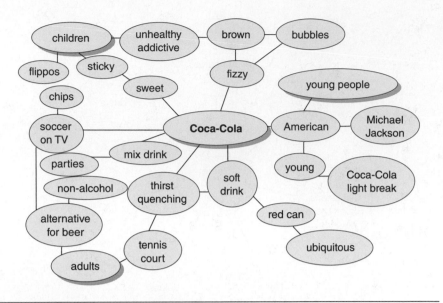

Figure 2.2   Associations With Coca-Cola

consistently introduce innovative ingredients and consumer benefits (e.g., L'Oréal, Nivea, Dove, Colgate) and communicate these effectively.

If a brand is associated with meaningful and distinctive benefits or values, this distinctiveness can be transferred to other areas. The British brand Virgin, owned by Richard Branson, carries associations of adventure, rebellion, and nonconformism that are linked to the personality of its owner. These values are used for all products of Branson's company: the airline, records, cola drink, vodka. However, these values may not be meaningful for the whole world.

Another example of an association network is one for Corona Extra, a Mexican beer brand exported to many countries in the world. It distinguishes itself by its transparent white bottle with a long neck and the ritual of drinking from the bottle with a slice of lime pushed into the neck. A mixed group of Spanish and German students developed the association network presented in Figure 2.3. This association network includes attributes and benefits as well as values. Two clusters of values can be distinguished. Those of the Germans are success, self-esteem, independence, and freedom; those of the Spanish are belonging, happiness, and sophistication. In later chapters (4 and 5), these values are shown to be distinctive of German and Spanish culture.

The purpose of advertising is to develop strong association networks in people's minds. The values selected to differentiate brands relate to the cultural mind-set of the strategist but should also relate to the cultural mind-sets of the target group. What makes advertising effective is the match between the values in the advertising message and the values of the receiver. A core problem in global advertising is a cultural mismatch between the advertisement and the target groups, which is rarely included in advertising tests. Although the large international companies try to measure the effectiveness of their advertising on a continuous basis, there is not

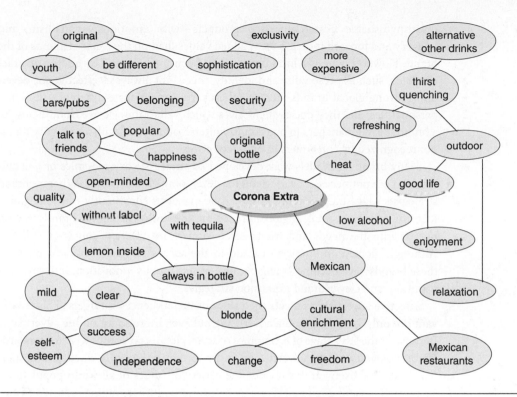

Figure 2.3 German and Spanish Associations With Corona Extra

much fundamental research on what makes advertising effective. There are, however, some rules of thumb.[65] Advertising, to be effective,

- must create meaningful associations;
- must be relevant and meaningful;
- must be linked with people's values;
- must reflect the role the product or brand plays in people's lives;
- must reflect or arouse people's feelings and emotions; and
- must be instantaneously recognized.

All these elements are influenced by the culture of both the advertiser and of the audience. Effective advertising reflects culture, is a mirror of culture. Understanding culture is a core topic of this book. With the advent of a variety of new channels of communication, the importance is increasing.

Summary

Brands add value to products. Global brands have values that can be measured in tens of billions of dollars, so proper brand management is of great importance. Increasingly, global companies have charged their products—those materially indistinguishable from competing products—with emotions, symbolism, and imagery and focused more on these added values than on the usage elements of the brand. However, whereas local brands have been made strong by adding abstract elements, such as personality and identity, this is not always as effective for developing strong global brands. Across cultures, consumers have different values and personalities, and they decide themselves which values they derive from the use of a brand. Brand managers in one country often load a brand with an identity that is not recognized by consumers in other countries.

Many branding models were developed by strategists or academics of one culture and are not necessarily as useful for developing global brands. Whereas brand strategists suggest a global brand should be managed consistently with one global identity, consumers look at global brands in different ways. Global brands that do not tie into the needs and wants of consumers in different countries will fail. Although global communications add to the success of global brands, many of these brands have become strong because of continuous innovation, intensive distribution, and clever brand expansion strategies.

Effective advertising reflects the values of the audiences it targets. This is relevant not only for classic media advertising but even more so for online advertising. Because of the advantage of economies of scale, global companies wish to standardize brands and/or their advertising. An important question is whether one standardized advertisement can include the variety of values of all world populations. The question can be ignored if one global world culture is waiting around the corner. To understand the improbability of a global world culture, the concept of culture must be understood. That will be the topic of the next chapter.

Notes

1. Schmitt, B. (1999). Experiential marketing. *Journal of Marketing Management, 15,* 53–67.

2. Kay, M. J. (2006). Strong brands and corporate brands. *European Journal of Marketing, 40*(7/8), 742–760.

3. Keller, K. L. (2009). Building strong brands in a modern marketing communications environment. *Journal of Marketing Communications, 15*(2–3), 139–155.

4. Kapferer, J. N. (2008). *The new strategic brand management: Creating and sustaining brand equity long term* (4th ed.). London: Kogan Page.

5. Reynolds, T. J., & Gutman, J. (1988, February–March). Laddering theory, method, analysis, and interpretation. *Journal of Advertising Research,* 29–37.

6. Foscht, T., Maloles III, C., Swoboda, B., Morschett, D., & Sinha, I. (2008). The impact of culture on brand perceptions: A six-nation study. *Journal of Product and Brand Management, 17*(3), 131–142.

7. Temporal, P. (2001). *Branding in Asia.* New York: Wiley, p. 31.

8. Holt, D. B. (2004). *How brands become icons: The principle of cultural branding.* Boston: Harvard Business School.

9. Holt, 2004, pp. 23–24.

10. Elliott, S. (2012, February 27). The Oreo turns 100, with a nod to the past. *New York Times.*

11. Roll, M. (2006). *Haier: An aspiring Chinese global brand.* Retrieved January 4, 2009, from http://www.asianbrandstrategy.com/2006/02/haier-aspiring-chinese-global-brand.asp

12. Cova, B., & Pace, S. (2006). Brand community of convenience products: New forms of customer empowerment—The case of "my Nutella the community." *European Journal of Marketing, 40*(9/10), 1087–1105.

13. Item found at http://www.macworld.co.uk/news, August 22, 2008.

14. Carlson, N., & Kovach, S. (2012, September 21). iPhone 5 lines from around the world. *Business Insider.* Retrieved September 30, 2012 from http://www.businessinsider.com/live-iphone-5-lines-at-apple-stores-around-the-world-2012-9?op=1

15. For more on the agency, go to http://www.interbrand.com

16. Interbrand. (2007). *All brands are not created equal: Best global brands 2007.* Retrieved January 4, 2008, from http://www.ourfishbowl.com/images/surveys/Interbrand_BGB_2007.pdf

17. Hollis, N. (2010). *The global brand.* Houndmills, UK: Palgrave Macmillan.

18. Hsieh, M.-H. (2004). Measuring global brand equity using cross-national survey data. *Journal of International Marketing, 12*(2), 28–57.

19. Roll, M. (2006). Asian brand strategy. *How Asia builds strong brands.* Trowbridge, UK: Cromwell Press, p. 23.

20. Macrae, C. (1993). Brand benchmarking applied to global branding processes. *Journal of Brand Management,* 289–302.

21. Monga, A. B., & Roedder, J. D. (2007, March). Cultural differences in brand extension evaluation: The influence of analytic versus holistic thinking. *Journal of Consumer Research, 33,* 529–536.

22. Sengupta, J. (2006). *Wraparound: Delivering a great brand experience.* New Delhi: Rupa & Co.

23. The power of private label. (2005). *The ACNielsen Global Online Consumer Opinion Survey.* For more, see http://www2.acnielsen.com/reports

24. Van Gelder, S. (2003). *Global brand strategy.* London: Kogan Page.

25. Whitelock, J., & Fastoso, F. (2007). Understanding international branding: Defining the domain and reviewing the literature. *International Marketing Review, 24*(3), 252–270.

26. Interbrand, 2007.

27. Private communication with Roie Yo Chia-Way, Taiwanese student at the master in retail design course at the Willem de Kooning Art Academy in Rotterdam.

28. Wiggins, J. (2007, March 5). McDonald's has a shake-up of image in Europe. *Los Angeles Times,* p. C-4.

29. Kay, 2006.

30. Hollis, N. (2009, May). Culture clash: Globalization does not imply homogenization. *Millward Brown's POV.* Retrieved from http://www.milwardbrown.com

31. De Swaan Arons, M., & Van den Driest, F. (2010). *The global brand CEO. Building the ultimate marketing machine.* New York: Airstream International.

32. Hollis, 2010.

33. Burkitt, L. (2012, September 26). Dispute tests Japanese brands. *The Wall Street Journal European Edition Online.* Retrieved from http://online.wsj.com/article/SB100008723963904445492045780020042284163884.html

34. Baker, M., Sterenberg, G., & Taylor, E. (2003, December). *Managing global brands to meet consumer expectations.* Brussels: ESOMAR, Global Cross-Industry Forum, Miami.

35. Amine, L. S. (2008). Country-of-origin, animosity, and consumer response: Marketing implications of anti-Americanism and Francophobia. *International Business Review, 17,* 402–422.

36. Pappu, R., Quester, P. G., & Cooksey, R. W. (2007). Country image and consumer-based brand equity: Relationships and implications for international marketing. *Journal of International Business Studies, 38,* 726–745.

37. Lee, C. W., Suh, Y. G., & Moon, B.-J. (2001). Product-country images: The roles of country-of-origin and country-of-target in consumers' prototype product evaluations. *Journal of International Consumer Marketing, 13,* 47–62.

38. Yasin, N. M., Noor, M. N., & Mohamad, O. (2007). Does image of country-of-origin matter to brand equity? *Journal of Product and Brand Management, 19*(1), 38–48.

39. Zhang, Y. (2009). *Design for global markets: Balancing unilateral global brands with local cultural values* (Master's thesis submitted to the Division of Research and Advanced Studies of the University of Cincinnati, Ohio). Retrieved from http://en.scientificcommons.org/56315892

40. Sharma, P. (2012). Advertising effectiveness: "Understanding the value of creativity in advertising," a review study in India. *Online Journal of Communication and Media Technologies, 2*(3). Retrieved from http://www.ojcmt.net/past2.asp?numara=23

41. Mihailovic, P., & De Chernatony, L. (1995). The era of brand culling—Time for a global rethink? *Journal of Brand Management, 2,* 308–315.

42. This story is from the German brand consultant Klaus Brandmeyer.

43. Seno, A. (2007, November 12). Homegrown luxe. *Newsweek,* p. 56.

44. Cayla, J., & Eckhardt, G. M. (2007). Asian brands without borders: Regional opportunities and challenges. *International Marketing Review, 24*(4), 444–456.

45. Amine, 2008.

46. For more, see http://www.rdtrustedbrands.com and http://www.rdasiatrustedbrands.com

47. Zambuni, R. (1993). Developing brands across borders. *Journal of Brand Management, 1,* 22–29.

48. Wang, J. (2008). *Brand new China. Advertising, media and commercial culture.* Cambridge, MA: Harvard University Press, p. 113.

49. Alcalde, M. C. (2009). Between Incas and Indians: Inca Kola and the construction of Peruvian-global modernity. *Journal of Consumer Culture, 9*(1), 31–54.

50. Schuiling, I., & Kapferer, J. N. (2003). Executive insights: Real differences between local and international brands: Strategic implications for international marketers. *Journal of International Marketing, 12*(4), 97–112.

51. Hollis, 2010.

52. Bhardwaj, V., Eickman, M., & Runyan, R. C. (2011). A case study on the internationalization process of a "born-global" fashion retailer. *The International Review of Retail, Distribution and Consumer Research, 21*(3), 293–307.

53. Douglas, S. P., & Craig, C. S. (2001). Integrating branding strategy across markets: Building international brand architecture. *Journal of International Marketing, 9*(2), 97–114.

54. Schuiling & Kapferer, 2003.

55. Wong, H. Y., & Merrilees, B. (2007). Multiple roles for branding in international marketing. *International Marketing Review, 24*(4), 384–408.

56. Sterenberg, G., & Baker, M. (2005, Autumn). Get real: The return of the product. *Market Leader,* pp. 43–47.

57. Dholakia, N., & Zwick, D. (2005, May). *Brand as mask* (Working Paper version v08, May 9). Kingston: University of Rhode Island, College of Business Administration.

58. Holt, D., Quelch, J. A., & Taylor, E. L. (2004, September). How global brands compete. *Harvard Business Review.*

59. Souiden, N., Kassim, N. M., & Hong, H-J. (2006). The effect of corporate branding dimensions on consumers' product evaluation. A cross-cultural analysis. *European Journal of Marketing, 40*(7/8), 825–845.

60. Taylor, C. R., & Okazaki, S. (2006). Who standardizes advertising more frequently, and why do they do so? A comparison of U.S. and Japanese subsidiaries' advertising practices in the European Union. *Journal of International Marketing, 14*(1), 98–120.

61. Bullmore, J. (1991). *Behind the scenes in advertising.* Henley-on-Thames, Oxfordshire, UK: NTC, pp. 79–82.

62. Lu, J. (2010). Multiple modernities and multiple proximities: McDonald's and Kentucky Fried Chicken in Chinese television commercials. *International Communication Gazette, 72*(7), 619–633.

63. Keller, 2009.

64. Duckworth, G. (1995, January). New angles on how advertising works. *Admap,* pp. 41–43.

65. Franzen, G. (1994). *Advertising effectiveness.* Henley-on-Thames, Oxfordshire, UK: NTC.

CHAPTER 3

Values and Culture

In modern marketing and advertising, values are used to differentiate and position brands vis-à-vis competitive brands. Values are said to be the basis for segmentation and positioning decisions. Values also are implicitly included in advertising, in the appeals and execution of advertising. Human values have been measured and compared within countries and across countries. Large, worldwide studies of human values are available, but those applied to marketing and advertising have mostly covered North America, Western Europe, and Asia. Little is available for Latin America and Africa.[1]

In most cases, the values people grow up with influence consumer behavior, but managers of global brands lack in-depth knowledge of the different values of people around the world. In particular, Western marketing managers are inclined to search for universals. By doing so, they ignore important differences. Also, perception is selective, so we tend to see what fits in our own value system, and so do marketing managers. We are also inclined to stereotype members of other cultures.

Most elements of consumer behavior are culture-bound, and so are the marketing strategies that marketers develop. In order to build relationships between consumers and brands, brands and brand communications must reflect people's values. For most people, culture is viewed as something abstract and intangible. The purpose of this chapter and the next is to make culture more concrete so that it is easier to deal with. This chapter defines culture and how it influences the various manifestations of culture, such as symbols, imagery, language, and thinking patterns.

The Value Concept

A *value* is defined by Rokeach[2] as "an enduring belief that one mode of conduct or end-state of existence is preferable to an opposing mode of conduct or end-state of existence." A *value system* is a "learned organization of principles and rules to help one choose between alternatives, resolve conflicts, and make decisions." Preferred alternatives are clean, not dirty; happy, not sad; healthy, not sick. One can feel emotional over such preferences. Preferences can lead to action: change dirty into clean by washing. When expressed in an abstract way, these preferences seem to be universal. But priorities vary, and how we express our values varies. We all want to be clean, but to reach that goal, people use various methods. The Belgians use twice as much soap powder as their neighbors, the Dutch. We all want to be healthy, but how we remain healthy varies. In the south of Europe, more antibiotics are used than in the north. In a value system, values are ordered in priority with respect to other values. This is why some authors use the term *value priority* interchangeably with values. Value priorities vary. For example, in the United States, individual happiness is a value of high priority, even a constitutional right, whereas in East Asia, personal happiness has lower priority than perseverance and harmony.

Values are taught at an early age and in an absolute manner. They describe what people in general think the world ought to be in an absolute way: freedom, peace (not a little bit of peace or a little bit of freedom). Values can serve as standards that guide our choices, beliefs, attitudes, and actions. Values are more stable than attitudes and occupy a more central position in a person's cognitive system.[3] We are not aware of our values; they operate unconsciously, like on automatic pilot.

Like other authors, Rokeach assumes (a) that the total number of values a person possesses is relatively small, (b) that all people everywhere possess the same values to different degrees, and (c) that the antecedents of human values can be traced to culture, society, and its institutions.

Values are distinguished between the values of individuals and collectives or between macro- and micro-level values. Macro-level values are called collective values or *cultural values*, and micro-level values are called *value orientations*.[4] A value orientation that becomes manifest in the actions of a smaller or larger group of people is a *cultural value*.

Values Are Enduring

Values are among the first things children learn, not consciously, but implicitly. Developmental psychologists believe that by the age of 10, most children have their basic value systems firmly in place.

Yet marketing researchers regularly try to demonstrate that values change. What they usually find are changes in how people express their values that basically are changes in the symbols and rituals of a culture. They might be misled by the behavior of members of a subculture, such as youth or businesspeople. Roland[5] gives the example of how an Indian man may dress in Western clothes at work and disregard intercaste rules in eating and other rituals, while strictly observing all of these codes and dressing traditionally at home.

The core values of national culture appear to be very stable. Data from Eurobarometer surveys (see Appendix B) between 1973 and 2011 show that across European countries, the levels of satisfaction with life in general have remained more or less the same, and there are remarkable cross-cultural differences: Consistently, the

Danish, Dutch, and British publics show a higher level of satisfaction than the Italian, French, and German. These differences have remained stable over time.

Figure 3.1 illustrates the stability of the differences. An important finding is that similar differences are found for young people 15 to 24 years old, as Eurobarometer surveys also asked young people in Europe to what degree they are satisfied with their lives. As the chart shows, this line runs parallel to the one of the general publics.

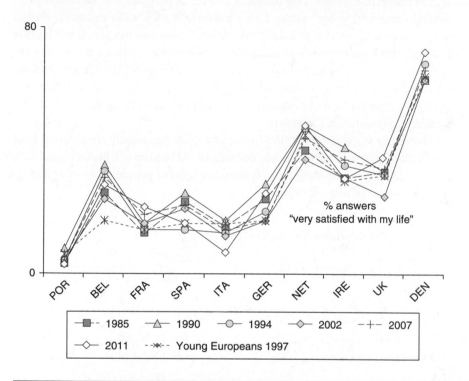

Figure 3.1   Satisfaction With Life 1985–2011

SOURCE: Data from Eurobarometer (1985–2011); Young Europeans (1997) (see Appendix B).

The Value Paradox: The Desirable and the Desired

There are two opposing aspects to values: the desirable and the desired, the distinction between what people think ought to be desired and what people actually desire, or, how people think the world ought to be versus what people want for themselves.[6] The desired and the desirable do not always overlap. The desirable refers to the general norms of a society and is worded in terms of right or wrong in absolute terms. The desired is what we want, what we consider important for ourselves. It is what the majority in a country actually do.

There is another paradox: the reflection of the gap between words and deeds, between what people say they do or will do, and what they actually do. Values that reflect the *desired* are closer to deeds than values that reflect the *desirable*. Because of the gaps between the desirable, the desired, and actual behavior, behavior may not correspond with the desirable, and norms for the desirable can be completely detached from behavior.

The *desired* relates to choice, to what is important and preferred; it relates to the "me" and the "you." The *desirable* relates to what is approved or disapproved, to what is good or right, to what one ought to do and what one should agree with; it refers to people in general (see Table 3.1).[7]

The distinction between the desirable and the desired leads to seemingly paradoxical values within one culture. This paradox may even make cultures appear to be similar or to be moving in a similar direction. It may confuse people in the sense that they think cultures are becoming alike. An example is the conclusion that the Japanese are becoming individualistic because of an increased focus on individuality in behavior and communication. In reality, individuality in Japan reflects the need for performance and competitiveness. The two aspects of values explain the paradoxes presented in Chapter 1.

The results of value surveys that ask for the desirable usually are different from the results of surveys that ask for the desired, as will be seen in Chapters 4 and 6. In order to understand different value systems and related paradoxes, we first have to understand the concept of culture.

Table 3.1   The Desirable Versus the Desired

The Desirable	The Desired
The norm, what ought	What people want for themselves
Words	Deeds
Approval, disapproval	Choice
What is good, right	Attractive, preferred
For people in general	For me and for you
Ideology	Pragmatism

SOURCE: Hofstede, G. (2001), *Culture's Consequences* (2nd ed.), Thousand Oaks, CA: Sage

Culture Defined

In the English language, as in many others, *culture* is a complicated word. It is used to describe high art (classical music, theater, painting, and sculpture), and it is often used to contrast these forms with popular art, or *popular culture*. It is used by biologists who produce cultures of bacteria; it is used in agriculture and horticulture. In advertising, cultural differences usually refer to the expressions of culture.

Culture is the glue that binds groups together. Without cultural patterns—organized systems of significant symbols—people would have difficulty living together. Culture is what defines a human community, its individuals, and social organizations. The anthropologist Clifford Geertz[8] views culture as a set of control mechanisms—plans, recipes, rules, instructions (what computer engineers call "programs")—for the governing of behavior. People are dependent on the control mechanisms of culture for ordering their behavior. In line with this, Hofstede[9] defines culture as "the collective mental programming of the people in an environment. Culture is not a characteristic of individuals; it encompasses a number of people who were conditioned by the same education and life experience."

Individuals are products of their culture; they are conditioned by their sociocultural environment to act in certain manners. Culture includes the things that have "worked" in the past. It includes shared beliefs, attitudes, norms, roles, and values found among speakers of a particular language who live during the same historical period in a specific geographic region. These shared elements of subjective culture are usually transferred from generation to generation. Language, time, and place help define culture.[10] Culture is to society what memory is to individuals.

Geertz[11] suggests that there is no such thing as a human nature independent of culture. Without interaction with culture, and thus the guidance provided by systems of significant symbols, our central nervous system would be incapable of directing our behavior. We are incomplete or unfinished animals who complete or finish ourselves through culture. Conclusions from psychoanalytic work in India, Japan, and the United States by the cross-cultural psychologist Roland are in accord with Geertz's statement. From Roland's[12] psychoanalytical work, it is apparent that the kinds of personalities persons actually develop, how they function and communicate in society, what their mode of being and experience is in the world and within themselves, and what their ideals and actualities of individuation are depend overwhelmingly on the given culture and society to which they belong.

Our ideas, our values, our acts, and our emotions are cultural products. We are individuals under the guidance of cultural patterns, historically created systems of meaning. Advertising reflects these wider systems of meaning: It reflects the way people think, what moves them, how they relate to each other, and how they live, eat, relax, and enjoy themselves.

Culture should not be viewed mainly as an environmental factor, something outside the consumer, to which the consumer is merely exposed, as expressed in some academic papers on international advertising.[13] Cultural values are not outside but inside the minds of people; they are part of their identity. Because of the stability of cultural values, some scholars are even beginning to suspect that some of them have a partially biological element.[14] The case for a link between biology and at least some cultural traits is getting stronger, as found by Allik and McCrae,[15] who compared group-level personality differences in 36 countries. See also Chapter 5.

Basically, there are two strands of thought: Are our behaviors, perception, and so forth determined by our genes or by our learning in specific societies; or in popular terms, are we driven by *nature or nurture*? A recent area of research that confirms a link between biology and culture is *cultural neuroscience*, which by using MRI technology, has given novel insights about cultural influences and mental processes. Cultural neuroscientists investigate the mutual constitution of culture, brain, and genes, discovering how "human culture" is manifested in neural activation patterns.[16] Findings have pointed at the interrelationship between cultural and neural processes. Cultural practices adapt to neural constraints, and the brain adapts to cultural practice. Learning and exposure to the cultural environment affects neural activation patterns, so culture equips its perceivers with culturally tuned perceptual processes to better navigate their cultural worlds. This is manifest both in perceptual outcomes and brain activity. Mind and culture are mutually constituted and engage in constant interaction.[17] Cultural neuroscience has, for example, an explanation for differences between North Americans and East Asians in performing numerical tasks and in the perception of background information or context.[18] When an American thinks about whether he is honest, his brain activity looks very different than when he thinks about whether another person is honest. When a Chinese man evaluates whether he is honest, his brain activity looks almost identical to when he is thinking about whether his mother is honest.[19] This is related to the difference between the independent and interdependent self as discussed in Chapter 5.

Levels of Culture

The term *culture* may apply to ethnic or national groups or to groups within a society at different levels: a country, an age group, a profession, or a social class. The cultural programming of an individual depends on the groups or categories to which he or she belongs. The expressions of culture that belong to a certain level of cultural programming will differ: Eating habits may differ by country, dress habits by profession, and gender roles by both country and social class. When discussing culture, it is important to be specific about the level, whether national culture, corporate culture, or age culture, in order not to create confusion. What is true at one level need not apply to another.

Cultural groups that share similar values exist at various levels with various degrees of homogeneity. These levels are illustrated in Figure 3.2. The widest group is the world, and what is shared is being human. It is being able to speak. But the language we speak and how we express ourselves varies. Continents can be viewed as being at a second level. In some continents or large parts of continents, shared values can be found that are different from the shared values in other continents, although there are large differences within these continents. For example, when comparing Asia with Europe, some common Asian values are very different from some common European values, and many African countries share values that are different from European values.

At the next level is the nation. Across continents, values of national culture can vary strongly. A country is not necessarily equivalent to a culture or society in the anthropological sense. A country (or nation-state) is a politically unified population; it may, and often does, contain more than one culture or society, anthropologically speaking. Some nation-states are very old, whereas others are of recent dates, such as ex-colonial countries, which consist of many cultural groups.

In some nations, different regions or provinces that historically have been governed separately, by local kings or princes, for example, Spain and Germany, may vary with respect to values. In particular in continents like South America and Africa, where nations have been constructed by foreign powers, their borders do

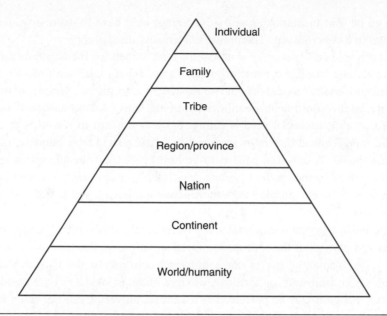

Figure 3.2 Levels of Culture

not delineate cultural groups. In such areas, tribes or clans cross national borders, and one cannot speak of national values, although across the continent some areas share more cultural values than others. So tribes, clans, or, at smaller scale, villages, or the Hispanic phenomenon of the Barrio can be placed at Level 5.

At Level 6 is the family, which can be the nuclear family of Western societies or the all-encompassing families of Africa or Asia, where the individual is integrated in the family, as opposed to Western individualistic societies where the individual is separate and unique.

Many people belong to a number of different groups at the same time, so we each carry several layers of mental programs within ourselves, corresponding to different layers of culture.[20] We can be part of a national culture; we can have a regional, linguistic, ethnic and/or religious affiliation; we can belong to a specific social class or profession or organization; we are born of a specific gender and sexual orientation, male, female, heterosexual, or homosexual.

Cultural Universals

Although people are not the same, some Western marketing and advertising professionals tend to perceive them to be the same. In particular, Western brand managers—because they are used to defining brands in abstract terms of personality and identity—are genuinely convinced of universality of consumers. Values and emotions, such as happiness, love and sadness, are assumed to be universal, but universals are always formulated in abstract terms. What makes people happy or how they express love varies not only by individual but even more so by culture. The more values are formulated in an abstract way, the more universal they seem to be. But in marketing and advertising, we'll have to express values and motives in a concrete way. Then most universality disappears.

Yet textbooks on international marketing tend to mention the search for cultural universals as a valuable orientation, referring to, among others, Murdock's list of cultural universals,[21] modes of behavior existing in all cultures. Examples of universals are bodily adornment, cleanliness, training, and cooking and food taboos. Indeed, a basic, universal need is eating. But it is not just to eat—it is to prefer certain foods cooked in certain ways and to follow a rigid table etiquette in consuming them.[22] A universal need is to be healthy. But how people act to remain healthy differs. In the south of Europe, for example, people use more medication, whereas in the north, people have a more active approach to health and exercise or play sports.

The ability to speak is universal, but it is not to talk, it is to utter the appropriate words and phrases in the appropriate social situations in the appropriate tone of voice. Also, romantic love is not a universal concept. In the United States, it includes friendship and comfort love, whereas Russians view it as unreal and temporary.[23] Religion may be perceived as a cultural universal, but the belief in one God or more, people's relationships with their Supreme Beings, and the rituals of worship are all part of culture and define the artifacts developed within a culture. Why are European cathedrals of a different structure than mosques or Hindu temples or American churches? Because they serve different religious practices. The concept of divinity is a Western concept. Ruth Benedict,[24] in her classic study on Japanese culture, describes how, after World War II, Japan was to adopt modern values, in which a concept of a divine monarch—as perceived through the eyes of the Americans—did not fit, and it was suggested to the Japanese emperor that he disavow his divinity. The emperor's reaction was said to be that it would be an embarrassment to strip himself of something he did not have. Religions are thought to create values, which in reality, they merely uphold and preserve.

Selective Perception

Perception is the process by which each individual selects, organizes, and evaluates stimuli from the external environment to provide meaningful experiences for him- or herself.[25] Selective perception means that people focus on certain features of their environment to the exclusion of others. This phenomenon plays a role in the discussion of an emerging *global culture*. Usually, the examples and illustrations accompanying the discourse are a few dominant global brands, such as Coca-Cola and McDonald's. Selective perception makes discussants see these and not the much larger number of local brands.

The selective perception phenomenon has strong consequences for advertising in an age in which the growing discrepancy between communication supply and consumption has led to the phenomenon of communication overload. Consumers are increasingly selective in what receives their attention. Culture reinforces this selective process. No two national groups see the world in exactly the same way. Medical studies of blind adults who were given sight through corrective surgery show that we have to be taught the "rules of seeing." These rules of seeing are not universal principles but are formed by the natural and social environments that teach us both what to look at and how to see it.[26] What people see is a function of what they have been trained or have learned to see in the course of growing up. Perceptual patterns are learned and culturally determined. You see what you want to see, and you don't see what you cannot see because it does not fit with your experience, your prior learning. We perceive what we expect to perceive. We perceive things according to our cultural map.[27] We become confused when things appear to be different from what we expected, and we may draw the wrong conclusions. Expecting guests at 8 in the evening but having them arrive at 9 will lead some of us to conclude that our guests are polite, others of us that they are impolite. Others, arriving at our house at dinnertime without invitation, may expect food because of their perception of hospitality. One reaction will be sharing whatever food there is, the other is embarrassment and waiting for dinner until the visitors have left. Some people nod their heads when they say yes, but that may mean no in quite a few other countries. We expect and see things from our own cultural frame of mind. We are prisoners of our own culture. Consumers are, and so are creative directors who follow their own cultural automatic pilot when developing advertising. So are the designers of social media and websites. This phenomenon enables them to develop effective communication for their own culture, but it limits their ability to develop effective advertising ideas, including meaningful values, for other cultures. Advertising in which the values do not match those of the culture of the receiver will be less noted or misunderstood and thus less effective.

Stereotyping

Stereotyping means mentally placing people in categories. Stereotypes can be functional or dysfunctional. Stereotyping is functional when we accept it as a natural process to guide our expectations. Stereotyping is dysfunctional if we use it to judge individuals incorrectly, seeing them only as part of a group. An example of a functional stereotype is that the Germans are punctual, which is correct. On average, they are more punctual than many other peoples. Certainly, the Italians and the Spanish have a different concept of time. For the Spanish, knowledge of this aspect of the German culture means that they can adapt their behavior: When they are expected for dinner, 8 o'clock means 8 o'clock, and not 9 or 10 as it does in Spain. An example of a dysfunctional stereotype would be for the British to say that the French are dirty, oversexed, and ludicrously obsessed with their culture and the French to say that the British are cold, uncultivated, hypocritical, and unreliable.[28] Yes, the British are more reserved in the eyes of the French, the Italians generally more chaotic in the eyes of the Germans, and the Germans rigid as perceived by the British.

It is important to realize that culture is relative: Stereotypes are in the eyes of the beholder's culture. Stereotypes are socially acquired knowledge and vary by social group. Because culture is stable, stereotypes can be found in literature from early times. An example is the way the Dutch have become part of the English language.

"Going Dutch," "a Dutch treat," and "a Dutch uncle" are expressions that reflect characteristics of the Dutch as observed by the English. Similar expressions about the Dutch do not occur in the German and French languages.

Advertising depends on the use of effective stereotypes because it must attract attention and create instant recognition. Advertising simplifies reality and thus has to use stereotypes. Advertising messages are generally short, and if audiences do not immediately recognize what the message is about, it is lost. Culture interferes. When we perceive or depict people of other cultures, we do so from the perspective of our own culture. Different cultures have different stereotypes of other cultures.

What are the characteristics of the stereotyped French? The Germans think the French are resourceful; the British think they are humorless and short tempered. The Dutch think the French are not very serious; the Spanish think they are cold and distant. The Finns think they are romantic yet superficial. The Americans think they are pleasant and intelligent yet pretentious. Asians think they are indiscreet.[29]

From this example, it is obvious that it is particularly dangerous to use strong national stereotypes in international advertising. The creative director's stereotyped perception may be different from the stereotyped perception of audiences in countries other than his or her own. Some stereotypes are shared by several cultures in Europe, for example, the stereotype of the German sense of humor not being understandable to others. The Spanish advertisement for Volkswagen (see Illustration 3.1) ties into that stereotype by saying, "People see this and smile. At last, they understand German humor."

Illustration 3.1
Volkswagen, Spain

Manifestations of Culture

Hofstede[30] distinguishes four manifestations of culture: symbols, rituals, heroes, and values. In Figure 3.2, these are depicted as the layers of an onion, indicating that symbols represent the most superficial and values the deepest manifestations of culture, with heroes and rituals falling somewhere in between.

Symbols are words, gestures, pictures, or objects that carry a particular meaning recognized only by those who share a culture. The words of a language or a particular kind of jargon belong in this category, as do dress, hairstyles, flags, status symbols, and brands. New symbols are easily developed, and old ones quickly disappear; symbols from one cultural group are regularly copied by others. This is why symbols are shown in the outer, most superficial layer in Figure 3.3. Coca-Cola, Nike, and Google are examples of brands that have become global symbols. Yet they may evoke different associations for Americans than they do for the Chinese.

Heroes are persons—alive or dead, real or imaginary—who possess characteristics that are highly prized in a society and who thus serve as role models for behavior. Even fantasy or cartoon figures, like Batman or Charlie Brown in the United States, Hello Kitty in Japan, and Astérix in France, can serve as cultural heroes. In the television age, outward appearances have become more important in choosing heroes than they once were. Fantasy heroes can become globally known, but the stories in which they play a part often are local. Astérix behaves in a different way than Donald Duck.

Rituals are the collective activities considered socially essential within a culture: They are carried out for their own sake. Examples include ways of greeting, ways of paying respect to others, and social and religious ceremonies. Business and political meetings organized for seemingly rational reasons often serve mainly ritual purposes: for example, to allow the leaders to assert themselves. Sporting events are rituals for both the players and the spectators. The rituals around American football are very different from those around European football. In particular, the phenomenon of cheerleaders is nonexistent in Europe.

In Figure 3.3, symbols, heroes, and rituals are included in the term *expressions of culture.* They are visible to an outside observer. Their cultural meaning is invisible, however; it lies in the way the expressions are interpreted by the insiders of the culture. Brands are part of a ritual, and advertising helps make the ritual. Manufacturers use and create rituals around their products to differentiate them from competitive products. The beer brand Corona Extra distinguishes itself from others by the suggestion that it should be consumed by drinking from the bottle after having pushed a piece of lime into the long neck of the bottle. Advertising displays the rituals around products and brands; it reflects how people behave and interact, how they are dressed, their language, their eating habits, and how their houses look. These elements are the expressions or artifacts of culture that express "How we do things here."

At the core of culture lie values. Values were defined in a previous section of this chapter. Researchers try to describe values by asking people to state a preference among alternatives. One of the difficulties in researching values is interpreting what people say. One problem is the distinction between the desirable and the desired, as discussed before. Language is another problem: Values don't translate easily because words expressing values have abstract meaning. They must be seen as labels of values. A word may serve as a label of a value in one culture but be the label of a different value in another culture. This explains the difficulty of translating advertising copy into languages other than the one in which it is conceived. This issue will be further discussed in Chapter 6.

A so-called global culture refers to the expressions of culture, the symbols,

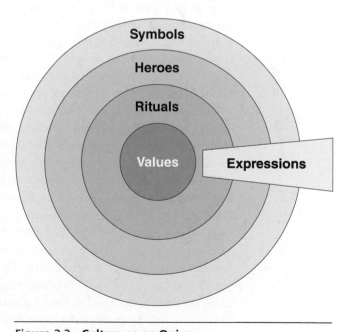

Figure 3.3 Culture as an Onion

SOURCE: Hofstede, G., Hofstede, G. J., & Minkov, M. (2010). *Cultures and organizations: Software of the mind* (3rd ed.). New York: McGraw-Hill.

converging eating habits, and global heroes. Fast food, and particularly the Big Mac or pizzas, have become a global ritual. Yet our values have not become global; they vary across cultures and are not likely to change during our lifetime. This stability of values is not well understood by advertising people, who tend to mistake superficial trends for changing values.

Large multinationals tend to shape a corporate culture with shared practices: ways of dressing, meeting, communicating, and presenting, all overriding the multitude of national cultures. This is useful to give cohesion to the worldwide group of employees and to give identity to the company.

National, historically defined cultures have strong emotional connotations for those who belong to them. These connotations define their identity, which means the subjective feelings and values of a population sharing cultural characteristics, a shared "memory," a "history." Global or cosmopolitan cultures cannot refer to such a common identity. Unlike national cultures, a global culture is essentially "memoryless."

Next to the visible signs and symbols, imagery, and music, other, not directly visible aspects influenced by culture, are intellectual styles and language. These will be discussed in the next sections.

Signs, Symbols, and Body Language

Pierce,[31] one of the founders of semiotics as a discipline, distinguishes three basic types of sign: icon, index, and symbol. An *icon* bears a resemblance to its object. An *index* is a sign with a direct existential connection with its object—smoke is an index of fire. A *symbol* is a sign whose connection with its object is a matter of convention, agreement, or rule. Words and numbers are symbols; so is the red cross. Globalization has led to increased use of icons. Airports, stations, and other places frequented by international travelers use icons because they are not linked with language. They also help with faster information processing. Other examples are the use of diagrams, such as bar or pie charts, in reports and presentations. Icons, indexes, and symbols are part of the fundamental semiotic instruments used for advertising. Language codes, signs, symbols, and gestures are all rituals of culture and define cultural groups. *Culture* is the shared ability to recognize, decode, and produce signs and symbols, so culture also is a combination of semiotic habits. Differences in semiotic habits delineate cultures.

Semiotics, the study of signs and symbols, is in many countries an integral part of advertising theory, although used more in some countries (France, Eastern Europe) than in others. Some cultures use more symbols in advertising than do others. This is related to writing and language. The Japanese and other Asians using the kanji script seem to have a greater ability to perceive and use symbols. Experience with Japanese students in a non-Japanese learning environment shows that, compared with Western students, they tend to be more comfortable with pictures and symbols than with language, particularly if the language is not their native language.

Signs and symbols are an important part of association networks in our memory: package, color, letters, signs. Color can have a particularly strong cultural meaning. Black is the color of mourning in the Western world. In China, white symbolizes mourning. Gold has a strong symbolic meaning for the Chinese, but not combined with black. For some cultures, symbolic language is much more important than verbal language. In Asia, numbers have significance unknown to Western cultures. Numbers can be particularly meaningful. An example is the 555 cigarette brand in Asia. Illustration 3.2 shows this brand in Cambodia. In China, the number 8 is auspicious. The Olympic Games of 2008 in China started on August 8, 2008 (8-8-8).

Gestures are important cultural signs: Gestures that in one culture have a positive meaning can be embarrassing to members of another culture. A Russian gesture meaning "friendship" means "winning" in the United States. Germans raise their eyebrows in recognition of a clever idea. The same expression in Britain and the Netherlands is a sign of skepticism. The Hungarian gesture, as shown in outdoor advertising for Pepsi in Illustration 3.3, is perceived as obscene, not only in West European countries but also in Bulgaria, close to Hungary. The U.S. OK sign means "zero" in France and Hungary, "money" in Japan. The thumbs-up gesture is used by pilots the world over, but in some countries, it is not so accepted. The V sign means "victory" for the English if the palm and fingers face outward; if the palm and fingers face inward, it means, "up yours."

Illustration 3.2 Cigarette Brand 555, Cambodia

Illustration 3.3 Pepsi, Hungary

Putting your feet up on your desk, as in the advertisement for Glenfiddich (Illustration 3.4), may demonstrate relaxation or a "Friday feeling" in the United States, but showing the soles of your shoes or feet is offensive in most other parts of the world, in particular in Asia and the Arab world. Showing your tongue to other people in Europe is a sign of contempt, but for children, it is a sign of challenging other children. In Asia, it is impolite, even for children. For the Maoris in New Zealand, it is a sign of great respect.

Making mistakes is easy, as every seasoned traveler will have discovered. What is considered polite in one culture may be considered obscene in another. What is friendly here is hostile there. A comprehensive guide to the meaning of gestures was developed by Desmond Morris,[32] who adds the note that signaling by gesture is a predominantly masculine pursuit. In some countries, it is so exclusively masculine that a female researcher had to withdraw before the local men would even discuss the subject.

The friday Scotch

Illustration 3.4   **Glenfiddich, USA**

Eye contact may communicate very different things to people of various cultures. Whereas in the West direct eye contact expresses boldness, which is viewed as positive, in East Asian countries, direct eye contact may make people feel uncomfortable or is even viewed as rude. In a 2007 global campaign by Nike with National Basketball Association (NBA) stars, the players were not engaged in a game, but their gaze was directed at the viewer, which was viewed as intimidating by the Chinese. In Shanghai, next to the global ads, a more culturally appropriate campaign was developed: featuring famous Chinese athletes who did not gaze at the public but were fixed on their goals, actually playing and providing a spectacle for the public.[33]

Proxemics, the study of people's use of space as a cultural artifact,[34] deals with the degree to which people want to be close to other people or to touch others. It is an aspect of body language and an expression of culture. When someone from the south of Europe makes a motion to a northern European to link arms while walking in the street, the latter may not know how to react, as touching in public is not something universal in Europe. Northern Europeans don't like to be close to other people. Observance of people's behavior in elevators will show that when a crowded elevator begins to empty, the French will stay where they are, yet the British will quickly increase space between each other.

The anthropologist Edward Hall,[35] in particular, has studied differences in proxemics in various cultures. In the United States, there is a commonly accepted invisible boundary around any two or three people in conversation that separates them from others. Distance alone serves to isolate, give privacy. Someone can be in a room with other people without disturbing their privacy. When a person stands still or sits down, even in a public place, a small sphere of privacy balloons around him or her, which is considered inviolate. Anyone who enters this zone and stays there is intruding. For the Germans, there is no such thing as being in the room without being inside the zone of intrusion of the other party present, no matter how far away. When an American wants to be alone, she or he goes into a room and shuts the door. The English have internalized a set of barriers that others are supposed to recognize. Use of space in countries around the Mediterranean can be seen in the crowded trains, buses, sidewalks, and cafés. These cultures are characterized by high sensory involvement, expressed in the way they eat, entertain, and crowd together in cafés. Isolating oneself is seen as an insult to others. Anglo-Saxons tend to go into their room and shut the door when they want to be alone. The Spanish don't do this. American students studying in Spain and living with families tend to become confused when their host families show concern everytime they are alone in their rooms with the door shut.

Another example is how professors and students relate. Spanish professors and students socialize outside class. They go to bars, dance, and touch. This is seen as inappropriate in the United States, where professors can even be accused of sexual harassment if the interaction is between people of different gender. Differences between Arabs and Americans or Europeans are even stronger. Arabs do not like enclosed space. Muslims have particularly strong rules for space between men and women. In advertisements, if showing men and women together is allowed at all, the distance must be carefully observed.

The American home compartmentalizes the family, so children grow up leading separate lives. This has consequences for media behavior. Americans are not used to watching television in groups, as are the Spanish.

When comparing cultures, it is important to learn which are the signs and symbols used by a culture and how they are recognized.

Imagery and Music

Imagery, or the use of pictures, symbols, or metaphors as a way of conveying meaning, is based on pictorial conventions. There are significant cross-cultural differences in pictorial perception and the construction of pictures. The selection of style and/or of point of view shown in a picture is based on the cultural learning of a photographer or creative director, with the cultural learning of the audience in mind. Audiences (consumers) use their learned pictorial skills in their response. More about this in Chapter 5.

Western people tend to think of the interpretation of pictures as a process occurring in time: the sequence of information processing as a function of visual layout. But not all cultures have a sequential thinking pattern. The concept of time varies, as well as the direction of viewing (left to right or right to left). Preferences for symbols or verbal expression and for movement or stills vary so much that art directors should think twice before developing an international campaign based on visuals. Yet the statement that visuals travel better than words is still often heard. Pictures, just like verbal language, have to be translated into the pictorial language of other cultures.

Metaphors, in particular, represent cultural artifacts. The advertisements for LG Corp. (Illustration 3.5) and Infonet (Illustration 3.6), both from *Newsweek,* represent metaphors that will not be understood universally. The Korean LG ad shows a fish in the desert, suggesting metaphorically that digital technology makes the impossible possible. In many Asian countries, the fish is also a symbol of luck and prosperity, which is not understood in most of the Western

Illustration 3.5 LG, International

Break
the spell,
communicate
globally

Whatever you wish for your global communications,
solutions from Infonet make it come true.

As a multinational, your wish is for a seamless global network that delivers the
full promise of your business systems investment. Infonet's global communications
solutions are customized, innovative, reliable, secure, cost-effective. And fully
managed end-to-end over our global multi-service network. Infonet offers local
support in more than 60 countries and connections in over 180. No need to wish.
We make it happen every day. Global communications services for multinationals.

infonet
www.infonet.com

Europe · Middle East · Africa + 32 2 627 39 11 Asia Pacific + 65 734 1199 North America + 1 310 335 2600 Latin America + 58 2 368 9400

Illustration 3.6   Infonet, International

world. The global advertisement for Infonet refers to an originally German fairy tale written by the brothers Grimm, which may not be well understood in all countries in the world.

Music is another aspect of culture. Although many types of music have proved able to travel (classical music, jazz, pop music), cultures tend to have their own rhythm. A people's music is inseparable from their lives, and songs represent an important part of their identity. Music represents a sort of rhythmic consensus, a consensus of the core culture. Technically, little is known about what human synchrony is, but rhythm is basic to synchrony. Being in sync with the core culture must be more effective than being out of sync.[36] Language has a rhythm, too. Those who have learned to speak a foreign language well, according to grammar and idiom, know that they will not be understood if they have not learned the music and rhythm of that language.

Thinking Patterns and Intellectual Styles

There is no single way of logical thinking. Linear externalized logic is part of Western philosophy and science and different from logic in other cultures, such as the more inward-looking Buddhist philosophies. Digital thinking and decision making are characteristic of the North American communication system. The Japanese are more inclined toward the analog and experience-based reasoning. North Americans are structural and analytical; they lack the dynamics of the Chinese yin-yang, the European dialectic (the process aimed at abolishing differences of opinion), or the Japanese holistic pattern-recognition approach, which involves recognizing the feeling of the overall situation before looking at the details. The North American approach works toward extremes in order to facilitate decision making. In continental European cultures, the emphasis is on making an analysis to generate ideological and theoretical arguments.

The way in which arguments are supported also varies across cultures. Some tend to rely on facts, some on ideology or dogma, and others on tradition or emotion. For the Japanese, the *kimochi,* or feeling, has to be right; logic is cold. The Saudis seem to be intuitive in approach and avoid persuasion based primarily on empirical reasoning. The French have a philosophy; Americans want data and proof of hypotheses. Usunier[37] distinguishes four different intellectual styles: the "Gallic" (French), the "Teutonic" (German), the "Saxonic" (English and American), and the "Nipponic" (Japanese). Saxons prefer to look for facts and evidence. Teutonic and Gallic styles tend to place theoretical arguments at the center of their intellectual process. Data and facts are there to illustrate what is said rather than to demonstrate it. The Teutonic style includes a preference for reasoning and deduction. The Gallic style is less occupied with deduction; it is directed more toward the use of persuasive strength of words and speeches in an aesthetically perfect way. The Nipponic intellectual style favors a more modest, global, and provisional approach: Thinking and knowledge are conceived of as being in a temporary state, avoiding absolute categorical statements.

Americans categorize virtually everything. Duality, a way of categorizing, is implicitly and explicitly part of American culture: concrete versus abstract, present versus past, new versus old, past versus future, harmony versus conflict, inner-directed versus outer-directed.[38] Japanese thought is not logical, but intuitive.[39] The Japanese are not familiar with polar thinking.

How people learn influences their thinking and response. Western learning methods are largely based on critical thinking and analysis. Asian learning systems are based more on memorizing. Different cultures teach different ways of gathering and weighing evidence, of presenting viewpoints, and of reaching conclusions. Particularly in the United States, if there are no facts to support an opinion, the opinion will not be considered legitimate or valid. There is an expression in the American language that expresses this: "the point," as in "Let's get right to the point" or "What's the point of all this?" Writers and speakers are supposed to "make their points clear," meaning that they are supposed to say or write explicitly the idea or piece of information they wish to convey. The directness associated with the point is not part of Chinese or Japanese languages.[40] Many such differences in intellectual styles were found by cross-cultural psychologists and are being confirmed by cultural neuroscience.[41]

Language

There are two ways of looking at the language-culture relationship: Language influences culture, or language is an expression of culture. Edward Sapir and Benjamin Lee Whorf hypothesized that the structure of language has a significant influence on perception and categorization.[42] The latter would imply that the worldview of people depends on the structure and characteristics of the language they speak. Users of markedly different grammars are led by their grammars toward different types of observations and different evaluations of similar acts of observation. According to this viewpoint, language is not only an instrument for describing events, but also it shapes events. Observers using different languages will posit different facts under the same circumstances, or they will arrange similar facts in different ways.

The other viewpoint is that language reflects culture. The approach is to realize that only the ability to speak is universal for humankind. Which language a person speaks is part of the culture in which she or he grows up. Holtgraves and Kashima[43] argue that language reflects and reinforces culture. Language use is patterned, and these patterns become linguistic practices. If linguistic practices are used widely in a linguistic community for a long period of time, they may be considered to have an influence on users' social cognitive processes—the process of encoding, storing, and retrieving knowledge related to other human beings—and as a matter of habit, people engage in their preferred linguistic practice. The use of language on any particular occasion reflects cultural orientations, and over time, these ways of representing culture linguistically become linguistic practices and eventually part of the language.

Thus, language may also provide identity, which is an essential aspect of language in ex-colonial countries. In Africa, where in many countries the ex-colonial language has become the lingua-franca, tribal language is connected with a sense of group identity, of loyalty to traditional ways. The lingua franca is a utilitarian instrument to get ahead in the world but doesn't provide a bond of solidarity.[44]

Many examples can be found of how cultures vary with respect to their languages. Whereas Western languages break down words into syllables and letters, Asian languages express contents by associative means which is most obvious in Chinese, Japanese, and Korean pictographic writing. Pictures or characters are associated with words.[45] An example of an illustrative language is Thai language that expresses abstract Western terms by more concrete terms. A fridge, for example, is *thu yen* or the cold box; heartbreak is *jay looy*, or heart flying away; *paak waan* means sweet mouth, meaning lying or glossing over.[46]

Other examples are dropping a pronoun, using adjectives as opposed to verbs, or using contextual qualifiers. The linguistic practice of pronoun drop (including the pronoun in the verb), a habit of mostly collectivistic cultures, is a specific example of a broad cultural pattern. Another example is the use of adjectives or verbs to describe human beings. Verbs retain contextual information, relating the person described to the social context. Korean speakers, for example, use verbs, but English speakers use adjectives to describe social objects, the self, and others. Speaking indirectly requires relatively greater attention to the context than does speaking directly. East Asian contextualizing linguistic practices reflect the view of individuals as embedded in the social context.

Expressions of culture are particularly recognizable in the use of metaphors. Examples are expressions like "he is a team player," "he drives me up the wall," a "ballpark estimate," and "the sweet spot," all derived from American baseball in the American language, whereas British English has a number of expressions relating to cricket. The elements used in metaphors will vary. In Egypt, for example, the sun is perceived as cruel, so a girl will not be described as "my sunshine" but may be compared with moonlight.[47] "Moonlighting" in English means having a second job in the evening.

It is the cultural environment which explains why some languages have more words for one thing than for others. Some languages have more different words for the different substances of ice or rain than others. The Norwegian language reflects a historic seafaring nation, having one strong word for "wind in your favor": *bør.* Some languages have words that do not exist in others. The English *pith,* the archaic word for marrow, refers to the white under the skin of oranges and other citrus fruit. This seems to be directly linked with the British marmalade culture. Some culture-specific words migrate to other languages if they express something unique. Examples of such words are *management, computer, apartheid, machismo, perestroika, geisha, sauna, Mafia,* and *kamikaze.*[48] Often, these words reflect the specific values of a culture. They cannot easily be translated into words of other cultures, or they have been borrowed from another culture from the start. The English language does not have its own words for *cousin* and *nephew.* These were borrowed from French (*cousin* and *neveu*). The way a person describes kin is closely connected with the way he or she thinks about them. In extended families, a father and a father's brother may both be termed *father.* The Hungarians differentiate between a younger sister (*húg*) and an older sister (*növér*). The Russian language has different names for the four different brothers-in-law. In Indonesian, *besan* is the word for "parents of the children who are married to each other."[49] Even terms of abuse vary: Whereas the most used abusive term of the Germans, Spanish, Italians, and Greek is related to lack of mental capabilities, the French, Brits, Americans, and Dutch use sexually loaded terms. Norwegians use *the devil.*[50]

Both the Spanish and the Dutch language show frequent use of diminutives. In both languages, use of the diminutive suffix reflects something positive, whereas using the enlargement suffix turns it into something negative.

The English language reflects the way Anglo-Saxons deal with action and time. They have a rich vocabulary expressing this, such as "down to earth," "feedback," "deadline." The English word *upset* expresses the way the English handle their emotions, with self-constraint. *Upset* is not translatable into most other languages. The English concept of *sharing* includes more values than a translation in other European languages can include. It includes "generosity," "participating," "caring for fellow people," "not totally concerned with the self," and "communicating positive things." It includes showing "how good you are" and "achievement." It covers both the German *teilen* and *mitteilen* or the Dutch *delen* and *mededelen* and more than that.

The Dutch and the Scandinavians have words for "togetherness" that express much more than "being together" and that do not exist in the Anglo-Saxon world. The words are *gezellig* (Dutch), *hyggelig* (Danish), *mysigt* (Swedish), and *kodikas* (Finnish). The Danes use it even in combinations like *hyggetime* ("together time") and *hyggemad* ("together food").[51] It means sharing your feelings and philosophies in a very personal and intimate way while being together in a small group. An Englishman living in the Netherlands, when asked his opinion, will shiver and say, "It is so intrusive." The concept means preferring a dinner party for four people to a larger group, whereas a small group is not considered to be a dinner party by the British or the Americans. For the Dutch and the Scandinavians, the concept can be used very effectively in advertising for the type of product used during such meetings, such as coffee, sweets, and drinks.

A German example is the word *Reinheit,* which has a wider meaning than the word *purity.* The word *ergiebig* is another example, meaning delivering quality and efficiency, or more for the same money. The Spanish word *placer* means much more than the translation *pleasure.* It includes pleasure while eating, enjoyment, sharing a social event, softness, warmth, the good life, contentment, and satisfaction. Some words represent interpersonal relations of one culture that do not exist in others.

The French notions of *savoir faire* and *savoir vivre* include a vast array of values specific to French culture and cannot be properly translated. The Japanese expression for "computer graphics" carries the meaning of a picture, a drawing, and illustration or sketch, but not of a graph. Another example is the Japanese word for *animation,* which in translation carries the meaning of comics or cartoons.[52] In Japan, the word for *heart* associates with *warmth,* not necessarily with *love,* as love is not expressed the same as in the Western world. There are no proper equivalents to the words *identity* and *personality* in the Japanese language, as the concept of personality separate from the social environment is alien to the Japanese people. The Japanese borrowed the word for brand (*burando*) from the English language because the Western brand concept is based on unicity and authenticity which are values that are not common in Japan.

The Ghanian philosopher Kwasi Wiredu[53] views the potential of human beings to adopt new concepts and ideas that previously didn't exist in their language as a remarkable and universal ability of human beings. We can understand and adopt concepts or problems expressed in another language even if these are not translatable in our own language. However, we have to be careful translating the untranslatable. Wiredu gives several examples of translation difficulties that can have grave interpretation consequences. In particular, translating concepts such as "mind," "person," "soul," "spirit," "truth," "fact," and "free will" and contrasts like "the natural and the supernatural" from English into the Akan language can cause misunderstandings because of conceptual problems. *Truth* in the sense of the opposite of "not false" doesn't have a linguistic equivalent in the Akan language; the related word *nokware* refers to "truthfulness," literally "being of one mouth." *Mind* is rarely directly translated because the Akan conception of mind is more a kind of capacity or function. There are several Akan words with which it can be identified but none that covers the exact meaning.

Untranslatable concepts often are so meaningful to members of a specific culture that they are effective elements of advertising copy. They refer to collective memory. This implies that words that are labels of culturally meaningful concepts are too ambiguous to use in international campaigns. A European campaign for the KitKat candy bar was based on the concept of the break: "Take a break, take a KitKat." The break was an English institution: the 11 o'clock morning tea break, when working people had their morning tea and brought a KitKat as a snack. Because of this, KitKat in the United Kingdom was called "Elevens." This type of break did not exist in any other country in Europe, so the break concept had to be translated in a different way for the other countries. Continental Europeans do not have the same break memory as do the British. Language is much more important than many international advertisers realize. It is common knowledge among those who are bi- or trilingual that copy, carrying cultural values, is difficult to translate. Monolingual people generally do not understand this. If translations are needed, particularly for research purposes, the best system is translating and back-translating the questions to be sure that at least the questions have the same meaning. Yet the values included in the words cannot be translated, and often conceptual equivalence cannot be attained.

Although English is the most spoken second language in the world, fluency varies widely, and advertisers have to understand that even in countries where most people seem to be able to understand English, this knowledge often is only superficial. Few Germans understand English language slogans like "Be Inspired" (Siemens) or "Impossible Is Nothing" (Adidas).[54] Certainly, colloquial English or American expressions will not be understood. The advertisement for Computer Associates (CA) International (Illustration 3.7) uses the word *schmortal,* which is not understandable for Europeans who speak English. Yet the ad was in the European edition of *Business Week.*

Often English language words are used in advertising more for symbolic reasons, for example, to convey modernity or an international image to the brand. Different languages can convey different symbolic meanings. For example, French symbolizes beauty and elegance and German reflects reliability and technicality. However, people tend to remember advertising in the local language better.[55]

Illustration 3.7
CA International

Comparing Cultures

The study of culture can be characterized by the dispute between those stressing the unique aspects of culture and those stressing the comparable aspects. A difficulty in comparing cultures is ethnocentrism. Because our own culture works as if on automatic pilot and we are all more or less prisoners of our own culture, it is difficult to exclude our own cultural value pattern from the way we perceive and classify other cultures. In a more extreme sense, *ethnocentrism* refers to a tendency to feel that the home-country people are superior to people of other countries, that they are more intelligent, more capable, or more reliable than people of other countries. Usually, ethnocentrism is more attributable to inexperience or lack of knowledge about foreign cultures than to prejudice.[56]

There are basically two approaches to comparing cultures, from the emic or from the etic point of view. *Etic* refers to what is general in cultures, *emic* to what is specific in one or more cultures. The usefulness of culture as an explanatory variable depends on our ability to "unpackage" the culture concept. To do so, the etic approach must be used, and cultural values must be arrayed along interpretable dimensions. Differences in the locations of cultures along these dimensions can then be used to explain variance of behavior patterns, norms, attitudes, and personality variables. The etic approach is followed in this book. Methodologies for measuring and comparing cultural values will be further discussed in Chapter 6.

Comparing Nations: Homogeneity and Heterogeneity

In this book we compare nations, or national cultures. A point of discussion is the delineation of cultural groups by national boundaries, although there is much diversity within national borders, as mentioned earlier in this chapter (Levels of Culture subsection). Many nations, however, are historically developed wholes that usually share one dominant language, mass media, a national education system, and national markets for products and services.[57] Because of the availability of national statistics collected by national governments, companies generally compare nations with respect to demographics and gross national income (GNI) per capita. National-level culture data add value to these comparisons.

With respect to values, some nations are more homogeneous than others, although differences between nations are substantially larger than differences within nations. Cross-cultural psychologist Shalom Schwartz[58] assessed cultural unity within nations by comparing the cultural distance between samples within countries with the cultural distance between samples from seven different countries. The cultural distance between samples from different countries was almost always greater than the distance between samples from the same country. Between-country distances were greater in 183 of 187 comparisons. This implies that the similarity of cultural value orientations within nations, when viewed against the background of cultural distance between nations, is considerable. Comparisons of, for example, younger and older subcultures yielded similar relative national scores.

Minkov and Hofstede,[59] by secondary analysis of data from the World Values Survey that offers data on values both at the national level and for country regions, found that 299 in-country regions from 28 countries in East and Southeast Asia, sub-Saharan Africa, Latin America, and the Anglo world overwhelmingly cluster along national lines on basic cultural values, with cross-border intermixtures being relatively rare. This was true even for countries like Malaysia, Indonesia, or Mexico and Guatemala, despite their shared languages and traditions.

Although differences between nations are substantially larger than differences within nations, one has to recognize the differences, in particular those existing in some large nations, such as Brazil, China, India, Indonesia, and the United States, which can be divided into regions differing along geographical, climatic, economic, linguistic, and/or ethnic lines.

A very heterogeneous nation is the United States, where the white American population is decreasing and other groups, in particular Americans of Hispanic origin, are increasing. According to the U.S. Census Bureau, in 2010, white Americans made up 72.4% of the population, but part of the white population is of Hispanic descent. African Americans made up 12.6%, and Americans of Hispanic origin composed 16.3% of the population.[60] Cross-cultural psychologists tend to measure value differences of these groups, but discussing these is beyond the scope of this book.[61]

Brazil is another example of a large country with mixed populations. As in other Latin American countries, the population of Brazil is the result of a mix of autochthonous, Hispanic, African, and non-Hispanic immigrant populations. In Brazil, the African influence comprises a variety of elements, not based on one single African source, but from many African peoples. Although a generic African origin can be recognized, it is not possible to identify a specific nation or people it comes from.[62]

Value differences of the original and later populations can be recognized in areas where these groups are more concentrated. Hofstede et al.[63] found that the Northeast, African-Brazilian region reflected more African values, and the North region with more indigenous populations reflected more values of the original populations.

Across Asia, some nations have a very long history and/or are more homogeneous than others. Other nations are very large and are expected to be more heterogeneous than smaller nations. Devinderpal Singh[64] found regional cultures in India that were quite different with respect to cultural values. For example, the state of Gujarat in western India is far more hierarchical, and power is distributed more unequally as compared to West Bengal and Punjab. Whereas Tamil Nadu is collectivistic, in West Bengal, people are more individualistic.

Sub-Saharan Africa is a geographically vast and culturally diverse region. It comprises more than 35 countries, each of them with an average of about ten culturally distinct communities within the national boundaries.[65] In Tanzania alone, there are 121 ethnic groups. Yet despite linguistic and cultural differences, most Africans live in a society where the key structures are the extended family, clans, villages, or tribes.[66]

Also, Europe is not a homogeneous region with respect to national values, and heterogeneity within nations varies. Some nations are clearly more homogeneous than others. Cross-cultural consultant Arne Maas used regional data from the European Social Survey[67] to calculate a measure of cultural cohesion by cluster analysis of 21 value questions that were answered by people from all provinces in a country. The questions measured value preferences, such as the importance of having friends and family and equality, or the importance of work or of being rich. These are not representative of the total value system of countries, but variety gives an indication of the degree of coherence of countries. The coherence measure for 19 countries ranged from 1.4 for Norway to 14.9 for Spain, indicating that of these 19 countries, Norway is most homogeneous and Spain most heterogeneous. The score for the whole region, including 19 countries, was 27.

The northern European countries are evidently culturally coherent. Their measures ranged from 1.4 for Norway to 2.4 for Sweden. Only Denmark appears to be less coherent with a measure of 5.3. The United Kingdom seems to be somewhere in the middle with 7.0, but this changes dramatically when Northern Ireland is left out of the analysis, and the measure changes from 7.0 to 1.6. A similar change occurs in Switzerland (coherence = 7.2); when Ticino, the Italian part of Switzerland, is left out. The figure then drops to 2.6. Spain is the least culturally coherent of all countries measured. It has a score of 14.9, the highest of all 19 countries. This is not so strange for a country with at least three regions with different languages and histories (Castillia, Cataluna, and Pais Vasco). Also, Greece is not very coherent (12.2), although the regions within Greece have more in common with other Greek regions than with regions in other countries. This means that Greek culture is quite different from other European cultures.

A third country that is culturally not very cohesive is Germany (8.5). It is interesting to see that the differences are especially large in former West Germany (13.7) and that the former DDR (East Germany) is quite cohesive (4.3). Some southern

German regions cluster with Austria and Switzerland rather than with other German regions. Also, Hamburg is quite different from the rest of Germany. Table 3.2 provides the measures for the 19 countries.

The consequences of heterogeneity of countries is that companies, when testing products or advertising, have to be careful which region to select as a test market in a particular country if it is a heterogeneous one. For international research, using a too homogeneous or too heterogeneous country as a test market is risky.

When heterogeneity was caused by immigration of large groups from other countries, in some cases, these immigrants kept living together and remained a separate culture within the host culture; in other cases, they mixed with the autochthonous population. Examples of the former are the Hispanics in the United States and Turkish and Moroccan immigrants in several European countries as well as the countries that were colonized by the British, who did not mix with the original populations. Examples of the latter are several Latin American countries where long-term colonizers and later immigrants mixed with the indigenous populations, resulting in so-called hybrid cultures. Yet results from measurements of cultural values at the national level in the various countries of Latin America tend to point at a greater influence from the values of the indigenous ancient civilizations than from the values of the colonizing powers.[68]

Both Africa and Latin America have been occupied by colonial powers, but the mix of populations is typical of Latin America. In most African countries, the colonizers did not mix with the indigenous population. One explanation may be that the cultural distance between Africans and the colonizers, being mostly from North Europe, was greater than the cultural distance between the Spanish and Portuguese and the indigenous populations of South- and Meso-America.

The degree of homogeneity is not related to people's feelings of national pride. The World Values Survey measures the degree to which people are proud of their country. This varies strongly across cultures. Whereas feelings of national pride are strong in the culturally heterogeneous South Africa where 74.9% of the population say they are proud of their country, they are weak in the culturally homogeneous Japan, where only 22.8% say so.

Table 3.2 Measures of Coherence for 19 Countries

1.	Norway	1.4	11.	Austria	5.7
2.	Finland	1.9	12.	Netherlands	5.7
3.	Sweden	2.4	13.	United Kingdom	7.0
4.	Hungary	2.9	14.	Switzerland	7.2
5.	Slovenia	3.0	15.	Israel	7.5
6.	Belgium	3.6	16.	Portugal	8.3
7.	Ireland	3.6	17.	Germany	8.5
8.	Poland	4.5	18.	Greece	12.2
9.	Czech Republic	5.0	19.	Spain	14.9
10.	Denmark	5.3	20.	All 19 countries	27.0

Summary

Values determine the way people think and behave. As most people are not aware of their values, they work as if on automatic pilot. There are paradoxical aspects to values. Cultural values are values shared by groups of people, for example, nations. International marketing and advertising people must understand these values of national culture because they influence consumer behavior, brand images, and the way advertising is made and perceived across countries. Cultural universals exist only when formulated in abstract terms. When dealing with people of cultures other than our own, stereotyping and selective perception can inhibit proper understanding of people's behavior. Because language is a reflection of culture, some words or concepts that are meaningful to people in one culture cannot be translated into the language of another culture.

The art of advertising is to develop symbols or advertising properties that must be understood by a target audience. In international advertising, these signs, or symbols, usually have originated in one culture and cannot be decoded the same way by members of other cultures. Understanding the concept of culture and the consequences of cultural differences will make marketing and advertising people realize that one message, whether verbal or visual, can never reach one global audience because there is no single global culture of people with identical values. Worldwide, there is a great variety of values. The problem is that we have to be able to recognize and to vocalize the differences. Models for understanding this variety will be described in Chapter 4.

Notes

1. Okazaki, S., & Mueller, B. (2007). Cross-cultural advertising research: Where we have been and where we need to go. *International Marketing Review, 24*(5), 499–518.

2. Rokeach, M. (1973). *The nature of human values.* New York: Free Press, p. 5.

3. Herche, J. (1994). *Measuring social values: A multi-item adaptation to the list of values* (MSI Report Summary, Report No. 94–101). Cambridge, MA: Marketing Science Institute.

4. Jagodzinski, W. (2004). Methodological problems of value research. In H. Vinken, J. Soeters, & P. Ester (Eds.), *Comparing cultures: Dimensions of culture in a comparative perspective* (p. 105). Leiden/Boston: Brill.

5. Roland, A. (1988). *In search of self in India and Japan.* Princeton, NJ: Princeton University Press, p. 94.

6. Hofstede, G. (2001). *Culture's consequences* (2nd ed.). Thousand Oaks, CA: Sage, pp. 6–7.

7. Hofstede, 2001.

8. Geertz, C. (1973). *The interpretation of cultures.* New York: Basic Books, p. 44.

9. Hofstede, G., Hofstede, G. J., & Minkov, M. (2010). *Cultures and organizations: Software of the mind* (3rd ed.). New York: McGraw-Hill, p. 5.

10. Triandis, H. (1995). *Individualism and collectivism.* Boulder, CO: Westview Press.

11. Geertz, 1973, p. 49.

12. Roland, A. (1988). *In search of self in India and Japan.* Princeton, NJ: Princeton University Press, p. 324.

13. Cheon, H. J., Cho, C.-H., & Sutherland, J. (2007). A meta-analysis of studies on the determinants of standardization and localization of international marketing and advertising strategies. *Journal of International Consumer Marketing, 19*(4), 109–147.

14. Minkov, M. (2007). *What makes us different and similar.* Sofia, Bulgaria: Klasika I Stil, p. 7.

15. Allik, J., & McCrae, R. R. (2004). Towards a geography of personality traits: Patterns of profiles across 36 cultures. *Journal of Cross-Cultural Psychology, 35*(1), 13–28.

16. Martínez Mateo, M., Cabanis, M., Cruz de Echeverría Loebell, N., & Krach, S. (2012). Concerns about cultural neurosciences: A critical analysis. *Neuroscience and Biobehavioral Reviews, 36*, 152–161.

17. Freeman, J. B., Rule, N. O., & Ambady, N. (2009). The cultural neuroscience of person perception. *Progress in Brain Research, 178*, 191–201.

18. Ambady, N., & Bharucha, J. (2009). Culture and the brain. *Current Directions in Psychological Science, 18*(6), 342–345.

19. Azar, B. (2010). Your brain on culture. *American Psychological Association Science Watch, 41*(10), 1–3. Retrieved October 4, 2012, from http://www.apa.org/monitor/2010/11/neuroscience.aspx

20. Hofstede et al., 2010.

21. Murdock, G. P. (1945). The common denominator of culture. In R. Linton (Ed.), *The science of man in the world crisis.* New York: Columbia University Press.

22. Geertz, 1973, p. 53.

23. De Munck, V. C., Korotayev, A., De Munck, J., & Khaltourina, D. (2011). Cross-cultural analysis of models of romantic love among U.S. residents, Russians, and Lithanians. *Cross-Cultural Research, 45*(2), 128–154.

24. Benedict, R. (1974). *The chrysanthemum and the sword: Patterns of Japanese culture.* Rutland, VT: Charles E. Tuttle, p. 301. (Original work published 1946)

25. Adler, N. J. (1991). *International dimensions of organizational behavior* (2nd ed.). Belmont, CA: Wadsworth, p. 63.

26. Scott, L. (1994). Images in advertising: The need for a theory of visual rhetoric. *Journal of Consumer Research, 21*, 260.

27. Adler, 1991.

28. Platt, P. (1989, January). An entente cordiale mired in stereotypes. *International Management*, p. 50.

29. Usunier, J. C. (1993). *International marketing: A cultural approach.* Englewood Cliffs, NJ: Prentice Hall.

30. This draws on Hofstede et al., 2010, pp. 7–10. Used with permission.

31. Pierce, C. S. (1990). Collected papers [1931–1958]. In J. Fiske (Ed.), *Introduction to communication studies* (2nd ed., pp. 47–48). New York: Routledge.

32. Morris, D. (1994). *Bodytalk: A world guide to gestures.* London: Jonathan Cape.

33. Wakefield, C. S. (2010). Nike's Shanghai advertising dialectic: A case study. *China Media Research, 6*(1), 68–85.

34. Hall, E. T. (1984). *The dance of life.* Garden City, NY: Doubleday/Anchor, p. 7.

35. Hall, E. T. (1969). *The hidden dimension.* Garden City, NY: Doubleday/Anchor, pp. 131–157.

36. Hall, 1984, pp. 190–191.

37. Usunier, 1993, p. 71.

38. Hall, 1984, p. 135.

39. Doi, T. (1973). *The anatomy of dependence.* Tokyo: Kodansha International.

40. Althen, G. (1988). *American ways.* Yarmouth, ME: Intercultural Press, pp. 30–31.

41. Freeman et al.. 2009.

42. As cited in Usunier, 1993, p. 99.

43. Holtgraves, T. M., & Kashima, Y. (2008). Language, meaning and social cognition. *Personality and Social Cognition Review*, 12(1), 73–94.

44. Greenberg, J. H. (1965). Urbanism, migration, and language. In Kuper, H. (Ed.), *Urbanization and migration in West Africa* (pp. 50–59). Berkeley: University of California Press.

45. Schütte, H. and Ciarlante, D. (1998). *Consumer behavior in Asia*. New York: New York University Press.

46. Kipping, N. (2007). *Intercultural marketing communication for global consumers?* Diplomarbeit im Studiengang Werbung und Marktkommunikation durchgeführt an der Hochschule der Medien, FH Stuttgart.

47. Hofstede, G., personal communication, 1996.

48. Hofstede et al., 2010, p. 389.

49. Burger, P. (1996, June). Gaten in de taal. *Onze Taal*, p. 293.

50. Van Oudenhoven, J. P., & De Raad, B. (2008). Eikels en trutten over de grens. (Abusive behavior across eleven countries). *Onze Taal, 77*(9), 228–231.

51. Burger, 1996.

52. Miracle, G. E., Bang, H. K., & Chang, K. Y. (1992, March 20). *Achieving reliable and valid cross-cultural research results* (Working paper). Panel of Cross-Cultural Research Design, National Conference of the American Academy of Advertising, San Antonio, TX.

53. Wiredu, K. (1996). *Cultural universals and particulars: An African perspective*. Bloomington: Indiana University Press.

54. Paulick, J. (2007, November 16). *Impossible is nothing, except understanding ads in English*. Deutsche Welle. Retrieved from http://www.dw-world.de/dw/article

55. Hornikx, J., Van Meurs, F., & De Boer, A. (2010). English or a local language in advertising? The appreciation of easy and difficult slogans in the Netherlands. *Journal of Business Communication, 47*(2), 169–188.

56. Miracle, G. E. (1982). Applying cross-cultural research findings to advertising practice and research. In A. D. Fletcher (Ed.), *Proceedings of the 1982 Conference of the American Academy of Advertising*. (Contact Robert King, AAA Executive Secretary, School of Business, University of Richmond, Richmond, VA 23173)

57. Hofstede et al., 2010, p. 21.

58. Schwartz, S. H. (2004). Mapping and interpreting cultural differences. In H. Vinken, J. Soeters, & P. Ester (Eds.), *Comparing cultures: Dimensions of culture in a comparative perspective*. Leiden, Netherlands: Brill.

59. Minkov, M., & Hofstede, G. (2011). Is national culture a meaningful concept? Cultural values delineate homogeneous national clusters of in-country regions. *Cross-Cultural Research, 20*(10), 1–27.

60. Humes, K. R., Jones, N. A. & Ramirez, R. R. (2011, March). Overview of Race and Hispanic origin: 2010. Retrieved April 30, 2013, from http://www.census.gov/prod/cen2010/briefs/c2010br-02.pdf

61. The *International Journal of Cross-Cultural Psychology* regularly publishes such studies.

62. Prandi, R. (2004). Afro-Brazilian identity and memory. *Diogenes, 51*(1), 35–43.

63. Hofstede, G., Garibaldi de Hilal, A., Malvezzi, S., Tanure, B., & Vinken, H. (2010b). Comparing regional cultures within a country: Lessons from Brazil. *Journal of Cross-Cultural Psychology, 41*(3), 336–352.

64. Singh, D. (2007). *Cross cultural comparison of buying behavior in India* (unpublished doctoral dissertation). Submitted to University Business School, Panjab University, Chandigarh.

65.   Mpofu, E. (2002, June–September). The cultural ecology of psychology in sub-Saharan Africa. *Cross-Cultural Psychology Bulletin*, 15–23.

66.   Darou, W. G., Bernier, P., & Ruano, C. (2003, March–June). Sow's African personality and psychopathology model. *Cross-Cultural Psychology Bulletin*, 30–35.

67.   See Appendix B. The 23 countries covered were Austria, Belgium, Czechia, Denmark, Finland, France, Germany, Greece, Hungary, Ireland, Israel, Italy, Luxembourg, Netherlands, Norway, Poland, Portugal, Slovenia, Spain, Sweden, Switzerland, Turkey, and United Kingdom. The survey provides answers to value questions that can be isolated for the various provinces of the participating countries.

68.   Private conversation with Salvador Apud, cross-cultural expert at ITIM America.

CHAPTER 4

Dimensions of Culture

When internationalizing, companies increasingly want to know to what extent host markets are different from the home market. International marketing and advertising professionals want to understand the impact of cultural differences. Both consumers and professionals know very well when "something does not fit," when "something is not right" in international marketing and communications. But this has to be vocalized to make people of other cultures understand why the "something" does not fit; one has to be able to explain and convince. Experience in a few different countries or language skills are not enough. For global marketing, we need to measure and document cultural differences.

Only in the past 25 years, constructs were developed that classified cultures for a better understanding of the consequences of culture for various aspects of management. Some of these can be applied to marketing, in particular for understanding differences in consumer behavior and communications. They help vocalize culture. Without systems for understanding and classifying cultural differences, objections to an imposed brand position or advertising concept from another culture can too easily be labeled as the "not-invented-here syndrome." Cultural differences have to be measured and documented. This chapter will discuss classification of cultures and various models.

Classifying Cultures

Cultural differences can be studied, described, classified, and compared in a variety of ways. One way is to look at the institutions that societies have created. Another is to observe and compare behavior. The third, most common approach is to ask people, by means of questionnaires, what they think. These studies measure beliefs or values. So, cultures can be described according to *descriptive characteristics* or classified into *value categories* or *dimensions* of national culture.

Examples of *descriptive characteristics* are works by Gannon and by Harris and Moran. Gannon[1] describes cultures by identifying metaphors that members of given societies view as very important, if not critical. He focuses mostly on the expressions of culture, among others, religion, family structure, small-group behavior, public behavior, leisure pursuits and interests, greeting behavior, humor, language and body language, sports, educational system, food and eating behavior, and social class structure. He provides a description of 16 cultures according to the following metaphors: the traditional British house, the Italian opera, the German symphony, French wine, the Swedish *stuga,* the Russian ballet, Belgian lace, the Spanish bullfight, Irish conversations, the Turkish coffeehouse, the Israeli kibbutzim and moshavim, the Nigerian marketplace, the Japanese garden, the Shiva's dance of India, American football, and the Chinese family altar. These metaphors provide good insight into the expressions of culture, but they are less useful for analyzing and comparing cultures and understanding consumer behavior across cultures.

Cultural characteristics distinguishing countries, described by international management consultants Harris and Moran,[2] are sense of self and space, communication and languages, food and feeding habits, time consciousness, values and norms, beliefs and attitudes, and work habits and practices. These characteristics are based on observations, and many of these are also found in dimensional models derived from large surveys.

Large-scale comparison of cultures by their manifestations is not possible because of the great variety of particulars, and this is why nowadays cultural differences between modern nations are measured and ordered along a set of dimensions representing different answers to universal problems of human societies. The function of cultural dimensions is that they group together a number of phenomena in a society, based on statistical relationships. Each dimension forms a scale, and countries have a score on these scales, so the scores for each country on one dimension can be pictured as points along a line. For two dimensions, they become points in a diagram or map. When using dimensions to explain cross-cultural variety of phenomena or people's behavior or attitudes, we use correlation analysis. Two measures (called *variables*) are said to be correlated if they vary together, and the *coefficient of correlation* (we use the Pearson product-moment correlation coefficient, r) expresses the strength of the relationship. If the correlation is perfect, the coefficient takes the value of 1.0. If the value is 0, then the two measures are completely unrelated. The coefficient is negative if the two measures are each other's opposite.[3] A correlation is said to be significant if it is sufficiently different from zero. Significant correlations point at relationships between variables, not necessarily at causal relationships, although these may exist. Dimensions that order cultures meaningfully must be empirically verifiable and more or less independent.

The most common dimension used for ordering societies is their degree of economic evolution or modernity, ordering societies from traditional to modern. One of two dimensions used by U.S. political scientist Ronald Inglehart,[4] who leads the World Values Survey, follows this order of societies. Inglehart arranges world values in two broad categories. The first is "traditional" versus "secular-rational," and the second looks at "quality of life" attributes ranging from "survival" to "well-being," the latter including so-called postmaterialist values. Inglehart's two dimensions are totally unrelated and so are independent.

Increasingly more complex models have been developed. Most of them define patterns of basic problems that are common to all societies and that have consequences for the functioning of groups and individuals. Few are true dimensions in the sense of being statistically independent. Such categories are better called *value orientations* or *value categories*.

The idea that basic common problems exist is not new. An early analysis was by Alex Inkeles and Daniel Levinson,[5] who suggested that the following issues qualify as common basic problems worldwide: (a) relation to authority; (b) the conception of self, including ego identity; and (c) primary dilemmas of conflict and dealing with them. These basic problems have been found in many later studies. American anthropologists Kluckhohn and Strodtbeck[6] proposed five value orientations on the basis of their investigations of small communities in the southwestern United States: (a) perception of human nature (good/evil); (b) relationship of man to his environment (subjugation-mastery); (c) time orientation (past-present); (d) orientation toward the environment (being and doing); (e) orientation toward human relationships (hierarchical-individualistic). Differences between cultures with respect to the relationship between man and his environment (nature) are still viewed as rather unique, so one section in this chapter will describe the various nature orientations.

The five value orientations are recognized in later studies, for example, by Fons Trompenaars,[7] who applied these orientations to countries and presented seven categories of work-related values. These are universalism-particularism, achievement-ascription, individualism-collectivism, emotional-neutral, specific-diffuse, time orientation, and orientation to nature. Trompenaars's concept of culture is defined as a way in which a group of people solves problems. Trompenaars's database was analyzed by the British psychologist Peter Smith,[8] who found only two independent dimensions in the data that basically measured various intercorrelated flavors of Hofstede's dimension of individualism. Trompenaars's dimensions are not statistically independent, and he produced no country scores, so his findings are not useful for marketing as they cannot be used to analyze consumption data.

Fiske[9] proposed four elementary forms of sociability that occur within and across cultures: (1) communal sharing, (2) authority ranking, (3) equality matching, and (4) market pricing. Fiske's theory was supported by ethnographic fieldwork and experimental studies covering five cultures. Authority ranking and equality matching are similar to forms found in classifications by others, such as Schwartz and Hofstede, models that we'll deal with in more detail. The anthropologist Edward Hall[10] distinguished patterns of culture according to context, space, time, and information flow. In particular, the context concept is useful for understanding communication behavior and advertising across cultures. Also, Hall did not develop country scores, but the context orientation is related to individualism-collectivism, one of Hofstede's dimensions. A separate section in this chapter will be dedicated to the context and time orientations.

Several dimensional models provide country scores that can be used as independent variables for the analysis of human behavior across cultures. Minkov[11] describes and analyzes 27 such models. This chapter describes three major large-scale models: by Geert Hofstede, by Shalom Schwartz, and project GLOBE.

The Dutch scholar Geert Hofstede[12] was the first who, starting in 1973, developed five independent dimensions of national culture. His five dimensions are labeled *power distance, individualism/collectivism, masculinity/femininity, uncertainty avoidance*, and *long-/short-term orientation*. Later, a sixth dimension was added called *indulgence/restraint*. The Israeli psychologist Shalom Schwartz[13] developed seven value types labeled *embeddedness versus intellectual and affective autonomy, hierarchy versus egalitarianism*, and *mastery versus harmony*. For comparison reasons, these seven value types can be viewed as three dimensions. One dimension is a pole with embeddedness on one end and autonomy (intellectual and affective) on the other; the next pole consists of hierarchy versus egalitarianism, and the third pole consists of mastery versus harmony. The most recent large-scale dimensional model is GLOBE,[14] developed by Robert House of the Wharton School of Management and his associates, who initiated a cross-national project for the study of leadership and societal culture. They searched for dimensions similar to Hofstede's and developed questions relating to these dimensions, which resulted in nine cultural dimensions for which they used similar labels as the Hofstede dimensions, but that are not the same; the labels are *uncertainty avoidance, power distance*, two types of *collectivism, gender egalitarianism, assertiveness, future orientation, performance orientation*, and *humane orientation*. Whereas the Hofstede dimensions are empirical, that is, resulting from a large database without prior theory, the GLOBE researchers first developed a theory, based on existing ideas.

Analysis of existing databases can also deliver useful classifications. From factor analysis of country means of items in the World Values Survey, Michael Minkov[15] defined three dimensions: *exclusionism versus universalism*, which is similar to Hofstede's dimension called individualism-collectivism; *monumentalism versus flexumility*; and *indulgence versus restraint*. The latter has been added to Hofstede's database as a sixth dimension, and the former has been developed into a new long-/short-term orientation dimension by Hofstede. Later Minkov[16] published an additional dimension, named *hypometropia versus prudence* and renamed indulgence versus restraint into *industry versus indulgence*.

Of the three major models, several dimensions overlap conceptually, but each model has dimensions that measure specific cultural values that do not appear in other models or that are only part of a dimension of another model. For example, Hofstede's power distance dimension, the GLOBE power distance dimension, and the Schwartz dimension hierarchy versus egalitarianism measure similar cultural values. So do Hofstede's dimension individualism-collectivism, GLOBE's in-group collectivism, and the Schwartz dimension embeddedness versus intellectual and affective autonomy. Several dimensions will be discussed in more detail in this chapter, others will only be mentioned, as they don't all equally contribute to understanding differences in consumer behavior and communication.[17]

When using dimensional models for understanding differences in behavior, we have to understand that at the basis of the dimensions are the questions posed in value questionnaires. Both content and form of the questions influence the results and the potential to apply them to global marketing and advertising. This will be further discussed in chapter 6.

Before describing the three major dimensional models, a few descriptive classifications are discussed that are useful for understanding consumer and communication behavior, such as high versus low context, differences in time orientation, and relationships with nature.

High-Context and Low-Context Cultures

Hall[18] distinguishes cultures according to the degree of context in their communication systems. In high-context communication, most of the information is part of the context or internalized in the person; very little is made explicit. The information in a low-context message is carried in the explicit code of the message. In general, high-context communication is economical, fast, and efficient. However, time must be devoted to programming. If this programming does not take place, the communication is incomplete. To the observer, an unknown high-context culture can be completely mystifying, because symbols that are not known to the observer play such an important role. Thus, high-context communication can also be defined as inaccessible to the outsider. Low-context cultures are characterized by explicit verbal messages. Effective verbal communication is expected to be direct and unambiguous. Low-context cultures demonstrate high value and positive attitudes toward words. The Western world has had a long tradition of rhetoric, a tradition that places central importance on the delivery of verbal messages.[19] In advertising, argumentation and rhetoric are found more in low-context cultures, whereas advertising in high-context cultures is characterized by symbolism or indirect verbal expression. An important consequence of context is that words and sentences as well as pictures have different meanings depending on the context in which they are embedded.

Hofstede suggested a correlation between collectivism and high context in cultures. In collectivistic cultures, information flows more easily between members of the group, and there is less need for explicit communication than in individualistic cultures.

Cultures are on a sliding scale with respect to context. Most Asian cultures are high context, whereas most Western cultures are low-context cultures, the extremes being Japan and China (high-context) and Germany, Switzerland, and the United States (low-context cultures).

Dimensions of Time

Time is more than what the clock reads. Different cultures have different concepts of time. Western advertisers tend to use clocks in their international advertising to symbolize efficiency. Clocks are not recognized as symbols of efficiency in cultures where people have a different sense of time. Time is a core system of cultural, social, and personal life. Each culture has its own unique time frame. Hall's[20] important study of time as an expression of culture provides an explanation of differences in behavior and language. He distinguishes different types of time, among others bio-logical time (light-dark/day-night, hot-cold/summer-winter), personal time (how time is experienced), and sync time (each culture has its own beat). Hall developed his theories during his stay with Native Americans, discovering how differently they dealt with time than did Anglo Americans. Different concepts of time can explain significant differences in behavior. A few aspects of time that are relevant to consumer behavior are summarized in the following sections: closure; past, present, and future orientation; linear versus circular time; monochronic versus polychronic time; and cause and effect.

Closure

Americans are driven to achieve what psychologists call *closure*, meaning that a task must be completed or it is perceived as "wasted." What Hall saw as characteristic of Hopi (Native Americans of the Southwest) villages was the proliferation of unfin-ished houses. The same can be seen in Turkey, in southern Europe, and in other collectivistic cultures where additional rooms will be built only when family needs arise. American novels or films always have a "happy ending," including solutions to problems; such conclusions are rare in Japanese novels.

Time Orientation Toward the Past, Present, or Future

North Americans tend to be future oriented; the future is a guide to present action, although the time horizon is short term. The old is easily discarded, and the new embraced. Most things are disposable, from ideas, trends, and management fads to marriage partners. Even the "old" is treated as new. Many Europeans are past ori-ented; they believe in preserving history and continuing past traditions.[21] Japan has a very long-term future time horizon, as have the Chinese, but they look to the past for inspiration. The Chinese tend to combine both the past and the future in one holistic view of life, including reverence for their forefathers and long-term respon-sibility for future generations, but they have less respect for cultural history. African time is said to be composed of a series of events that are experienced. The future is of little meaning because future events have not yet occurred.[22] Destiny as an aspect of time and referring to a future is part of the Indian magic-cosmic world that the Western world has regarded as superstition and ignorance.[23]

Time Is Linear or Circular

Time can be conceived as a line of sequential events or as cyclical and repetitive, compressing past, present, and future by what these have in common: seasons and rhythms. The latter time orientation is linked with Asian culture; the former is the Western time orientation. The linear time concept causes people to see time as compartmentalized, schedule dominated. Americans have a linear time concept with clear structures, such as beginning, turning point, climax, and end. Time is used as a measuring instrument and a means of controlling human behavior by setting deadlines and objectives. Time is tangible, like an object; it can be saved, spent, found, lost, and wasted. Temporal terms, such as *summer* and *winter,* are nouns; they are treated as objects. For Native Americans, summer is a condition: hot. The term is used as an adverb, not related to time but to the senses.

In Japan, time is circular and is related to the special meaning of seasons. Japanese time thinking is not in terms of today, tomorrow, or the day after tomorrow. The seasons form an automatic, upward spiral; everything returns automatically. Saying "back to the old values" in Japan does not imply a step backward but a step forward. It means progressing through an upward spiral, using what was good in the past for progress.

Monochronic and Polychronic Time

Hall[24] also looked at how people handle time, distinguishing between monochronic (M-time) and polychronic (P-time) cultures. People from monochronic cultures tend to do one thing at a time; they are organized and methodical, and their workdays are structured to allow them to complete one task after another. Polychronic people, on the other hand, tend to do many things simultaneously. Their workday is not a chain of isolated, successive blocks; time is more like a vast, never-ending ocean, extending in every direction. The Germans adhere to the more rigid and compartmentalized way of dealing with time. To people who do many things at the same time, however, such as the Spanish, Arabs, Pakistani, or South Americans, punctuality is nice but by no means an absolute necessity in the middle of a hectic day. In monochronic cultures, time spent on the Internet takes time from other activities, such as TV viewing. In polychronic cultures, people do both at the same time.

When two people of different time cultures meet, they may easily offend each other because they have different expectations related to time. In particular, the fact that in polychronic cultures people interrupt during meetings is very annoying to people of monochronic cultures. Not all M-time cultures are the same, however. In Japan, tight M-time is for business, and P-time is for private life.

Cause and Effect

Time also relates to the concept of cause and effect that is used to explain a sequence of events. The cause-effect paradigm appears particularly in North American decision-making culture. Things don't just happen. Something makes them happen. Symbolic and mystical explanations of events are not accepted. Preference is given to concrete and measurable causes that precede the consequence or effect. With the Chinese, on the other hand, causes and results do not have to follow each other. They often happen simultaneously. One event can be explained by another unrelated event that is happening at the same time.[25] The American way of decision making often leads to suboptimization due to the too simplified cause-and-effect model they use. The Japanese use a holistic cause-and-effect model that takes into account a multitude of causes that have a joint effect.[26]

Relationship of Man With Nature

There are basically three types of relationships between humanity and nature: *mastery over nature* (man is to conquer nature), *harmony with nature* (man is to live in harmony with nature), and *subjugation to nature* (man is dominated by nature).[27]

In the Western world, humanity is viewed as separate from nature. In particular, the North American relationship to nature is that it should be conquered, controlled. Nature and the physical environment can be and should be controlled for human convenience. To most North Americans, the expression "to move a mountain" is not a metaphor symbolizing the impossible but rather an optimistic challenge based on past experience. The outlook of U.S. culture is that it is the person's responsibility to overcome obstacles that may stand in his or her way. The harmony-with-nature orientation draws no distinction between or among human life, nature, and the supernatural; each is an extension of the others. The Japanese experience of nature is one of communion, of exchange, characterized by a subtle intimacy. It is an experience of identification with nature. Westerners tend to explain the Asian reverence for nature as a relationship with God that involves living in harmony with the world of nature. Takeo Doi,[28] a Japanese psychiatrist, says that in Japan, God as a creator is absent, and human beings therefore seek comfort by attempting to immerse themselves completely in nature. Other cultures, such as many African cultures, see people as dominated by nature, and supernatural forces play a dominant role. This subjugation to nature involves the belief that nothing can be done to control nature.

The Three Major Large-Scale Dimensional Models

The three major large-scale worldwide dimensional models overlap in some ways but vary with respect to purpose, sampling, and type of questions used. What they have in common is aggregating responses by individuals drawn from a series of different national or regional samples. The predominant emphasis has been upon characterizing cultures in terms of shared values, shared beliefs, or shared sources of guidance.[29] What they also have in common is measuring various elements of human behavior in business or organizations. None of the models were developed for explaining differences in consumer behavior, although some can be applied to help understand cross-cultural differences in product ownership, buying, communication, and media behavior. This chapter summarizes the similarities and differences of the three models.

The purpose of the Hofstede model[30] was to understand differences in work motivations of all levels of employees, caused by the nationality of the employees. Schwartz, as a psychologist, searched for basic values on which individuals in all cultures differ and from there developed a theory of cultural values on which societies differ.[31] House,[32] the initiator of GLOBE, was interested in the effectiveness of leadership styles; he wanted to find out if charismatic leader behavior is universally acceptable and effective.

The samples used for the three models are different. Hofstede used matched groups of employees in seven occupational categories within one global company in 66 countries in order to understand differences in work-related behavior. By doing this within one global company, he eliminated the influence of corporate culture. Schwartz used students and teachers in 54 countries. GLOBE surveyed middle managers in 951 local organizations in food processing, financial services, and telecom services in 62 societies.

The types of questions used follow different patterns. Hofstede asked respondents for behavioral preferences. Schwartz asked respondents for guiding principles in people's lives with respect to social issues,[33] and the GLOBE researchers measured respondents' perceptions of the organizations or societies in which they live or work in terms of ideological abstractions, about society *as it is* and *as it should be,* which they call *practices* and *values*; these represent the *desired* and the *desirable*. What the GLOBE researchers call *values* are in fact *norms*, how people state the way other people should behave. As the desired and desirable often are opposed, for seven of the nine GLOBE dimensions, cultural values and practices are negatively correlated.[34] Only for in-group collectivism and gender egalitarianism do the two correlate positively, which may be due to the fact that the questions for these dimensions are more closely related to people's daily lives than those for the other dimensions. Both GLOBE and Schwartz in their questions refer to the society in which the respondents live, whereas Hofstede asks for personal preferences. In Chapter 6, we'll elaborate on the effects of the different types of questions.

In the following sections, the dimensions of the three major models will be described in clusters of dimensions that overlap. When describing or using the GLOBE dimensions, we refer to the practices, not the values, as the latter result in confusing relationships with consumer behavior. The dimensions are described in order of importance for consumer behavior and in particular communication behavior.

Individualism and Collectivism

Several dimensions of the different models include values that can be viewed as individualistic or collectivistic. It is the most important dimension for understanding differences in communication. We use Hofstede's label *individualism-collectivism* as an umbrella term for the various values covered by the Schwartz dimension autonomy-embeddedness that measures several aspects of individualism-collectivism and the GLOBE dimension in-group collectivism that measures collectivism on the one pole and on the other individualism. The various dimensions measure similar values, although not exactly the same. There are different collectivistic and individualistic patterns and not all individualistic or collectivistic cultures are the same. Correlations with various communication related databases show that the GLOBE dimensional scale of in-group collectivism delivers the strongest explanations for differences with respect to communication behavior. What the different dimensions have in common are differences in definition of the self, emphasis on personal preferences versus duties and obligations, and emphasis on rationality versus giving priority to relationships and taking into account the needs of others.[35]

Hofstede[36] points at the following core characteristic of individualism-collectivism: In individualistic cultures, people look after themselves and their immediate family only, and in collectivistic cultures, people belong to in-groups which look after them in exchange for loyalty. In individualistic cultures, identity is in the person, and people want to differentiate themselves from others. In collectivistic cultures, identity is based in the social network to which one belongs. In individualistic cultures, people are "I" conscious and express private opinions. People attach priority to variety and adventure. Intellectual autonomy encourages individuals to pursue their own ideas and intellectual direction independently. There is more explicit, verbal communication. In collectivistic cultures, people are "we" conscious—their identity is based on the social system. Harmony with in-group members and avoiding loss of face is important, resulting in preference for indirect communication.

The roots of individualism are in England. In early English society, as early as the 13th century, children at the age of 7 or 9 years—both males and females—did not grow up in an extended family but were put out to hard service in the houses of other people.[37]

Between 70% and 80% of the world's population is more or less collectivistic. The Anglo-Saxon world is individualistic, and so are the northern countries of Europe, whereas the South and East countries are more collectivistic. In Italy, Hofstede's data were collected in the north, where people appeared to be individualistic. Other studies[38] indicate that the Italians as a whole are collectivistic. All of Asia, Africa, and Latin America are collectivistic, although to varying extent and with different manifestations.

Individualistic cultures are universalistic cultures, whereas collectivistic cultures are particularistic. People from individualistic cultures tend to believe that there are universal values that should be shared by all. People from collectivistic cultures, on the other hand, accept that different groups have different values. Being individualistic, most North Americans believe that democracy, especially North American democracy, should ideally be shared by all. People from collectivistic cultures find such a view hard to understand.[39] Hall[40] observes, "Americans, more than most, seem dominated by the need to shape other people in their own image." This is particularly reflected in American marketing and advertising philosophies. A statement by Cristina Martinez, Latin American regional account director for Eastman Kodak at J. Walter Thompson Co., Miami, reflected this attitude: "We're finding that teenagers are teen-agers everywhere and they tend to emulate U.S. teen-agers."[41] The Japanese, the Chinese, and other Asians feel so unique that they cannot and will not imagine that Westerners will ever be able to adopt their values and behavior.

The United States is one of the most individualistic cultures in the world, but it also is a society with large ethnic minorities that mostly differ with respect to individualism-collectivism. Various cross-cultural psychologists have examined differences in the cultural orientations of the large U.S. minority groups, African, Asian, and Hispanic Americans. Several studies have found that these groups are more collectivistic than European Americans, but African Americans are found to be more individualistic than the other groups. Some researchers explain this by claiming that becoming individualistic has been a survival mechanism for former slaves, who had a different position in society than the other groups. However, across several studies, a major criterion for measuring individualism was the degree of self-esteem, which appears to be high among African Americans.[42] High self-esteem is not an exclusive characteristic of individualistic cultures but is also an aspect of short-term orientation (see pp. 114–115).

Some cross-cultural psychologists have tried to refine the individualism-collectivism dimension by distinguishing between vertical individualism (VI) and horizontal individualism (HI) and between vertical collectivism (VC) and horizontal collectivism (HC).[43] These distinctions reflect values that are also found in configurations of the dimensions individualism and power distance where HI is the configuration of individualism with low-power distance, and VI with high power distance; VC is the combination of high power distance and collectivism and HC combines with low power distance. Whereas VI also includes achievement values, HI includes more egalitarian values and lower achievement needs. For example, whereas Americans are individualistic and achievement oriented, the Danes are also individualistic, but less oriented toward success and achievement and more toward social justice and equality.[44]

In the sales process in individualistic cultures, parties want to get to the point fast, whereas in collectivistic cultures, it is necessary to first build a relationship and trust between parties. This difference is also reflected in the different roles of advertising (see Chapter 7). In collectivistic cultures, corporate brands are favored over product brands. You can build a relationship between a company and consumers better than between (abstract) brands and consumers. In collectivistic cultures, people are more interested in concrete product features than in abstract brands. Individualists tend to see brands as unique human personalities. In the extremely individualistic United States, even children have been named after big brands, such as L'Oréal, Chevrolet, and Armani.

Individualism/collectivism explains different behaviors in the private and public domain. Whereas in individualistic cultures people entertain their friends in the home or private garden, collectivists tend to meet their friends in public places like bars, cafés, and restaurants. The number of cafés is negatively correlated with individualism. In collectivistic cultures, people have relatively few private gardens. Within Europe, there is a positive correlation between individualism and ownership of private gardens. Although in the south of Europe more and more one-family houses are being built, many of these have communal gardens, a phenomenon that is unthinkable in individualistic cultures, such as the United Kingdom and the Netherlands. Across Europe, in the collectivistic cultures, people take more part in activities in the public domain, such as visits to the cinema, theater, and festivals.[45]

At the start of the Internet, how and where people accessed it varied in relation to the private-public domain distinction. Figure 4.1 illustrates the way people access the Internet in different places in individualistic and collectivistic cultures. In the latter, people are used to doing all sorts of activities in the public domain, both in the streets and in bars or cafés, as reflected in the numbers of cafés per 10,000 people. Because of these habits, people also have no problems accessing the Internet in the cyber café, whereas in individualistic cultures, people will not want to access the Internet outside the home.

Individualism is increasing worldwide because it is linked with wealth, but it remains a relative concept. If it is said that Japanese society is individualizing, that does not mean Japanese values will come close to American values. The relative difference is expected to remain.

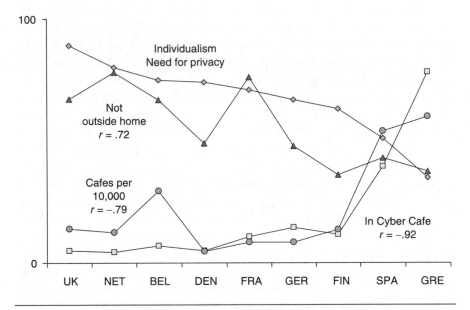

Figure 4.1   Internet Access Inside or Outside Home, Europe

SOURCE: Data from Hofstede (2001) (see Appendix A); Eurostat (2001) (see Appendix B); Hotrec data on numbers of cafés per 10,000 people (1997) (www.hotrec.com).

Power Distance

Values related to people's relationships with elders and authority, or dependence and independence values, are included in dimensions called power distance (Hofstede and GLOBE) and in Schwartz's dimension hierarchy versus egalitarianism. The dimensions overlap, but are not totally the same.

Power distance measures the extent to which less powerful members of a society accept and expect that power is distributed unequally. It is reflected in the values of both the less powerful and more powerful members of society. It influences the way people accept and give authority. In large power distance cultures (those scoring high on the power distance indexes or those scoring high on the hierarchy scale), everyone has his or her rightful place in a social hierarchy, and as a result, acceptance and giving of authority come naturally. People take the hierarchical distribution of roles for granted and comply with the obligations and rules attached to their roles. To the Japanese, behavior that recognizes hierarchy is as natural as breathing. It means "everything in its place." In small (low-scoring) power distance cultures, the focus is on equality in rights and opportunity. In high power distance cultures, there are strong dependency relationships between parents and children, bosses and subordinates, professors and students, as well as between governments and citizens. In low power distance cultures, children are raised to be independent at a young age. Americans will avoid becoming dependent on others, and they do not want others, with the possible exception of immediate family members, to be dependent on them. Whereas independence is an important value for low power distance cultures, dependence and obedience characterize high power distance cultures. D. Lawrence Kincaid,[46] authoring about Asian communication theory, formulated power distance as follows: "Each person has a specific place within the scheme of the world, which is by definition hierarchical. Those in higher positions always have more power and this is taken for granted as the natural scheme of things."

Generally, Asian, Latin American, and African countries score high and mostly the Anglo-Saxon world and North Europe score low on power distance. Although the Schwartz Hierarchy pole is related to Hofstede's power distance, there are some differences with respect to country scores. For example Greece, Italy, and Portugal, which score high on Hofstede's power distance scale, score relatively low on the Schwartz hierarchy scale, which may indicate that the values measured by the two may not be exactly the same.

In high power distance cultures, one's social status must be clear so that others can show proper respect. Global brands serve that purpose. In continental Europe, some luxury alcoholic drinks have such social status value in the high power distance cultures. There is a significant correlation between power distance and consumption of Scotch whisky in continental Europe.

In high power distance cultures, appearance is important, and people are well groomed, in particular when going out in the streets as your position in the social hierarchy is defined by the clothes you wear, your shoes, your posture, and your makeup. In low power distance cultures, people take less care of their outer appearance and wear in public what they wear in private. Presidents go jogging in shorts, and film stars wear jeans and T-shirts. According to a study by Nielsen, 87% of Brazilians and 79% of the Portuguese try to look stylish at all times, whereas 76% of Norwegians and 69% of New Zealanders *don't* try to look stylish.[47]

The rightful-place concept implies that in high power distance cultures, being the "number one" brand is important. A brand that has entered markets early and is viewed as the number one brand will remain so more easily than it would in low power distance cultures where challengers are favored with a "we try harder" approach.

In low power distance cultures, parents play with their children as equals, whereas in high power distance cultures, children play more with each other, and adults and children live in different worlds. This explains why the Danish Lego (toys, building blocks) did not sell as well in France as in Denmark. The concept is based on parents and children constructing buildings together.

The degree of power distance tends to decrease with increased levels of education. As a result, it is expected that improved education worldwide will lead toward decreased power distance, but relative differences between countries are not expected to change.

Differences in the degree to which people inform themselves of current affairs or politics are best explained by Hofstede's power distance dimension. Various sources show that this dimension explains differences in communication behavior and information needs, such as information gathering for making a buying decision and reading newspapers or watching the news on television. It also explains differences in usage of the Internet and mobile phones.

High power distance and collectivism include some similar values. Both include dependency values which means people make an effort to live up to expectations of others.[48] However, power distance and individualism/collectivism both are also related to wealth. High GNI per capita correlates with low power distance and with individualism. So when using the dimensions for understanding differences in communication behavior or media usage, we always have to control for wealth. An example is newspaper readership, which is higher in low power distance and individualistic cultures. However, worldwide, a stronger explanatory factor is wealth. Generally, in a worldwide sample of countries that vary strongly with respect to wealth, the latter is the variable that explains the difference, but in a sample of countries of more similar wealth, as in Western Europe, it is power distance that explains the difference (see also Chapter 8 on culture and the media).

Long-/Short-Term Orientation

The difference between long-term and short-term orientation is measured by Hofstede's dimension long- versus short-term orientation (LTO), and a similar GLOBE dimension labeled *future orientation*, but the latter seems to be less clear-cut and includes a mix of elements of various other dimensions. It correlates negatively with in-group collectivism and thus includes individualistic values, which results in relationships that are different from Hofstede's dimension. At societal level, it finds similar relationships as Hofstede's dimension, such as reading ability and newspaper readership, but less information on personal values, such as degrees of self-enhancement.

Included in Hofstede's short-term orientation are values of national pride, tradition, low thrift, self-esteem, self-enhancement, religion, magnanimity, and generosity. Included in long-term orientation are longer-term thinking, thrift, perseverance, and pragmatism. In long-term oriented cultures, parents are more lenient toward children than in short-term oriented cultures. In short-term oriented cultures, people tend to be religious, often with a strong belief in a God that will solve their problems, regardless of what they do themselves. This can be viewed as opposed to the self-reliance of long-term oriented cultures.[49] Most East Asian countries score high on this fifth dimension. Anglo-Saxon societies, Latin America, and Africa score low, whereas Europe shows a great variety (see Appendix A).

An example of how the time perspective is reflected in behavior is the time spent eating, which correlates with this dimension, as illustrated in Figure 4.2.

With respect to communication behavior, Hofstede's long-/short-term orientation dimension differentiates between collectivistic cultures. Short-term oriented cultures are more oral cultures whereas long-term oriented cultures are more literate. Long-term oriented cultures score higher in literacy and reading ability[50] and are more reliant on written information whereas in short-term oriented cultures, people depend more on communication from TV, friends, and family. Facebook is most popular in the short-term oriented cultures. The reason is that Facebook stimulates more self-enhancement than some social media in long-term oriented cultures do, such as Mixi in Japan. This will be further discussed in Chapter 8. Long-/short-term orientation also explains adoption of all sorts of applications of the Internet as well as relationships between parents and children with respect to media usage. Whereas in short-term oriented cultures parents guide their children with respect to Internet usage, they do less so in long-term oriented cultures. The dimension weakly correlates negatively with Hofstede's indulgence versus restraint (IVR) dimension, so short-term oriented cultures tend to give priority to indulgence, and long-term oriented cultures are more restrained. Procrastination, or the

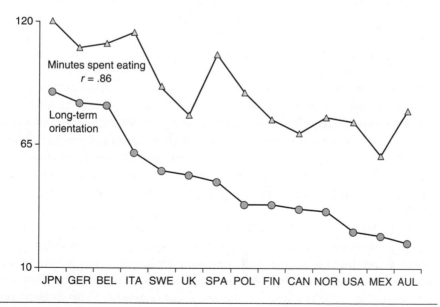

Figure 4.2   Minutes Spent Eating

SOURCE: Hofstede et al. (2010) (see Appendix A); OECD (2009), *Society at a Glance* (see Appendix B).

avoidance of a task or work that needs to be done, is related to a tendency to engage in short-term pleasurable activities, an aspect of short-term orientation. GLOBE's future orientation dimension provides less clear explanations for understanding differences in communication behavior.

Something that is often perceived as paradoxical in the measurements on this index is the combination of strong respect for tradition and short-term orientation in a large part of the Western world, whereas respect for old age and ancestor worship are such strong elements of Asian value systems. This reflects the desirable versus the desired: Tradition is important, but it is innovativeness that is desired. Particularly in China, pragmatism tends to overrule respect for tradition. An example is the 10-year Cultural Revolution, which destroyed a priceless cultural heritage. It is not the first time such a frenzy has happened. Mao Zedong, the instigator of the Cultural Revolution, was inspired by the first emperor, Shi Huangdi, who unified China in 220 B.C.[51] He had all books destroyed and 463 philosophers buried alive in an attempt to remove the traditional Confucian thought from the collective Chinese memory. It was in vain: The emperor died after 11 years, and the scriptures of Confucius and other philosophers, which had been memorized, were reissued.[52] Yet pragmatism in accepting foreign habits in China has a limitation; they must fit *guo qing,* or "the Chinese national context." Good ideas applicable to China must be promoted; corrupted and inapplicable ideas must be discarded.

Assertiveness and Male-Female Roles

Several dimensions measure societal differences with respect to the degree of assertiveness, average performance orientation of people, and relationships between males and females, such as gender equality and role differentiation or overlapping roles of males and females. Hofstede's dimension masculinity-femininity is a complex dimension as it measures the degree of assertiveness or achievement orientation versus quality of life as well as the degree of role differentiation versus overlapping roles of males and females. GLOBE measures several aspects of Hofstede's masculinity-femininity dimension through different dimensions. The *assertiveness* dimension measures the degree of assertiveness and *gender egalitarianism* measures gender equality. Schwartz's mastery pole of his dimension *mastery/ harmony* also has some conceptual overlap with masculinity. Both emphasize assertion and ambition.[53] However, the harmony pole is not the same as Hofstede's femininity pole.

The dominant values in societies that score high on the masculinity or assertiveness dimensions are achievement and success; the dominant values in societies that score feminine and low on the assertiveness dimension are caring for others and quality of life. In masculine and assertive societies, status is important to show success, and being a winner is positive. Big and fast are beautiful. Societies that score low have a people orientation and regard small as beautiful. There is a tendency to strive for consensus. Quality of life is more important than competition. Status is not so important to show success.

Hofstede's *masculinity-femininity* dimension explains more than the other dimensions with regard to variation in the degree of role differentiation: small in feminine societies, large in masculine societies. In feminine cultures, a male can take a typical female job without being seen as a "sissy." In masculine cultures, both males and females can be tough; in feminine cultures, both males and females can be tender. This is the essence of the dimension. It explains differences in household roles such as cleaning, child care, cooking, and shopping as well as differences in working part-time, by both males and females. In Europe, in the feminine cultures, women spend more time in employment, and in the masculine cultures, women spend more time on domestic activities.[54] In the masculine cultures of Latin America, men must be "real men." For example, in a Latin American survey across seven countries, the percentages of answers agreeing with the statement "Real men don't cry" correlated with masculinity.[55] We should not confuse a term like *machismo* with the masculinity concept. Machismo or manliness in popular culture is often associated with chauvinism, aggression, and hypermasculinity, but it can also represent qualities such as dignity, honor, responsibility, and treating others with respect.[56]

The GLOBE dimension *gender egalitarianism* measures equal opportunity for women versus male domination. High scores point at the same opportunities for females and males; low scores indicate greater male domination. This is, however, more about equal opportunity in education and in the workplace than about the existence or absence of specific male-female roles in society and in family life and households. The female-male ratio of enrollment in tertiary education and adult literacy rates correlate positively with gender egalitarianism whereas the percentage of women in parliaments correlates negatively with Hofstede's masculinity dimension, and there is no relationship with gender egalitarianism. The percentage of women in parliament is more a matter of roles in society as it is not only about women's opportunities but also about men, for example, whether they are willing to vote for women.

The GLOBE dimension *assertiveness* reflects the degree to which individuals in organizations or societies are assertive, dominant, and aggressive in social relationships. It correlates significantly with Hofstede's masculinity. Assertive societies are viewed as dominant, as are masculine cultures. The United States is an example of an assertive culture. Competition is viewed as a fundamental aspect of human nature and people live in a dog-eat-dog world. However, other items of the assertiveness dimension are part of other dimensions. For example, Den Hartog[57] links assertiveness with a direct communication style, making one's wants known to others and in no uncertain terms, which points at low-context communication. That characteristic presupposes that Asian societies that are low context societies, are not competitive, which is not the case. Competitive Japan scores quite low on this dimension, whereas it scores high on the Hofstede dimension masculinity that also measures the degree of competitiveness.

Another GLOBE dimension, *performance orientation*, includes values related to the hard and soft aspects of culture, but it includes puzzling elements. Javidan[58] links it to the work ethic of protestant Calvinism and summarizes it as a characteristic of high performance oriented cultures that they value education and learning, emphasize results, take the initiative, and prefer explicit and direct communication. Those that score low value social and family relations; loyalty, tradition, and seniority; and use subtle and indirect language, which points at high-context communication. Japan and Korea are cultures with high performance ethics and score medium to high on this dimension, but people are certainly not direct in their communication.

Although the performance orientation may help explain differences in advertising appeals with respect to winning, hardly any conclusive findings have been published. Hofstede's dimension also measures assertiveness, but it is of more interest for consumer behavior in measuring role differentiation and ownership of products that are meant for showing success; this, together with power distance, explains differences in status needs.

A core value of feminine cultures is modesty, or not showing off. So if one excels, it should not be shown. For some of the Scandinavian countries, this is illustrated by Jante's law (*Janteloven*), 10 rules that give a fairly accurate depiction of the moral code in Sweden and Scandinavia today. Jante's law comes from the novel by 19th-century Dano-Norwegian author Aksel Sandemose, titled "*En flygtning krysser sitt spor*" (*A Fugitive Crosses His Own Track*).[59]

Du skal ikke tro . . . (You should not "feel" that . . .)

du er noget (you are anything)

du er lige så meget som os (you are equal to us, i.e., at our level)

du er klogere end os (you are more clever than we are)

du er bedre end os (you are better than we are)

ved mere end os (you know more than we do)

er mere end os (you are more than we are)

at du du'r til noget (you are good at anything)

Du skal ikke le ad os (you must not make fun of us)

Du skal ikke tro . . . (you should not think that . . .)

nogen bryder sig om dig (anybody likes you)

at du kan lære os noget (you can teach us anything)

Envy is a principal part of Jante's law. If you break the social code, it means that your neighbors will despise you for your uniqueness or an excess show of wealth. The desire of people of feminine cultures to not stand out in a crowd is reflected in the dislike of "employee of the month" schemes, which are effective human resource instruments in the United States. A U.S. TV commercial for Tylenol used this to demonstrate the effectiveness of the product. Carolina hears she has just been elected Employee of the Month for the 11th time because she didn't use a single sick day (Illustration 4.1).

 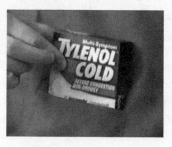 

Illustration 4.1 Tylenol, USA

For marketing purposes, the most important aspect of this dimension is role differentiation or overlap in shopping and buying decisions. Men do more household shopping in the feminine cultures. Low masculinity explains 52% of variance of the proportion of men who spend time on shopping activities.[60] In the feminine cultures, more men work part-time than in the masculine cultures because both partners want to share the task of raising the children. Across Europe, in the masculine cultures, more people agree with the statement "A university education is more for a boy" than in the feminine cultures.[61]

If advertising doesn't reflect the right male-female roles, it doesn't work well. A TV commercial for Danone in France showed a grandfather who brought his grandson to school. The same commercial was used in Poland, where it didn't work. Although in both countries grandparents are important, as both score high on power distance, France scores feminine and Poland masculine. In Poland, it is the grandmother who would accompany the grandchild to school, not the grandfather.

Japan is a very masculine society with strong role differentiation. This combined with collectivism can explain the way men and women relate. There is no such thing as the Western love relationship between men and women in marriage. "You are there, exist together, and you take each other for granted." Literally, You are like air for each other. Kumiko Hashimoto, the wife of a former Japanese prime minister Ryutaro Hashimoto, was quoted as saying the following about her relationship with her husband: "I give way to him almost as if he were a feudal lord, with everything done as he wishes."[62]

U.S. researchers seem reluctant to use the masculinity dimension, possibly because of the label. Masculine/feminine can be misinterpreted as politically incorrect wording. At the time Hofstede labeled this dimension, there was no such thing as a political correctness movement. The problem can be solved by using the terms "gender of nations" or "tough versus tender."

Uncertainty Avoidance

Both Hofstede and GLOBE use the term *uncertainty avoidance* for dimensions that are quite different and have an opposite relationship. Hofstede's[63] definition is "the extent to which people feel threatened by uncertainty and ambiguity and try to avoid these situations." Some people do not mind ambiguity, whereas others hate uncertainty or ambiguity and try to cope with it by making rules and prescribing behavior. In cultures of strong uncertainty avoidance (those scoring high on the index), there is a need for rules and formality to structure life and belief in experts. People are more interested in the process of how things work than in the results. People in high uncertainty avoidance cultures have a higher level of anxiety, and conflict and competition are threatening. High uncertainty avoidance also leads to intolerance, low trust, inflexibility, and dogmatism. Weak (low-scoring) uncertainty avoidance cultures feel that there should be as few rules as possible. They are more result oriented than process oriented. They believe more in generalists and common sense, and there is less ritual behavior. Conflict and competition are not threatening. Uncertainty avoidance explains, for example, differences in the adoption of innovations, including the Internet and ownership of personal computers. It explains differences in traveling, foreign language speaking, and contacts people have with foreigners.

The name and definition of GLOBE's dimension uncertainty avoidance suggests similar aspects, but it is very different from Hofstede's uncertainty avoidance. It is more a variant of collectivism, pointing at the high importance of in-groups and relative lack of interest in out-groups.[64] It is defined as the extent to which members of collectives seek orderliness, consistency, structure, formalized procedures, and laws to cover situations in their daily lives.[65] This is not exactly the same as avoiding ambiguity, anxiety, and stress, for which all sorts of other coping mechanisms than orderliness and laws may serve to handle them. The GLOBE country's scores for this dimension correlate negatively with Hofstede's scores, resulting in opposing correlations with other variables. For example, measures of general life satisfaction and happiness correlate negatively with Hofstede's uncertainty avoidance dimension and positively with the GLOBE dimension. Reading ability tends to correlate negatively with Hofstede's dimension but positively with the GLOBE dimension. Whereas frequent use of the computer is found more in cultures that score low on Hofstede's dimension, it is found less in cultures that score low on GLOBE's dimension.[66] A possible cause of confusion is the use of complex questions that contain two different concepts. For example, for measuring uncertainty avoidance, GLOBE asks the following question: "In this society, orderliness and consistency are stressed, even at the expense of experimentation and innovation," as if innovation is not possible in an orderly fashion. This GLOBE dimension is not very useful for understanding differences in consumer behavior.

The expert in cultures that score high on Hofstede's uncertainty avoidance scale must be a true expert with degrees in specialized areas in order to allow him- or herself to be called an expert. This is different from countries that score lower such as the United States, where anyone can become an expert because no one says what an expert is or must know. Americans can get themselves listed in the *Yearbook of Experts* for a few hundred U.S. dollars.[67] Differences in usage of some products like food and drink reflect varying needs for purity which are stronger in high uncertainty avoidance cultures than in cultures that score low. Examples are mineral water and washing powder. "In Europe, with increased wealth and improved quality of the tap water, the correlation between mineral water consumption and uncertainty avoidance has become more significant over time. Figure 4.3 illustrates the correlation between bottled water consumption and uncertainty avoidance for 15 countries worldwide. In high uncertainty avoidance cultures, mineral water also tends to be advertised by its purity attribute, which is often symbolized by showing the brand in a nature setting. Illustration 4.2 shows TV images of mineral water brands from Spain, France, and Italy.

Whereas high uncertainty avoidance cultures have a passive attitude toward health by focusing on purity in food and drink and using more medication, low uncertainty avoidance cultures have a more active attitude toward health by focusing on fitness and sports. The percentage of people who say they never play sports correlates with high uncertainty avoidance.[68] The percentage who say they have used antibiotics in the past year also correlates with high uncertainty avoidance.[69]

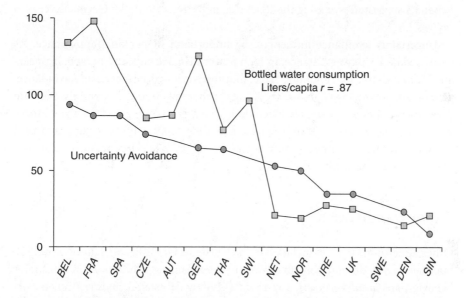

Figure 4.3 Bottled Water Consumption

SOURCE: Data from Hofstede (2010) (see Appendix A); Beverage Marketing Corporation. (www.beveragemarketing.com) (2003).

Illustration 4.2 Aquarel, Spain; Volvic, France/Germany; Allegra, Italy

Cultures of strong uncertainty avoidance feel the need to structure reality, but they will do this in different ways. Configurations with other dimensions will show differences in how reality is structured. If combined with individualism, the rules are explicit and written. Combined with collectivism, the rules are implicit and rooted in tradition. Combined with low power distance, the rules are internalized; one accepts the rules and that one has to abide by them. Combined with high power distance, one need not abide by the rules because they are externalized. Germans and French, both strong uncertainty avoidance cultures, like rules; but the Germans use them to structure themselves, the French to structure others. In French culture, reality is structured through conceptualization. This difference explains the propensity for the conceptual or the "grand idea" of the French, which is so different from the German thinking model. When the artist Christo suggested wrapping the Pont Neuf in Paris, it did not take the French long to agree. When he suggested wrapping the Reichstag in Berlin, it took the Germans years to say yes.

Uncertainty avoidance influences the importance of personal appearance. As discussed under power distance, in high power distance cultures, personal appearance is important for upholding "face," but this varies with uncertainty avoidance. The Japanese, scoring high are very much concerned about how nicely they are dressed, and they judge people by clothes, which is less the case with the Chinese who score low. Also, in Japan, the rituals or the proper way things are done and one's social status are important, whereas for the Chinese, face is more related to one's economic capability.[70]

Other Dimensions

Other dimensions that are included in the Hofstede, GLOBE, and Schwartz models, but that as yet do not contribute much to explaining differences in consumer behavior, are *indulgence versus restraint* (Minkov, Hofstede), *mastery versus harmony* (Schwartz), and *humane orientation* (GLOBE).

The dimension indulgence versus restraint (IVR) was developed by Minkov[71] and was added as a sixth dimension to Hofstede's model. Indulgence includes the degree of happiness people experience, the control they have over their own lives, and the importance of leisure. Restraint, the pole that Minkov[72] later named *industry* includes values like hard work and thrift. Many Latin American countries score high on this dimension. Low scores are found for ex-Soviet dominated countries. Low IVR includes buying something only if really needed; it also includes traditional values, such as the belief that a woman's first priority should be her family. High IVR includes wanting to pay for extra quality and indulging in the latest gadgets. For example, in 2012 across the wealthy inhabitants of Europe, ownership of an iPad was positively related to IVR.[73] The dimension correlates negatively with Hofstede's long-term orientation and positively with the Schwartz dimension egalitarianism. Although explanations of cross-cultural consumer behavior differences are not clear-cut, we include the countries' scores in this book—which may motivate researchers to do more exercises with this dimension.

The Schwartz dimension *mastery-harmony* deals with the treatment of human and natural resources. Harmony cultures emphasize fitting into the social and natural world, trying to appreciate and accept rather than to change, direct, and exploit, whereas mastery cultures encourage active self-assertion in order to master, direct, and change the natural and social environment. Correlations with consumption-related variables have not delivered enlightening results.

The GLOBE dimension *humane orientation* is defined as the degree to which an organization or society encourages and rewards individuals for being fair, altruistic, friendly, generous, caring, and kind to others.[74] In cultures that score low, self-interest is more important and so are values of pleasure and self-enjoyment as well as self-enhancement. This dimension is a mix of several other dimensions, such as individualism-collectivism and long-/short-term orientation. It is also a puzzling dimension, because the title suggests different value preferences than are found in correlations with other phenomena. For example, humane orientation correlates with the degree of racism and preferences for the death penalty.[75]

Not all dimensions contribute equally to understanding differences in consumer behavior, marketing, and advertising. The analysis presented here is based on a comparison of the models by correlation analysis and regression analysis of a number of large databases, using the dimensions of the three major models. The result of this exercise was that only the GLOBE dimension in-group collectivism resulted in clear explanations although the results were similar to those of Hofstede's individualism-collectivism. As a result, for this book we continue using the Hofstede dimensions which appear to be most practical and useful for understanding marketing and advertising related differences.

Configurations of Dimensions

The cultural dimensions described in this chapter can be used to generalize the specific. Countries can be described according to a number of characteristics. As examples, we do this for three countries: the United States, the Netherlands, and Japan.

The United States

The cultural dimensions of the United States are as follows: an M-time culture, linear time pattern, low-context, below average on power distance, high on individualism, high on masculinity, relatively weak in uncertainty avoidance, and with a short-term orientation.

The United States shows the following cultural characteristics:

- Short-term thinking, which influences all aspects of American life: the bottom line, success now rather than in the future, extremely short-range schedules
- Obsession with change, "new," and "better"
- More a credit card than a debit card culture
- Linear thinking; time is compartmentalized

- Hype, persuasive communication, and rhetoric
- Education valued only if it allows the individual to compete more effectively
- Expression of private opinions
- Equal opportunity
- Independence
- Need for privacy, universalistic thinking, ethnocentrism
- Importance of winning, power, success, and status
- Strong role differentiation
- Humor, innovativeness, creativity
- Man must conquer nature
- Importance of leisure
- Education teaches students to "be critical," makes them think. Students ask "why?" not "how?"

The Netherlands

The cultural dimensions of the Netherlands (and the Scandinavian countries) are as follows: M-time culture, linear time concept, low-context, low power distance, high on individualism, low on masculinity, of relatively weak uncertainty avoidance, relatively long-term orientation.

The Netherlands shows the following cultural characteristics:

- Longer term thinking
- More a debit card than a credit card culture
- Traditional; reverence for the past
- Linear thinking, rhetoric
- Time is compartmentalized
- Need for privacy
- Equality, not so much in opportunity as in freedom and care
- Independence
- Universalistic thinking, preachers
- Winning is OK, but not its display; status not important
- Small role differentiation
- Consensus seeking, jealousy
- Thrift, perseverance
- Caring rather than winning is the ideal
- Education beyond the basic ability to get a job
- Leisure is important

Japan

The cultural dimensions of Japan are as follows: a P-time culture, circular time concept, high-context, above average power distance, collectivistic, masculine, strong uncertainty avoidance, long-term orientation.

Japan shows the following cultural characteristics:

- Pressure on every Japanese person to know his or her place, to behave like his or her neighbors, not to shame his or her family, and to avoid jolting social harmony
- Dependence
- Private opinions not expressed
- Status is important to show power and success, but people avoid standing out in a crowd: "the nail that sticks out will be hammered down"
- Long-term thinking
- A cash culture or debit card culture, not a credit card culture
- Thrift, perseverance
- Strong role differentiation
- Education is not based on teaching students to be critical: The very meaning of "to think" is differently understood. In Japanese culture, it means something like, "to find an answer that can be shared by others." Students ask "how?" instead of "why?"
- Education has an intrinsic value, which cannot be measured purely in terms of the labor market
- "New" is accepted as a collective necessity, but basically the Japanese do not like change
- Obsession with cleanliness, purity
- Harmony with nature rather than conquest over nature
- Duty more important than leisure

Summary

Classification of cultures is necessary to understand differences in cross-cultural consumer behavior and to differentiate marketing and advertising strategies across countries. Classifying cultures by dimensions has proved to be a constructive method. It helps in vocalizing and labeling cultural differences and similarities.

A broad classification is the degree to which cultures contextualize, which is reflected in the type of communication cultures use. The difference between high- and low-context communication cultures helps us understand why, for example, Japanese and American advertising styles are so different, why the Japanese prefer indirect verbal communication and symbolism over the direct assertive communication approaches used by Americans.

In the past decades, several classifications of culture have been developed that were reviewed in this chapter in detail. When new dimensional models are introduced researchers tend to have high expectations, but before using a specific model, it should be analyzed with respect to its appropriateness for the specific purpose.

The Hofstede model proves to be most useful for comparing cultures with respect to consumption-related values. As a result, it can explain the variety of values and motives used in marketing and advertising across cultures. This will be particularly useful for companies that want to develop global marketing and advertising strategies. The model helps explain differences of various aspects of consumer behavior across cultures. These will be discussed in Chapter 5.

Notes

1. Gannon, M. J. (1994). *Understanding global cultures.* Thousand Oaks, CA: Sage.

2. Harris, P. R., & Moran, R. T. (1987). *Managing cultural differences.* Houston, TX: Gulf, pp. 190–195.

3. Hofstede, G., Hofstede, G. J., & Minkov, M. (2010). *Cultures and organizations: Software of the mind* (3rd ed.). New York: McGrawHill; throughout this book, significance levels are indicated by $*p < .05$; $**p < .01$; and $***p < .005$. When regression analysis is used, multiple linear regression analysis is done stepwise. The coefficient of determination or R^2 is the indicator of the percentage of variance explained. The examples in the charts in the various chapters in this book are of significant correlations between secondary data and one or more dimensions. Usually, for presentation clarity, not all countries are included. If more countries are available than presented in the chart, the original number of countries with the related correlation coefficient is included in an endnote.

4. Inglehart, R., Basañez, M., & Moreno, A. (1998). *Human values and beliefs.* Ann Arbor: University of Michigan Press. Data files are downloadable at http://www.worldvalues survey.com

5. In Inkeles, A., & Levinson, D. (1997). *National character.* New Brunswick, NJ: Transaction, pp. 45–50.

6. Kluckhohn, C. (1952).Values and value orientations in the theory of action. In T. Parsons & E. A. Shils (Eds.), *Toward a general theory of action.* Cambridge, MA: Harvard University Press; Kluckhohn, F., & Strodtbeck, F. (1961). *Variations in value orientations.* Evanston, IL: Row, Peterson.

7. Trompenaars, F. (1993). *Riding the waves of culture: Understanding cultural diversity in business.* London: Nicholas Brealy.

8. Smith, P. B., Dugan, S., & Trompenaars, F. (1996). National culture and the values of organizational employees: A dimensional analysis across 43 nations. *Journal of Cross-Cultural Psychology 27,* 231–264.

9. Fiske, A. P. (1992). The 4 elementary forms of sociality: Framework for a unified theory of social relations. *Psychological Review, 99,* 689–723.

10. Hall, E. (1984). *Beyond culture.* New York: Doubleday; Hall, E. (1994). *The dance of life.* New York: Doubleday, pp. 85–128.

11. Minkov, M. (2013). *Cross-cultural analysis: The science and art of comparing the world's modern societies and their cultures.* Thousand Oaks, CA: Sage.

12. Hofstede, G. (2001). *Culture's consequences* (2nd ed.). Thousand Oaks, CA: Sage; Hofstede et al., 2010.

13. Schwartz, S. H., & Bilsky, W. (1987). Toward a universal psychological structure of human values. *Journal of Personality and Social Psychology, 53,* 550–562; Schwartz, S. H., & Bilsky, W. (1990). Toward a theory of the universal content and structure of values: Extensions and cross-cultural replications. *Journal of Personality and Social Psychology, 58,* 878–891; Schwartz, S. H. (1994). Beyond individualism/collectivism. In U. Kim, H. C. Triandis, et al. (Eds.), *Individualism and collectivism: Theory, method, and applications: Vol. 18. Cross-cultural research and methodology.* Thousand Oaks, CA: Sage, pp. 85–119.

14. House, R. J., Hanges, P. J., Javidan, M., Dorfman, P. W., & Gupta, V. (2004). *Culture, leadership, and organizations: The GLOBE study of 62 societies.* Thousand Oaks, CA: Sage.

15. Minkov, M. (2007). *What makes us different and similar.* Sofia, Bulgaria: Klasika I Stil.

16. Minkov, M. (2011). *Cultural differences in a globalizing world.* Bingley, UK: Emerald.

17. The author of this book has compared the models for the purpose of understanding culture-based differences in consumer behavior, communication behavior and media usage by correlation analysis and regression analysis of a number of large databases using all dimensions of the three models. For the three dimensions, country scores for 45 countries were available. For the Hofstede dimensions, the scores are published in Hofstede, Hofstede, and Minkov (2010), as well as in this book (Appendix A). The GLOBE scores are available from the book by House et al. (2004), and Shalom Schwartz personally provided the most recent scores for his model. These country scores are not published. It appeared that two important Schwartz dimensions, intellectual and affective autonomy, are basically one dimension and provided results that were so similar that later only the data for intellectual autonomy were used, although Schwartz suggests it is better to use the average scores of the two. For the GLOBE model, only the practices were used as the value data are too far from reality. The dimension institutional collectivism practices didn't provide any meaningful results, in contrast to in-group collectivism, so only the latter was used.

18. Hall, 1994, pp. 85–128.

19. Ferraro, G. P. (1994). *The cultural dimension of international business.* Englewood Cliffs, NJ: Prentice Hall, pp. 50–51.

20. Hall, 1984, pp. 16–27, 32–34.

21. Adler, N. J. (1991). *International dimensions of organizational behavior.* Belmont, CA: Wadsworth, pp. 30–31.

22. Ferraro, 1994, p. 94.

23. Roland, A. (1988). *In search of self in India and Japan.* Princeton, NJ: Princeton University Press, p. 302.

24. Hall, 1984, pp. 17–24.

25. De Mooij, M. (1994). *Advertising worldwide.* London: Prentice Hall International, pp. 135–136.

26. This is demonstrated by the cause-and-effect approach in the Ishikawa or fishbone diagram, in Oakland, J. S. (1989). *Total quality management* (2nd ed.). Oxford, UK: Butterworth Heinemann.

27. Kluckhohn & Strodtbeck, 1961.

28. Doi, T. (1985). *The anatomy of self.* Tokyo: Kodansha International, pp. 147–148.

29. Smith, P. (2006). When elephants fight, the grass gets trampled: The GLOBE and Hofstede projects. *Journal of International Business Studies, 37,* 915–912.

30. Hofstede, 2001; Hofstede et al., 2010.

31. Schwartz, S. H. (2011). Studying values: Personal adventure, future directions. *Journal of Cross-Cultural Psychology, 42*(2), 307–319.

32. House et al., 2004.

33. Schwartz, S. H. (2004). Mapping and interpreting cultural differences. In H. Vinken, J. Soeters, & P. Ester (Eds.), *Comparing cultures: Dimensions of culture in a comparative perspective.* Leiden, Netherlands: Brill.

34. Javidan, M., House, R. J., Dorfman, P. W., Hanges, P. J., & Sully de Luque, M. (2006). Conceptualizing and measuring cultures and their consequences: A comparative review of GLOBE's and Hofstede's approaches. *Journal of International Business Studies, 37,* 897–914.

35. Gelfand, M. J., Bhawuk, D. P. S., Nishi, L. H., & Bechtold, D. J. (Eds.). (2004). Individualism and collectivism. In House, R. J., Hanges, P. J., Javidan, M., Dorfman, P. W., & Gupta, V. (2004). *Culture, leadership, and organizations. The GLOBE study of 62 societies.* Thousand Oaks, CA: Sage. pp 437–512.

36. Hofstede, 2001.

37. Macfarlane, A. (1978). *The origins of English individualism.* Cambridge, MA: Blackwell, pp. 146, 174.

38. Michael Hoppe, a German American management educator, replicated the IBM study on a population of political and institutional elites and found that Italy is much more collectivistic than the IBM scores lead one to believe. Hoppe's study also found differences with respect to Finland, which may be more individualistic than the IBM scores indicate. Contradictory information about the level of individualism or collectivism in Italy is probably due to the fact that Italy is bicultural: The north is individualistic, but the rest of the country is collectivistic. Hofstede's IBM data were mainly collected in the north, and he found strong individualism. Consumption and media behavior data are based on a country average; where these relate to individualism or collectivism, Italy tends to score similar to Spain, which is much more collectivistic.

39. Adler, 1991, p. 47.

40. Hall, 1984, p. 86.

41. Malkin, E. (1994, October 17). X-ers. *Advertising Age International,* 1–15.

42. Coon, H. M., & Kemmelmeier, M. (2001). Cultural orientations in the United States. *Journal of Cross-Cultural Psychology, 32,* 348–364.

43. Shavitt, S., Lalwani, A. K., Zhang, J., & Torelli, C. J. (2006). The horizontal/vertical distinction in cross-cultural consumer research. *Journal of Consumer Psychology, 16*(4), 325–356; Triandis, H. C. (1995). *Individualism and collectivism.* Boulder, CO: Westview Press, pp. 44–47.

44. Nelson, M. R., & Shavitt, S. (2002). Horizontal and vertical individualism and achievement values. *Journal of Cross-Cultural Psychology, 33,* 439–458.

45. See Appendix B Data Sources, European Media and Marketing Surveys (EMS) 2012.

46. Kincaid, D. L. (1987). Communication East and West: Points of departure. In D. L. Kincaid (Ed.), *Communication theory: Eastern and Western perspectives* (pp. 331–340). San Diego, CA: Academic Press.

47. Nielsen. (2007, March). *Health, beauty and personal grooming, a global Nielsen consumer report.* Retrieved from http://pt.nielsen.com/documents/0705_PersonalGrooming .pdf

48. See Appendix B Data Sources, World Values Survey, 2005.

49. Minkov, M., & Hofstede, G. (2012). Hofstede's fifth dimension: New evidence from the World Values Survey. *Journal of Cross-Cultural Psychology, 43*(1), 3–14.

50. See Appendix B Data Sources, OECD Programme for International Student Assessment (PISA) study (2009). *OECD Society at a Glance.* Unesco Institute for Statistics.

51. Suyin, H. (1994). *Eldest son.* London: Jonathan Cape, p. 392.

52. Ross, J. (1990). *The origin of Chinese people.* Petaling Jaya, Malaysia: Pelanduk (M) Sdn. Bhd. (Original work published 1916)

53. Schwartz, 2004.

54. *Harmonised European Time Use Survey, 2007.* European Commission, Eurostat report. See http://epp.eurostat.ec.europa.eu/portal/page/portal/eurostat/home

55. Soong, R. (2003, December 23). Argentina, Brazil, Chile, Colombia, Ecuador, Mexico and Peru. Message posted to TGI Latina (www.zonalatina.com/Zldata332.htm).

56. Davis, R. E., Resnicow, K., & Couper, M. P. (2011). Survey response styles, acculturation, and culture among a sample of Mexican American adults. *Journal of Cross-Cultural Psychology, 42*(7), 1219–1236.

57. Den Hartog, D. N. (2004). Assertiveness. In R. J. House, P. J. Hanges, M. Javidan, P. W. Dorfman, & V. Gupta (Eds.), *Culture, leadership, and organizations: The GLOBE study of 62 societies* (pp. 395–436). Thousand Oaks, CA: Sage.

58. Javidan, M. (2004). Performance orientation. In R. J. House, P. J. Hanges, M. Javidan, P. W. Dorfman, & V. Gupta (Eds.), *Culture, leadership, and organizations: The GLOBE study of 62 societies* (pp. 239–276). Thousand Oaks, CA: Sage.

59. Sandemose, A. 1938. En flygtling krydser sit spor [A fugitive crosses his own track]. Copenhagen: Gyldendals Bogklub. [Danish translation. Originally published in Norwegian, 1933.] English translation provided by Donald Nekman, personal communication.

60. *How Europeans spend their time.* (2002). Eurostat. Data 1998–2002. Europe, 9 countries. The proportion of men who spent any time on shopping activities—percentage per day correlated with masculinity, $r = -.72^{**}$. $R^2 = .52$.

61. *Social values, science, and technology.* (2005, June). Special Eurobarometer Report (EBS 225). For 27 countries, $r = .60^{***}$ and masculinity explains 36% of variance; for a selection of 16 wealthy countries, $r = .72^{***}$ and masculinity explains 52% of variance.

62. Perspectives. (1996, April 22). *Newsweek,* p. 7.

63. Hofstede, 2001.

64. Minkov, M. and Blagoev, V. (2011). What do project GLOBE's cultural dimensions reflect? An empirical perspective. *Asia Pacific Business Review,* 1–17.

65. Sully de Luque, M., & Javidan, M. (2004). Uncertainty avoidance. In R. J. House, P. J. Hanges, M. Javidan, P. W. Dorfman, & V. Gupta (Eds.), *Culture, leadership, and organizations: The GLOBE study of 62 societies* (pp. 602–653). Thousand Oaks, CA: Sage.

66. See Appendix B Data Sources, World Values Survey.

67. Samuelson, R. J. (1995, June 5). A nation of experts: If you think you're one, well, maybe you are. *Newsweek,* p. 33.

68. *Citizens of the European Union and sport.* (2004). Special Eurobarometer Report (EBS 213), Europe. For 21 countries, $r = .68^{***}$, uncertainty avoidance explains 47% of variance.

69. *Antibiotics.* (2003). Special Eurobarometer Report (EBS 183.3), Europe. For 14 countries, UAI: $r = .57^{**}$, PDI: $r = .62^{**}$.

70. Suedo, K. (2004). Differences in the perception of face. In F. E. Jandt (Ed.), *Intercultural communication* (pp. 293–301). Thousand Oaks, CA: Sage.

71. Minkov, 2007.

72. Minkov, 2011.

73. See Appendix B Data Sources, European Media and Marketing Survey (EMS) 2012.

74. Kabasakal, H., & Bodur, M. (2004). In R. J. House, P. J. Hanges, M. Javidan, P. W. Dorfman, & V. Gupta (Eds.), *Culture, leadership, and organizations: The GLOBE study of 62 societies* (pp. 564–601). Thousand Oaks, CA: Sage.

75. Minkov & Blagoev, 2011.

CHAPTER 5

Culture and Consumer Behavior

How people behave and what motivates them is largely a matter of culture. Consumer behavior theories are rooted in Western psychology and sociology and not necessarily applicable for understanding how consumers behave in other parts of the world. Much of Western psychology may be irrelevant in Asia.[1] Across cultures, people have different concepts of self, which influence their buying motives. Concepts like personality and identity are Western concepts, and so is the practice of attaching personal traits to brands. Emotions and how people express emotions are related to culture. Differences in how people process information, how they make decisions, whether they are innovative, all aspects are related to culture. For effective global marketing, branding, and advertising, these differences must be known and understood. This chapter provides an overview of consumer behavior theory and points out the influences of culture.

Consumer Behavior

Consumer behavior can be defined[2] as the study of the processes involved when people select, purchase, use, or dispose of products, services, ideas, or experiences to satisfy needs and desires. In this definition, consumer behavior is viewed as a process that includes the issues that influence the consumer before, during, and after a purchase. Various components of human behavior are involved in this process. These can be summarized as *what people are* ("who am I"), the self and personality, defined by people's attributes and traits ("what sort of person am I"), *how people feel, how people think and learn,* and *what people do.* The terms of the social sciences for feeling, thinking, and doing are *affect, cognition,* and *behavior.*

The model presented in Figure 5.1[3] structures the cultural components of the person in terms of *consumer attributes* and *processes,* and the cultural components

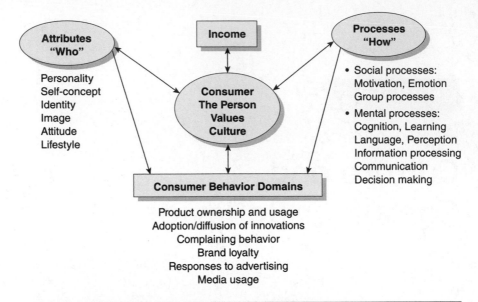

Figure 5.1   Cross-Cultural Consumer Behavior Framework

SOURCE: Adapted from Manrai, L. A., & Manrai, A. K. (1996). Current issues in cross-cultural and cross-national consumer research. In L. A. Manrai & A. K. Manrai (Eds.), *Global perspectives in cross-cultural and cross-national consumer research* (p. 13). New York: International Business Press/Haworth Press.

of behavior in terms of *consumer behavior domains*. Income interferes. If there is no income, there is little or no consumption, so income is placed in a separate box. The attributes of the person refer to *what people are* and the processes refer to *what moves people*—the *who* and the *how*. The central question is "Who am I?" and in what terms people describe themselves and others—their personality traits and identity. Related to the *who* are attitudes and lifestyle because they are a central part of the person. How people think, perceive, and what motivates them—*how* the aspects of "me" process into behavior—are viewed as processes.

Consumer Attributes

One aspect of Western marketing is the focus on product attributes, benefits, or values that are to distinguish the user's self from others. Another aspect is the distinction between the actual self and the ideal self. People will buy products that are compatible with their self-concept or, rather, that enhance their "ideal self" image. In that sense, our self-concept is the image we carry in our mind of the type of person we are and who we desire to be. Frequently mentioned drives related to the ideal self are self-esteem, self-respect, and self-actualization. The concepts of self, the ideal self—personality, identity, and image—have been derived from psychological studies in the United States and northwest Europe, so these and other psychological models presented in consumer behavior textbooks are derived from an individualistic worldview. Increasingly, other models are being developed for other groups.[4] This and following sections present such different worldviews.

The Concept of Self

The concept of self, as used in consumer psychology, is rooted in individualism. It includes the following ideas about a person. A person is an *autonomous entity* with a distinctive set of attributes, qualities, or processes. The configuration of these internal attributes or processes causes behavior. People's individual behavior varies, and this distinctiveness is good. People's attributes and processes should be expressed consistently in behavior across situations, and this consistency is good. Behavior that changes with the situation is viewed as hypocritical or pathological.

In the collectivistic model of the self, persons are fundamentally interdependent with one another. The self cannot be separated from others and the surrounding social context. This concept of self is characteristic of Asia, South America, Russia, the Middle East, Africa, and the south of Europe. The interdependent view of human nature includes the following ideas about a person. A person is an *interdependent entity* who is part of an encompassing social relationship. Behavior is a consequence of being responsive to the others with whom one is interdependent, and behavior originates in relationships. Individual behavior is situational; it varies from one situation to another and from one time to another. This sensitivity to social context is good.[5] Next to the term *interdependent* self in collectivistic cultures, the term *familial*[6] self is used. It is a "we" self, relational in different contexts. It includes a private self and a public self. The *private self* operates in interdependence with others of a person's in-group. There is emotional connectedness, empathy, and receptivity to others. It is through the *public self* that the social etiquette of relationships with the outer group is maintained in varying interpersonal contexts.

In individualistic cultures, a youth has to develop an identity that enables him or her to function independently in a variety of social groups apart from the family. Failing to do so can cause an identity crisis. In collectivistic cultures, youth development is based on encouragement of dependency needs in complex familial hierarchical relationships, and the group ideal is being like others, not being different.[7]

The very first words of little children in China are people-related, whereas children in the United States start talking about objects.[8] In Japan, feeling good is more associated with interpersonal situations, such as feeling friendly, whereas in the United States, feeling good is more frequently associated with interpersonal distance, such as feeling superior or proud. In the United Kingdom feelings of happiness are positively related to a sense of independence, whereas in Greece good feelings are negatively related to a sense of independence.[9]

For individualists, the norms are self-reliance, self-assertion, and self-actualization and a high degree of verbal self-expression. Members of collectivistic cultures conceive of the self as part of the group to which they belong. As a result, for members of collectivistic cultures, self-esteem, if used as a concept, is not linked to the individual but to relationships with others. The self is not defined as a set of abstract, unique characteristics but defined through a web of social and personal relationships. In Japan, "respecting yourself" means always showing yourself to be the careful player; it does not mean, as in English usage, consciously conforming to a worthy standard of conduct. In India, "we" self-regard means that feelings of inner regard or esteem are experienced not only around oneself but equally around the "we" of the extended family, particular community (*jati*), and other groups to which one belongs.[10] These are called in-groups, or inner circle, as opposed to out-groups, or outer circle.

In collectivistic cultures with increased wealth, some consumption habits may suggest that consumers are adopting Western individualistic values, such as personal freedom, but this may be misleading. In modern China, if encouraged, young consumers may be attracted to freely express their own taste, but such personal freedom is only tolerated as long as it remains personal, does not conflict with collective moral standards, and does not challenge common interests.[11]

Next to individualism, masculinity explains variation of the self-concept. A relationship orientation, including family values, not only is specific to collectivistic cultures but also is found in individualistic cultures that are also feminine.[12] Whereas in feminine cultures, modesty and relations are important characteristics, in masculine cultures, self-enhancement leads to self-esteem, which is a valid barometer of psychological health. In cultures of the configuration individualism/masculinity (Anglo-Saxon cultures), self-enhancement, or ego-boosting, is most pronounced. It can be recognized in a TV commercial for Discover Card, pictured in Illustration 5.1. The card is used to buy Christmas decorations. Whatever the actor buys, the neighbor has more. The actor cannot stand having less. In the end, his whole house is illuminated, all bought with the card.

The influence of masculinity can also be recognized in answers to a question in the European Social Survey[13] that asks respondents across Western and Eastern European countries to mark the importance of getting respect from others. Collectivism explains 47% of variance, and masculinity explains an additional 13% of variance. The relationship between respect from others and collectivism is illustrated in Figure 5.2, which also shows that feminine cultures like Sweden, Norway, and Finland score lower than masculine cultures like Ireland, Switzerland, and Poland.

Illustration 5.1   Discover Card, USA

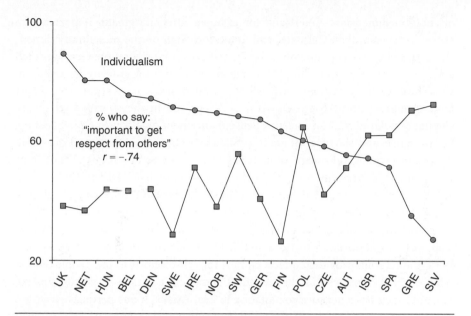

Figure 5.2 Importance of Getting Respect From Others

SOURCE: Data from Hofstede (2001) (see Appendix A); European Social Survey (2002/2003) (see Appendix B).

Self-enhancement and self-esteem are essential concepts for marketing and advertising, as many consumption activities can reinforce both. The concepts are also important for understanding differences in the functioning of social media because of the different ways people tend to present themselves. Perceptions of self in relation to others and society are related to self-esteem. Yet different routes have been found to reaching self-esteem. To North Americans, *self-enhancement* leads to self-esteem, whereas in East Asian cultures it is *self-improvement*. Self-enhancement or a general sensitivity to positive self-relevant information, confirms competence to European Americans.[14] In East Asia, self-esteem is tied to maintaining face, which implies that meeting the consensual standards associated with their roles and the pursuit of face is facilitated by self-improvement motivations.[15]

One of the fundamental needs of Asian societies that are influenced by Confucianism is to be respected by others. Respect indicates social superiority. Owning the right brands establishes superiority. According to Lu, brands have different functions in this respect. "While having a Ferrari or a Porsche is a clear display of the owner's wealth, owning a Rolls Royce or a Bentley not only displays wealth, but also indicates power and social status."[16]

For some time, self-enhancement and self-esteem have been thought to be phenomena typical of individualistic cultures, because the tendency to maintain and enhance self-esteem through efforts to stand out or be superior to others was assumed to be associated with individualism.[17] However, among individualistic cultures, differences in self-enhancement are also considerable. These differences can be explained by cultural masculinity, but even better by the long-/short-term orientation dimension. Americans, for example, attribute greater importance to self-enhancement than Germans, and both score high on the masculinity dimension, but they score very differently on long/short-term orientation: Germans high and the United States medium.[18] Feelings of pride and self-esteem are strong in short-term oriented cultures, such as in the United States, but even more in many Latin American and African cultures, as recognized in the so-called self-praise singing popular in African societies. Self-enhancement practices like ego boosting, performance, and showing off are integrated aspects of the North American self. American sociologist Erving Goffman[19] saw the structure of self in terms of "how we arrange for performances in Anglo-American society." Differences in self-enhancement are substantial, both across individualistic and collectivistic cultures.

Related are differences in self-disclosure. Several Internet facilities, such as social networks, may induce people to disclose more about themselves than they would do in face-to-face situations, but this varies across cultures. Whereas in the West, the Internet provides an ideal context for self-disclosure, and people tend to release verbal emotions that they wouldn't express in a person-to-person context, self-disclosure has a negative connotation to East Asians. If one partner reveals too much about himself or herself, the other may take it as inappropriate or as an indicator of incompetence.[20] This will be further discussed in Chapters 7 and 8.

Understanding the cultural aspects of the self should make marketers careful with extending the Western concept of self to other cultures. Examples are personal drives, such as self-esteem, self-confirmation, self-consistency, self-actualization, recognition, exhibition, dominance, independence, and the need for achievement.

Personality

Broadly defined, *personality* is the sum of the qualities and characteristics of being a person in individualistic cultures where the person is defined as an "independent self-contained, autonomous entity who comprises a unique configuration of internal attributes (e.g., traits, abilities, motives, and values) and who behaves primarily as a consequence of these internal attributes."[21] This personality is unique and cross-situationally consistent; that is, people are assumed to behave in a consistent way in different situations, to act *in character*. Personality is usually described in terms of traits such as autonomy or sociability. This concept of personality as an autonomous entity separate from the social environment includes the characteristics of an independent self of individualistic cultures. In collectivistic cultures, people's ideal characteristics vary by social role. Behavior is more strongly influenced by contextual factors.[22] East Asian thinking does not make a sharp person-situation distinction and has a more holistic notion of the person without a boundary between the person and the situation. Easterners believe in the continuous shaping of personality traits by situational influences.[23] Among speakers of Nguni languages in South Africa, personality characteristics vary with situation and relational context; Nguni languages also have fewer words for traits, and personal descriptions referring to pro-social or antisocial behavior are larger in number than found in Western personality traits descriptions. The fact that there is no consistency in personality, which is the essence of the Western concept, implies that the personality concept is not universal.[24]

Personality Traits

The Western habit of describing oneself and others in terms of abstract characteristics has led to the development of characterization systems of personal traits. Examples of such traits are *nervous, enthusiastic,* or *original.* Although there are thousands of trait-descriptive adjectives in English, only a few major groups of traits have been found in the Western world. The most used set of traits is called the five-factor model, the most recent version being named the Revised NEO Personality Inventory (NEO-PI-R), by Hofstede and McCrae.[25] This model consists of five factors labeled Neuroticism (N), Extraversion (E), Openness to experience (O), Agreeableness (A), and Conscientiousness (C). Each factor is defined by six specific traits or facets. For example, conscientiousness is represented by competence, order, dutifulness, achievement striving, self-discipline, and deliberation. These five factors have been found in many different cultures, although varying in weight across cultures. The relationship with culture was found by correlating Hofstede's cultural variables with culture-level means of individual-level scores on the five factors for 36 cultures. All five factors were related to one or more cultural dimensions. For example, neuroticism scores are higher in cultures of strong uncertainty avoidance and high masculinity. Extraversion scores are higher in individualistic cultures where autonomy and variety are valued more highly than duty and security.

Although research using the same set of questions has resulted in similar five-factor structures across cultures, this doesn't imply that these are the only existing conceptions of personhood. It merely shows that a set of English-language questions, when translated, results in similar five-dimensional structures.[26] There may be other conceptions of personality that are not found. The different factors may also vary as to different facets. Openness, for example, is not commonly used as a distinct dimension in the set of personality traits in Chinese culture. This is understandable as openness was not encouraged in traditional Chinese culture. For measuring an "open" person, interpersonal tolerance and social sensitivity are more relevant.[27]

Western individualists view traits as fixed; they are part of the person. East Asian collectivists view traits as malleable; they will vary with the situation. When individualists describe themselves or others, they use elements of the personal self in objective, abstract terms, out of context (I am kind, she is nice). People from collectivistic cultures tend to use mostly elements of the collective self or describe actions of people in context (my family thinks I am kind, she brings cake to my family).[28]

In individualistic cultures, personality traits are used to predict behavior because of emphasis on consistency between psychological traits and behavior. As collectivists place a higher value on situational cues, the utility of personal traits for predicting behavior may not be as strong in collectivistic cultures as it is in individualistic cultures.[29]

Identity and Image

Identity is defined as the idea one has about oneself, one's characteristic properties, one's own body, and the values one considers important. *Image* is how others see and judge a person.[30] Definitions of identity—as for personality—refer to an independent individualistic self.

In most Western cultures, people tend to assess the identity of self and others based on personality traits and on other individual characteristics such as age and occupation.[31] In collectivistic cultures, people are not used to doing so. They will assess themselves in terms of their ability to maintain harmonious relationships with others. One's identity is the group: the family, neighborhood, school, or the company where one works.

Western consumer behavior theory states that individuals can be pleased with personality traits that form a part of their *real* identity, or they may want to change them as a function of an image they would like to have. This produces an identity that reflects what psychoanalysts have termed the *ideal self.* If these two aspects of identity are far apart from each other, efforts are usually made to reduce the gap, and in individualistic cultures, material possessions can serve this purpose. Whereas in individualistic cultures, brands can contribute to an ideal and unique identity, in collectivistic cultures, brands serve the need for social status to demonstrate one's position in society.

In Western psychology, the body is viewed as part of the identity. Body esteem is related to self-esteem, and people attribute more desirable characteristics to physically attractive persons. The vast majority of research on what constitutes physical attractiveness has been conducted in Western societies, but mostly in the United States, where physical attractiveness of women is judged according to strict criteria, which leads to a tendency of self-criticism. The typical American woman begins to voice dissatisfaction with her body early in life and continues to do so right into the adult years. The general idea is that a desirable appearance leads to greater self-esteem. In Japan, where people attribute success more to external than to internal sources, there is less emphasis on the body as a source of esteem.[32] Confucian philosophy suggests that in the development of self-esteem and happiness, external physical appearance is less important than success in social role performance.[33] What is considered attractive varies. The Japanese, for example, rate large eyes and small mouths and chins as attractive whereas Koreans prefer large eyes, small and high noses, and thin and small faces.[34] Whereas obesity is frowned upon in the West, in some parts of Africa, it is perceived as a symbol of wealth in men and of fertility in women.[35]

From a Western worldview, Unilever developed a worldwide "Campaign for real beauty" for its personal care brand Dove, showing ordinary women and saying that real beauty can be found only on the inside; that every woman deserves to feel beautiful. The message is that real beauty is not portrayed by fashion models only. Unilever published a study of women's self-descriptions and statements about physical attractiveness in different countries.[36] The percentages of women who find themselves attractive correlate with individualism, low power distance, and low uncertainty avoidance. The latter explains 78% of variance. This is the configuration of the Western world where people are more preoccupied with the self. The opinion that the media and advertising should show more everyday women correlated with the same configuration, with low uncertainty avoidance explaining 53% of variance. In the high power distance and high uncertainty avoidance cultures, women's opinions are that physically attractive women are more valued by men. High power distance explains 75% of variance. In these cultures, the self is viewed in relation to others. This demonstrates that opinions of female beauty and the importance of female attractiveness vary across cultures and in particular between East and West. Also, in the West, being old makes women less attractive, which was another theme Dove used in advertising for its Dove pro-age brand. This is not an issue in most of Asia.[37] The Dove pro-age campaign presents nude women over 50 with the message that beauty doesn't have an age limit. Illustration 5.2 shows pictures of the pro-age campaign: A Dutch ad saying "Know yourself, know your skin; Let your skin shine" includes a picture of a nude grey-haired woman. The two other pictures are from the international TV commercial. In the United States, the TV ads did not adhere to Federal Communications Commission regulations and were banned because of too much nudity.

Illustration 5.2   Dove Pro-Age Print Advertisement (Netherlands) and Pictures from International Film

Personality and Identity in Marketing

In Western marketing practice and theory, identity and personality are used to define brand positions. At the basis of the Western practice of adding personalities to brands is the so-called self-brand congruity, that is, the tendency among consumers to use brands that are congruent with their self-image to create and communicate their self-concepts. However, self-brand congruity effects seem to be more evident in individualistic cultures than in collectivistic cultures, related to the differences in self-consistency across cultures.[38]

The concepts of brand personality and brand identity also are metaphors from individualistic cultures that are less understandable and less useful to collectivistic cultures. Words for the concepts *identity* and *personality* do not even exist in the Chinese and Japanese languages. There is a Japanese translation of the English word *identity*—"to be aware of one-self as oneself"—but its significance lies in the suggestion that this awareness of self is based on connections with others. The *katakana* (the Japanese language system that uses foreign words) word for *identity* is used. But using the word does not necessarily imply conceptual equivalence.

Even among individualistic cultures, a brand personality that can be recognized by, or is attractive to, the average public of one culture will not necessarily be recognized or found attractive by the average public of another culture. Brands acquire their personalities over time, and these are largely derived from the market context in which they develop. This context consists of a series of peculiarities that might not repeat itself in the same ways in other intended markets.[39]

If the human personality trait construct is culture-bound, so also the brand personality construct will be culture-bound. Jennifer Aaker[40] has conducted several studies to define brand personality dimensions across cultures. She found five brand personality factors in the United States that she labeled *Sincerity, Excitement, Competence, Sophistication,* and *Ruggedness.* The first three resemble the human personality factors Agreeableness, Extraversion, and Conscientiousness. Similar studies in Japan and Spain led to additional but country-specific factors: *Peacefulness* in Japan and Spain and a specific Spanish dimension, which she labeled *Passion.* A study of Korean brand personalities[41] of well-known global brands like Nike, Sony, Levi's, Adidas, Volkswagen, and BMW found two specific Korean brand personalities. The first, labeled *Passive Likeableness* included traits like easy, smooth, family oriented, playful, and sentimental. The second was labeled *Ascendancy* and included traits like strict, heavy, intelligent, and daring. These findings suggest that, even if companies wishing to be consistent have connected one specific personality trait to a global brand, consumers across cultures attach different personalities to these brands. These are the traits that may be viewed as fitting by consumers, but they can be very different from what the company wanted. A cross-cultural brand value study[42] showed that a brand characteristic like *friendly* is most attributed to strong global brands in high uncertainty avoidance and low power distance cultures. In low power distance cultures (also individualistic), friendship is viewed as important as people have to make an effort to make friends, as described in Chapter 4 under individualism-collectivism. Findings from two surveys asking about the importance of friends show correlations with power distance.[43] *Prestigious* is a characteristic attributed to global brands in high power distance cultures, and *trustworthy* is most attributed to strong brands in high uncertainty avoidance cultures. In the low power distance and low uncertainty avoidance cultures, people attributed *innovative* and *different* to these brands. So consumers project their own personality preferences onto global brands. Figure 5.3 presents a map of different brand personalities attributed to strong global brands.

A general aspect of the brand personality concept is that it is less relevant for members of collectivistic cultures than for members of individualistic cultures. If people are not used to describing themselves in abstract terms, out of context, they are not likely to be able to do so for brands either. If in collectivistic cultures people tend to describe themselves in relation to other people, they may also prefer to associate brands in relation to real people they view as a role models. This may explain the Japanese habit of linking brands to celebrities instead of abstract personal traits.

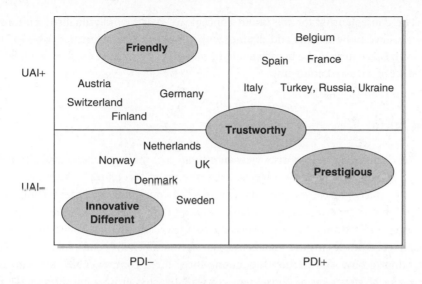

Figure 5.3 Brand Personality Traits Attributed to Strong Global Brands

SOURCE: Data from Hofstede (2001) (see Appendix A); Crocus study.

It is easier for a creative team to explain a proposed campaign by showing the client a popular talent around whom the campaign is to be built than by talking about abstract creative concepts. Generally, there is a significant correlation between collectivism and the use of celebrities in advertising.[44]

For members of collectivistic cultures where context and situation are so important, the brand concept is too abstract to be discussed the way members of individualistic cultures do. The Reader's Digest Trusted Brands survey in 2002 asked people in 18 different countries[45] in Europe about the probability of buying unknown brands. The responses "extremely/quite likely to consider buying a brand which I've heard of but haven't tried before" correlated significantly with individualism ($r = .82***$). A brand out of context is less relevant to members of collectivistic cultures than to members of individualistic cultures.

Where context and situation are important, people may easily adjust their brand choice to different situations. Peter Hessler,[46] in his book *Country Driving*, writes how one of his protagonists carries different cigarette brands for use in town or country.

Brands function differently across individualistic and collectivistic cultures. Whereas in individualistic cultures brands are made into unique personalities, in collectivistic cultures, they should generate trust in the company. Whereas American companies have developed product brands with unique characteristics, Japanese companies have generally emphasized the corporate brand. In essence, this means inspiring trust among consumers in a company and so persuading them to buy its products. Japanese and Korean companies, in their television advertisements, display corporate identity logos more frequently than U.S. and German companies do.[47] In China, the first association with a well-known brand tends to be trust.[48]

The consequences for the brand concept are that in individualistic cultures, brands have to be unique and distinct with consistent characteristics, whereas in collectivistic cultures, the brand should be viewed as being part of a larger whole, a product of a trusted company.

Attitude

Western consumer behaviorists view an *attitude* as a lasting, general evaluation of people (including oneself), objects, advertisements, or issues.[49] Attitudes have affective and cognitive components. The affective component includes feelings and emotions one experiences in response to an attitude object.[50] Both are related to behavior. In Western branding theory, the cognitive, affective, and behavioral components of attitudes toward brands translate as brand belief, brand evaluations, and intention to buy. The relationship among these three components is known as a *hierarchy of effects*, as if consumers consistently step from one component to another.

In the Western definitions, attitudes help to organize and structure one's environment and to provide consistency in one's frame of reference. Individualists want consistency between their attitudes, feelings, and behaviors.[51] This need for consistency between attitude and behavior implies that under certain conditions (in individualistic cultures), the behavior of consumers can be predicted from their attitudes toward products, services, and brands, and a purchase prediction is derived from a positive attitude. In collectivistic cultures, however, people form attitudes that fulfill their social identity functions, and there is not a consistent relationship between attitude and future behavior. It may be a reverse relationship: Behavior (product usage) comes first and defines attitude. In collectivistic cultures, shared experience influences brand attitude positively more than in individualistic cultures.[52]

For assessing advertising effectiveness, attitude toward the advertisement (A_{ad}) tends to be measured, and that information is used as an indication of buying intention. This is a logical practice in individualistic cultures, but the practice will not work the same way in collectivistic cultures.

The most widely known model that measures the relationship between attitude and behavior is the Fishbein behavioral intentions model, also referred to as the theory of *reasoned action*. Fishbein hypothesizes that a person's behavioral intentions are determined by an attitudinal or personal component and a normative or social component. The personal component or attitude toward the act refers to personal judgment of behavior, whereas the normative, or social, component refers to social pressures on behavior such as expectations of others.[53] What in Western terms is called "social pressure" has relatively weak influence on individualists, who will refer to their own personal attitudes as having influenced their buying decisions.[54] The individualistic social norm has a different loading in collectivistic cultures, as it does not capture "face." Face motivates collectivists to act in accordance with one's social position. If one acts contrary to expectations of one's social position, "a shadow is cast over one's moral integrity."[55] Thus, in collectivistic cultures, the norm is to live up to the standards of one's position whereas the social norm component of the Fishbein model measures perceptions of opinions of other persons.

Attitudes and intentions are what we feel and know and are derived from what we say. Intentions are often poor predictors of behavior, with large variance across cultures. Intentions must be measured, and differences in response styles are a cause of varying relationships between buying intention and actual buying. For example, if 55% of the people who try a new product in Italy say they will definitely buy it, the product will probably fail. If in Japan 5% say they will definitely buy it, the product is likely to succeed. If people are used to external, uncontrollable factors, such as fate or power holders, interfering at any time in the realization of an expressed intention, people will more readily express positive intentions that will not transform into behavior. This difference is reflected in the way people answer in semantic scales in survey research (see Chapter 6).

Consistency needs of individualistic cultures have led to measuring buying intention as a predictor of sales. There is however, a gap between intention and actual behavior, and this gap varies across cultures. In Europe, the difference is related to uncertainty avoidance, that is, the higher the countries score on this dimension, the larger the gap. Table 5.1 illustrates this with a few data from a Eurobarometer study of attitudes toward the environment.

Across cultures, people's attitudes toward specific product, product categories, or consumption habits vary. Examples are attitudes toward food safety, toward health, and toward consumption in general or the degree of materialism.[56] Attitudes at the national level that can have strong influences on brand choice are consumer ethnocentrism or consumer animosity, which influence the choice of a brand. Consumers are sensitive to the country of origin of products and brands. The *country of origin* (COO) of a brand or a foreign-sounding brand name influences consumer perceptions.[57] Consumers who have positive or negative attitudes toward a particular country will show favorable or unfavorable responses to country-related advertisements.[58] Attitudes toward foreign products vary by country of origin of the product. For example, whereas Japan is judged best for technologically advanced and

Table 5.1 **Relationships Between Buying Intention and Actual Buying of Environmentally Friendly Products**

	Ready to buy environmentally friendly products (%)	Bought environmentally friendly products (%)	Difference
Greece	88	13	75
Portugal	75	7	68
Poland	77	13	64
Germany	76	18	58
Austria	81	33	48
Sweden	88	42	46
Denmark	86	41	45

SOURCE: Eurobarometer (2008). Attitudes of European Citizens Towards the Environment (EBS 295) (see Appendix B).

attractively priced products, Germany is the home of reliable, solid products. France and Italy share the preeminence for style, design, and refinement.[59]

When consumers prefer products or brands from their own country to products or brands from other countries, this is called consumer *ethnocentrism*. Generally, in developed countries, preferences for domestic products are stronger than in developing countries.[60] Consumer ethnocentrism is related to the degree of national pride, which is measured by the long-term orientation dimension. Across Latin America, where feelings of national pride generally are strong, 67% agree with the statement "I prefer to buy products manufactured in my own country."[61]

Whereas consumer ethnocentrism refers to a preference of domestic products instead of products from *all* foreign nations, *consumer animosity* refers to the reluctance to purchase products of a *specific* country because of military, political, or economic events. Hence, someone low in ethnocentricity may still avoid purchasing products from a specific country as a form of punishment for that country's past (or current) military, political, or economic behavior. Examples of such consumer animosity are those against Japanese products in Nanjing, China, due to brutal treatment during the 1931 to 1945 Japanese occupation and against French products in Australia due to the French nuclear testing in the South Pacific. In ex-colonial countries, consumer animosity is found to turn to the ex-colonizing countries. Animosity has not been shown to affect the perception of the quality of products from the target country, but it does affect willingness to buy products from that country.[62]

Lifestyle

Lifestyle is described in terms of shared values or tastes as reflected in consumption patterns. Personal characteristics are viewed as the raw ingredients to develop a unique lifestyle. In an economic sense, one's lifestyle represents the way one allocates income, but lifestyle is viewed more as a mental construct that explains, but is not identical with, actual behavior.[63]

Lifestyle may be viewed as a useful within-country criterion, but it is less useful for defining segments across cultures because lifestyles are country-specific. No one has ever produced an empirical base to support the argument that across countries, lifestyle similarities are stronger than cultural differences. In contrast, increasingly, evidence is found that culture overrides lifestyle. Even if across cultures certain groups of people can be identified with respect to ownership of specific products, the motives for buying these products vary so strongly that for developing international advertising, these lifestyle groups are not useful.

Social Processes

Social processes deal with the *how*s of consumer behavior and include motivation, needs, drives, emotion, and group processes. All are processes that steer behavior. Although some emotions are internal, many result from interaction with the social environment.

Needs

Consumption can be driven by functional or social needs. Clothes satisfy a functional need; fashion satisfies a social need. A car may satisfy a functional need, but the type of car can satisfy a social need. Many global brands that seem universal are bought for different reasons across cultures. What in one culture may be a functional need can be a social need in others. The bicycle is a functional need to many Chinese, who need it for transportation, whereas it is a social need to most Americans, who use it for socializing or fitness.

Differences in sensitivity to certain product attributes and varying buying motives can be explained by the underlying cultural values that vary by product category. For example, in high uncertainty avoidance cultures, the generic need related to mineral water is purity, which is irrelevant in low uncertainty avoidance cultures. Alcoholic beverages have status value in masculine cultures, not in feminine cultures, and whiskey consumption is related to social status in high power distance cultures. For cars, needs vary between safety, status, design, and environmental friendliness, all related to different cultural values.

Maslow[64] categorized human needs in a hierarchy of importance: physiological needs, safety needs, social needs, esteem needs, and self-actualization. His hierarchy of needs concept is based on the assumption that a person's behavior is directed at satisfying needs and that some needs will take precedence over others when the individual is faced with choices as to which needs to satisfy. Physiological needs will take precedence over security or safety, group membership, or esteem needs. The supreme category then is self-actualization. Figure 5.4 depicts Maslow's hierarchy.

Maslow's hierarchy of needs is generally presented as a universal model, but the cross-cultural relevance is increasingly questioned. There is little evidence to support Maslow's hypothesis that there is a universal order among the non-physiological goals. A universal human pattern may be that physiological

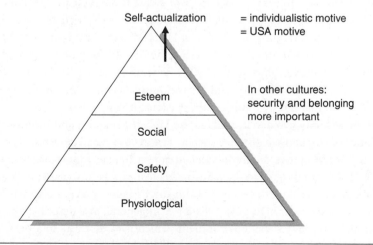

Figure 5.4   Maslow's Hierarchy of Needs

needs take precedence over higher order needs, but the ranking of the non-physiological needs varies across cultures.

Self-actualization is a highly individualistic U.S. motive. In collectivistic cultures, what will be actualized is not the self but the interest and honor of the in-group (not its individual members). In collectivistic cultures, belonging and safety will converge: It is very risky to distinguish oneself from the group. Security or safety is likely to prevail over other needs where uncertainty avoidance is strong. Belonging will prevail over esteem in feminine cultures, but esteem over belonging in masculine cultures.[65]

Motivation

Motivation can be defined as the internal state of an organism that drives it to behave in a certain way. *Drives* are the motivational forces that cause individuals to be active and to strive for certain goals. The study of motivation, the mixture of wants, needs, and drives within the individual, is seen as of prime importance to understanding behavior. Motivation research seeks to find the underlying "why" of our behavior; it seeks to identify the attitudes, beliefs, motives, and other pressures that influence our purchase decisions. In the 1950s, researchers such as Ernest Dichter used Freudian psychoanalytical ideas to explain behavior on the basis of unconscious motivation. Motivation theories are particularly based on Freud's idea of anxiety.

Freud's concepts related to the self, quoted in many textbooks on consumer behavior, are culturally determined. In developing his concepts of the id, ego, and superego, Freud was a true product of Austrian-Hungarian culture. Austria and Hungary score extremely low on power distance and high on uncertainty avoidance. Strong uncertainty avoidance implies that parents raise their children with the message that life is threatening or dangerous, so children have to create structures to cope with threat. If combined with large power distance, this attitude does not pose a problem for children, as parents will create the structures for them. Small power distance, however, implies that children become independent at an early age and have to structure reality for themselves. This leads to frustration. Freud's superego is meant to control the id, thus, taking the role of the parent. It serves as an inner uncertainty-absorbing device.[66] One conclusion is that if Freud's theory is true or useful, it will be most useful for the Austrians and Hungarians and other cultures of a similar configuration of dimensions. It will be less useful for cultures of weak uncertainty avoidance, such as the United Kingdom and Scandinavia, or for cultures of large power distance such as France and Asian cultures.

Cross-cultural motive differences that are of particular importance to branding and advertising are differences in status needs. An expression related to social status that entered the English language from the Chinese is *face*, a characteristic of collectivistic cultures of high power distance. In general, *face* describes the proper relationship with one's social environment, which is as essential to a person (and that person's family) as the front part of his or her head. Social roles shape peoples identities and constitute desirable images, and the more a person is expected to fulfill his or her social role, the more he or she is perceived as losing face when failing to do so.[67] Other collectivistic cultures have linguistic equivalents, for example, the Greek *philotimos*. Face is lost when an individual, either through his action or that of people close to him, fails to meet essential requirements placed upon him by his social position.[68] Upholding face goes with avoiding social embarrassment. Social embarrassment occurs when an individual is seen by others when buying, for example, intimate products. In India, avoidance of social embarrassment has been used in advertising as an appeal for several product categories such as deodorants or detergents: for example, being punished by your teacher for not wearing clean clothes.[69]

Buying Motives

Understanding the variations in what motivates people is important for positioning brands in different markets. Motives underlie brand loyalty, brand preference, brand image, and the importance of luxury brands. The diagram in Figure 5.5 maps the different motives for luxury brands in cultures of the configuration of individualism and masculinity.

In collectivistic cultures in the two right hand quadrants (of the figure) that are also of high power distance, people have the need to conform, and luxury brands provide social status. Russians, being both collectivistic and very high on power distance, are very status sensitive. When combined with low masculinity, harmony and a relationship orientation prevail, and luxury brands mainly serve a social

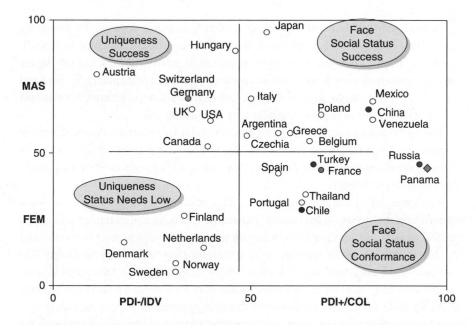

Figure 5.5   Motives for Luxury Brands

SOURCE: Data from Hofstede (2001) (see Appendix A).

function. When combined with high masculinity, status needs are reinforced to enhance group identity, to show that you belong to an important social class. Consumption of luxury goods is regarded as a behavior to maintain and enhance one's face.[70] In 2004, 29% of the total turnover of Moët Hennessy-Louis Vuitton SA (LVMH), owner of Louis Vuitton and Dior, and 58% of turnover of Cognac producer Remy Martin were concentrated in Asia.[71] In China, status appeals are also heavily used in advertising.[72] In fact, there are two Chinese consumption phenomena linked with the face concept: a gifting culture and "face" consumption. Some products or brands are mainly bought as gifts and others serve as a display of social position. Because gift giving also provides social status, gifts are often of higher quality and/or price than the same products bought for one's own consumption. Wang provides, as an example, the gift status of moon cakes bought for the Autumn festival by the saying "those who buy premium moon cakes won't eat them and those who eat them don't purchase them."[73] The need for luxury brands to show social position and success is strongest in the right upper quadrant where countries score high both on masculinity and collectivism/power distance. Also, across Europe in the cultures that score highest on this configuration of dimensions, people tend to enjoy it when people see how successful they are.[74]

The face concept does not apply to the cultures shown in the left quadrants that are individualistic. When combined with high masculinity, luxury brands help to enhance the unique self. In the individualistic and low masculine cultures, people have low status needs. They want to be unique but don't need to stand out and will not need luxury brands to demonstrate their success, only to some degree their uniqueness, with the exception of the few countries that combine high power distance with individualism, such as France and Belgium, where the social status motive does apply.

Several scholars have developed lists of consumption motives by analyzing advertising. Pollay's[75] list of values in advertising is an early inventory of North American buying motives. Some motives may exist across cultures, but the degree of importance will vary. Some motives are category-bound (e.g., purity for food and drink). For other categories, motives can strongly vary across cultures. An example is how motives for buying automobiles vary by culture.

Figure 5.6 shows motives for buying automobiles by cultural clusters according to two of Hofstede's dimensions, masculinity and uncertainty avoidance. These motives are recognized in the design of cars and in the appeals used by advertisers of successful car brands.

The lower left quadrant shows the configuration of low masculinity and weak uncertainty avoidance. In this culture cluster, people have a preference for safety to protect their family and to receive value for money. Safety (to protect the weak) and the functional aspects of a car are more important than technology or design. The Swedish Volvo car brand is well known for the safety claim. In feminine cultures, people have little interest in the motor of their car. Data from several surveys show that they don't even know the power of their car engines, as compared with people in masculine cultures. The lower right quadrant shows a cluster of cultures with the configuration of masculinity and weak uncertainty avoidance. People in these cultures have status needs to show their success and prefer cars with big, powerful

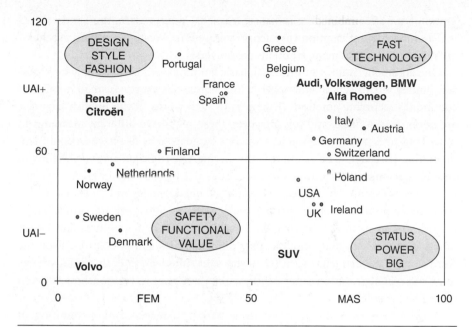

Figure 5.6   Car-Buying Motives Across Europe

SOURCE: Data from Hofstede (2001) (see Appendix A).

motors. This is the culture cluster where people will be most attracted to the sturdy SUV type. The upper right quadrant shows the cluster of cultures with the configuration of masculinity and strong uncertainty avoidance. People in these cultures are aggressive drivers, and they prefer cars with rapid acceleration. This seems paradoxical, as one would expect to see risk aversion translated into a safety motive. Not so: The explanation is that people of strong uncertainty avoidance cultures build up stress, which they also want to release. Fast and aggressive driving serves as an emotional safety valve. It demonstrates that uncertainty avoidance is not the same as risk avoidance. But cars must also be technologically advanced, well designed, and well tested. These are the cultures where people prefer the German brands like Audi and BMW and the Italian Alfa Romeo. Volkswagen's claim, "Vorsprung durch Technik" (headstart through technology), reflects the technology motive. In the upper left quadrant, in the combination of low masculine and strong uncertainty avoidance, one sees the need for "sporty" driving, fast acceleration but not so aggressive. This is combined with a preference for design (but more in the art/fashion sphere), pleasure, and enjoyment. This is the area where the stylish brands like Renault and Citroën originate and are preferred.

Emotion

Emotion tends to be described as a process that involves an interaction between cognition and physiology. Emotions consist of various components like experience, facial expression, and physiological response that are closely linked together.

Emotions are affective responses that are learned. Concept, definition, understanding, and meaning of emotion vary across cultures. Yet Western emotion psychologists have argued that many emotions are universal.

One argument in favor of universal, basic emotions is that most languages possess limited sets of central emotion-labeling words, referring to a small number of commonly occurring emotions. Examples of such words in the English language are *anger, fear, sadness,* and *joy.* However, these may have different meanings in other languages. Many emotion terms in one language may not have an equivalent in another language. One example is the German word *Schadenfreude,* the joy in another person's misfortune; a word that does not exist in the English language. Other examples are the Korean concepts of *dapdaphada* and *uulhada,* which include components such as sadness and loneliness and have no equivalent in English or German. The fact that such words exist in some cultures and not in others demonstrates that emotions play different roles across cultures. Even the word *emotion* as such refers to different states. In American English, *emotion* refers to an internal state, but in other cultures, emotions refer to relationships between people and events.[76]

Another argument for universality is based on research of recognition of facial expressions. The question is whether it is justified to take facial expression as an index of the presence of emotions because it is possible that in some societies emotions occur without facial expressions, and in others, facial expressions occur without emotions.[77] Seeing a facial expression allows an observer to draw a conclusion about a situation, but one specific facial expression is not necessarily connected to one specific emotion. For example, a smile is generally viewed as an expression of happiness. However, seeing a friend can make a person smile, but this does not imply that the person is happy. He or she can, in fact, be sad or lonely.

Across cultures, people weigh facial cues differently. When interpreting emotions of others, the Japanese focus more on the eyes, whereas Americans focus on the mouth. This difference may explain why stylized facial icons seem to differ between Japan and the United States. In Internet text mails, Americans use emoticons that vary the direction of the mouth, e.g. :) and :(. Japanese emoticons vary the direction of the eyes and may not vary the direction of the mouth, e.g. ^_^ and ;_;.[78]

The psychologists Mesquita and Frijda[79] reviewed various elements of emotions across cultures and concluded that several elements of emotion, but not all, are related to culture. For example, among individualistic independent selves, "ego focused" emotions like anger, frustration, and pride, are more marked than among collectivistic interdependent selves, where "other focused" emotions, such as sympathy, shame, and feelings of interpersonal communion, are more marked.

Intensity and meaning of emotions vary and are culturally defined. Emotions are, for example, more subdued in hierarchical, high power distance, and collectivistic cultures.[80] In individualistic cultures, personal feelings and their free expression are more important than in collectivistic cultures. A comparison of emotion expression across 32 countries showed a significant correlation with individualism

for overall emotion expressivity and in particular expressing happiness and surprise.[81] East Asian collectivists try to display only positive emotions and tend to
control negative emotions. Probably, this is the reason why, in emotion-recognition
studies, Chinese people are less able to identify expressions of fear and disgust.[82]
People in weak uncertainty avoidance cultures are less inclined to show emotions
than cultures of strong uncertainty avoidance. The British "stiff upper lip" can serve
as an example. Also, the vocal expression of emotion by Chinese young adults is
more restrained than by Italian young adults.[83]

The same expressions may have different meanings in different cultures. Children in Western societies protrude their tongue to show contempt; among Chinese,
the same gesture means surprise. A smile may be an expression of pleasure or
embarrassment. Instead of suppressing an expression of displeasure, Asians may
display an expression of polite intercourse, what Westerners may perceive as a
smile. In personal encounters, the author of this book has often seen Chinese or
Indonesians smile or even laugh to hide their embarrassment. This sort of smile is
certainly not a reflection of happiness.

Emotions in Advertising

The concept of global (standardized) advertising as first introduced by the advertising agency Saatchi & Saatchi in the early 1980s was based on the assumed universality of basic emotions such as happiness or love. This has led to parity
advertising, showing happy people connected to the brand. Because the ways people show their emotions are so different across cultures, the use of emotions in
global advertising is not advisable. Those who rely on so-called mood boards to
visualize different brand positions have found they cannot use the same visuals to
express moods across cultures. Experience at international advertising agency
BBDO has taught that for its "photo sort" method, which it used to position brands,
photographs of facial expressions produced in the United States to represent and be
recognized as "mood" could not be transplanted to Europe. The way American
actors expressed specific moods could not be recognized by European respondents.
The same is true within Europe: No single "photo deck" could be developed for the
whole of Europe.

Group Processes

Western consumer behavior theory distinguishes between formal (associations)
and informal groups (family and friends) that may influence behavior and decision
making. Another group that is distinguished as influencing consumer behavior is
the reference group.

The Western individualistic assumption is that people can choose group membership. Individuals select other people, groups, or associations that match or reinforce their identity. In collectivistic cultures, members of the in-group, also called

inner circle, are part of one's identity. They are not selected; they are part of your being. Whereas in individualistic cultures, few other people will influence the buying process, which is an individual activity, Japanese housewives refer to an average group of eight other housewives who influence their decision making.[84] This explains the success of network marketing in collectivistic cultures.

In consumer decision making, the degree to which group members depend on others, in particular family members, varies with collectivism and power distance. Comparative content analysis of Chinese and American advertising demonstrates that group consensus and conformity to family preference rather than individual choice is found in Chinese advertising more often than in American advertising.[85] When in individualistic cultures people refer to friends and family as influencing their decisions, this process is not the same as in-group influence in collectivistic cultures. Although across Europe in collectivistic cultures people do consult family and friends for comparison,[86] this is part of frequent in-group interpersonal communication, and people are not inclined to view this process as influencing decisions or as an active information-gathering process. (See also the section on information processing.) Although interdependence between family members is strong in collectivistic cultures, peers have more influence on buying and media behavior as media behavior and ownership of certain products or brands adds to group identity. Japanese sociologists state that by owning a Vuitton purse, anonymous young women can feel kinship with other Vuitton owners and not feel "excluded."[87] Singh[88] reports that in India, too, young people are more influenced by peers than by family members. Conformance to peers may be more important than family influence.

In feminine cultures, the marriage partner plays a stronger role in the buying process than in masculine cultures. An example of how strongly this difference can affect advertising was a television commercial for the Renault Mégane (automobile). It depicted a man who wanted to surprise his wife with the new Renault Mégane, at the same time demonstrating the short stopping distance. He stops in front of what he thinks is his house, shouting, "Darling, I have bought the Renault Mégane," and it appears he has entered his neighbor's (similar) house because he is not used to the short stopping distance. The text of this Belgian commercial was changed radically for the Netherlands, although it was in the same language (as part of Belgium and the Netherlands share the same language). In masculine Belgium, apparently, the husband can buy a car without consulting his wife, but this is not done in feminine Netherlands.

Reference group generally is defined as an actual or imaginary individual or group that is relevant for an individual's evaluations, aspirations, or behavior.[89] The terms *reference group* and *aspirational group* tend to be used more loosely to describe any external influence that provides social clues. In individualistic cultures, the degree to which peers influence an individual in nuclear families is stronger for public than for private products and brands whereas this is not the case for individual members of extended families. This occurs because in nuclear families, the number of immediate family members and their importance to the individual is limited whereas in extended families, there are numerous family members available to influence the individual's decision making.

Public and Private Space

Behavior in private space can be different from behavior in public space. Members of individualistic cultures have a greater need for privacy than have members of collectivistic cultures, which has implications for usage of several product categories, such as beer, but also for media usage, such as watching television in the home versus in public space, or the use of the mobile phone. Collectivists socialize more in public space, whereas individualists do so more in the home. In Europe, in the more collectivistic countries where people more frequently visit cafés and bars, they also access the Internet more in cyber cafés. Mixing home and work life is also related to individualism. Whereas in individualistic cultures people may want to take work into their homes, this is not the usual behavior in collectivistic cultures. In Chapter 8, we'll see how this has influenced penetration of the personal computer and Internet across individualistic and collectivistic cultures. An example of how the difference influences mobile phone use is seen in Spain, where users have an option of two different lines on the same mobile handset: one for personal use and another for professional use, to maintain a differentiation between the public and private spheres.[90]

Opinion Leaders

In Western decision-making theory, specific individuals are assumed to influence the decision-making process through word-of-mouth communication, generally within a certain product category. Opinion leaders are strong, informal sources of product information. They achieve their status through technical competence and social accessibility. They serve as role models and play an important role in the process of diffusion of innovations. The concept of opinion leadership is basically an American concept, derived from the diffusion of innovation theory by Rogers,[91] which resulted from investigation of the speed and pattern of the spread of new farming techniques across the United States.

The roles of opinion leaders vary across cultures. People with technical competence, or competent people in general, are likely to be favored in strong uncertainty avoidance cultures. Masculine cultures have high regard for the successful. In high power distance cultures, the power holders may have an important role as opinion leaders.

An important difference is in the way opinion leaders get their information. Whereas the theory says they get their information from the mass media in individualistic cultures, in collectivistic cultures, they obtain their information from the social network.

Mental Processes

How people see, what they see and do not see, how they think, how language structures their thinking, how they learn, and how people communicate are mental processes. These processes—called cognitive processes in psychology—deal with understanding of several *how*'s of behavior. The term *cognition* covers the main internal psychological processes that are involved in making sense of the environment and deciding what action might be appropriate. Mental processes include learning and memory, thinking and reasoning, understanding and interpreting stimuli and events, attention, perception, language, and categorization. A few of these topics are reviewed in the following sections.

Learning, Memory, Language, and Perception

Most human behavior is learned. When people act, they learn. *Learning* describes changes in an individual's behavior arising from experience. Cultural values are also acquired by learning. This is a semi-conscious process which is called *socialization*. Socialization is the process whereby the young of a society learn the values, ideas, practices, and roles of that society. The major participants in socialization of young people, the family, would not see themselves consciously in this learning process, whereas others, such as educators, function deliberately for this purpose.

Memory involves acquiring information and storing it for later retrieval. Learning and memory have great practical significance for many activities in life. Culture also affects memory. There is evidence for better recall of stories consistent with people's own cultural knowledge.[92]

The information a person has acquired must be *organized* in order for it to be placed in one's memory. The human memory is arranged according to *schemata,* structures of knowledge a person possesses about objects, events, people, or phenomena. To place the acquired information in memory, it must be *encoded* according to the existing schemata. A schema relating to activity is called a *script.* The independent self of individualistic cultures forms context-independent schemata, whereas the interdependent self of collectivistic cultures forms context-dependent schemata.[93] Thus, East Asians are more likely to remember information in terms of the context within which it is presented, whereas Westerners will remember the various components separately.

The structure of a language (e.g., its grammar and type of writing system) has consequences for basic consumer processes, such as perception and memory. Structural differences, such as in scripts of Indo-European and Asian languages, seem to affect mental representations, which in turn influence memory. Chinese native speakers rely more on visual representations whereas English speakers rely primarily on phonological representations (verbal sounds). In the English language, verbal sounds are most used to encode the brand name and facilitate memory. Explicit repetition of words enables consumers to encode and recall the brand name. An example is, "If anyone can, Canon can," used as payoff in ads for Canon in the United Kingdom, or the more recent "You can, Canon" payoff that is used in international advertising, as in Illustration 5.3.

Illustration 5.3 Canon, International

Because of their own focus on sound and pronunciation, Western companies are inclined to adapt their brand names to other cultures more vocally than visually. Chinese consumers, however, are more likely to recall information when the visual memory is accessed and are more likely to recall brands when they can write them down.[94] Visually distinct brand name writings or calligraphy and logo designs that enforce the writing will be more effective in China whereas for English native speakers the sound qualities of brand names should be exploited by the use of jingles and onomatopoeic names (names resembling the sound made by the object).

Categorization

How people categorize other people and objects varies with individualism-collectivism. Collectivists tend to pay attention to relationships between objects whereas individualists categorize objects according to rules and properties. Chinese children will group items together that share a relationship, whereas Canadian children will group items together that share a category.[95] Ask an African to sort a few objects, say some tools, food items, and clothes, and he will put a knife with a potato as a knife is needed to slice a potato.[96] The difference is related to analytical thinking of individualists versus holistic thinking of collectivists. The difference has implications for brand strategy. American consumers view a brand extension of a different product category as not fitting with the parent brand. A brand extension must "fit," and this fit is judged on the basis of product class similarity. Collectivists view the parent brand in terms of the overall reputation of or trust in the company. So they perceive a higher degree of brand extension fit also for extensions in product categories far from those associated with the parent brand than individualists would.[97] Whereas companies of individualistic cultures carefully select line or brand extensions that fit the product category, companies from collectivistic cultures stretch their brands in wider directions. The European brand Nivea has been careful to limit line extensions to related personal care products and linked them all consistently to the core brand values *purity* and *value for money.* Japanese Shiseido, a cosmetics company, has extended its brand into the food category. The overall category Shiseido covers is *beauty,* and both cosmetics and beauty food appear to fit this category. Examples of beauty food are sweets for shiny eyes, lollipops for full hair, and self-tanning chewing gum.[98] The Spanish brand Chupa Chups, characterized by the yellow-red logo designed by Salvador Dali, includes many different products: from lollipops to sunglasses, clothes, shoes, and stationery.[99]

Related to this is the use of classifiers. A classifier is a measure that is used in conjunction with numerals (one, two, three, etc.) or determiners (*a, the, that, this*) and that refer to common physical features of objects, such as shape, size, thickness, or length, as well as other perceptual or conceptual properties associated with objects, such as "bendability" or "graspability." Classifiers categorize a given object into a larger set of objects and describe classes of objects. As such, they are different from adjectives that describe specific instances within a class. Adjectives answer the question, "What kind of object is it?" whereas classifiers answer the question, "What kind of object is this a member of?" The use of classifiers is not found in Indo-European languages, but in many others, such as in Chinese, Japanese, Korean, and Thai languages as well as Navajo and Yucatan-Mayan languages. The classifier system has to be exploited carefully, as it can have positive and negative effects. For example, a classifier for pipe-like, thick objects will lead to positive expectations for lipstick, but a classifier for long, thin objects can lead to negative expectations that it will provide less quantity and will not last long. When existing products are modified and change shape, inconsistency can occur. Classifiers used for telephones (objects standing on a frame) cannot be used for cellular phones.[100]

Field Dependency

Research from various areas suggests that members of individualistic and collectivistic cultures differ with respect to the degree to which they perceive objects either as single and independent entities (field independent) or as being related to the context in which they appear (field dependent). *Field dependent* people are influenced in their perception by characteristics of their physical and social environment. *Field independent* people will perceive an object separately from its environment.[101]

The amount of field information is restricted in classic Western art—painters include field information only to the extent that it can realistically be observed given the perspective within a given scene. East Asians, in contrast, have employed various ways of emphasizing field information. The Chinese developed the scroll form to depict a panoramic view of landscape that could include a whole succession of mountain ranges, near and far. The bird's-eye view used in Japanese landscape depiction is another mode of representing field information. The artist's standpoint is higher than the objects depicted.

In Western portraits, the intention is to distinguish the figure from the ground. For this reason, the model occupies a major fraction of the space. East Asian portraiture is unlikely to emphasize the individual at the expense of the context. For this reason, the size of the model is relatively small, as if the model is embedded in an important background scene. Analyses of paintings of groups of people show similar results: East Asian paintings of people place the horizon higher and present models smaller than do Western paintings of people. When making photographs, East Asians are more likely than Westerners to set the zoom function in order to make the model small and the context large.[102] Field dependents are likely to see more in a message than intended by the sender. Illustration 5.4. shows how this phenomenon applies to design. The traditional design of the package of

Illustration 5.4 Fruittella packages in China

SOURCE: Visser, E. (2009). *Packaging Design: A Cultural Sign.* Barcelona: Index Book, s.l.

Fruittella sweets features monsters with no background. This is unacceptable in China, so an exception was made and a landscape was added.[103]

The Creative Process

Artistic creativity refers to the creativity expressed in any aspect of the arts, but also in design and advertising. The extent to which a person or a product is judged as creative may be influenced by where the person or the product originates. It is assumed that the Western conception of creativity is primarily concerned with innovation, whereas the Eastern conception of creativity is more dynamic, involving the re-use and reinterpretation of tradition rather than breaks in tradition.[104] Two aspects of creativity are *creative expression* (i.e., production of creative products) and *judgment of creative products.* Several studies have measured judgment, but the number of cross-cultural studies measuring differences in production of creativity is limited. A general finding is that judges evaluate in-group creations more positively than out-group creations.[105]

A Western assumption is that the creative process is based on divergent thinking. If that were the core of creativity, the need for conformity in collectivistic cultures would inhibit the creative process, but there is no empirical evidence of that. Yet there is some variation in the ways creativity can be fostered in different cultures. Countries high on uncertainty avoidance prefer creative individuals to work through organizational norms, rules, and procedures, and countries high on power distance prefer creative individuals to gain support from those in authority before action is taken. In individualistic cultures that are also low on uncertainty avoidance and power distance, creativity can best survive outside organizational constraints. High power distance means individuals are restricted in challenging others, and deviant ideas tend to be suppressed. Thus, conceptions and definitions of creativity in one culture should not be applied thoughtlessly and uncritically to evaluate and judge creativity in another.

Locus of Control

An important mental phenomenon that explains the influence of others on behavior is *locus of control,* as introduced by Julian Rotter.[106] Internal or external locus of control refers to the degree to which persons expect that an outcome of their behavior depends on their own behavior or personal characteristics versus the degree to which persons expect that the outcome is a function of chance, luck, or fate; is under the control of powerful others; or is simply unpredictable.[107] At the culture level, the difference suggests that in some cultures, people are more inclined to take social action to better life's conditions (also called "civic competence") whereas in other cultures, people are more dependent on institutions, such as authorities and governments. The belief in the West that the locus of control resides in the individual and that behavior is a function of the individual's own action is deeply implanted in decision theory. In collectivistic cultures, however, where people are used to the fact that other people may make decisions about them and for them, external locus of control operates; and this is reinforced by high power distance, where the power holders will ultimately make the decisions. Particularly, the combination of high power distance, collectivism, and strong uncertainty avoidance appears to be linked with external locus of control. An example is how, across 12 countries in Europe, people answer the question when asked how globalization should be controlled.[108] The higher the countries score on power distance, the higher the percentage of people who say there should be more regulation by their governments to control globalization. The percentage of people who agree with the statement "I have little influence over things that happen to me" correlates significantly with high power distance ($r = .55^{***}$), with low individualism ($r = -.54^{***}$), and with strong uncertainty avoidance ($r = .54^{***}$).[109] In Figure 5.7, countries are mapped according to internal-external locus of control.

Understanding the difference is important because internal locus of control is part of the fundamental assumptions in behavior intention models and in decision-making theories. When testing new product concepts, buying intent is regarded as one of the key performance indicators. In external locus of control cultures, people will be more inclined to express buying intention than internally driven consumers would. If one is used to fate or power holders interfering at any time in the realization of an expressed intention, then this is just part of daily life, and it is reflected in the way buying intention is expressed. It will predict behavior less than it does in internally driven cultures. So it affects survey results, which will be discussed in more detail in Chapter 6.

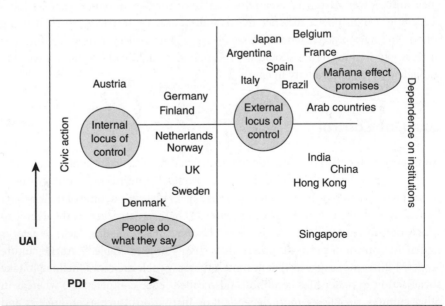

Figure 5.7   Power Distance and Uncertainty Avoidance: Locus of Control

SOURCE: Data from Hofstede (2001) (see Appendix A).

Information Processing

Information processing theory is a psychological approach to analyze how people acquire, organize, and use information to assist choice behavior. The underlying assumption is that people want to solve problems and choose rationally. This assumption is increasingly disputed in the Western world and can be even less generalized for consumers of non-Western cultures. There are several culture-bound concepts that influence information processing. How people acquire information mostly varies with individualism. In collectivistic cultures, people will acquire information more via implicit, interpersonal communication and base their buying decisions more on feelings and trust in the company whereas in individualistic cultures, people will actively acquire information via the media and friends to prepare for purchases.

Differences in categorization and field dependency that also vary with individualism-collectivism affect how people process information. The way an individual attends to information in the environment can result in different organizations of knowledge. Field dependents have stored information differently and thus will access information in the memory in a different way than field independents do. This applies to processing information about products and brands; it influences brand associations and the measurement of brand image as what people store in memory and what they retrieve from memory will differ. The Western concept of brand image depends on so-called global beliefs that consumers may have about a brand that are relatively more abstract than thoughts about specific products or categories. Interdependent Easterners are more inclined to focus on concrete information. They do have abstract beliefs, but concrete information is more accessible in the memory. The implication is that even if a brand association is made equally accessible across cultures, people use the same piece of information differently. If, for example, people are asked for beliefs regarding Sony, to an Easterner, the name Sony may prompt concrete information, such as Sony TV, and an overall image of the Sony brand may be less accessible, as compared to Westerners who may access abstract traits.[110] It has implications for the types of advertising preferred. Field independents are more likely to connect the same brand level beliefs to various products by brand, whereas field dependents are more likely to store and retrieve product specific beliefs. The different processing styles affect the type of information focused on and the importance placed on different information, which affects the way information is stored and structured in memory. In the end, the differences affect brand equity based on brand associations (see Chapter 11).[111]

Such differences in processing styles may also influence the way and degree to which people use information for making buying decisions. Whereas in individualistic cultures of low power distance, people will actively acquire information via the media and friends, in collectivistic and/or high power distance cultures, people will acquire information more via implicit, interpersonal communication and base their decisions on feelings or trust. In collectivistic cultures, frequent social interaction causes an automatic flow of communication between people, who as a result acquire knowledge unconsciously. Information is like air, it is there, you don't search for it. This is confirmed by Cho et al.[112] who state that in China, consumers rely more on word of mouth communication because of the high contact rate among group members.

Eurobarometer[113] asks people to what degree they view themselves as well-informed consumers. The percentages of respondents who say they are "well-informed" correlate with low power distance, low uncertainty avoidance, and individualism; the latter explains 61% of variance. One of the early Eurobarometer surveys in 1976[114] among the eight countries of the then-European Community asked if consumers shopping for food had sufficient information. The percentages of positive answers also correlated with low power distance and low uncertainty avoidance. Many other studies show data that confirm this relationship. From a Eurobarometer survey on consumer empowerment,[115] a significant correlation is found between people who view themselves as an informed consumer when choosing and buying goods and individualism ($r = .65***$). Conversely, the degree to which people do not find themselves well informed, correlates with collectivism. A Eurobarometer survey on science and technology,[116] asking for levels of knowledge on a variety of scientific matters, shows significant negative correlations between individualism and the percentages of respondents who feel poorly informed about science, culture and the arts, politics, and sports news.

These data show how, across cultures, information needs and perception of information vary, and this is not related to actual available information. Consistently, respondents in the more collectivistic south of Europe feel less informed than those in the individualistic north of Europe, and they also express a greater need for information, although objectively there is not a lack of information. The percentage of British who feel well informed about sports news[117] is about three times as high as that of the Spanish. Yet the amount of sports news on Spanish television is about five times as high as on British television.[118]

Generally, we have to realize that most acquired information is organized in schemata that already exist in the memory. When processing advertising, most information presented in an advertisement will fit an existing schema. Often, only the information relevant and important to the activated schema is selected; the rest is lost. Many things can go wrong in information processing. First, one's own cultural roots may inhibit the perception of stimuli coming from another cultural perspective. Second, interpretation of the meaning may not be as intended. Third, the evaluation and decision-making process may vary.

Decision Making

The fundamental assumption in decision-making theory is that decisions do not "happen," someone "makes them." This is a Western view. The Japanese are more likely to prefer events to shape whatever actions are required, to stand back from an event rather than attempt to control it by decision making.[119] Next to this, various aspects of decision making vary by culture, for example, the need for information and who influences the decision.

The need for information and the type of information desired will vary. Buyers in collectivistic cultures seek less information and do so less consciously than buyers of individualistic cultures do. Strong uncertainty avoidance will lead to the need for more and detailed information. Club Méditerranée "learned that Japanese tourists crave infinite detail in their travel plans. So, along with brochures and activity schedules for the villages they'll visit, Club Med sends them maps of airports at both ends of the trip, showing toilets, customs booths, and other facilities."[120] The Japanese are more thorough in the decision-making process than Chinese and North-Americans. However, the thoroughness with which people go about in their deliberations to support their decisions tends to cause indecisiveness. The latter is evaluated positively in Japan, but negatively in the United States.[121]

Western thinking is that the chances of making an optimal choice are better when choosing among a large number of options. This cannot be generalized. Self-expression needs and ideals of uniqueness lead individualists to see greater value in having choices than collectivists do.

The underlying thought of most Western *consumer decision-making* models is that all consumers engage in shopping with certain fundamental decision-making modes or styles, including rational shopping and consciousness regarding brand, price, and quality. The search for a universal instrument that can describe consumers' decision-making styles across cultures seems to be problematic.

An approach that focuses on consumers' orientations in making decisions is the consumer characteristics approach by Sproles and Kendall,[122] who developed an instrument to measure consumer decision-making styles analogous to the personality traits concept, called the consumer style inventory (CSI). The CSI identifies eight mental characteristics of consumer decision making: (1) perfectionism or high-quality consciousness; (2) brand consciousness; (3) novelty-fashion consciousness; (4) recreational, hedonistic shopping consciousness; (5) price and "value-for-money" shopping consciousness; (6) impulsiveness; (7) confusion over choice of brands, stores, and consumer information; and (8) habitual, brand-loyal orientation toward consumption.

This approach has been applied to different cultures with varying results. For example, among Koreans[123] the brand-conscious, perfectionist style was found most, and price-consciousness and value for money were not found in Greece and India.[124]

In the *business or industrial decision-making* process, the number of members in the decision-making unit (DMU) varies; so does the importance of the individual members. Also, the members of the DMU behave differently, and this is related to the country's management style and culture. In Britain, specialist expertise is not highly regarded. Decisions tend to come about by informal consensus developed in meetings, discussions, and out-of-office contacts among middle managers. Top management normally refuses any routine contacts with suppliers. This is due to the high level of delegation, a characteristic of small power distance cultures. In France, although middle or specialist managers may be consulted, in the end, the president directeur général must give permission. In the Netherlands, business relationships are more relaxed and informal. In Italy, businesses have to take relatively large amounts of time and resources to deal with industrial relations problems. Successful managers have to be flexible improvisers. Authority may be delegated to trusted individuals rather than to holders of particular job titles so that finding the right decision maker is an art. Interpersonal contact is of great importance. A distinctively Spanish company is likely to have a strong leader, an entrepreneurial autocrat with boldness and personal charisma. Good personal relations are necessary to prevent middle management blocking approaches, and anything important may have to be sent "up the line" for final approval.

In high power distance cultures, the boss will make the decision, and the roles of influentials below his or her level will be less pronounced than in small power distance cultures. In the latter cultures, secretaries have an important influence on decisions related to their work, such as those related to office equipment. The decision-making process will also vary according to the degree of masculinity. In feminine cultures, where reaching consensus is important, all people concerned must be allowed to give their opinion, whereas in masculine cultures, decisiveness is seen as a virtue that will make the decision-making process more expedient.

Finding the influence of others in decision making is not easy, as culture influences the degree to which people think they are involved in decision making, which may be different from actual decision-making power. Because of egalitarian values in low power distance cultures, more people think they are involved in decision making on corporate buying aspects than in high power distance cultures. Whereas in Denmark a secretary who assists her or his boss in gathering information on products to buy may view this as involvement in decision making, a secretary in France giving the same assistance probably will not view this as being involved in making the decision, as the boss implicitly makes all decisions.[125] In a Eurobarometer survey, low power distance explained 50% of variance of the answer *strongly agree* with the statement "my job allows me to take part in decisions."[126]

Consumer Behavior Domains

Behavior refers to the physical actions of consumers that can be directly observed and measured by others. It is also called overt behavior to distinguish it from mental activities. A trip to a shop and usage and ownership of products involve behavior. All processes such as motivation, emotion, cognition, and affect are involved in behavior, but they operate differently across the various consumer behavior domains, such as product acquisition, ownership and usage, shopping and buying behavior, complaining behavior, brand loyalty, and adoption of innovations.

Product Acquisition, Ownership, and Usage

There are substantial differences between countries with respect to product ownership and usage, and many of these can be explained by culture. People's values have a direct and an indirect effect on product ownership. A product has physical characteristics (attributes) that have functional or psychosocial consequences or benefits. Product ownership or usage can also express the (desired) values of the consumer. A car not only is a means of transportation, but also says something about its owner. Each product category has its own cultural relationship. In this section, we give a few such examples, but we do not cover motives for buying luxury goods as these are discussed in Chapter 9.[127]

Food consumption varies with climate and historical, economic, and cultural factors. Food carries cultural meaning. In collectivistic cultures, the symbolic function of food is much stronger than in individualistic cultures, and variety of food is important. Food should be available in the house for any unexpected guest. In high uncertainty avoidance cultures, purity is an important attribute of many food and drink products. In Chapter 4, the example of bottled water consumption was used. The relationship between uncertainty avoidance and mineral water consumption has been consistent over time. Although in the past 30 years the quality of tap water has improved everywhere in Europe, the differences between countries have remained similar since 1970 or have become even larger. Since 1970, high uncertainty avoidance has explained between 44% and 53% of variance of various data on mineral water consumption in Europe (see the chart in Chapter 1).

Expenditures on *clothing and footwear* as a percentage of household expenditures are higher in collectivistic and high uncertainty avoidance cultures. In collectivistic cultures, for reasons of face, people want to be well groomed when going out into the streets. In high uncertainty avoidance cultures, it is one way of facing a threatening world. In large power distance cultures, people dress according to occasion and spend more on expensive accessories such as expensive briefcases or shoes.[128]

Many *consumer electronics* serve the individualistic need for variety and stimulation. Worldwide, television ownership (numbers per 1,000 people) is linked with individualism. The frequency of watching and the programs viewed are culture-bound (see Chapter 8). The role of television in social life varies. Owning the latest model may be a symbol of wealth in high power distance cultures. In Asia, a television set also serves a social need, as an important application is karaoke.

PC ownership is a matter of wealth, but an important explanation of differences in ownership is uncertainty avoidance, which generally explains variance of adoption of innovations. Worldwide data on percentages of households with computer correlate with GNI per capita, but across wealthy countries uncertainty avoidance also explains variance.[129] Ownership of computers does not say much about using them, as in collectivistic cultures people may share computers. Similarly *Internet in households* worldwide is related to wealth and individualism, and across wealthy countries that also are of low uncertainty avoidance. Variation in how people use computers and the Internet is discussed in Chapter 8.

Until recently, GNI per capita explained most of variance of the numbers of cars per 1,000 population, as well as car usage, but in 2009 for 78 countries worldwide, it was individualism that explained 57% of variance, with GNI per capita together with high uncertainty avoidance explaining an additional 16%.[130] The relationship is illustrated in Figure 5.8.

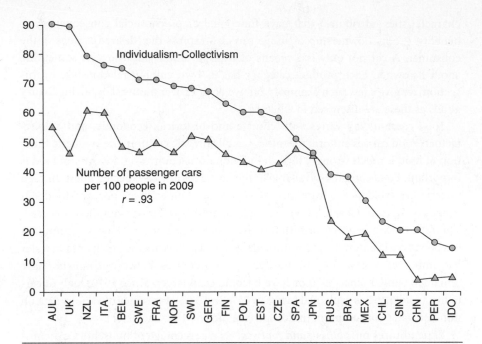

Figure 5.8   Number of Passenger Cars per 1,000 People

SOURCE: Data from Hofstede (2001) (see Appendix A) and World Development Indicators 2009 (see Appendix B).

For many durables like consumer electronics, differences in national wealth usually explain variance of ownership. But after some time, countries converge with respect to ownership of such products and mainly usage differences vary with culture. Another phenomenon is that at a certain point, convergence turns into divergence. An example is ownership of television sets in Europe where countries converged with respect to national wealth; where also ownership of TV sets converged, but only until 1997 when countries started to diverge, as illustrated in Figure 5.9.

Whereas national wealth explains variance of *leisure expenditures* worldwide, culture explains such differences in the developed world. In Europe, leisure expenditures are highest in individualistic cultures of low power distance and low uncertainty avoidance. The heavy spenders are Sweden and the United Kingdom; the low spenders are Spain and Portugal. An explanation is that in the latter cultures, free time is spent with family and relatives whereas in the former people spend more time on paid organized leisure activities. Elements of low uncertainty avoidance that explain expenditures on leisure products and services are low anxiety, innovativeness, and a culture of fitness. Relevant individualistic values are pleasure, stimulation, variety, and adventure, so the sale of "pleasure" products and services like travel, theme parks, and sports activities tends to be higher in individualistic than in collectivistic cultures. On the other hand, in collectivistic and high power distance cultures in Europe, people pay more visits to the theatre, museums, and the cinema.[131]

Also *financial products* vary by culture. More life insurance policies, for example, are sold in individualistic cultures than in collectivistic cultures. In the former,

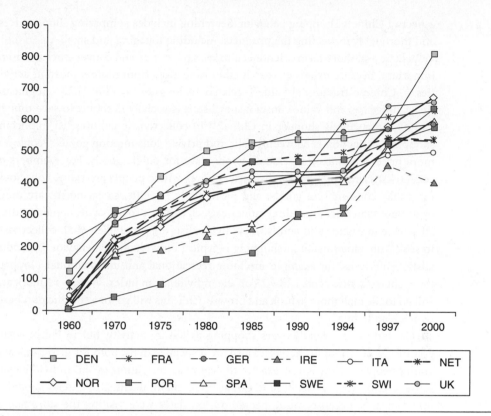

Figure 5.9 TV Sets per 1,000 Population, Europe 1960–2000

SOURCE: United Nations Statistical Yearbooks and World Bank Development Indicators (see Appendix B).

should one die early, one cannot count on family to support one's dependents. Other relationships are with low power distance and low masculinity. In the feminine cultures, people are emotionally more sensitive to the needs of their dependents. In high power distance cultures, people rely on their superiors to take care of them.[132] There is no relationship with uncertainty avoidance, which confirms that uncertainty avoidance is not the same as risk avoidance.

Shopping and Buying Behavior

Shopping and buying behavior concerns shopping activities, shopping purposes, who does the shopping and with whom, shopping frequency, buyer-seller relationships, and retail preferences. In addition to the conventional retail options, there is the Internet, which has introduced a new dimension to buyer-seller relationships.

Shopping activities and purposes in addition to buying can be *searching, learning about product supply, bargain hunting, price bargaining, spending money, recreation, avoiding boredom,* and *self-gratification.* Self-gratification is an unlikely motive for the interdependent self of collectivistic cultures. Searching and price bargaining are activities common in collectivistic cultures. Widespread haggling is an important aspect of Chinese shopping behavior. Searching includes comparing shops, prices, and thoroughly inspecting the products, including touching and smelling. In individualistic and short-term oriented cultures, saving time and convenience are more important, because extensive search takes time away from more important activities.[133] Chinese traditional values—related to long-term orientation—emphasize thrift, diligence, and value consciousness, so it is socially desirable to save money and be a meticulous shopper in China.[134] In collectivistic cultures, an important shopping distinction is between public and private consumption goods. People are more price conscious for personal goods than for public goods. For members of collectivistic and high power distance cultures where people are status conscious, for public consumption goods, and particularly for gifts, social norms are more important than price. Spending money as such can be a social value, demonstrating allegiance to friends and family. As individualists are more likely than collectivists to seek "fun" situations, fun shopping is typical individualistic behavior. Individualistic Americans, for example, are more recreational and informational shoppers than Chileans, who score a low 23 on the individualism index. Whereas Americans will go to the mall more to look and browse, Chileans will go for a specific purchase, with a plan to buy.[135]

The term *recreational* covers shopping as leisure activity, but in collectivistic cultures, some shopping activities also are a social activity, both for grownups and young people, which is not exactly the same as recreation in the individualistic sense. Donquixote, a Japanese discount retail chain, decided to extend shopping hours in 2002 because young people out on dates were visiting the store late at night.[136] In India, shopping has become a leisure activity for urban nuclear family women. They love visiting various retail formats and comparing prices and bargaining.[137] In Malaysia, shopping malls offer all sorts of entertainment, like cinemas, bowling, ice skating, and other indoor entertainment, which makes visiting shopping malls a leisure activity.[138]

Both in the search and buying process, social relationships between buyers and sellers vary among individualistic and collectivistic cultures. In collectivistic cultures, buyers want a relationship with the seller and involve in-group members more than in individualistic cultures. The importance of in-group members doesn't imply that people always go shopping with their in-group members. Although teenagers may shop in groups when shopping as a leisure activity, for some purposes, Chinese prefer to shop anonymously, attracting little community and extended family attention to avoid any resulting gossip and the risk of losing face. They prefer crowded places. The Chinese concept of *renao*—meaning lively, bustling with noise and excitement, opposite to a negative state of being alone—explains preference for crowded and noisy shopping places like markets.[139] Knowing these different shopping habits can prevent costly mistakes. Mattel built a bright-pink, six-floor $30 million flagship stand-alone Barbie store in Shanghai which had to close after just 2 years.[140]

Living conditions influence shopping habits, including who does the daily shopping. Whereas in the United States or the United Kingdom, or even in France, people go to a mega-store once a week to do bulk buying, Japanese housewives make it their routine to visit a familiar nearby supermarket where their friends gather. One reason is the social influence; another is that refrigerators and storage space at Japanese homes are limited.[141] Where more women work full-time, shopping habits will differ from those in countries where women work part-time or are full-time housewives. The dimension masculinity–femininity explains differences in male-female shopping, as explained in Chapter 4.

Other differences in buying behavior are between *planned buying* and *impulsive buying*. Impulsive buying is involved when a person has no intention to buy a product, yet buys it. A consumer can also intend to buy a product and decide only in the shop which brand to buy. A completely planned purchase occurs if both the product and the brand purchase were planned. Impulsive buying is related to thrill, variety, and sensation seeking as well as stimulation, traits that are related to individualism and low uncertainty avoidance. A comparison of impulsive buying behavior across five Western and Asian countries[142] showed that the individualistic emphasis on the self, individual needs, and desires encourage impulsive buying behavior. Collectivistic notions of the self that emphasize interdependence, emotional control, and moderation tend to discourage impulse buying behavior. Also, high power distance cultures tend to display less impulsive buying tendencies, and conversely more impulsive buying behavior is found in low power distance cultures.[143]

Next to the physical retail environment—also called *brick-and-mortar retailing*—there are various means for out-of-home shopping and buying: mail order, television shopping, and Internet shopping. In many countries, physical shopping is being replaced by Internet shopping, but preferences vary by culture (see Chapter 8).

Complaining Behavior

Consumer complaining behavior can be classified into three categories: (a) voice response to the party directly involved in the complaint; (b) negative word of mouth or brand switching; and (c) legal action.[144] With varying concepts of self, consumers across cultures vary with respect to these three types of responses. Because of harmony needs, collectivistic consumers are relatively loyal and are less likely to voice complaints when they experience post-purchase problems, but they do engage in negative word of mouth to in-group members. There is evidence that compared with Australians, the Chinese are less likely to lodge a formal complaint for a faulty product.[145] When collectivists do exit, it is particularly difficult for the offending supplier to regain them as customers.[146]

An aspect of American culture is the frequent use of legal action. It is related to the configuration of individualism and masculinity, which makes people want to get the most out of life. This explains the high use of litigation in the United States. Also, consumers will take more legal action. For years, the cigarette industry has been sued for damaging smokers' health. In 2002 in the United States, obese people have even started suing fast food chains, holding them responsible for their gaining weight.

Brand Loyalty

Conformance and harmony needs make collectivists relatively brand loyal. Purchasing products that are well known to the in-group may help to decrease uncertainty about in-group approval of the purchase.[147] Choosing another brand than the group members' brand or changing brands distinguishes a person from the group. It is preferable to choose the popular or perceived popular brands. This will be reinforced by uncertainty avoidance. Trying a new product or brand involves the willingness to change, and it may also satisfy a variety-seeking motive.[148] Variety seeking and stimulation are elements of individualistic cultures.

High power distance implies respect for the status quo, the "proper place" of the power brand, the brand with the highest market share. In Asia, big market-share brands are the kings of their "brand world," and consumers in Asia believe in them implicitly.[149] This is the reason brands like Coca-Cola, Nescafé, and San Miguel have such high and sustained market shares in a number of Asian countries. Being "big" automatically provides trust. This trust, combined with harmony and conformance needs of collectivistic cultures, leads to high brand loyalty. Consequently, it will be difficult for new entrants in these markets to gain market share.

Brand credibility is an important motive for brand loyalty in collectivistic and high uncertainty avoidance cultures.[150] For consumers in East Asian cultures, the reputation of the firm contributes to customer loyalty, more than in individualistic and low power distance cultures.[151] Brands that people know are preferred to unknown brands, and this even more applies to luxury brands. According to Lu, "Beijing consumers are quite conservative when they meet an unknown luxury brand. It takes time and a strong marketing campaign to communicate your brand and reach your targeted clients effectively."[152]

Diffusion of Innovations

Consumers' degree of innovativeness influences their propensity to try new products. As innovativeness is related to tolerance for ambiguity and deviant ideas, members of weak uncertainty avoidance cultures are more innovative than members of strong uncertainty avoidance cultures. Several studies have demonstrated the relationship between uncertainty avoidance and consumer innovativeness[153] and new product take-off across wealthy countries.[154]

How innovativeness operates in cultures depends on its configuration with other dimensions. Power distance and individualism influence innovativeness in cultures in another way. Whereas it is internalized in the person in small power distance and individualistic cultures, in large power distance and collectivistic cultures, it is externalized. In the latter, the degree of innovation depends on the power holders and group process. Although the Chinese are a weak uncertainty avoidance culture and in the far past have proved to be extremely innovative, for some time, their power holders have not stimulated innovativeness. The Chinese invented a number of processes or instruments that were not discovered or acknowledged in the West until more than 1,000 years later. Examples of inventions are the process of making steel from crude iron (2,000 years), deep drilling for natural gas (1,900 years), and the wheelbarrow (1,300 years); they were also the first to discover the circulation of blood (1,800 years).[155] In China, the incentive for inventions was service to the overlord or emperor, not personal ambition.

Rogers[156] identified five categories of (American) consumers according to their degree of acceptance of new products. These five categories of adopters are often illustrated in a normal distribution curve, as illustrated in Figure 5.10. They are called Innovators, Early Adopters, Early Majority, Late Majority, and Laggards. Innovators represent 2.5% of (American) society; they are described as venturesome individuals who are willing to take risks. Early adopters (13.5%) are those who take up new ideas that have already been taken up by the innovators, who serve as role models. The early majority (34%) are risk avoiders, but they are relatively deliberate in their purchasing behavior. The late majority (34%) are skeptical and cautious of new ideas. Laggards (16%) are very traditional.

The percentages as well as the time span of the adoption process vary by culture. More innovative cultures have a larger percentage of early adopters than less innovative cultures. Collectivism plays another role. In Asia, few consumers are prepared to take the social risk of being the first to try a new product.[157] However, if people think others have tried it, acceptance goes fast. Particularly in Japan, after acceptance, the spreading of new products is rapid. On the one hand, change is not appreciated, so adoption of new ideas and products takes longer. Yet the need for conformance leads to faster adoption as soon as a group member has taken the lead. In individualistic and strong uncertainty avoidance cultures, the adoption process takes longer because what is new is dangerous, and that relates to each person individually.

Dutch marketing professor Jan-Benedict Steenkamp[158] calculated percentages of adoption categories for packaged goods in five countries in Europe (Table 5.2). These were based on household panel data on the occurrence and timing of first purchases for 239 new consumer packaged goods over a 52-week period after introduction. Correlations with the cultural variables confirm the relationships with uncertainty avoidance and individualism.

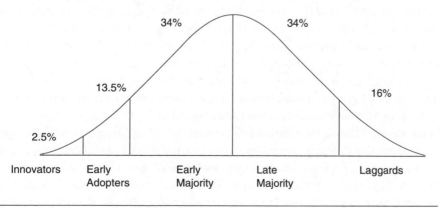

Figure 5.10 Adoption of Innovations, USA

The category innovators in the five European countries plus the United States correlates with low uncertainty avoidance and individualism, whereas the category late majority correlates with high uncertainty avoidance and collectivism. Also, in Latin America, where all countries are high on uncertainty avoidance, the percentage of early adopters tends to be lower than in the United States. A Target Group Index (TGI) study in Chile found 7.5% of the average population that could be viewed as early adopters of technological innovations.[159]

Table 5.2   Diffusion of Innovations and Culture

	Innovators (%)	Early Majority (%)	Late Majority (%)	Laggards (%)
USA	16.0	34.0	34.0	16.0
UK	23.8	43.4	26.4	6.4
France	15.1	25.5	35.6	23.8
Germany	16.8	26.1	34.2	22.9
Spain	8.9	34.1	43.9	13.1
Italy	13.4	30.8	41.0	14.8
Correlation coefficients				
IDV	.75*		−.74*	
UAI	−.83*		.83*	

SOURCE: Steenkamp, J.-B. E. M. (2002, November 17). *Global consumers.* Presentation at Tilburg University. Based on *Consumer and market drivers of the trial probability of new consumer packaged goods* (Working paper). Tilburg University, Tilburg, Netherlands.

Summary

Most concepts and theories of consumer behavior are Western-centric. The concepts of self, identity, and personality are integral parts of consumer psychology, which originated in the West. They are used in theory, in practice, in research, and in strategy. To use them properly, they must be adapted, or better, specific concepts for collectivistic cultures must be developed. What people buy and why they buy certain products are influenced by their cultural values. A number of theories of consumer behavior commonly found in textbooks were reviewed in this chapter. Both mental and social processes vary by culture, and this influences decision making and choice behavior. Motives for buying products vary among and within geographic areas. Countries may share a border but be far apart with respect to buying motives. Finding relationships between actual buying behavior and cultural dimensions is exciting and assuring. Most value research relies on what people say about their values. Finding the relationship between actual consumption behavior and measured value differences provides strong proof of the influence of culture, which cannot be ignored and which also brings understanding that can be used for developing effective cross-cultural marketing strategies. As proper communication is an essential element of effective branding and advertising, much attention was given to the various differences in perception and information processing across cultures.

Notes

1. Miyahara, A. (2004). Toward theorizing Japanese interpersonal communication competence from a non-Western perspective. In F. E. Jandt (Ed.), *Intercultural Communication* (p. 181). Thousand Oaks, CA: Sage.

2. Solomon, M., Bamossy, G., & Askegaard, S. (1999). *Consumer behaviour: A European perspective.* London: Pearson Education, p. 8.

3. This model is based on Manrai, L. A., & Manrai, A. K. (1996). Current issues in cross-cultural and cross-national consumer research. In L. A. Manrai & A. K. Manrai (Eds.), *Global perspectives in cross-cultural and cross-national consumer research* (p. 13). New York: International Business Press/Haworth Press.

4. Oyserman, D. (2006). High power, low power, and equality: Culture beyond individualism and collectivism. *Journal of Consumer Psychology, 16*(4), 352–356.

5. Markus, H. R., & Kitayama, S. (1991). Culture and the self: Implications for cognition, emotion and motivation. *Psychological Review, 98*(6), 224–253.

6. Roland, A. (1988). *In search of self in India and Japan.* Princeton, NJ: Princeton University Press, pp. 3–13.

7. Roland, 1988; Triandis, H. C. (1995). *Individualism and collectivism.* Boulder, CO: Westview Press.

8. Tardiff, T., Fletcher, P., Liang, W., Zhang, Z., Kaciroti, N., & Marchman, V. A. (2008). Baby's first ten words. *Development Psychology, 44*(4), 929–938.

9. Nezlek, J. B., Kafetsios, K., & Smith, V. (2008). Emotions in everyday social encounters. *Journal of Cross-Cultural Psychology, 39*(4), 366–372.

10. Roland, 1988, p. 242.

11. Lu, P. X. (2008). *Elite China: Luxury consumer behavior in China.* Singapore: John Wiley & Sons (Asia) PTE. LTD.

12. Watkins, D., Akande, A., Fleming, J., Ismail, M., Lefner, K., Regmi, M., et al. (1998). Cultural dimensions, gender, and the nature of self-concept: A fourteen-country study. *International Journal of Psychology, 33*, 17–31.

13. Jowell, R., et al. (2003). *European Social Survey 2002/2003* (technical report). London: Centre for Comparative Social Surveys, City University.

14. Kitayama, S.; Markus, H. R.; Matsumoto, H., & Norasakunkit, V. (1997). Individual and collective processes in the construction of the self: Self-enhancement in the United States and self-criticism in Japan. *Journal of Personality and Social Psychology, 72*, 1245–1266.

15. Heine, S., & Hamamura, T. (2007). In search of East Asian self-enhancement. *Personality and Social Psychology Review, 11*(1), 4–27.

16. Lu, 2008, p. 6.

17. Twenge, J. M., & Crocker, J. (2000). Race and self-esteem: Meta-analysis comparing whites, blacks, Hispanics, Asians and American Indians and comment on Gray-Little and Hafdahl. *Psychological Bulletin, 128*, 371–408.

18. Koopmann-Holm, B., & Matsumoto, D. (2011). Values and display rules for specific emotions. *Journal of Cross-Cultural Psychology, 42*(3), 355–371.

19. Goffman, E. (1959). *The presentation of self in everyday life.* Harmondsworth, Middlesex, UK: Penguin.

20. Chen, G.-M. (1995). Differences in self-disclosure patterns among Americans versus Chinese. *Journal of Cross-Cultural Psychology, 26*, 84–91.

21. Markus, H. R., & Kitayama, S. (1998). The cultural psychology of personality. *Journal of Cross-Cultural Psychology, 29*, 63–87.

22. Church, A. T., et al. (2006). Implicit theories and self-perceptions of traitedness across cultures. *Journal of Cross-Cultural Psychology, 37*(6), 694–716.

23. Norenzayan, A., Choi, I., & Nisbett, R. E. (2002). Cultural similarities and differences in social influence: Evidence from behavioral predictions and lay theories of behavior. *Personality and Social Psychology Bulletin, 28,* 109–120.

24. Valchev, V. H., Van de Vijver, F. J. R., Nel, J. A., Rothmann, S., Meiring, D., & De Bruin, G. P. (2011). Implicit personality conceptions of the Nguni Cultural-Linguistic Groups of South Africa. *Cross-Cultural Research, 45*(3), 235–266.

25. In Hofstede, G., & McCrae, R. R. (2004). Personality and culture revisited: Linking traits and dimensions of culture. *Cross-Cultural Research, 38*(1), 52–88.

26. Schmitt, D. P., Allik, J., McCrae, R. R., & Benet-Martínez, V. (2007). The geographic distribution of big five personality traits. *Journal of Cross-Cultural Pscyhology, 38*(2), 173–212.

27. Cheung, F. M., Cheung, S. F., Zhang, J., Leung, K., Leong, F., & Yeh, K. H. (2008). Relevance for openness as a personality dimension in Chinese culture. *Journal of Cross-Cultural Psychology, 39*(1), 81–108.

28. Triandis, H. C. (2004). Dimensions of culture beyond Hofstede. In H. Vinken, J. Soeters, & P. Ester (Eds.), *Comparing cultures: Dimensions of culture in a comparative perspective* (p. 37). Leiden/Boston: Brill; Kashima, Y., Kashima, E. S., Kim, U., & Gelfand, M. (2005). Describing the social world: How is a person, a group, and a relationship described in the East and the West? *Journal of Experimental Social Psychology, 42,* 388–396.

29. Eap, S., DeGarmo, D. S., Kawakami, A., Hara, S. N., Hall, G. C. N., & Teten, A. L. (2008). Culture and personality among European American and Asian American men. *Journal of Cross-Cultural Psychology, 39*(5), 630–643.

30. Antonides, G., & Van Raaij, W. F. (1998). *Consumer behaviour: A European perspective.* Chichester, UK: Wiley, pp. 162–163.

31. Belk, R. W. (1984). Cultural and historical differences in concepts of self and their effects on attitudes toward having and giving. In T. C. Kinnear (Ed.), *Advances in consumer research* (pp. 753–760). Provo, UT: Association for Consumer Research.

32. Kowner, R. (2002). Japanese body image: Structure and esteem scores in a cross-cultural perspective. *International Journal of Psychology, 37,* 149–159.

33. Prendergast, G., Leung K. Y., & West, D. C. (2002). Role portrayal in advertising and editorial content, and eating disorders: An Asian perspective. *International Journal of Advertising, 21,* 237–258.

34. Matsumoto, D. (2000). *Culture and psychology: People around the world* (2nd ed.). Belmont, CA: Wadsworth, p. 411.

35. Oyedele, A., & Minor, M. S. (2012). Consumer culture plots in television advertising from Nigeria and South Africa. *Journal of Advertising, 41*(1), 91–107.

36. Etcoff, N., Orbach, S., Scott, J., & Agostino, H. (2006, February). *Beyond stereotypes: Rebuilding the foundation of beauty beliefs.* Retrieved from http://www.vawpreventionscotland.org.uk/sites/default/files/Dove%20Beyond%20Stereotypes%20White%20Paper.pdf

37. Sulaini, K. E. (2006). *Blink: Tackling the communication flux within the Asia-Pacific region.* A research project submitted in fulfillment of the requirements for the degree of bachelor of Communication, RMIT University, Melbourne, Australia, and MARA University of Technology, Malaysia.

38. Sung, Y., & Choi, M. (2012). The influence of self-construal on self-brand congruity in the United States and Korea. *Journal of Cross-Cultural Psychology, 43*(1), 151–166.

39. Campana C., & Paulo R. (1999, November). Evaluating the value of global brands in Latin America. *Marketing and Research Today,* pp. 159–167.

40. Aaker, J. L., Benet-Martínez, V., & Garolera, J. (2001). Consumption symbols as carriers of culture: A study of Japanese and Spanish brand personality constructs. *Journal of Personality and Social Psychology, 81,* 492–508.

41. Sung, Y., & Tinkham, S. F. (2005). Brand personality structures in the United States and Korea: Common and culture-specific factors. *Journal of Consumer Psychology, 15*(4), 334–350.

42. Crocus (Cross-Cultural Solutions, 2004) was a cross-cultural study that measured brand value (called "brand pull") and provided a cultural explanation of strong or weak brand value in different countries. It was conducted by the research agency chain Euronet, in co-operation with the advertising agency chain Interpartners. Unpublished.

43. *European Social Reality.* (2007). Special Eurobarometer Report (EBS 225), 24 countries. The percentages of answers saying that friends are very important correlates with low power distance ($r = -.59***$). *European Social Survey* (2002/2003), 21 countries. Answers to the same question correlate with low power distance ($r = -.52**$).

44. Praet, C. (2001). Japanese advertising, the world's number one celebrity showcase? A cross-cultural comparison of the frequency of celebrity appearances in TV advertising. In M. S. Roberts & R. L. King (Eds.), *The proceedings of the 2001 special Asia-Pacific conference of the American Academy of Advertising*; Praet, C. (2004). The influence of culture on the use of celebrities in advertising: A multi-country study. NOW/JSPS report 2004, unpublished; Praet, Carolus L. C. (2008). The influence of national culture on the use of celebrity endorsement in television advertising: A multi-country study. *Proceedings of the 7th International Conference on Research in Advertising (ICORIA).* Antwerp, Belgium.

45. Belgium, Czech Republic, Denmark, Finland, France, Germany, Hungary, Italy, Netherlands, Norway, Poland, Portugal, Russia, Slovakia, Spain, Sweden, Switzerland, United Kingdom.

46. Hessler, P. (2010). *Country driving: A Chinese road trip.* New York: HarperCollins, p. 232.

47. Souiden, N., Kassim, N. M., & Hong, H. J. (2006). The effect of corporate branding dimensions on consumers' product evaluation, a cross-cultural analysis. *European Journal of Marketing, 40*(7/8), 825–845.

48. Hofstee, M. (2006, June 29). 2 weken in 14 indrukken. *Adformatie,* pp. 34–35.

49. Solomon et al., 1999, p. 121.

50. Cervellon, M.-C., & Dubé, L. (2002). Assessing the cross-cultural applicability of affective and cognitive components of attitude. *Journal of Cross-Cultural Psychology, 33,* 346–357.

51. Gudykunst, W. B., Matsumoto, Y., Ting-Toomey, S., Nishida, T., Kim, K., & Heyman, S. (1996). The influence of cultural individualism-collectivism, self construals, and individual values in communication styles across cultures. *Human Communication Research, 22,* 510–543.

52. Chang, P. L., & Chieng, M. H. (2006). Building consumer-brand relationship: A cross-cultural experiental view. *Psychology and Marketing, 23*(11), 927–959.

53. Antonides & Van Raaij, 1998, pp. 202–205.

54. Lee, C., & Green, R. L. (1991). Cross-cultural examination of the Fishbein behavioral intentions model. *Journal of International Business Studies, 22,* 289–305.

55. Malhotra, N. K., & McCort, J. D. (2001). A cross-cultural comparison of behavioral intention models. *International Marketing Review, 18,* 235–269.

56. De Mooij, M. (2011). *Consumer behavior and culture. Consequences for global marketing and advertising* (2nd ed.). Thousand Oaks, CA: Sage.

57. Diamantopoulos, A., Schlegelmilch, B. B., & Du Preez, J. P. (1995). Lessons for pan-European marketing? The role of consumer preferences in fine-tuning the product-market

fit. *International Marketing Review, 12,* 38–52; Keillor, B. D., & Hult, G. T. (1999). A five-country study of national identity: Implications for international research and practice. *International Marketing Review, 16,* 65–82.

58. Moon, B. J., & Jain, S. C. (2002). Consumer processing of foreign advertisements: Roles of country-of origin perceptions, consumer ethnocentrism, and country attitude. *International Business Review, 11,* 117–138.

59. Dubois, B., & Paternault, C. (1997, May). Does luxury have a home country? An investigation of country images in Europe. *Marketing and Research Today,* 79–85.

60. Usunier, J. C. (1999). *Marketing across cultures* (3rd ed.). Harlow, UK: Pearson Education.

61. *Patriot games: Consumer preferences for national products.* (2004, May). Retrieved May 2004, from http://www.zonalatina.com/Zldata19.htm

62. Mosley, G. G., & Amponsah, D. K. (2011). The effect of consumer animosity and ethnocentrism on product evaluations and willingness to buy: An example from Ghana. Retrieved July 10, 2011, from http://business.troy.edu/Downloads/Publications/TSUSBS/2006SBS/2006ConsumerAnimosity.pdf

63. Grunert, K. G, Brunsø, K., & Bisp, S. (1997). Food-related lifestyle: Development of a cross-culturally valid instrument for market surveillance. In L. R. Kahle & L. Chiagouris (Eds.), *Values, lifestyles, and psychographics.* Mahwah, NJ: Lawrence Erlbaum, p. 343.

64. Maslow, A. H. (1954). *Motivation and personality.* New York: Harper & Row.

65. Hofstede, G., Hofstede, G. J., & Minkov, M. (2010). *Cultures and organizations: Software of the mind* (3rd ed.). London: McGraw-Hill, p. 129.

66. Hofstede, G. (2001). *Culture's consequences* (2nd ed.). Thousand Oaks, CA: Sage.

67. Lin, C-C., & Yamaguchi, S. (2011). Under what conditions do people feel face-loss? Effects of the presence of others and social roles on the perception of losing face in Japanese culture. *Journal of Cross-Cultural Psychology, 42*(1), 120–124.

68. Hofstede, 2001, p. 230.

69. Information from Vivek Gupta, Senior Vice President IMRB Brand Science at Kantar Group, Bangalore, India.

70. Jiang, Y., & Li, N. (2009). An exploratory study on Chinese only-child-generation motives of conspicuous consumption. In H. Li, S. Huang, & D. Jin (Eds.), *Proceedings of the 2009 American Academy of Advertising Asia-Pacific conference* (pp. 121–129). American Academy of Advertising in conjunction with China Association of Advertising of Commerce and Communication University of China.

71. Roll, M. (2006). *Asian brand strategy.* London: Palgrave McMillan, pp. 50–51.

72. Zheng, L., Phelps, J., & Hoy, M. (2009). Cultural values reflected in Chinese Olympics advertising. In H. Li, S. Huang, & D. Jin (Eds.), *Proceedings of the 2009 American Academy of Advertising Asia-Pacific conference* (pp. 26–27). American Academy of Advertising in conjunction with China Association of Advertising of Commerce and Communication University of China.

73. Wang, J. (2008). *Brand new China. Advertising, media, and commercial culture.* Cambridge, MA: Harvard University Press, p. 17.

74. European Media and Marketing Survey 2012, among the affluent European populations of 21 countries, including Turkey. High power distance and masculinity together explain 60% of variance.

75. Pollay, R. W. (1984). The identification and distribution of values manifest in print advertising 1900–1980. In R. E. Pitts, Jr., & A. G. Woodside (Eds.), *Personal values and consumer psychology* (pp. 111–135). Lexington, MA: Lexington Books, D. C. Heath.

76. Matsumoto, D., & Hwang, H. S. (2012). Culture and emotion: The integration of biological and cultural contributions. *Journal of Cross-Cultural Psychology, 43*(1), 91–118.

77. Russell, J. A. (1995). Facial expressions of emotion: What lies beyond minimal universality? *Psychological Bulletin, 118,* 379–391.

78. Yuki, M., Maddux, W. W., & Masuda, T. (2007). Are the windows to the soul the same in the East and West? Cultural differences in using the eyes and mouth as cues to recognize emotions in Japan and the United States. *Journal of Experimental Social Psychology, 43,* 303–311.

79. Mesquita, B., & Frijda, N. H. (1992). Cultural variations in emotions: A review, *Psychological Bulletin, 112,* 179–204.

80. Kağitçibaşi, Ç. (1997). Individualism and collectivism. In J. W. Berry, M. H. Segall, & Ç. Kağitçibaşi (Eds.), *Handbook of cross-cultural psychology* (Vol. 3, p. 23). Boston: Allyn & Bacon.

81. Matsumoto, D., with 19 co-authors. (2008). Mapping expressive differences around the world: The relationship between emotional display rules and individualism versus collectivism. *Journal of Cross-Cultural Psychology, 39*(1), 55–74.

82. Wang, K., Hoosain, R., Lee, T. M. C., Meng, Y., Fu, J., & Yang, R. (2006). Perception of six basic emotional facial expressions by the Chinese. *Journal of Cross-Cultural Psychology, 37*(6), 623–629.

83. Anolli, L., Wang, L., Mantovani, F., & De Toni, A. (2008). The voice of emotion in Chinese and Italian young adults. *Journal of Cross-Cultural Psychology, 39*(5), 565–598.

84. Interview with K. Ushikubo, November 1995.

85. Lin, C. (2001). Cultural values reflected in Chinese and American television advertising. *Journal of Advertising, 30,* 83–94.

86. *Consumer empowerment.* (2011). Special Eurobarometer Report (EBS 342). 26 countries. The question was, "Thinking of the last time you purchased a good, e.g., a household appliance or electronic good, which of the following did you consult: Family and friends." Collectivism explains 26% of variance.

87. Zielenziger, M. (2002, September 6). Young Japanese gobble up luxury items. *Free Press.* http://www.freep.com/news/nw/japan

88. Singh, D. (2007). Cross cultural comparison of buying behavior in India. A thesis submitted to the faculty of business management & commerce Panjab University, Chandigarh, for the degree of Doctor of Philosophy. University Business School.

89. Solomon et al., 1999, p. 296.

90. García-Montes, J. M., Caballero-Muñoz, D., & Pérez-Álvarez, M. (2006). Changes in the self resulting from the use of mobile phones. *Media, Culture & Society, 28*(1), 67–82.

91. Rogers, E. M. (1962). *Diffusion of innovations.* New York: Free Press.

92. Mishra, R. C. (1997). Cognition and cognitive development. In J. W. Berry, P. R. Dasen, & T. S. Saraswathi (Eds.), *Handbook of cross-cultural psychology* (Vol. 2, pp. 143–175). Boston: Allyn & Bacon, p. 160.

93. Kühnen, U. (2001). The semantic-procedural interface model of the self: The role of self-knowledge for context-dependent versus context-independent modes of thinking. *Journal of personality and social psychology, 80,* 397–409.

94. Schmitt, B. H., Pan, Y., & Tavassoli, N. T. (1994). Language and consumer memory: The impact of linguistic differences between Chinese and English. *Journal of Consumer Research, 21,* 419–431.

95. Unsworth, S. J., Sears, C. R., & Pexman, P. M. (2005). Cultural influences on categorization processes. *Journal of Cross-Cultural Psychology, 36*(6), 662–688.

96. Ramdas, A. (2008, March 10). Geef mij maar onzin kennis. *NRC/Handelsblad,* p. 7.

97. Monga, A. B., & Roedder John, D. (2007). Cultural differences in brand extension evaluation: The influence of analytic versus holistic thinking. *Journal of Consumer Research, 33,* 529–536.

98. Gemmen, P. (2002, September 12). Eet u smakelijk. [Enjoy the food]. *Adformatie,* pp. 24–26.

99. Jahn, R. (2001, March 29). Laat de zon schijnen in merkenland [Let the sun shine in brand country]. *Adformatie,* p. 50.

100. Schmitt, B. H., & Zhang, S. (1998). Language structure and categorization: A study of classifiers in consumer cognition, judgment, and choice. *Journal of Consumer Research, 25,* 108–122.

101. Kühnen, U., Hannover, B., Roeder, U., Shah, A. A., Schubert, B., Upmeyer, A., & Zakaria, S. (2001). Cross-cultural variations in identifying embedded figures: Comparisons from the United States, Germany, Russia, and Malaysia. *Journal of Cross-Cultural Psychology, 32,* 365–371.

102. Masuda, T., Gonzalez, R., Kwan, L., & Nisbett, R. E. (2008). Culture and aesthetic preference: Comparing the attention to context of East Asians and Americans. *Personality and Social Psychology Bulletin, 34*(9), 1260–1275.

103. Visser, E. (2009). *Packaging design: A cultural sign.* Barcelona: Index Book, s.l.

104. Paletz, S. B. F., & Peng, K. (2008). Implicit theories of creativity across cultures. *Journal of Cross-Cultural Psychology, 39*(3), 286–302.

105. Chen, C., Kasof, J., Himsel, A. J., Greenberger, E., Dong, Q., & Xue, G. (2002). Creativity in drawings of geometric shapes. A cross-cultural examination with the consensual assessment technique. *Journal of Cross-Cultural Psychology, 33,* 171–187.

106. Rotter, J. B. (1966). Generalized expectancies for internal versus external control of reinforcement. *Psychological Monographs, 80*(609).

107. Rotter, J. B. (1990). Internal versus external control of reinforcement. *American Psychologist, 45,* 489–493.

108. *Globalisation.* (2003, October). Flash Eurobarometer Report (151b).

109. *Social values, science, and technology.* (2005). Special Eurobarometer Report (EBS 225), 27 countries.

110. Ng, S., & Houston, M. J. (2006, March). Exemplars or beliefs? The impact of self-view on the nature and relative influence of brand associations. *Journal of Consumer Research, 32,* 519–529.

111. Ng, S., & Houston, M. J. (2008). Field dependency and brand cognitive structures. *Journal of Marketing Research, 45.*

112. Cho, B., Kwon, U., Gentry, J. W., Jun, S., & Kropp, F. (1999). Cultural values reflected in theme and execution: A comparative study of U.S. and Korean television commercials. *Journal of Advertising, 28*(4), 60–73.

113. *Consumer survey.* (2002, January). Flash Eurobarometer Report (117).

114. *European consumers, their interests, aspirations, and knowledge on consumer affairs.* (1976, May). Special Eurobarometer Report (EBS 007).

115. *Consumer empowerment.* (2011). Special Eurobarometer Report (EBS 342).

116. *Science and technology.* (2010). Special Eurobarometer Report (EBS 340).

117. Ibid (EBS 340).

118. Léon, B. (2008). Science related information in European television: A study of Prime-Time News. *Public Understanding of Science, 17,* 443–460.

119. Stewart, E. C. (1985). Culture and decision making. In W. B. Gudykunst, L. P. Stewart, & S. T. Ting-Toomey (Eds.), *Communication, culture, and organizational processes* (pp. 177–211). Beverly Hills, CA: Sage.

120. Toy, S. (1995, October 16). Storm, terrorists, nuke tests: Why is Club Med smiling? *BusinessWeek*, p. 20.

121. Yates, J. F., Ji, L-J., Oka, T., Lee, J-W., Shinotsuka, H., & Sieck, W. R. (2010). Indecisiveness and culture: Incidence, values, and thoroughness. *Journal of Cross-Cultural Psychology, 41*(3), 428–444.

122. Sproles, G. B., & Kendall, E. L. (1986). A methodology for profiling consumer decision making styles. *Journal of Consumer Affairs, 20,* 267–279; Lysonski, S., Durvasula, S., & Zotos, Y. (1996). Consumer decision-making styles: A multi-country investigation. *European Journal of Marketing, 30,* 10–21.

123. Hafstrom, J. I., Jung, S. C., & Young S. C. (1992). Consumer decision-making styles: Comparison between United States and Korean young consumers. *Journal of Consumer Affairs, 26,* 146–158.

124. Lysonski, Durvasula, & Zotos, 1996.

125. De Mooij, M. (2011). *Consumer behavior and culture: Consequences for global marketing and advertising.* (2nd ed.). Thousand Oaks, CA: Sage.

126. *European social reality.* (2007). Special Eurobarometer Report (EBS 273), Europe, 24 countries.

127. For a more in-depth description and evidence of relationships between culture and various product categories, see De Mooij, 2011 (in this note section).

128. *European Media and Marketing Survey.* (2012). The percentages of respondents who last year bought a suit costing over €1,000 correlates positively with power distance ($r = .61^{***}$) and uncertainty avoidance. Having bought shoes or boots over € 500 correlated positively with power distance ($r = .64^{***}$).

129. ITU (International Telecommunications Union). (2010). Key ICT indicators. Retrieved from http://www.itu.int/en/ITU-D/Statistics/Pages/stat/default.aspx. For 76 countries worldwide the percentages of households with a computer correlate positively with GNI/capita ($r = .90^{***}$) and with individualism ($r = .72^{***}$).

130. *World Development Indicators.* (2009). Number of passenger cars per 1,000 population for 78 countries.

131. *European Media and Marketing Survey.* (2012). Percentage of respondents who said they paid three or more visits to the theatre, museum or cinema in the last 12 months.

132. Chui, A. C. W., & Kwok, C. C. Y. (2008). National culture and life insurance consumption. *Journal of International Business Studies, 39,* 88–101.

133. Ackerman, D., & Tellis, G. (2001). Can culture affect prices? A cross-cultural study of shopping and retail prices. *Journal of Retailing, 77,* 57–82.

134. Cai, Y. (2007, September 4–6). Investigating the relationship between personal values and mall shopping behavior: A generation cohort study on the new generation of Chinese and their previous generation. In E. Howard (Ed.), *Proceedings of the Fourth Asia Pacific Retail Conference* (pp. 62–87). Bangkok: Manidol University and Oxford: Said Business School.

135. Nicholls, J. A. F., Mandakovic, T., Li, F., Roslow, S., & Kranendonk, C. J. (1999). Are U.S. shoppers different from Chilean? A comparative study of shopping behaviors across countries. In *Proceedings of the Seventh Cross-Cultural Consumer and Business Studies Research Conference.* Retrieved July 9, 2010, from http://marketing.byu.edu/htmlpages/ccrs/proceedings99/nicholls.htm

136. Botting, G. (2002, May 23). Buyers be wares—Shopping consumes Japan. *The Japan Times.* Retrieved September 16, 2002, from http://www.japantimes.co

137. Mishra, A., & Vishas, R. (2009, August 25–27). Classification and store affiliation of Indian retail consumers: A case study with Bangalore women. In *Proceedings of the Fifth Conference on Retailing in Asia Pacific* (pp. 248–274). Oxford Institute of Retail Management and The Hong Kong Polytechnic University, Institute for Enterprise.

138. Kamarulzaman, Y., & Madun, A. (2009, August 25–27). Attracting patrons to shopping malls: A case of Malaysia. In *Proceedings of the Fifth Conference on Retailing in Asia Pacific* (pp. 174–185).

139. Warden, C. A., Huang, S. C. T., Liu, T. C., & Wu, W. Y. (2008). Global media, local metaphor: Television shopping and marketing-as-relationship in America, Japan, and Taiwan. *Journal of Retailing, 84*(1), 119–129.

140. Gordon, A. (2011, March 10). Barbie stumbles out, but "lifestyle" door is still open. *Forbes.* Retrieved March 10, 2011, from http://www.forbes.com/sites/adamgordon/2011/03/09/barbie-walks/

141. Tanikawa, M. (2001, October 5). French supermarket struggles to fit in. *International Herald Tribune.* http://www.iht.com

142. Kacen, J., & Lee, J. A. (2002). The influence of culture on consumer impulsive buying behavior. *Journal of Consumer Psychology, 2,* 163–176.

143. Zhang, Y., & Mittal, V. (2008). Culture matters: The impact of power-distance belief on consumers' impulse buying tendency. *Advances in Consumer Research, 35,* 643.

144. Chelminski, P. (2001, December). The effects of individualism and collectivism on consumer complaining behavior. *Proceedings Eighth Cross-Cultural Research Conference,* Association for Consumer Research and American Psychological Association. Kahuku, Oahu, Hawaii.

145. Lowe, A., Chun-Tung, A., & Corkindale, D. R. (1998). Differences in "cultural values" and their effects on responses to marketing stimuli: A cross-cultural study between Australians and Chinese from the People's Republic of China. *European Journal of Marketing, 32,* 843–867.

146. Watkins, H. S., & Liu, R. (1996). Collectivism, individualism, and in-group membership: Implications for consumer complaining behaviors in multicultural contexts. In L. A. Manrai & A. K. Manrai (Eds.), *Global perspectives in cross-cultural and cross-national consumer research.* New York/London: International Business Press/Haworth Press.

147. Lee, J. A. (2000). Adapting Triandis' model of subjective culture and social behavior relations to consumer behavior. *Journal of Consumer Psychology, 2,* 117–126. Countries studied were Australia, United States, Hong Kong, Singapore, and Malaysia.

148. Baumgartner, H., & Steenkamp, J.-B. E. M. (1996). Exploratory consumer buying behavior: Conceptualization and measurement. *International Journal of Research in Marketing, 13,* 121–137.

149. Robinson, C. (1996). Asian culture: The marketing consequences. *Journal of the Market Research Society, 38,* 55–66.

150. Erdem, T., Swait, J., & Valenzuela, A. (2006). Brands as signals: A cross-country validation study. *Journal of Marketing, 70,* 34–49.

151. Jin, B., Park, J. Y., & Kim, J. (2008). Cross-cultural examination of the relationships among firm reputation, e-satisfaction, e-trust, and e-loyalty. *International Marketing Review, 25*(3), 324–337.

152. Lu, 2008, p. 117.

153. Yeniurt, S., & Townsend, J. D. (2003). Does culture explain acceptance of new products in a country? *International Marketing Review, 20*(4), 377–396.

154. Tellis, G. J., Stremersch, S., & Yin, E. (2003). The international take-off of new products: The role of economics, culture, and country innovativeness. *Marketing Science,*

22(2), 188–208; Singh, S. (2006). Cultural differences and influences on consumers' propensity to adopt innovations. *International Marketing Review, 23*(2), 173–191.

155.   Temple, R. (1986). *China.* London: Multimedia Publications.

156.   Rogers, 1962.

157.   Lu, 2008, p. 101.

158.   Steenkamp, J.-B. E. M. (2002, November 17). *Global consumers.* Presentation at Tilburg University. Based on *Consumer and market drivers of the trial probability of new consumer packaged goods* (Working paper). Tilburg University, Tilburg, Netherlands.

159.   *Early adopters of technological innovations.* (2003). TGI Chile. Retrieved November 5, 2004, from http://www.zonalatina.com/Zldata99.htm

CHAPTER 6

Researching and Applying Cultural Values

I n the previous chapters, we reviewed different value orientations of the inhabitants of different countries and how these can explain differences in consumer behavior that are important for global marketing and advertising strategy. Those who want to use value studies and cultural models for researching differences in marketing and advertising now have a wide choice of different models that measure different concepts and are only similar to a certain extent. Dimensions and culture are products of the mind that help us to simplify the overwhelming complexity of the real world, so as to understand it. There is not just one way to simplify it. Different researchers' minds produce different sets of dimensions.[1] Differences result from different study goals, different research concepts, and different research methods.

This chapter is mostly meant for students who want to understand the research on which theory is based or who want to do some research themselves as it further pursues the value concept and the difficulties encountered when measuring values, such as the role of language, the type of questions used in surveys and the level of measurement. Do we measure individuals or nations? Do we ask for the desired or the desirable? Usually values are derived from verbal statements of respondents and other behaviors, and the results from different countries are compared. This asks for equivalence of research design, type of questions, scales, and the like. This chapter explains the pitfalls of cross-cultural research.

Value Research

In the 1960s, American scholar Milton Rokeach[2] made an inventory of American values. The Rokeach Value Survey was one of the first and is still used as the basis for many value- and lifestyle studies. Rokeach distinguished two levels of values: terminal values and instrumental values. *Terminal values* refer to desirable end-states of existence. *Instrumental values* refer to desirable modes of conduct. Instrumental values are motivators to reach end-states of existence. Table 6.1 shows Rokeach's instrumental and terminal values, alphabetically arranged.[3]

How enduring values are was demonstrated by Yankelovich[4] who in the 1990s found that despite increased affluence and other changes, many of America's most important traditional values had remained firm and constant. Despite the transformations in America's lifestyles, a number of core values shared by virtually all Americans have endured unchanged:

- Freedom (valuing political liberty, free speech)
- Equality before the law
- Equality of opportunity (the practical expression of freedom and individualism in the marketplace)
- Fairness (placing a high value on people getting what they deserve as a consequence of their own individual actions)
- Achievement (a belief in the efficacy of individual effort: the view that education and hard work pay off)
- Patriotism (loyalty to the United States)

Table 6.1   Rokeach's Terminal Values and Instrumental Values

Terminal Values	Instrumental Values
a comfortable life	ambitious
exciting life	broad-minded
a sense of accomplishment	capable
a world at peace	cheerful
a world of beauty	clean
equality	courageous
family security	forgiving
freedom	helpful
happiness	honest
inner harmony	imaginative
mature love	independent
national security	intellectual
pleasure	logical
salvation	loving
self-respect	obedient
social recognition	polite
true friendship	responsible
wisdom	self-controlled

SOURCE: Reprinted with the permission of The Free Press, a Division of Simon & Schuster, Inc., from *The Nature of Human Values* by Milton Rokeach. Copyright © 1973 by The Free Press. Copyright © renewed 2001 by Sandra Ball-Rokeach. All rights reserved.

- Democracy (the belief that the judgment of the majority should form the basis of governance)
- American exceptionalism (a belief in the special moral status and mission of America)
- Caring beyond the self (concern for others, such as family or ethnic group)
- Religion (a reverence for some transcendental meaning)
- Luck (good fortune can happen to anyone at any time)

Yankelovich adds that this tiny cluster of values holds Americans together as a single people and nation; it is the unity amid the variety of American life.

These values can be recognized in much of American advertising. An example is a TV commercial for Tele King Communications Corporation that offers people the opportunity to be their own boss, independence, big money, and leisure time. Being your own boss means independence and equality. The examples of leisure time reflect an exciting life (cruises, mountaineering) and pleasure. Earning big money reflects a comfortable life (Illustration 6.1).

Illustration 6.1   Tele King, United States

A simpler approach to values, called List Of Values (LOV), was developed by Kahle and Goff Timmer.[5] LOV consists of nine values: a sense of belonging, excitement, fun and enjoyment in life, warm relationship with others, self-fulfillment, being well respected, a sense of accomplishment, security, and self-respect. Both Rokeach's list and LOV have been used for value studies worldwide, also in marketing and advertising. Although Rokeach realized that values vary by culture, quite a few research agencies keep applying American lists of values to other cultures. However, surveys developed in one environment and used to measure values of another environment will lead to irrelevant results. International value studies from the start should take into account the different value systems of the participating countries. There are several consequences of using lists of values developed in one culture for other cultures: Value priorities may vary; terminal values of one culture may serve as instrumental values in other cultures; and values that are relevant in one culture may not exist at all in another culture, and thus, there are no linguistic or conceptual equivalents in other languages. The following sections discuss these problems.

There are several cross-cultural value studies, the results of which are available in the public domain. A European cross-cultural value study is the European Values Study (EVS),[6] which has been extended to the World Values Survey (WVS) by Ronald Inglehart.[7] Another study, conducted by a number of European academics is the European Social Survey (ESS).[8] Some international media studies have included questions that measure value differences. Examples are surveys by the *Reader's Digest* and the European Media and Marketing Surveys (EMS).[9] Also, various surveys by Eurobarometer include questions about values (see Appendix B). For a limited number of countries in Asia, data are available from Asiabarometer.[10]

Values, Beliefs, Traits, and Norms

What Rokeach calls instrumental values are more like personal traits, and his terminal values are a mix of what people desire for themselves and what they desire for their society. As most value studies mix these, it is important to distinguish between values, personal traits, beliefs, and norms or ideologies. *Values* are preferences for states of being. *Beliefs* generally are expressed as agreements or disagreements with worldviews. *Personal traits*—in the Western definition—are a consistent pattern of thought or action. *Norms* or *ideologies* are about what people in general should or should not do. Many value surveys mix the four, asking questions about what people think about themselves, about others (in their opinion), and what they themselves or others should be. Values are usually studied by asking people what is important to them in their own lives and how important it is, usually expressed in abstract terms. The answers reflect personal values, which are not necessarily the same as what others may consider important, or their own actual traits. For example, people can value creativity without being creative. Beliefs, when based on opinions of groups of people may result in stereotypes. Confusions between values and personal traits generally do not cause serious research problems, but values and norms or ideologies should be clearly distinguished.[11] As these differences are the basis of the different results of the various value studies and cultural models, the effects of question formulation on the outcome of cultural models will be discussed in more detail on pages 176–178.

Value Priorities Vary

Some values may exist everywhere, but there is a difference in *rankings of priorities of values*. This has been found in various studies based on both the Rokeach and LOV values. In an exercise to find cross-cultural differences among American, Australian, Israeli, and Canadian students, Rokeach found differences in the ranking of the importance of the values in his list.[12] The Israeli students, in particular, deviated. For example, they cared more about being capable than being ambitious, and they were less individualistic and more group oriented than the other students, all of whom were from Anglo-Saxon cultures (American, Australian, and Canadian). This supports Hofstede's findings on the Israeli culture, which is more collectivistic and of high uncertainty avoidance, resulting in a higher regard for competence than is found in U.S. culture.

Grunert, Grunert, and Beatty[13] compared values for two age groups in three countries (United States, Germany, and Denmark) based on Kahle's LOV instrument and found that ratings varied, particularly with respect to the values fun and enjoyment and self-fulfillment. Danish respondents, independent of their age, rated fun and enjoyment much higher than both German and U.S. respondents. The latter, on the other hand, rated self-fulfillment higher.

Kamakura and Mazzon[14] found substantial differences between the United States and Brazil for the Rokeach terminal values. Whereas family security, world peace, and freedom have consistently been important values in the United States, true friendship, mature love, and happiness appear to be the most important values in Brazil. Comparison of rankings from 1971 and 1981 also showed that the ranking of values in the United States had been quite stable over time.

Mixing Terminal and Instrumental Values

Terminal values of one culture may be the instrumental values of another culture. Rokeach listed obedience, getting along well with others, and self-control as instrumental values.[15] In high power distance as well as in collectivistic cultures, however, obedience may well be a terminal value. Respect for elders, parents, or any higher placed person is ingrained in these cultures. Similarly, if the division between terminal and instrumental values were used in Asian cultures, getting along with others, or harmony, might be a terminal value rather than an instrumental one. A Belgian value, listed as the first terminal value by the Belgian Patrick Vyncke,[16] is having one's own house, one's own place under the sun. The Dutch would consider this to be an instrumental value. The house is the instrument of security or care. However, specific to the Belgians is strong linkage to the soil of their birthplace, which is expressed by the saying, "a stone in your belly." For practical reasons, in cross-cultural value studies, the distinction between instrumental and terminal values is better avoided.

Stability and Value Shift

We pointed at the stability of values in Chapter 3 (pp. 54–55). Several long-term value studies, such as the World Value Survey, demonstrate such stability. Many elements of culture are stable and do not change within a short period. The degree of stability depends, however, on the type of item. For example, answers to questions about religion, hard work, or obedience appear to be more stable than those to questions about tolerance and imagination. One of the causes may be that hard work and obedience are concepts that may make sense in all modern nations whereas tolerance and imagination may be too abstract for some respondents.[17]

Some values may change in the long term with different causes. Value shift can be caused by economic change, modernization, maturation and generation effects, Zeitgeist, and seniority effects.

Wealth leads to individualism, and poverty leads to collectivism. With better education, the level of power distance goes down. Yet relative differences remain, and some differences may even become stronger. At face value, people tend to become more individualistic, but individuation follows different patterns. Modernization, including industrialization and urbanization, is assumed to turn collectivistic societies into individualistic societies. Although urbanization tends to break up the joint household of the extended family in favor of more nuclear households, this does not imply decreasing extended family values. Roland[18] states that the Indian family remains an extended one. The extended family maintains strong family ties, gets together on holidays, makes mutual decisions on important matters, and sometimes maintains joint ownership. Indian society and culture modernize by traditionalizing various foreign innovations. A class society has formed, but classes do not predominate over caste. Instead, caste associations have been formed to provide assistance for jobs, marriages, or loans; and castes have participated in the political process. The Japanese remain enmeshed within traditional family and group hierarchical structures although new skills and greater education have led to increased individuation. Modernization for the Japanese has reinforced the traditional Japanese ego-ideal into a total dedication to the task, which contributes to the good of the group. The system of structural hierarchy and unquestioned subordination in high power distance cultures may change, but dependency values, including deep respect for superiors and reciprocal relationships, remain.

An example of how in modern life extended family traditions keep playing a role is a commercial for Maruha cat food (illustration 6.2). Family members who still live in rural areas tend to send food packages to family members who live in the city. Also, the cat is nostalgically thinking about his extended cat family, their rural environment, and the food.

Maturation[19] effects mean that people's values shift as they grow older. Stress, for example, is highest at middle age. Masculinity decreases with increasing age. Young people who want to make it in life generally adhere more to masculine values than do those who have already made it. Youngest and oldest age categories are less individualistic.

Generation effects occur when values are fixed in the young from a certain period and then stay with that age cohort over its lifetime. Drastic changes in the conditions of life during youth may lead to generations having different fixed values. The value shift of the generation of the 1960s in Europe and the United States is an example of a generation effect.

Zeitgeist effects occur when drastic systemwide changes in conditions cause everyone's values to shift, regardless of age. In times of recession, the degree of power distance may increase because equality is less functional, or it may lead to increased bureaucracy and shift to a stronger level of uncertainty avoidance.

Illustration 6.2   Maruha cat food, Japan

Seniority effects occur when the values of people who are more senior in an organization are measured. Seniority and age effects cannot be separated easily.

The degree of uncertainty avoidance of countries can change with environmental factors. Natural disasters and war will cause higher levels. In 1996, when we
measured the dimensions in the EMS survey, Finland's score on uncertainty avoidance had lowered and the score of the United Kingdom had become higher than the
original Hofstede score. The United Kingdom was in an economic crisis at that
time, and Finland had been delivered from the pressure of the Soviet Union.

Culture-Specific Values

Some important values are culture-specific. Relevant values of one culture may not
exist in another culture. For example, in Rokeach's list of values, two important
Asian values are missing: perseverance and thrift. Relevant, culture-specific values
can be found by looking at the important cultural concepts that appear to be
untranslatable into any other language, or only translatable into the languages of
similar cultures. Due to the fact that there are no linguistic or conceptual equivalents for some value-expressive words, using a single value list for cross-cultural
research can cause errors. In the translation process, values can become incomprehensible or get a different loading. Nowadays, lists of values can be found for many
different countries. Some are based on behavioral guides from old philosophies like
Confucianism and Buddhism that also explain differences in communication
behavior (see Chapter 7). We are providing here only a few examples, to show how
specific some of these values can be. Examples of lists of national values are from
Belgium, the Netherlands, India, and Japan.

Belgian Values

A list of values developed by a Belgian scholar Patrick Vyncke[20] shows values not found in Rokeach's list (see Table 6.2). The Belgian list includes individualistic values such as self-esteem, self-interest, and "doing your own thing." It reflects individualistic values as well as the masculine and high power distance values of success, status, and prestige. Most interesting is the fact that the first eight values all seem to be a reflection of strong uncertainty avoidance, which is a characteristic of Belgian culture. Owning your own house is a form of security; so are thrift, progeny, health, safety, being able to count on people, and being without pain. In particular, the statement "keep everything, all you have, as it is," reflects reluctance to change. The value progeny is reflected in the importance of children in Belgian society.

Table 6.2   List of Belgian Values

1. Having your own house, place "under the sun"
2. Thrift, frugality
3. Progeny, having descendants
4. Health, a healthy life
5. Safety, living in a safe world
6. Security, being able to count on people
7. Being without pain, fear, or misfortune
8. Keeping everything, all one has, as it is
9. Paying attention to oneself, self-interest
10. Romanticism, being in love, romantic love
11. Erotic love, sex, sensuality, seduction
12. A strong, intimate, and mature partner relationship
13. Love for children
14. Strong friendship, comradeship, "mateship"
15. Strong family ties, good family relationships
16. A better world for one's fellow man
17. A better environment, love of nature
18. Self-esteem, self-respect
19. Being respected by others
20. Being admired, having prestige, status, success
21. Leadership, power
22. Ability to be oneself as one is
23. Freedom, independence, doing one's own thing
24. Development of one's own abilities, creativity
25. Having one's own lifestyle
26. Being without stress, having peace, inner harmony
27. An active, exciting, adventurous life
28. Enjoying the simple things in life
29. Leading a prosperous, comfortable, luxurious life

SOURCE: Vyncke, P. (1992). *Imago-Management*. Used with permission of Mys & Breesch, Ghent, Belgium.

Dutch Values

Dutch Joke Oppenhuisen[21] found six dimensions of Dutch values that are summarized in Table 6.3. Each of the dimensions reflects the paradox that is typical of individualistic cultures that are also low on masculinity: freedom versus affiliation, which is also found in Scandinavian value studies. For each dimension, this paradox is related to different societal aspects: social relations, fellow human beings, society, security, family life, and dependence on approval by others. Each dimension consists of a set of 10 items. In Table 6.3, the first three of each dimension are presented. The study doesn't provide value priorities. Several values were similar to the Rokeach values, but additional values were found that do not occur in the Rokeach list.

Table 6.3   Dutch Values: Six Dimensions

Dimension 1		*Dimension 2*	
Affiliation	*Achievement*	*Social*	*Individual*
Cuddling	Ambition	Empathy	Enjoyment
Friendship	Fanatic	Understanding	Attractive
Love	Power	Helpful	Carefree
Dimension 3		*Dimension 4*	
Old values	*New values*	*Security*	*Challenge*
Patriotism	Hobbies	Tidy	Challenge
Respectable	Education	Rich	Spontaneous
Proud	Have time	Clean	Break new ground
Dimension 5		*Dimension 6*	
Family life	*Freedom*	*Conformist*	*Go it alone*
Be a mother	Freedom	Well-groomed	Go it alone
Have children	Ordinary	Attractive	Believe
Cuddling	Peace and quiet	Prestige	Rebel

SOURCE: Oppenhuisen, J. (2000). *Een schaap in de bus? Een onderzoek naar waarden van de Nederlander* [A sheep in the bus? A study of Dutch values]. Unpublished doctoral dissertation, University of Amsterdam, The Netherlands.

Indian Values

In Indian culture, the values of the extended family are predominant, although individuality is richly developed in Indians, including a large degree of freedom in feeling, thinking, and cultivation of one's inner life. Competitive individualism, however, is severely frowned on in Indian society because it can disrupt relationships.[22]

For UNESCO, Dr. Srivastava[23] made an inventory of Indian values in the form of a list of personality attributes. These were classified in four categories: *Me and me* attributes that are practiced by the individual alone, without reference to his or her social relationships and without assistance from others; *Me and you* attributes that necessitate interaction between two or more individuals; *Me and society* attributes that involve wider interactions with the society, nation, and the world; *Me and God* attributes that involve an individual's relationship with her or his maker. Each category includes a set of attributes that are summarized in Table 6.4.

Table 6.4   Indian Values

Me and me	Me and you	Me and society	Me and God
Cleanliness	Patience	Sharing	Prayer
Dignity of labor	Dutifulness	Team spirit	Worship
Diligence	Courtesy	Dialogue	Gratitude
Perseverance	Love	Justice	Service
Determination	Magnanimity	Sympathy	Witnessing God in nature
Fortitude	Humility	Hospitality	
Courage	Being a good sports-person	Non-violence	Righteous behavior
Self-reliance		Peace	Pursuits for salvation
Excellence	Honesty	Harmony	
Hope	Tolerance		
Meditation	Charity		
Self-analysis			

SOURCE: Srivastava, H. S. (2004). Indian core values of peace and harmony. In Z. Nan-Zhao & B. Teasdale (Eds.), *Teaching Asia-Pacific core values of peace and harmony*. Bangkok: UNESCO Asia and Pacific Regional Bureau for Education.

Japanese Values

First, we describe Japanese values that are also found in other East Asian cultures and that are frequently recognized in marketing and advertising: harmony with fellow human beings and harmony of man with nature. They are characteristic of the combination of long-term orientation and collectivism and, although here explained for Japanese culture, are applicable to other East Asian cultures.

Harmony. One of the most important basic Japanese values is harmony (*wa*): walk together, think together, dine together. Related is empathy (understand and anticipate the feelings of others), respect for age, and honesty. Honesty cannot be related to the Western concept of truth. The Japanese concept of honesty is linked to respect. For example, government should not treat us as children, but as grown-ups.

Nature. When the Japanese speak of the providence of nature, they refer to a natural order that they believe to be the fountainhead of all existence. In the Christian world, God is the fountainhead of all existence, and humans seek comfort from God. In Japan, human beings seek comfort by attempting to immerse themselves in nature. Another explanation of the reverence for nature is that the Japanese turn to nature because there is something unsatisfying in the way they deal with human relations, where the surface is always glossed over and conflict is kept in the shadows. Living with the strong distinction between dealing with people in one's inner circle and one's outer circle can be very complicated and stressful. Nature does not have this distinction and can therefore be trusted completely.[24] Relating to nature is not as confusing as relating to human beings. Thus, nature has a relaxing function.

Other, typical Japanese values can be recognized in a model developed by the late Kazuaki Ushikubo[25] who studied people's wants in Japan and developed a model for structuring wants. This structure is based on 12 Japanese core values. From 1982 onward, he carried out an annual survey among 3,000 respondents, presenting them with 12 statements. Respondents received a number of stickers to distribute over the value statements to show their preference. This technique circumvents the problem of Asians' dislike of thinking in opposites. Ushikubo found four clusters of basic values, which he named *Change, Participation, Freedom,* and *Stability,* as presented in Figure 6.1.

The cluster *Change* includes the statements "Want to learn knowledge faster than other people," "To create something and upgrade my ability," and "Want to have stimulation, change in my life, new things."

The cluster *Participation* includes the statements "To keep friends is very important," "Have a happy time with friends and family" (Japanese *danran*), and "Do well with all people around me."

The cluster *Stability* includes the statements "Want to refresh from a tired brain or body" (meaning relaxation), "To live without fear—safety," and "Want to be healthy."

The cluster *Freedom* includes the statements "Identity of myself is important," "Live easy, I do not care about my surroundings," and "To live in loneliness, have a lonely time."

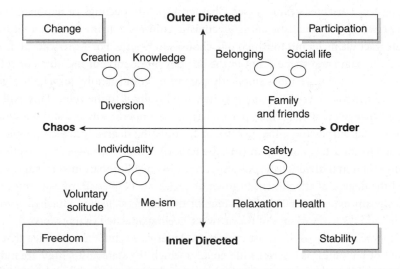

Figure 6.1   Japan (Ushikubo): "Freedom and Order"

SOURCE: Ushikubo, K. (1986). A method of structure analysis for developing product concepts and its applications. *European Research, 18,* 174–184.

These descriptions show some terms that have different meanings in the West. The term *friends* under Participation does not relate to the Western concept of friendship but to "correct behavior versus the others in your group." *Danran* means having a happy time, enjoying open-hearted conversation with your family and good friends. The term *identity* under Freedom is an example of a value that is emphasized because it is lacking in society. The Freedom cluster, defining individuality (individuality, me-ism, and voluntary solitude) was indicated by only 10% of the respondents, which illustrates the different meaning of freedom in Japan: individuality, me-ism, thus, escaping the (sometimes) stifling conformity of the group.

Important Values Don't Translate

Values have to be labeled, and if the labels are translated but the values are not comparable, they tend to represent different values. Thus, translation of values of American value lists into other languages can result in meaningless concepts or may even turn positive concepts into negative ones. A few examples of untranslatable words and concepts were given in Chapter 3. Such words and concepts are very important for advertising because in the specific culture, they can communicate a message instantly. Because American lists of values are so frequently used for cross-cultural studies, in this section, the translation problems of a few of the typical Rokeach values are described.

Values like patriotism and nationalism are more meaningful in some countries than in others, often depending on their histories. For countries that have always had open borders, such as the Netherlands, these values are neither meaningful nor important. If someone in the Netherlands were to declare himself ready to die for his country, people would start laughing. Anyway, patriotism is a culture-bound concept. Feelings of national pride are stronger in short-term oriented cultures than in long-term oriented cultures (see Chapter 4, p. 94). Feelings of nationality also vary between individualistic and collectivistic cultures. For the former, a *nation* is the abstract ultimate unit to which one chooses to belong. For Americans, it is loyalty to the "stars and stripes," not to the current president. For members of collectivistic cultures, one is more implicitly part of a "grand family" in which a good ruler has the role of the benevolent father, and loyalty is to the ruler. This explains how in Japan, a culture based on personal ties, the emperor was and still is a symbol of loyalty far surpassing a flag.[26] Also, in Europe, the degree to which people feel attached to their town or region (not the nation) is much stronger in collectivistic cultures than in individualistic cultures, according to a Eurobarometer[27] survey that asked the degree of attachment to town or region in 14 West European countries. Collectivism explained 62% of variance of the answers "feeling attached to one's region" and 43% of variance of the answers "feeling attached to one's town."

Happiness is one of the most important American values. Yet the idea that the pursuit of happiness is a serious life goal by which the state and family are judged is unthinkable to the Japanese. To the Japanese, the supreme task in life is fulfilling one's obligations. Pleasure or happiness is a relaxation that can easily be given up in order to fulfill one's obligations.[28] Advertisers often present happiness as a universal value, but the above makes clear that the priority varies. Next to that, what makes people happy varies even more.

Another Western value, romantic love, is underplayed by the Chinese but is cultivated by the Japanese. Erotic pleasure, on the other hand, is a moral issue or even a taboo to the Americans, whereas the Japanese see no need to be moralistic about sex pleasures. In Indian culture, too, the erotic is accepted and expressed.[29]

Salvation, an American value, when translated into Dutch seems to be irrelevant. The literal translation is the same word as delivering a baby. In the Dutch value study, it was listed as problem solving. All concepts related to religion or to belief in higher beings are culture-bound. The Japanese cannot cope with concepts relating to God at all. For them, the concept of salvation is nonexistent. When they seek comfort, they seek it in nature.

The word *freedom* has different connotations across cultures. The concept of freedom as described by U.S. students means "free enterprise." Dutch students tend to describe *freedom* as "freedom to express your feelings, to be yourself." In 1996, Russian students from western Siberia associated the word *freedom* primarily with "not being in prison" and secondarily with freedom from pollution and freedom of speech.[30] To the Japanese, *freedom* means "to behave as you please, to transcend the group." It is experienced as "having individual ideas, escape from spiritual bondage," which is not the same as the Western individualistic notion of freedom that serves as a basis for asserting the precedence of the individual over the group, which is not seen as desirable in Japanese society. The Japanese word used to translate the English word *freedom* (*jiyu*) is of Chinese origin. It means to behave as one pleases, without considering others, which for a collectivistic society basically means disharmony and thus is negative. As liberty and freedom in the West signify respect for the human being, the concept has become ambiguous, to say the least, to the Japanese.[31]

The Rokeach value *a comfortable life* is linked with material prosperity. To the Japanese it means to be rich, not in money, but spiritually, to be without fear, have stability, no change, good relations, a good house. In the Dutch value study, it was listed as enjoyment.

The Rokeach values *self-respect* and *self-esteem* are related to the concept of "self" in an individualistic culture as was described in Chapter 5. *Self-respect* (*jicho*) in Japan means restraint, which is the opposite of the American value, which includes values like character, reputation, and prestige. A major dimension of Japanese self-esteem relates to reflecting well on the family and work group through high performance thus gaining their respect. Indians' inner feelings of esteem are deeply tied up with family reputation.[32]

Asking people of different cultures to define a word like *pleasure* may lead to long sentences and explanations, which suggests that it has different connotations in different cultures. Because it is frequently used in advertising, understanding its meaning and connotations in other cultures is important. In Japan, *pleasure* is a personal feeling of pleasure, related only to the inner circle. The Spanish concept of *placer* reflects a wide variety of feelings of social and inner enjoyment.

The concept of friendship is ambiguous. In the Western sense, it does not exist in Japanese society. It is known and used because it is an often encountered English-language word, but those whom you call your friends are basically members of the inner circle. True friendship is made to mean "understanding how to communicate." This is very different from the North American concept of friendship, in which you can make friends and lose friends. In the Japanese outer circle, you have no friends. Rarely might you find a new friend in your work. As a result, asking Japanese respondents to choose the degree of importance of true friendship is a nonsense question. Japanese cannot express the importance of true friendship. This also holds true in China and in other collectivistic cultures, although more strongly in some than in others.

Americans call people friends who are merely acquaintances in the European context. In most of continental Europe, only close friends are on a first-name basis. Dealing with everybody on a first-name basis, as the Americans do, confuses the friendship concept. It is particularly confusing to Germans, for whom the wider usage of the word *friendship* is too ambiguous, as is illustrated by the reaction to a *Newsweek* article about service.[33]

> Germans, like most Europeans, are more distant with customers than Americans are used to, but can hardly be summed up as unfriendly. The artificial friendliness commonly practiced by shop assistants and restaurant staff in America would be off-putting to Germans. Who wants to be on a first-name basis with a waiter who'll be forgotten promptly after the meal?

Western abstract concepts like "world at peace" or "quality of life" are beyond understanding to many Asians. To the Japanese, peace, not the large concept of peace, but peace nearby, means health, safety, and having good people around you.

Measuring Cultural Values

The very first thing to have in mind is that, whatever measurement system chosen, researchers start with their own subjective cultural views, whether they study other cultures through firsthand experiences or from a distance by collecting and analyzing data. Researchers carry their own culture; what they observe and the questions asked in surveys are selected from the researchers' point of view.

The values that characterize a society cannot be observed directly. They can be inferred from various cultural products (fairy tales, children's books, or advertising) or by asking members of society to score their personal values by stating their preferences among alternatives and then calculating the central tendency of the answers. When value differences are derived from cultural products, or artifacts of culture, we run the risk of circular reasoning.[34] Values should be related to information about cultures derived from the study of individuals. This information generally is gathered by way of value questionnaires among representative or matched samples, asking people about their value priorities or practices that reflect values. In order to structure the information, the results are aggregated to the culture- or country-level and are then factor analyzed. The mean of a construct for a collection of individuals can then be interpreted as the central tendency of individuals.[35] So dimensions are generally developed from large numbers of variables by statistical data reduction methods (e.g., factor analysis) and provide scales on which countries have different positions.

Reducing culture to dimensions with numbers on scales has been criticized. But we have to understand that dimensions are useful constructs that explain behavior. As Hofstede[36] states,

> We cannot directly observe mental programs. What we can observe is only behavior: Words or deeds. Mental programs are intangibles and the terms we use to describe them are *constructs*. A construct is a product of our imagination, supposed to help our understanding. Constructs do not "exist" in an absolute sense: We define them into existence. In the same way values and dimensions do not exist. They are constructs, which have to prove their usefulness by their ability to explain and predict behavior. . . . Culture is not the only thing we should pay attention to. In many cases economic, political or institutional factors provide better explanations. But sometimes they don't, and then we need the construct of culture.

Dimensions also are based on Western, individualistic thinking and categorization. Yet collectivists tend to have few problems with the system as it categorizes on the basis of groups, not unique individuals.

The most influential aspect that inhibits comparability of cross-cultural studies is the conceptual foundation of cross-cultural research. All too frequently, theories or constructs developed in one country are used in the study of another, which can result in bias. No matter how accurate and refined the analytical procedures, if the underlying conceptual model is flawed, the findings and their interpretation will, at best, be biased.[37] An example from advertising research is applying the Resnik and Stern coding scheme, developed in the United States, to analysis of advertising in other countries.

The bases of the dimensions are the questions posed in value questionnaires. Both content and form of the questions influence the results. Questions have to be translated, and meanings must have conceptual equivalence across all cultures where the questions are used. Across cultures, people also respond differently to scales in surveys, which can cause biased results. Also, the culture of the researcher plays a role. Most value surveys have been conducted by Western scholars and their Western background can be recognized in their hypotheses, purpose, topics, and questions of their studies. For example, quite a few Western cross-cultural management researchers are obsessed by typical Western leadership issues. As noted before, the Rokeach list of values that is used for value studies worldwide lacks questions relating to important Asian values, such as perseverance and duty, values that are viewed as negative in most Western societies. For many Westerners, "duty" connects with negative feelings. Connecting feelings of pleasure with duty, as in several East Asian cultures, is alien to Western researchers.[38] The next sections will describe the various research aspects that can cause bias.

Measuring the Desired Versus the Desirable

In Chapter 3, we presented the differences between the desired and the desirable. Questions about the desirable are worded in terms of right/wrong or important/unimportant, and answers will reflect people's views of what is right or wrong. The desired is worded in terms of you and me, including our less virtuous desires. Statements about the desired are close to actual behavior, although even these do not always correspond to the way people really behave.[39] Value studies that ask for the desirable lead to different results than those that measure the desired. Some studies ask respondents questions about what they should prefer for themselves or what they think their society should look like. These questions reflect the desired and the desirable. For example, the GLOBE[40] researchers ask respondents— next to measuring their views on how things are done in their societies (the practices)—to express what is desirable in their societies, so they measure values in terms of preferences about the behavior of others in their society. This is not the same as individual behavior. For example, if I want to be powerful, it doesn't follow that I shall want others to be powerful. Questions about personal behavior are relatively easy to answer. Thinking about how others behave, or even an abstract item, such as society, is much more difficult to answer; such questions can cause bias.[41]

Survey Questions

The usefulness of cultural models mostly depends on the type of questions asked in surveys and the way these influence answers. Understanding how these questions make a difference is necessary to understand the usefulness of the different models. The common approach is to ask people what they think by means of questionnaires, asking respondents to agree or not agree with statements about themselves (e.g., "I tend to do my own thing"). Several problems arise when asking people for their preferences. People may sometimes not say what they think; they may distort their answers for various psychological or cultural reasons or misinterpret some questions. The culture and context of respondents can influence the answers. For example, a Korean student in the Netherlands would express pride to be Korean, which she would not do in her own country, as expressing pride is not done there. The way questions are formulated can cause bias. The answers may not accurately reflect people's feelings or behavior in actual social settings.[42] In particular, collectivists are sensitive to context. Requests to make statements about the self or the self as part of the group without specifying which group or in which situation may not lead to useful results.[43] Next to the difference between the desirable and the desired, major elements of questions that influence the results are conceptual differences, taboos, and intelligibility problems. Minkov[44] mentions that in some countries there are whole domains that may be closed to researchers. An example is asking female respondents about sex in most Arab countries. Intelligibility is a more important element. Some surveys ask respondents about topics they have never thought about and cannot judge. Examples are when nationally representative samples of respondents in developed and developing economies are asked to assess the desirability of a market economy or democracy. One of the GLOBE questions reads "The economic system in this society is designed to maximize: individual interests/collective interests."[45] Also, when there are no linguistic equivalents to concepts in questions, they tend to become incomprehensible.

Generally five types of questions can be distinguished in the three major dimensional models discussed in Chapter 4 that affect the results:

1. Questions about what is important to people in their daily lives, questions about oneself, one's behavior or feelings, or personal preferences (self-reports) that reflect cultural values. Examples of such questions are about personal feelings of happiness, the frequency of feeling tense or nervous, the importance of having time available for family life. The Hofstede model is based on such self-reports of actual behavior of individuals or preferences related to people's daily lives at all layers of society. Hofstede asks people about individual behavioral preferences, preferred or actual states of being, which is the desired. Questions relate to recognizable aspects of daily life.

2. Judgmental self-reports, like asking people to define themselves according to personal characteristics, such as judging oneself as an honest, friendly, or aggressive person. Such definitions tend to be relative. When individuals make certain judgments about themselves, they implicitly draw comparisons with others. These referent others, however, are different for people in different cultures. For example, in a society where, on average, people are aggressive car drivers, an individual driver may not judge himself to be an aggressive driver whereas he would notice his driving as being aggressive in a society where most people are more tolerant drivers. We see a similar phenomenon in cross-cultural measurement of personality traits. In a large study[46] of personality traits across cultures, the researchers were surprised to find Chinese, Korean, and Japanese people in the very bottom on the scale representing the degree of conscientiousness. It seems unlikely that most people would think of individuals of these cultures as extremely undisciplined and weak willed—a profile indicative of low conscientiousness. However, where the standards for being punctual, strong-willed, and reliable are very high, respondents may report that they are less disciplined than is generally the case in that particular culture.

3. Questions about value preferences, asking respondents to rate the importance of values "as guiding principles in my life" on a scale. Examples of such values are equality, politeness, wealth, and respect for tradition. The answers may not be the same as answers to actual behavioral questions. What people view as a guiding principle more reflects the norm, the desirable or what one ought to view as the right behavior. The Schwartz model uses this type of questioning. As the formulation of value priorities tends to be quite abstract, such questions are best answered by well-educated people. The respondents sought for the Schwartz Value Survey are teachers and students.

4. Questions about behavior in relation to the society in which people live, which imply people's judgment of other members of their society (referent questions). Examples are statements to which respondents can agree or not: "In this society people are generally assertive," or "In this society people are generally very concerned about others." When answering the question, respondents have to think about what their society actually is, and many may not be aware of characteristics of people outside their own group; some may answer in the context of the nation whereas others may refer to their family or neighborhood only. Asking ordinary respondents to describe their societies or their fellow citizens produces meaningful results only when the discussed issues are very simple, such as some types of relationships within families.[47] Thinking about how others behave or an abstract item, such as society, is much more difficult than thinking about oneself. When questions refer to issues that people cannot be expected to be knowledgeable about, the answers may not make much sense or result in stereotypes that are far from reality. Basically, when referring to societal behavior, we measure a mix of two variables: the individual's personal values, reflected in their opinion and the society or group referred to. When the referent group is simple and nearby, such as family or nearby contacts in daily life, respondents will have no problem with such questions, but when referring to an abstract phenomenon, like society, problems may arise. Maybe highly educated people can estimate the average values of their society without projecting their own values, but most people will project their own values or norms onto the desirable ones for the society in which they live. These may not represent reality. The GLOBE study uses this type of question.

5. Judgmental referent questions, asking people to express judgments about societal norms. These are questions asking respondents how other people in their society *should* behave. The GLOBE study uses such questions, and the GLOBE researchers call the results *values*. Here, three variables are at work: the respondents' personal values reflected in their opinion, the society of which he or she is part, and the norms for "others" in society. It is very complex questioning. Examples are agreement or disagreement with statements like "In this society students should strive for improved performance," or "In this society followers should obey their leaders" (GLOBE). Other examples are agreement or disagreement with abstract statements like "There should be more emphasis on family life" or "Less importance should be placed on work" or "There should be greater respect for authority" (World Values Survey). Generally, the use of judgmental questions relating to people's own society, be it direct or indirect, asks for invalid results as people will give answers relative to the behavioral standards of their own culture. For example, people's level of agreement with the statement "There is too much sex on TV" will depend not only on whether they think sex should be allowed on TV but also on how much sex there in fact is on TV in their particular country. A similar problem exists with the following statement: "We drink more wine at home these days." To agree with this statement in a wine-drinking country like Italy would imply something very different from the same response in the United Kingdom.[48]

Individual and Culture Level

In cross-cultural research, a clear distinction must be made between the individual and culture level. In comparative cross-cultural research at the national level, individuals are sampled from a population in order to reach conclusions on that population. The *average* value priorities of individual members of one society are compared with the *average* value priorities of individual members of other societies. There is overlap between individual values and cultural values because institutions reflect the values shared by the individual members of a society. If they would not do so, individuals would not be able to function adequately. Individual members of a society have internalized values that help them conform to the requirements of societal institutions. Individuals are guided by their cultural priorities and in their behavior reinforce the social system.[49]

At the cultural level, the properties of individuals as observed within a country or group (e.g., age or literacy) are aggregated and then treated as country-level variables. To find explanations for some phenomena at country level (e.g., level of literacy across countries), the aggregate data can be correlated to other country-level variables (e.g., gross national income [GNI] per capita). This is called "between-system" or "between-country" comparison, although data are used that were originally collected among individuals of countries. Because the data have been aggregated, we cannot use them anymore to explain within-system differences. The aggregated data represent a mix of different people because a society consists of a variety of people, so patterns of associations observed at the culture level (also called ecological level) can be different from patterns at the individual level. Using a culture-level correlation to interpret individual behavior can lead to misinterpretations. One example is the positive correlation between obesity and national wealth, but within rich countries, the poorer individuals are more likely to be obese because they cannot afford healthy food. So obesity is positively correlated with wealth at the national level, but negatively within nations.[50] An example for value measurement is from Schwartz[51] who has shown that patterns of associations with "freedom" are different at the individual and at the cultural (national) level. Within countries, individuals who score high on the importance of "freedom" also tend to score high on the importance of "independence of thought and actions." But if the scores for all individuals in each nation are averaged, the nations where on average "freedom" is scored as more important than in other nations are not those scoring higher on the importance of "independence" but those scoring higher on "protecting the welfare of others." The individual associations are based on psychological logic, the national associations on the cultural logic of societies composed of different, interacting individuals.[52] Also, Fischer,[53] through analysis of time-series data of the European Social Survey (ESS), finds that the importance of pursuing one's own interests versus emphasizing the welfare of others appears to have different functions at individual and country level. Thus, value scores based on country-level constructs cannot be used to compare individuals across countries.[54] Measuring individual respondents on scales based on aggregate data is called an *ecological fallacy*. Reverse ecological fallacy is committed in the construction of ecological indexes from variables correlated at the individual level. An example of a reverse ecological fallacy is the use of a ready-made U.S. scale for comparing cultures, for example, Rokeach's structure of central and instrumental values for comparing countries.

Because of their strong belief in the uniqueness of individuals, generally, individualists are in favor of individual-level studies; they feel reluctant about categorizing people on the basis of group characteristics and insist that people should be treated, analyzed, and interpreted as individuals, not as group members. In more collectivistic cultures, the opposite bias can be found. Group differences are exaggerated and viewed as absolute. There is a tendency to treat people on the basis of the group that they belong to rather than as individuals.[55]

Equivalence of Survey Data

For making international comparisons, data should have the same meaning across countries—they must be equivalent—because biased information leads to ambiguous or even erroneous conclusions.[56] Several types of equivalence can be distinguished: *sample* equivalence, *linguistic* and *conceptual* equivalence, *metric* equivalence, *categorical* and *functional* equivalence.

The first three types of equivalence are discussed in separate sections. The latter two types of equivalence are also relevant for marketing research. Categorical equivalence refers to comparability of product category definitions between countries. For example, beer belongs to the category soft drinks in southern Europe, but it is considered to be an alcoholic beverage in northern Europe. Functional equivalence relates to the question of whether the concepts, objects, or behaviors studied have the same role or function in all countries included in the analysis. The bicycle is considered mainly as a means of transport in the Netherlands, China, or India, whereas it is mainly used for recreational purposes in the United States.[57]

Sample Equivalence

Cross-national value research should use representative national samples or matched samples, similar in all respects except nationality. When we compare cultural aspects of nations, we should try to match for different categories. It is obviously not very meaningful to compare Spanish nurses with Swedish policemen. One strategy for matching is to make samples very broad, so that subcultural differences are randomized out. This is what is done by drawing representative samples from populations, as done in public opinion polls. The opposite strategy is drawing from similar subcultures. We can compare Spanish nurses with Swedish nurses or Spanish policemen with Swedish policemen. When doing this, we have to be careful about generalizing to a nation as a whole. We have to check if both professions have similar functions in society. The matching is adequate if the differences we find between cultures in one sample set are confirmed by those found by others in other matched samples.[58]

Students constitute seemingly equivalent samples but are not. Next to having limited consumption experience, students' living circumstances are different. Students in the United States generally live on campus; students in Europe live by themselves, which makes them more independent, whereas students in Asia still live with their families. Next to that, students overrepresent a young, high-status, and prosperous slice of any given society.[59] In particular, in high power distance cultures with large income differences they represent the rich layer of society. Many studies published in the major academic journals relevant for marketing and advertising are based on experiments conducted by psychologists based in the United States. The reader should be aware of the fact that the study of American psychology students may not be representative of humanity as a whole.[60]

Linguistic and Conceptual Equivalence

Often, for global surveys, questionnaires are developed in the home country, phrased in the English language, and translated for use in many other countries. The accuracy of results depends in part on respondents' ability to understand the questions being posed. The translation and back-translation method helps to avoid some mistakes, but it doesn't guarantee conceptual equivalence. In Chapter 3, several problems caused by language were discussed, which are particularly important when translating questionnaires.

A question that is relevant for one culture is not necessarily relevant for another culture. Even if correctly translated, the same question can mean different things in different cultures because people interpret the meaning of questions, and give answers, relative to the norms of their own culture. Meanings and associations with concepts often vary. For example, in some cultures, the meaning of the concept of shame is humiliation and loss of face, whereas in others it tends to be related to modesty.[61] Another example is the difficulty of conveying the meaning of value questions as in one of the VALS statements that seems particularly tied to U.S. culture: "Just as the Bible says, the world literally was created in six days." This may simply confuse a Buddhist in Japan.[62] Another conceptual problem can arise when using scales with opposites. Words that are seen as opposites in one culture may not be viewed as opposites in another.[63]

Metric Equivalence

Cross-national studies may be flawed through borrowing scales used in domestic studies without examining their relevance and equivalence in other countries and contexts.[64] A scale that has been developed in one culture will not always have a similar effect in another culture. Differences in response style and tendencies to use extreme points on verbal rating scales (Extreme Response Style, ERS), as well as yea-saying and nay-saying (acquiescence, ARS), have been found to differ from country to country.[65] Italians, for example, like extremes and mark toward the end of any semantic scale, whereas the Germans are more restrained and mark toward the middle. The effect is that a *completely agree* answer in Italy is not worth the same as a *completely agree* answer in Germany.[66]

One cause of ERS is the type of Likert scale. If high-ERS participants are given a survey using a 7-point Likert-type scale, their responses tend to be either 1 *(strongly agree)* or 7 *(strongly disagree)*. If low-ERS participants are given the same survey, their responses will tend to cluster around 4 *(neither agree nor disagree)*.[67] The smallest between-group differences in ERS were found with the use of a 3-point scale.[68] Also, responses to Likert scales that contain a mixture of positive-worded and reverse-worded items will vary with culture.[69]

An ARS difference occurs when one group systematically gives higher or lower responses than another group, resulting in a scale displacement. To American respondents, a response of 3 on a 5-point Likert scale may mean no opinion, whereas it may mean mild agreement to Korean respondents. As a result of this scale displacement, Korean 3s are equivalent to American 4s, and Korean 4s are equivalent to American 5s.[70]

Across 19 countries, ERS is positively related to Hofstede's dimensions masculinity and power distance. However, taking an extreme position also is related to short-term orientation. The long-term orientation dimension contrasts nations where people tend to agree and disagree strongly with nations where people are more moderate. According to Smith,[71] this is a reflection of communication style, not just a source of measurement error. ARS is related to four dimensions. Persons from individualistic cultures are less likely to engage in ARS, and this also applies to persons from high uncertainty avoidance cultures. But also persons in high masculine and high power distance cultures are less likely to respond in an acquiescence manner.[72]

The effect of ERS and ARS can be reduced or eliminated by statistically standardizing the data. If scores are standardized per cultural group, cross-cultural differences in means, standard deviations, or both are eliminated. However, meaningful differences may also be lost. Some response styles may not be illogical. If Latin Americans score high on most values, regardless of their content, they just may have strong values that are expressed accordingly whereas East Asians may not be so strongly attached to their values and thus express them less strongly. Van de Vijver and Leung,[73] cross-cultural research methodologists, state that standardization requires justification because cross-cultural differences in average scores may not be exclusively due to response sets or other unwanted sources but may reflect valid differences. Too often, adjustments have thrown out valuable construct information in the effort to remove bias.[74] Dolnicar and Grün suggest,

> Difference between cultures can be checked by performing an ANOVA on the answer patterns given the different cultures. If the difference is not significant the data can be safely combined. If, however, this difference is significant, the researcher has to decide whether the differences encountered are meaningful findings in terms of cross-cultural differences or whether they are likely to represent differences in response behavior, in which case the original data set should be corrected before analysis.[75]

Comparing Dimensional Models

The above sections have provided the various criteria for comparing dimensional models. In the description of the three major large-scale worldwide dimensional models in Chapter 4, we pointed at several basic differences with respect to purpose, sampling, and type of questions used. The three models are different and can be applied for different purposes. Those who want to study both individual-level values and culture-level values may opt for the Schwartz model. The Hofstede model is suggested to be more useful in predicting behavior, and the GLOBE value dimensions could prove more useful in studying aspects of intergroup and international relations.[76]

The models by Hofstede and Schwartz both provide country scores that can be used for analysis of consumption data. There are several relationships between the dimensions of the three models. For 45 countries worldwide as expected, there are positive correlations between Hofstede's power distance, GLOBE's power distance, and Schwartz's hierarchy. Also, Hofstede's individualism correlates negatively with GLOBE's in-group collectivism and positively with Schwartz's autonomy. Other comparisons are somewhat disturbing, as explained in Chapter 4. There is a negative correlation between Hofstede's and GLOBE's uncertainty avoidance. Hofstede's masculinity correlates positively not only with GLOBE's assertiveness dimensions but also with power distance. There is no significant correlation between Hofstede's long-term orientation and GLOBE's future orientation. These correlations also vary for different groups of countries. Thus, before doing any research with the different dimensions, it is wise to first find correlations between the models' dimensions.

Comparing the Hofstede and Schwartz dimensions for 20 European countries,[77] we find that harmony correlates significantly with low individualism and high uncertainty avoidance, egalitarianism with low masculinity and short-term orientation, and hierarchy with high masculinity. For these 20 countries, all Schwartz value categories correlated significantly with each other. When correlating them with consumption data, the Schwartz dimensions tend to deliver opposing results to those of Hofstede. For example, whereas PC ownership and Internet users per 1,000 people (data 2005) correlate significantly with Hofstede's dimensions individualism and low power distance, which include values of equality, there is a significant negative correlation of the same data with Schwartz's egalitarianism. These opposing findings may be due to the differences in questioning the desired versus the desirable.[78]

Several inventories of cultural classifications applied to international marketing show that of available models, the Hofstede model has been used most frequently to understand differences across markets. It has been used for analyzing market entry modes; for innovation, research, and development; for personality and motivation studies; for understanding emotions across cultures, and for analyzing advertising.[79] It is useful to segment the world on a country level so international marketers can adopt similar advertising campaigns in a country segment.[80]

Applying Cultural Dimensions to Marketing and Advertising

In this book, the Hofstede model is used to explain consumer behavior differences, motives, advertising appeals, and executional forms. An often posed question is whether Hofstede's country scores, produced in the late 1960s and early 1970s, are valid to use some 30 years later. Several replications of Hofstede's study on different matched or non-matched samples have proved that his data are still valid.[81] In the second edition of his book, *Culture's Consequences,* Hofstede describes over 200 external comparative studies and replications that have supported his indexes.[82] Comparison with later models has also shown that the basic value differences found in his model were also found in later models.

The Hofstede dimensions are practical because they are limited in number and because they overlap relatively little and cover most countries in the world. Advertising strategists can utilize Hofstede's framework as a guide to provide direction in selecting country-specific advertising appeals.[83] As the model was developed for understanding work-related motives, analytical skills are needed when applying the model to analyze consumption motives and advertising. Problems can arise in the formulation of hypotheses and in selecting countries or groups of countries for analysis. Sometimes, researchers challenge the predictive value of the model because their hypotheses were not supported instead of challenging the formulation of the hypotheses. A few general points of caution are dealt with in the next sections.

Understanding Manifestations of Dimensions

When working with the dimensions, the content of each dimension must be studied carefully before formulating hypotheses or explaining results. Some manifestations of each dimension are more work-related whereas others can be applied to consumer behavior. For example, power distance is about the relationship between bosses and subordinates, but it also is about everyone having his or her rightful place in society versus equality. The latter explains the need for luxury brands as status symbols in high power distance cultures because they can be used to demonstrate one's place in the hierarchy. In any hierarchy, it is important to display your status through outward appearances of rank and wealth. Collectivism is not about subordinating oneself to the group. This is the typical description from an individualistic view of the person. The group itself is one's identity, and there is interdependency.

Long-term orientation is not the same as forecasting the future.[84] Uncertainty avoidance is not risk avoidance. "Natural" is a motive for high uncertainty avoidance cultures, less a feminine appeal.[85] Showing people in relation to others can be a reflection of collectivism but also of affiliation needs of feminine cultures. In content analysis of advertising, the picture of a family is assumed to be a reflection of collectivism, but paradoxically, it can also be a reflection of individualism where people are afraid that family values are disappearing. In individualistic cultures, even more families may be found in advertising, because it is the desirable. Advertisers may feel a lesser need to depict families in advertising in collectivistic cultures because the family is a part of one's identity; it is not the desirable. Expecting community relations in websites of collectivistic cultures is a similar example.[86] These may be expected to be found more in individualistic cultures where one has to make an effort to preserve community relations. To collectivists, this is an automatic process. One has to take into account such value paradoxes when formulating research hypotheses.

The culture of researchers tends to play a role in selecting dimensions for analysis. North American researchers tend to ignore the masculinity dimension, which in their cultures may be problematic because of political correctness standards. It seems to conflict with strongly felt values, and many researchers seem unable to understand the essence.[87] For analyzing advertising, the difference between role differentiation and overlapping roles can be a useful observation. Others are overt display of success and the use of strong typography or power words. Female nudity in advertising should not be confused with sex appeal. There is no relationship with masculinity.

One of the most difficult things to overcome for any researcher from any culture is ethnocentrism, that is, the tendency to apply the dimensional frameworks we use and judge the scores obtained from these from one's own culture's point of view and value system.[88]

Sampling Countries for Research

In several cases, different samples of countries lead to different results. The choice of which nations to compare can influence the validity of the findings and reduce the possibility of generalizing findings. Comparisons that include both modern and developing countries produce differences that are hard to interpret. It is not easy to get subclasses of cultures for which valid comparison is possible. Correlations of different groups of countries will have different results. Hofstede's dimension power distance can serve as an example of how different groups of countries show different relationships. Worldwide, for a group of 33 countries of mixed levels of economic development, power distance is correlated with wealth, that is, the higher the GNI per capita, the lower the countries score on power distance, so there is a negative correlation between national wealth and power distance. This relationship does not exist among a group of developed countries. When data for a large group of countries are available, the best advice is to do calculations for the whole sample and for a selection of higher income countries as well.

The relationships between dimensions can vary for different regions. For example, Hofstede's dimension uncertainty avoidance correlates positively with power distance in a wealthy subgroup of countries, but this relationship is nonexistent in a poorer subgroup of countries.[89] This may be related to findings that in richer countries, uncertainty avoidance is negatively related to the penetration of new products, but this relationship tends to be positive under poorer economic conditions.[90]

Different samples of countries can result in different significance of correlations. For several communication technology products, our finding is that the wealthier the group of countries, the more significant the correlations with culture. Finally, when comparing cultural relationships over time, the same countries have to be selected.

Cause-Effect

A frequently asked question is about the cause-effect relationship between culture and social phenomena. Are the characteristics of a social system (e.g., legal, political, or economic system) produced by the personal qualities of the population, or are the personal qualities of people generated by the nature of the social system in which they live?

Also, the relationship between cultural values and behavior is not clear-cut. Collective values can only indirectly influence individual-level behavior, and the causality between values and behavior is complex. A relationship may be found between a country's position on a collective value dimension and societal phenomena, but understanding the causal relationship between the two is quite complicated.[91]

In many cases, common historical learning that has shaped national culture is the best factor to explain variance. But problems of determining whether what is observed is caused by history or is a functional relationship are frequent. A classical controversy of this nature concerns the meaning of the Weberian hypothesis relating Protestant values to capitalist orientations. Is it a "functional" relationship between Protestant values and entrepreneurship, or is the relationship based on shared contacts or common historical learning?[92] The latter is probably the case. Capitalism thrived in countries of a specific cultural configuration that also harbored Protestantism.[93] Weber did not consider Protestantism as a justification for values that were taking root in northern Europe as a result of economic and social developments: increased international trade and personal enrichment. Religious affiliation by itself is less culturally relevant than it is often assumed. If we trace the religious history of countries, what religion a population has embraced seems to have been a result of previously existing cultural value patterns more than a cause of cultural differences. Also, in many cases, cultural values are stronger comparison factors than religious beliefs. Minkov[94] uses as example the fact that Nigerian Muslims are far closer in their values to Nigerian Christians than to Bulgarian Muslims.

Another example is the relationship (in continental Europe) between low English-speaking skills and low usage of the Internet. Both are related with Hofstede's dimension uncertainty avoidance. In strong uncertainty avoidance cultures, people avoid difficulties of language learning[95] as well as innovative behavior with respect to new technology (see also Chapter 5). So the functional relationship is with uncertainty avoidance (see Chapter 4).

Other assumed cause-effect relationships are between economic development and culture. Some theorists see culture as a major determinant of socioeconomic success whereas others see national wealth as a determinant of culture. Schwartz[96] states that socioeconomic and cultural variables powerfully influence each other. Inglehart's findings suggest that economic development is related to culture change away from traditional values and toward self-expression values. However, further analysis of the WVS data by Van de Vliert led to the conclusion that higher levels of economic growth are not related to decreases in traditional values and increases in secular-rational values.[97]

Commercial Value and Lifestyle Research

Lifestyle research for marketing aims to group people according to their value systems as expressed by their lifestyle. For such research, usually large numbers of questions on activities, interests, and opinions are reduced to two basic and bipolar dimensional structures resulting from factor analysis, and the resulting factors are given labels that cover the factor items, as interpreted by the creators of the studies. As a result, the labels will reflect the culture of the developers of the study. This leads to labels like "strivers," "devouts," or "fun seekers" if the study is directed by Americans or to labels like "mythical" or "emotional" by French researchers, whereas British researchers tend to include class-based segment labels. Both concepts and dimensions used in value studies reflect the culture of the home country and cannot be extended to other cultures without losing meaning.

The Stanford Research Institute's values and lifestyles (VALS) program was one of the first value and lifestyle studies. VALS, developed by SRI International, Menlo Park, California,[98] is based on the Rokeach value system. It uses a questionnaire asking about motivations and demographic characteristics that are seen as predictors of consumer preferences. Later, a parallel system called RISC International (after the International Research Center for Social Change in Paris) emerged in Europe. In several other countries, such studies were developed.

The common aspect of these studies is the use of two-dimensional space in which consumption, respondents, and values are placed. The primary dimensions of VALS are *motivations* and *resources*, distinguishing segments or VALS Types labeled *innovators, thinkers, achievers, experiencers, believers, strivers, makers* and *survivors*. RISC distinguished three dimensions: *expansion-stability* (openness to new ideas vs. resistance to change), *enjoyment-responsibility,* and *flexibility-structure.*[99] A consumer styles model by the market research agency GfK-Roper[100] uses two dimensions in terms of consumer needs of which one is labeled *to have* versus *to be* and the other *to lead a passionate life* versus *peace and security*. Segments are formulated in terms of traits (e.g., *open-minded*) and attitudes or desires (e.g., *search for sustainability*).

The VALS segmentation system was developed in the United States, and the values included are typical for the United States. Nevertheless, international research and advertising agencies apply it to other cultures. The questionnaire includes referent statements, such as "I dress more fashionably than most people," and ideological statements, such as "The Federal Government should encourage prayers in public schools,"[101] which makes the survey not very useful for cross-cultural comparison.

CCA, a French system developed in the 1990s, worked with the dimensions *progressive-conservative* and *material-spiritual.* The first dimension reflects the paradox of high power distance and high uncertainty avoidance cultures where people want progress and innovation, but the need for stability makes them conservative.

The Belgian market research agency Censydiam uses theories by the psychoanalyst Adler.[102] According to this theory, consumers develop basic strategies for the management of tension. This focus on anxiety reflects the high score of Belgium on uncertainty avoidance. The results of such studies are often presented without saying that the findings are based on a study among respondents of one specific culture and are not applicable to subjects that are of a totally different culture.

A commercial segmentation system developed by Gallup in Scandinavia, Kompas, works with the dimensions *modern* versus *traditional* and *individual* versus *social* values.[103] The latter dimension reflects the freedom-affiliation paradox: Expressing one's individuality is important, but affiliation needs are even more important and can be conflicting.

A Japanese model developed by advertising agency Dentsu used the dimensions *achiever* versus *membership dependent* and *group merit* versus *intelligent, nonconformist,* which both reflect the individualism-collectivism paradox.

An originally German study of social milieus extended its study to other markets in Europe.[104] In other countries, the structures have become quite different. Social milieus describe the structure of society in terms of social class and value orientations. Within cultures, groups of people are delineated who share a common set of values and beliefs about, for example, work, leisure, and relationships. Groups are labeled in terms of *modern, conservative, proactive,* or *materialist.* These groups are not necessarily similar across cultures.

Sometimes, studies of different countries use similar English-language labels for different typologies or classification cues that can be misleading. One example is the difference between the group *achievers* in VALS and in a Japanese lifestyle study by Dentsu. The achievers in VALS have goal-oriented lifestyles that center on family and career. They avoid situations that encourage a high degree of stimulation or change. They prefer premium products that demonstrate success to their peers. Hiroe Suzuki of Dentsu's information technology center distinguished four life models in Dentsu's lifestyle study:[105] *Achiever, Intelligent, Group Merit,* and *Membership Dependent.* Key words in the description of the achiever in this study were "enterprising," "importance of individuality," and "importance of human relationships," a description that is rather different from the VALS description.

The above may have demonstrated that most lifestyle studies have strong local roots. The cross-cultural validity of international lifestyle instruments remains to be demonstrated.

Summary

This chapter described the value concept and how to research values. Value studies based on the Rokeach Value Survey are used worldwide, although the values are typical for American culture. When translated into other languages, some values become meaningless, and meaningful values of other cultures are overlooked. There are several pitfalls to cross-cultural research, the most important being equivalence of research design and methods. Too many researchers follow the ethnocentric approach of using research designs, questions, or scales developed in one culture for others, resulting in incomparable findings.

The cultural models described in Chapter 4 are based on different measurement concepts of which the most important is the difference between measuring the desirable or the desired. As a result, they will provide different results when using them for understanding differences in consumer behavior and advertising effects.

Transplanting surveys developed in one environment to another that differs significantly cannot lead to an effective strategy. People's values vary by culture, and researchers' values differ as well. If there is no match between the culture reflected in a research model and the culture of the country where it is applied, the outcome will not be meaningful. Using axes of one culture to position brands in another culture is an interesting but not very effective exercise. Increasingly, dimensional models are developed that can be used for secondary analysis of consumption or attitude data. Before using such a model, the research design and the questions must be carefully reviewed. Understanding that the values of one culture cannot be used indiscriminately in another culture should lead toward more refined value studies for developing effective global marketing and advertising strategies.

Notes

1. Hofstede, G. (2004). Epi-dialogue. In H. Vinken, J. Soeters, & P. Ester (Eds.), *Comparing cultures: Dimensions of culture in a comparative perspective* (p. 272). Leiden/Boston: Brill.

2. Rokeach, M. (1973). *The nature of human values.* New York: Free Press.

3. Rokeach, 1973, p. 28.

4. Yankelovich, D. (1994). How changes in the economy are reshaping American values. In H. J. Aaron, T. E. Mann, & T. Taylor (Eds.), *Values and public policy* (pp. 23–24). Washington, DC: Brookings Institution.

5. Kahle, L. R., & Goff Timmer, S. (1983). *A theory and method for studying values and social change: Adaptation to life in America.* New York: Praeger.

6. Halman, L. (2001). *The European Values Study: A third wave.* WORC Tilburg University. PO Box 90153, 5000 LE Tilburg, The Netherlands. E-mail evs@kub.nl.

7. Inglehart, R., Basañez, M., & Moreno, A. (1998). *Human values and beliefs.* Ann Arbor: University of Michigan Press. The complete data files can be downloaded from www.worldvaluessurvey.org

8. European Social Survey (ESS). http://ess.nsd.uib.no (see Appendix B).

9. Reader's Digest Surveys: A Survey of Europe Today, 1970; Eurodata, 1991; Reader's Digest Surveys: Trusted Brands, 2001, 2002, 2003, 2004, continuing on an annual basis, although for recent years the data are less accessible; European Media and Marketing Surveys (EMS), 1995, 1997, 1999, 2007, 2012 (see Appendix B).

10. Asiabarometer. http://www.asiabarometer.org

11. Minkov, M. (2013). *Cross-cultural analysis: The science and art of comparing the world's modern societies and their cultures.* Los Angeles: Sage.

12. Rokeach, 1973, p. 90.

13. Grunert, K. G., Grunert, S. C., & Beatty, S. E. (1989, February). Cross-cultural research on consumer values. *Marketing and Research Today,* pp. 30–39.

14. Kamakura, W. A., & Mazzon, J. A. (1991). Value segmentation: A model for the measurement of values and value systems. *Journal of Consumer Research, 18,* 208–218.

15. Rokeach, 1973, p. 15.

16. Vyncke, P. (1992). *Imago-Management: Handboek voor Reclamestrategen.* Ghent, Belgium: Mys & Breesch, Uitgevers & College Uitgevers, p. 134.

17. Minkov 2013, p. 34.

18. Roland, A. (1988). *In search of self in India and Japan.* Princeton, NJ: Princeton University Press, pp. 90–93, 102–103, 131.

19. Hofstede, G. (2001). *Culture's consequences.* Thousand Oaks, CA: Sage, p. 35.

20. Vyncke, 1992, pp. 133–135.

21. Oppenhuisen, J. (2000). *Een schaap in de bus? Een onderzoek naar waarden van de Nederlander* [A sheep in the bus? A study of Dutch values]. Unpublished doctoral dissertation, University of Amsterdam, The Netherlands.

22. Roland, 1988, p. 240.

23. Srivastava, H. S. (2004). Indian core values of peace and harmony. In Z. Nan-Zhao & B. Teasdale (Eds.), *Teaching Asia-Pacific core values of peace and harmony.* Bangkok: UNESCO Asia and Pacific Regional Bureau for Education.

24. Doi, T. (1985). *The anatomy of self.* Tokyo: Kodansha International, pp. 147–156.

25. Kazuaki Ushikubo was president of Research and Development, Inc., Japan. He developed a model describing Japanese values that is described in Ushikubo, K. (1986). A method of structure analysis for developing product concepts and its applications. *European Research, 18,* 174–184. Quotes in this chapter are from a conversation I had with Mr. Ushikubo in November 1995. Research and Development gave permission to use Mr. Ushikubo's statements and model with the note that the text only partially represents the total concept of CORE, R&D's proprietary lifestyle analysis.

26. Benedict, R. (1974). *The chrysanthemum and the sword: Patterns of Japanese culture.* Rutland, VT: Charles E. Tuttle, p. 129.

27. Eurobarometer survey. (2001). Eurobarometer Report (55). (see Appendix B).

28. Benedict, 1974, p. 192.

29. Benedict, 1974, p. 183; Roland, 1988, pp. 109–110, 262.

30. Students' answers during a seminar on marketing and culture for Russian students from western Siberia, organized by the Finnish Marketing Institute, Brussels, October 2, 1996.

31. Doi, 1985, pp. 84–86.

32. Roland, 1988, pp. 131, 203; Benedict, 1974, p. 290.

33. Letters: A failing role model? [Letter from Mike Dunn of Bamberg, Germany] (1996, April 16). *Newsweek.*

34. Inkeles, A. (1997). *National character.* New Brunswick, NJ: Transaction.

35. Fischer, R. (2009). Where is culture in cross cultural research? An outline of a multilevel research process for measuring culture as a shared meaning system. *International Journal of Cross-Cultural Management, 9*(1), 25–49.

36. Hofstede, G. (2002). Dimensions do not exist: A reply to Brendan McSweeney. *Human Relations, 55*(11), 1355–1361.

37. Douglas, S. P., & Craig, C. S. (2006). On improving the conceptual foundations of international marketing research. *Journal of International Marketing, 14*(1), 1–22.

38. Buchtel, E. (2011, Summer). Triandis Award: A sense of obligation. *Cross-Cultural Psychology Bulletin, 44*, 15–19.

39. Hofstede, G., Hofstede, G. J., & Minkov, M. (2010). *Cultures and organizations: Software of the mind* (3rd ed.). New York: McGraw-Hill.

40. Javidan, M., House, R. J., Dorfman, P. W., Hanges, P. J., & Sully de Luque, M. (2006). Conceptualizing and measuring cultures and their consequences: A comparative review of GLOBE's and Hofstede's approaches. *Journal of International Business Studies, 37*, 897–914.

41. Smith, P. (2006). When elephants fight, the grass gets trampled: The GLOBE and Hofstede projects. *Journal of International Business Studies, 37*, 915–912.

42. Kitayama, S. (2002). Culture and basic psychological processes: Toward a system view of culture: Comment on Oyserman et al. *Psychological Bulletin, 128*, 89–96.

43. Harb, C., & Smith, P. B. (2008). Self-construals across cultures: Beyond independence-interdependence. *Journal of Cross-Cultural Psychology, 39*(2), 178–197.

44. Minkov, 2013.

45. Gelfand, M. J., Bhawuk, D. P. S., Nishi, L. H., & Bechtold, D. J. (2004). Individualism and collectivism. In R. J. House, P. J. Hanges, M. Javidan, P. W. Dorfman, & V. Gupta (Eds.), *Culture, leadership, and organizations: The GLOBE study of 62 societies* (pp. 437–512). Thousand Oaks, CA: Sage.

46. Schmitt, D. P., Allik, J., McCrae, R. R., & Benet-Martínez, V. (2007). The geographic distribution of big five personality traits: Patterns and profiles of human self-description across 56 nations. *Journal of Cross-Cultural Psychology, 38*(2), 173–212.

47. Minkov, 2013.

48. Williams, J. (1991, August). Constant questions or constant meanings? Assessing intercultural motivations in alcoholic drinks. *Marketing and Research Today*, pp. 169–177.

49. Hofstede, 2001, pp. 15–17; Schwartz, S. H. (1994). Beyond individualism/collectivism. In U. Kim, H. C. Triandis et al. (Eds.), *Individualism and collectivism: Theory, method, and applications: Vol. 18. Cross-cultural research and methodology* (pp. 92–93). Thousand Oaks, CA: Sage.

50. Minkov, 2013.

51. Schwartz, 1994, p. 104.

52. De Mooij, M., & Hofstede, G. (2010). The Hofstede model: Applications to global branding and advertising strategy and research. *International Journal of Advertising, 29*(1), 85–110.

53. Fischer, R. (2012). Value isomorphism in the European Social Survey: Exploration of meaning shifts in values across levels. *Journal of Cross-Cultural Psychology, 43*, 883–898.

54. Fischer, R., Vauclair, C. M., Fontaine, J. R. J., & Schwartz, S. H. (2010). Are individual-level and country-level value structures different? Testing Hofstede's legacy with the Schwartz Value Survey. *Journal of Cross-Cultural Psychology, 4*(2), 135–151.

55. Minkov, M. (2007). *What makes us different and similar.* Sofia, Bulgaria: Klasika I Stil, p. 35.

56. Van Herk, H., Poortinga, Y. H., & Verhallen, T. M. M. (2005). Equivalence of survey data: Relevance for international marketing. *European Journal of Marketing, 39*(3/4), 351–364.

57. Van Herk et al., 2005.

58. Hofstede, 2001, p. 463.

59. Oyserman, D. (2006). High power, low power, and equality: Culture beyond individualism and collectivism. *Journal of Consumer Psychology, 16*(4), 352–356.

60. Minkov, 2013.

61. Minkov, 2013, p. 86.

62. Beatty, S. E., Homer, P. M., & Kahle, L. R. (1988). Problems with VALS in international marketing research: An example from an application of the empirical mirror technique. *Advances in Consumer Research, 15,* 375–380.

63. Harzing, A. (2006). Response styles in cross-national survey research: A 26-country study. *International Journal of Cross Cultural Management August 2006, 6* (2), 243–266.

64. Douglas, S. P., & Nijssen, E. J. (2003). On the use of "borrowed" scales in cross-national research. *International Marketing Review, 20*(6), 621–642.

65. Douglas, S. P., & Craig. C. S. (1983). *International marketing research.* Englewood Cliffs, NJ: Prentice-Hall International Editions, p. 192.

66. Williams, 1991.

67. Cheung, G. W., & Rensvold, R. B. (2000). Assessing extreme and acquiescence response sets in cross-cultural research using structural equations modeling. *Journal of Cross-Cultural Psychology, 31,* 187–212.

68. Clarke, I., III. (2001). Extreme response style in cross-cultural research. *International Marketing Review, 18,* 301–324.

69. Wong, N., Rindfleisch, A., & Burroughs, J. E. (2003). Do reverse-worded items confound measures in cross-cultural consumer research? The case of the material values scale. *Journal of Consumer Research, 30,* 72–91.

70. Cheung & Rensvold, 2000.

71. Smith, P. B. (2011). Communication styles as dimensions of national culture. *Journal of Cross-Cultural Psychology March, 42,* 216–233.

72. Johnson, T., Kulesa, P., Cho, Y. I., & Shavitt, S. (2005). The relation between culture and response styles: Evidence from 19 countries. *Journal of Cross-Cultural Psychology, 36*(2), 264–277.

73. Van de Vijver, F., & Leung, K. (1997). *Methods and data analysis for cross-cultural research.* Thousand Oaks, CA: Sage, p. 15.

74. Clarke, 2001.

75. Dolnicar, S., & Grün, B. (2007). Cross-cultural differences in survey response patterns. *International Marketing Review, 34*(2), 127–143.

76. Smith, 2006.

77. Schwartz, S. H. (2007). Cultural and individual correlates of capitalism: A comparative analysis. *Psychological Inquiry, 18*(1), 52–57.

78. A more detailed comparative analysis of the models by Hofstede and Schwartz can be found in De Mooij, M. (2011). *Consumer behavior and culture: Consequences for global marketing and advertising* (2nd ed.). Thousand Oaks CA: Sage, pp. 39–45.

79. Magnusson, P., Wilson, R. T., Zdravkovic, S., Zhou, J. X., & Westjohn, S. A. (2008). Breaking through the cultural clutter: A comparative assessment of multiple cultural and institutional frameworks. *International Marketing Review, 25*(2), 183–201.

80. Vanderstraeten, J., & Matthyssens, P. (2008). Country classification and the cultural dimension: A review and evaluation. *International Marketing Review, 25*(2), 230–251.

81. Søndergaard, M. (1994). Research note: Hofstede's consequences: A study of reviews, citations and replications. *Organization Studies, 15,* 447–456.

82. Hofstede, 2001.

83. Milner, L. M., & Collins, J. M. (2000). Sex-role portrayals and the gender of nations. *The Journal of Advertising, 29,* 67–79.

84. Minkov, 2007, pp. 24–25.

85. Rhodes, D. L., & Emery, C. R. (2003). The effect of cultural differences on effective advertising: A comparison between Russia and the US. *Academy of Marketing Studies Journal, 7*(2), 89–105.

86. Singh, N., Kumar, V., & Baack, D. (2005). Adaptation of cultural content: Evidence from B2C e-commerce firms. *European Journal of Marketing, 39*(1/2), 71–86.

87. Hofstede, G. (2006). What did GLOBE really measure? Researchers' minds versus respondents' minds. *Journal of International Business Studies, 37,* 882–896.

88. Yaprak, A. (2008). Culture study in international marketing: A critical review and suggestions for future research. *International Marketing Review, 25*(2), 215–229.

89. Müller, H. P., & Ziltener, P. (2004). The structural roots of values: An anthropological interpretation of Hofstede's value dimensions. In H. Vinken, J. Soeters, & P. Ester (Eds.), *Comparing cultures: Dimensions of culture in a comparative perspective* (p. 139). Leiden/Boston: Brill.

90. Yeniurt, S., & Townsend, J. D. (2003). Does culture explain acceptance of new products in a country? *International Marketing Review, 20*(4), 377–396.

91. Jagodzinski, W. (2004). Methodological problems of value research. In H. Vinken, J. Soeters, & P. Ester (Eds.), *Comparing cultures: Dimensions of culture in a comparative perspective* (p. 118). Leiden/Boston: Brill.

92. Przeworski, A., & Teune, H. (1970). *The logic of comparative social inquiry.* New York: Wiley-Interscience, pp. 51–56.

93. Hofstede, 2001, p 114.

94. Minkov, 2013.

95. Several data on foreign language speaking show a relationship with uncertainty avoidance: The higher countries score on this dimension, the fewer foreign languages people speak. With respect to the English language, the argument can be that the countries with a language structure that is similar to the English language (all Germanic languages) have an advantage in learning English. However, also within the group of Germanic language countries (United Kingdom and Ireland excluded), a significant correlation is found between English speaking and low uncertainty avoidance (e.g., the percentage of people who say they speak English well enough for conducting a conversation, in EMS 1997, 7 countries, $r = -.82^*$).

96. Schwartz, 2004, p. 65.

97. Van de Vliert, E. (2007). Climatoeconomic roots of survival versus self-expression cultures. *Journal of Cross-Cultural Psychology, 38*(2), 156–172.

98. Holman, R. H. (1984). A values and lifestyles perspective on human behavior. In R. E. Pitts, Jr., & A. G. Woodside (Eds.), *Personal values and consumer psychology* (pp. 35–54). Lexington, MA: Lexington Books, D. C. Heath.

99. RISC International. (1995). *Why people buy* [Brochure]. Paris (www.risc-int.com).

100. GfK Roper Consumer Styles, 2007–2008. Retrieved November 26, 2012 from http://www.intomartgfk.nl/imperia/md/content/intomart/presentation_roper_consumer_styles.pdf

101. VALS survey, retrieved November 26, 2012, from http://www.strategicbusinessinsight.com/vals/surveynew.shtml

102. Callebaut, J., Janssens, M., Lorré, D., & Hendrickx, H. (1994). *The naked consumer: The secret of motivational research in global marketing.* Antwerp: Censydiam Institute, p. 106.

103. Hansen, F. (1998). From lifestyle to value system to simplicity. *Advances in Consumer Research, 25,* pp. 181–195.

104. Homma, N., & Ueltzhoffer, J. (1990, June 18–20). The internationalization of everyday-life research markets and milieus. *ESOMAR Conference on America, Japan and EC '92: The Prospects for Marketing, Advertising and Research,* Venice, Italy. See also http:// www.motivaction.nl

105. Received from Hiroe Suzuki, November 1995. Earlier description in Suzuki, H. (1998, June 18–20). *Japanese lifestyle, life models and applications to creative concepts.* Paper presented at a meeting of the ESOMAR Conference on America, Japan and EC '92: The Prospects for Marketing, Advertising and Research. Venice.

CHAPTER 7

Culture and Communication

Because the United States is the birthplace of marketing and advertising theory and techniques, American cultural assumptions are at the root of philosophies of how advertising works, not only in the United States but also in other parts of the world. If we want to understand how advertising works across cultures, we'll first have to learn how communication works. Styles of communication vary by culture and are influenced by deeply ingrained habits and philosophies. One of the clearest distinctions is between high-context and low-context communication. Related to this distinction is how people process information and their expectations of the role, purpose, and effect of communication. Is advertising persuasive by nature, or can it have another role in the sales process? Understanding how advertising works across cultures is of great importance for international companies. With advanced information technology, new forms of communication have emerged. These are hybrid forms of communication, a mix of oral and literate communication. Understanding this is the basis for proper usage of these new media for marketing communications. Like advertising, the way people use these and how the content is designed, such as website design, are influenced by culture.

Communication

All living human beings communicate through sounds, speech, movements, gestures, and language. Communication involves many human activities: speaking, listening, reading, writing, viewing, and creating images. How people communicate is based on cultural conventions that are adhered to in interacting with other people, in producing and sending messages and in interpreting messages.

In Western communication studies since the 1960s, many definitions, theories, and models of communication have been developed, varying from process-oriented models to models that focus on signs, symbols, and the conveying of meaning. Scholars in other parts of the world have developed different theories of the purpose of communication and how communication works, but theories of marketing communication have mainly been derived from Western communication theory that defines communication more or less as a linear process. According to Asian scholars,[1] the Western process approach is not appropriate for understanding communication in most of Asia.

A central element of this book is that in order to understand communication, we have to be interested in people, their being, needs, motives, and so on. Wilbur Schramm, one of the founders of North American communication theory already pointed at this stating,

> Let us understand clearly one thing about it: communication (*human* communication, at least) is *something people do*. It has no life of its own. There is no magic about it except what people put into it. There is no meaning in a message except what the people put into it. When one studies communication, therefore one studies people—relating to each other and to their groups, organizations and societies, influencing each other, being influenced, informing and being informed, teaching and being taught, entertaining and being entertained—by means of certain signs which exist separately from either of them. To understand the human communication process one must understand how people relate to each other.[2]

When studying communication and its effects, we have to understand how individuals communicate and their effects on others, in particular how communication and its effects are influenced and modified by the social systems in which they take place. Understanding interpersonal relationships across cultures is important for understanding how forms of mass communication work and even more for understanding the new electronic media that are hybrid forms of personal and mass communication. Many of the topics discussed in Chapter 5 serve as the basis for understanding the differences in how people relate to each other across cultures that apply to communication across cultures.

Communication Theory

In classic North American communication theory, communication in a broad sense includes all the procedures by which one mind may affect another. All communication is viewed as persuasive, and communication is information based. Communication in its most general sense refers to a process in which information is shared by two or more persons and which has consequences for one or more of the persons involved. Implicit in the North American models is a separate self of individuals whose decisions are information based. This tends to be illustrated by a model of communication, as depicted in Figure 7.1, which includes the source or sender of a message (person, organization, company, brand), the message itself

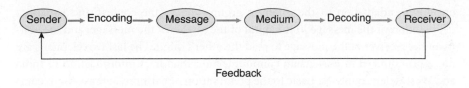

Figure 7.1 Classic Model of Communication

(story, picture, advertisement), the medium (any carrier of the message: a story-teller, newspaper, television, Internet), and the receiver of the message (person, consumer).

In this communication process, a message is selected and encoded in order to transfer meaning. The receiver of the message must be able to receive the message via the medium and decode it. The sender is responsible for effective communication by properly coding the message. The model is sender-oriented. Yet the sender of the message, after the message has been sent, wants to get feedback to find out if the message has been received and understood. The model doesn't include empathy with the receiver on the part of the sender of the message before or while sending a message. The sender who formulates and shapes the message uses his or her cultural framework, which will be reflected in the content and in the form of the message. In mediated communication, the media are also shaped by the culture of the people who produce them, both in content and in form. The receiver of the message uses his or her cultural framework when decoding the message. In the decoding process, selective perception will operate in the sense that people will best understand messages that fit existing schemata. This concerns content, form, and style of the message.

The sender orientation of Western communication models is like a monologue and mostly valid for North American and North European communication. In South and East Europe, the dialogue provides a different representation of the communication process, including empathy with the receiver of the message. For example, the Russian scholar Michael Bakhtin[3] views communication as a dialogue. In the dialogue, there is *utterance*, which refers to language spoken in context, so communication by definition is *contextual*. It includes the content of the conversation, the communicator's attitude toward the subject, and responsiveness on the part of the person being addressed. The speaker anticipates the viewpoint of the other and adapts communication to that anticipation. This anticipation or empathy that is also recognized in Asian communication is not found as an essential aspect in Western communication theory which generally is presented as a one-way process where feedback is mainly necessary to be certain that persuasion has taken place.

Next to empathy, several other aspects are central to communication in Asia, where, as in most other collectivistic cultures, communication varies with roles and relationships, with concern for belonging to the community and fitting in and occupying one's proper place.[4] Included are the need for harmony in interpersonal relationships, causing indirectness in communication; distinction of in-group and out-group; adaptation to the different groups and to the context and situation; deliberation of the message in the mind of the sender of the message; and the ability of the receiver of the message to read the other's mind. The last two elements are more pronounced in East Asian communication than in communication in India and West Asian countries. Basic to the preservation of harmony in East Asian communication is what Miike[5] describes as a narrow exit and a wide entrance. The "exit" of the sender of a message is small as the message will exit only after careful internal evaluation. This evaluation causes pauses and silence. The "entrance" of the receiver of the message is wide open. Not only is the message indirect, but both parties also use nonverbal cues that have to be interpreted. This is the mind-reading process. Also during the interpretation process, there will be some periods of silence to help the internal evaluation process. Whereas in the Western communication model, the sender is responsible for effective communication, in the East Asian model, both receiver and sender are responsible.

Whereas the purpose of North American communication is persuasion and communication theory has been derived from Aristotle's rules for persuasive communication, in Asia, communication takes place according to rules for behavior inherited from the old Confucian and Buddhist philosophies.[6] Buddhism offers guidelines for how people should communicate, following the Buddhist ideal of social order.[7] Communication must be socially appropriate. Also in Hinduism, the positions of the sender and the receiver are not static. Communication is a two-way process resulting in mutual understanding. It does not emphasize dominance of the sender. Commonness of experience has to take place. The effectiveness of any message depends on the communication environment. The same message may have different meanings in different contexts.[8]

Of the differences between Western and Asian communication, silence is one of the most distinguishing elements of communication. Whereas in the United States each day on average time spent on conversation is 6 hours 43 minutes, it is 3 hours, 31 minutes in Japan. Silence as a form of speech in East Asian cultures is greatly influenced by both the Buddhist and Taoist emphasis on tranquility. It is the mind sounding inside, rather than the mouth talking outside. Silence, then, becomes an effective nonverbal expression for mutual understanding.[9]

Silence in communication is found mostly in collectivistic cultures that are also long-term oriented. In collectivistic cultures that are short-term oriented, communication is a continuous stream of dialogue, of speaking and listening. For the Akan of Ghana, silence, unless requested for some scared practices, is considered an insult. Communication is a two-way street, and several proverbs confirm this. For example, "One mind cannot deliberate communal issues by itself."[10] African communication is influenced by commonness and a central African concept, *Ubuntu,* that includes concepts such as humanity, affection, and caring. An individual owes his or her existence to the existence of others. "I am" because "you are," and "you are" because "I am." We can be human only through others. The African conception of being and communication is also musical. As stated by the Senegalese philosopher Senghor, the African being can be formulated as "I feel, I dance the other; I am."[11] One of the most distinguishing aspects of African communication is that oral literacy is at the base. Oral literacy uses all sorts of mnemonic devices to help memory, such as repetitions and metaphors, which are indirect modes of communication. The love of speech, the word, dialogue, the rhythm of talk is thought to be the soul of Africa. The love of speech is reflected in the many artistic forms of rhetoric as by praise singers and storytellers.[12]

Also in Latin America, where in most areas the combination of collectivism and short-term orientation is found, speech is more important than silence although in some areas silence is part of communication. Discourse-related studies among the peoples of Lowland South America at the end of the 20th century have found dialogue in which the addressed repeats the utterances of the principle speaker in whole or part, a means to indicate understanding, assent, and respect. Findings are also of elaborate greeting processes, body language, and use of prolonged silence.[13] The elaborate and sometimes extreme style of these cultures is recognized in the extreme response styles in survey research, which is very different from the moderate style of East Asians.[14]

In sum, in such collectivistic cultures as are found in Asia and Africa, but also Latin America, human communication is an exchange or interaction, more than merely a way that information moves from one place to another.[15] Yet there are important differences across collectivistic cultures with respect to long-/short term orientation that are also related to literacy and orality.

Orality and Literacy

Countries have trodden different paths toward literacy, and the impact of writing has never everywhere been the same. Communication and the cultural products originating in oral cultures are structured in a different way than those developed in literate cultures. These differences can be recognized in communication styles, literary genres, the media, advertising, and electronic communication today.

Oral communication is simply said mouth to mouth communication, a speech or conversation, but derived forms are specific literary genres, such as legends, tales, and stories. Any non-literal communication is a process where information is exchanged between individuals or groups through a common system of orality or visual features, such as symbols, signs, or behaviors. Today, primary oral culture hardly exists as every culture knows of writing and has some experience with its effects. Yet many cultures to varying degrees preserve much of the mind-set of primary orality. Oral cultures, even when becoming literate, tend to keep their oral style.[16] Oral literacy includes several forms of communication that are found less in textual or literate cultures, such as redundancy and repetition. These characteristics, for example, use of metaphors and flowery and elaborate language can still be found in various communication styles such as in Russian, Arabic, and Spanish.

Literacy generally points at writing, reading, learning, and developing knowledge. Reading and writing developed in a different way and at different places in the various parts of the world. In northern Europe, literacy developed with the advent of Protestantism because individuals were expected to read the Bible personally or individually, not hear it read by others. Countries dominated by Catholicism, such as Spain and Italy lagged.[17] In East Asia, it was Confucianism which had emphasized written communication and de-emphasized oral communication.[18]

Generally, literacy is described as the ability to read and write, understand, interpret, create, communicate, compute, and use printed and written materials. In 2009, the 10 countries scoring highest on average reading ability of 15-year-olds were in East Asia and Northern Europe. The degree of literacy as measured by UNESCO[19] correlates significantly with the long-term orientation dimension. An explanation of the relationship with long-term orientation is from Tannen,[20] who finds that oral tradition is strong in cultures that are oriented toward the past. In more future-oriented Asian thinking, the spoken word is viewed as existent only in the moment it is spoken. Writing is the tool for permanent recording, whereas an oral utterance has vanished as soon as it is uttered. However, in writing, something can be totally and completely deleted, whereas in speaking, what is said cannot be unsaid. Nonverbal features as in oral conversation are not available in writing.

> You may wrinkle your face up until it cracks while you write, but this expression will not show up on the written page. You may yell or whisper or sing as you compose sentences, but the words as they fall on the page will not reflect this behavior.[21]

Literate tradition has not replaced oral. No individual is either "oral" or "literate." Rather, people use devices associated with both traditions in various settings. Oral formulaic thought and expression do not disappear as soon as one starts writing, and many modern cultures that have known writing for centuries have never fully interiorized it, such as Arabic and Mediterranean cultures. Ong[22] argues that "many of the contrasts often made between 'Western' and other views seem reducible to contrasts between deeply interiorized literacy and more or less residually oral states of consciousness."

Oral residues have an impact on people's thinking patterns, people's mind-sets. People in an oral society had to rely on real situations for the understanding of abstract things; they had to conceptualize and verbalize all their knowledge with more or less close reference to the human life world. Concepts are used in situational, operational frames of reference that are minimally abstract and that are close to the living human world.[23] This may relate to the differences in abstract and concrete thinking and the differences found in information needs between the Mediterranean countries of Europe and the North. Knowledge is not necessarily gained by active information seeking, but is an implicit part of human communication flows, as described in Chapter 5 (p. 140). As literacy is said to influence all sorts of cognitive processes like categorization and abstract and logical reasoning, in literate cultures, people may prefer searching for facts and data on the Internet whereas more oral cultures may get their information from interpersonal contacts and/or social media. Across Europe, it is in the North that people first started reading books, and it is individualism-collectivism that still explains differences in book reading. Several European surveys have asked people how many books they read. Since 1970 in Europe, heavy book reading has been related to individualism, low power distance, and low uncertainty avoidance, representing Northwest Europe, the same area where people started reading the Bible individually. Figure 7.2 shows how, for Europe, the relationship between individualism and book reading has remained constant between 1990 (12 or more) and 2007 (5 or more).

The need to understand the difference between orality and literacy is growing with the electronic age because of the hybrid communication function of the various Internet and mobile media where we can see a form of communication that can be called digital orality: informal spoken conversation, but written. The difference definitely is more than that between writing and talking; it distinguishes between ways of information seeking and decision making. These influences can be found through individualism/collectivism and the long-/short-term orientation dimension. For example, in cultures scoring high on the long-term orientation dimension, people trust the typical literate Internet-facilitating features, such as search engines and product reviews, whereas in the short-term oriented cultures, people trust more in their family and friends.[24]

The electronic media, in particular the mobile phone, are hybrid forms of oral and literate communication, and oral cultures use it in different ways than literate cultures do. Searching for hard facts on the Internet is an activity found more in literate cultures whereas electronic Word-of-Mouth (eWOM), as via social media, can be viewed as an oral communication form. A logical consequence of orality is preference for the talking, or speaking, function of the mobile phone. An interesting

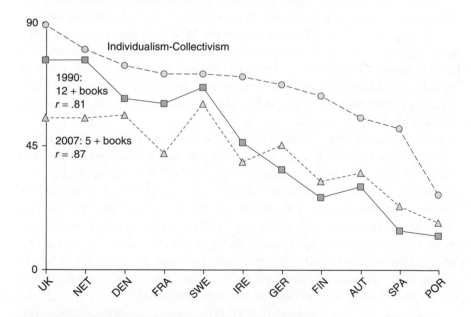

Figure 7.2 Individualism and Book Reading in Europe

SOURCE: Data from Hofstede (2001) (see Appendix A); *Reader's Digest* 1991 and Eurobarometer European Cultural Values, 2007 (see Appendix B).

development is usage of some of the social media, such as Twitter. Basically, this is oral communication, talk written down. But it goes against Tannen's observation that what is said cannot be unsaid and that what is written down can be deleted. What is written on the Internet is not easily deleted.

Culture and Communication Styles

The need for context, directness versus indirectness, literacy or orality, and the purpose of communication, altogether make up communication styles of cultures, both interpersonal communication style and mass communication styles. Various other factors explain differences in communication style. Rapid speech rate, for example, suggests to Americans that the speaker makes true and uncensored statements, whereas for Koreans, slow speech implies careful consideration of others and context.[25]

Interpersonal Communication Styles

Gudykunst and Ting-Toomey distinguish interpersonal communication styles between *verbal* and *nonverbal* each with further distinctions, and found these differences explained by power distance and uncertainty avoidance by which they mapped different cultures.[26]

Verbal styles can be distinguished between *verbal personal* and *verbal contextual*. The two styles focus on personhood versus situation or status. Verbal personal style is individual-centered language; it enhances the "I" identity and is person oriented (e.g., English). Verbal contextual style is role-centered language; it emphasizes a context-related role identity (e.g., Japanese, Chinese), which includes different ways of addressing different persons according to their status and/or situation. For example, the Japanese language adapts to situations where higher- or lower-placed people are addressed.

Verbal personal style is linked with low power distance (equal status) and individualism (low context), whereas verbal contextual style is linked with high power distance (hierarchical human relationships) and collectivism (high-context).

Another distinction is between elaborate, exacting, and succinct verbal style. *Elaborate* verbal style refers to the use of rich, expressive language which often is a remnant of orality and mostly found in collectivistic and short-term oriented cultures. *Exacting* or *precise* style is a style where no more or no less information than required is given, mostly found in individualistic cultures that have been literate for a long time. *Succinct* or *understated* style includes the use of understatements, pauses, and silences. Silences between words carry meaning.

Gudykunst and Ting-Toomey[27] found that high-context cultures of moderate to strong uncertainty avoidance tend to use the elaborate style. Arab cultures, for example, show this elaborate style of verbal communication, using metaphors, long arrays of adjectives, flowery expressions, and proverbs. Low-context cultures of weak uncertainty avoidance (e.g., United States, United Kingdom) tend to use the exacting style. The succinct style is found in high-context East Asian cultures (e.g., Japan).

Nonverbal style possibilities are *unique-explicit* and *unique-implicit* style and *group-explicit* and *group-implicit* style, which echo the self-orientation of individualism versus the group orientation of collectivism, and *accessibility-inaccessibility,* which refers to the degree to which the home environment emphasizes the openness or closedness of occupants to outsiders. Strong uncertainty avoidance cultures perceive outsiders as more threatening than do weak uncertainty avoidance cultures, and power distance reinforces that.

Together, verbal and nonverbal styles can explain how we communicate. Figure 7.3 clusters countries according to these styles and summarizes the different interpersonal communication styles.

Communication in the cultures in the two left quadrants is direct, explicit, verbal, and personal. People like written communication. In business, they prefer using e-mail to using the phone. They use the exacting style and like data. The sender is responsible for effective communication. Communication in the mostly collectivistic cultures in the two right quadrants is more implicit and indirect. France and Belgium, which are individualistic, are exceptions, and communication can be both explicit and implicit. Communication is role centered. In cultures in the top right quadrant, the elaborate style is used, and communication can be inaccessible. In the lower right quadrant, the succinct style is found. Particularly

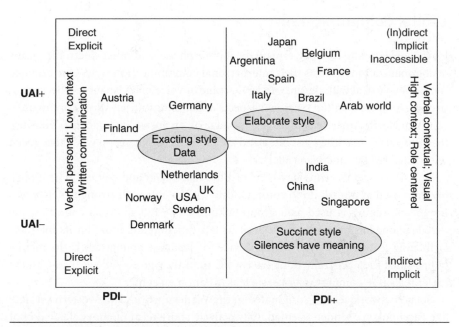

Figure 7.3 Interpersonal Communication Styles

SOURCE: Gudykunst, W., & Ting-Toomey, S. (1988). *Culture and interpersonal communication.* Newbury Park, CA: Sage, adapted by De Mooij 2004; Data from Hofstede (2001) (see Appendix A).

in East Asia, communication implies empathy or "understanding without words."[28] Children learn to "read the other's mind," to read subtle cues in the communication from others. They are expected to feel the mood or air of each interpersonal situation and improvise appropriate social behavior and communication depending on the reading of the contextual features.[29] So here, the receiver is responsible for effective communication. In particular, the difference between the indirect style of the East and the direct style of the West can cause grave misunderstandings in international business.[30]

The most pronounced difference is between the direct versus the indirect style, or the extent to which speakers reveal their intentions through explicit verbal communication. In the direct style, wants, needs, and desires are expressed explicitly. The indirect verbal style refers to verbal messages that conceal the speaker's true intentions. Wordings such as *absolutely* and *definitely* to express buying intentions are an example of the direct style, whereas *probably* or *somewhat* are examples of the indirect style.

Different communication styles influence writing styles, so academic writing styles also vary across cultures. Editorial boards of most marketing and advertising journals are dominated by Americans who set strict rules and formats for academic papers, according to American writing style. Authors who do not follow this tend to be rejected. As a result, scholars from outside the United States are poorly represented in marketing journals. Thus, American students are deprived as so few studies from outside the United States can be accessed.[31]

Digital Communication

How people use the Internet, e-mail, the mobile phone, and other electronic means of communications reflects their interpersonal communication style. One example is how people deal with the answering machine or voice mail. Japanese—because of stronger emphasis on the relational aspects of communication—find it more difficult than North Americans to leave a message on an answering machine. They use their answering machines less often and are more likely to hang up when they reach one, compared to American callers.[32]

In Asia, usage of technology is related to relationship and context. The mobile phone is used as a medium to communicate with people with strong ties, whereas instant messaging is used as a group-talking tool.[33] But in some countries, the mobile phone has been adopted less for its talk function and more for its Internet-facilitating features. The key digital device for Japanese youngsters is the mobile phone since they generally don't have a PC until they go to college. The Chinese prefer real-time communications, such as instant messaging.[34]

Social network services originated in the Western world, and Western services like Facebook are sender oriented; they activate short-term memory. They do not allow for dialogue. Yet people in collectivistic cultures have become the leaders in social networking on the Internet as they allow for continuous flows of information. However, people use social network services in different ways, and local services have adjusted to local cultural habits. The number of contacts (what in Western terms are called *friends*) vary enormously (see Chapter 8).[35] The numbers of friends people have across cultures correlate with short-term orientation. It is a manifestation of self-enhancement.

Blogging has become a global phenomenon, but the degree to which people blog, their motives, and their topics, vary by country. In 2006, there were more blogs in the Japanese language than in the English language, and the French spent five times as much time blogging as the Americans. For the French, the blog is like the café where they discuss everyday life and politics, fitting in with French argumentative culture.[36] Japanese tend to care less whether their blog influences others, and they are reluctant to reveal their identity, even with the use of aliases. Generally, Asians tend to disclose themselves less to friends and strangers than Westerners do.

Whereas in the West, the Internet provides an ideal context for self-disclosure and people tend to release verbal emotions more than they would in a person-to-person context, self-disclosure has a negative connotation for East Asians. If one partner reveals too much about himself or herself, the other may take it as inappropriate or as an indicator of incompetence.[37] However, for collectivists also, the Internet appears to be a context that allows for more self-disclosure than face-to-face relationships do. Yet North Americans do not perceive East Asians as self-disclosing near as much as East Asians perceive themselves to be.[38] North Americans view their East Asian partners as indirect without sufficient self-disclosure. At the same time, East Asians feel that their North American partners are overexplicit and rude.[39]

The combination of talking and texting on the mobile phone makes it the most hybrid medium of all new technology. It allows illiterate people to connect with others who are not close by, and it also allows literary expressiveness. In many countries, the texting (SMS) function has created a new type of language. Across cultures, people have also adopted the mobile phone to express themselves in their own culturally appropriate way. Whereas in individualistic cultures people use texting for efficiency reasons, in collectivistic culture, also those with oral literacy, people use it to express themselves in style. One example is Senegal, where students tend to send SMS poems, in particular romantic poems, in their own language (Wolof), which generally is not used for writing, as the language in which students learn to write is French. One example of such poetry[40] is the following:

> May the sun of godsend lighten up your way, may the sky of peace be above you, may you walk on the earth of happiness, (with) the wind of love refreshing you.

When people of different communication styles interact with each other online, they may encounter unexpected communication behaviors and barriers due to cultural differences. Across cultures, people construct culturally specific norms and patterns of online interactions and relationships and will continue to do so as the role of the Internet evolves and expands.

Chapter 8, on media and culture, will deal with the electronic media in more depth.

Mass Communication Styles

Three aspects determine mass communication styles: content, form, and style. Differences in form and style of mass communications reflect interpersonal communication styles as well as differences in orality and literacy. The influence of culture on content, form, and style can be recognized in literature, mass media programs, public relations, and advertising.

American television, for example, is more action oriented than Finnish television. Domestically produced Finnish video dramas are much more static. They sacrifice action and setting for dialogue and extreme close-ups.[41] Both the Russians and the Japanese depict boredom in their novels whereas American novels do not do much with the theme. "Fun is not a Russian concept," says Moscow sociologist Maria Zolotukhina, speaking of the difficulties faced by the creators of a Russian version of the popular American children's television program *Sesame Street*.[42] The "happy ending" is rare in Japanese novels and plays whereas American popular audiences crave solutions. This is reflected in American TV dramas and commercials. The essence of much drama in Western, individualistic literature is an eternal struggle of the hero ("to be or not to be"). Chinese essayist Bin Xin has noted that real tragedy has never existed in Chinese literature because the Chinese have hardly any struggles in their minds.[43] Also, how people behave in literature and what motivates them reflect cultural values. An example from literature is the Italian *Pinocchio*, by Carlo Collodi; Pinocchio is an obedient and dependent child, as compared with the nephews of Disney's Donald Duck, who are much more independent and less obedient. Strong uncertainty avoidance is reflected in the novel *Das Schloss (The Castle)*, by Franz Kafka, in how the main character K. is affected by bureaucracy. *Alice in Wonderland*, where the most unreal things happen, is a typical work to originate in a culture of weak uncertainty avoidance, England. It is no surprise that in the same culture, the Harry Potter books originated and *The Lord of the Rings*. Press releases from American public relations agencies reflect U.S. culture. They are short and to the point. A characteristic of Latin American literature is a general aesthetic outlook, moving into a world of the fantastic and bizarre, a *baroque artistic style*. The mystic and supernatural is reflected in Latin American novels in which fantastic and incredible things may occur in mythical cities as in Gabriel Garcia Márquez's novel *One Hundred Years of Solitude*.

Underlying Models

The basis of communication styles of the different world regions are the age-old philosophies of these regions: those of Aristotle, the Buddha, and Confucius.

At the base of Western mass communication theory is Aristotle's *On Rhetoric*. It is, in the broadest sense, the theory and practice of spoken or written eloquence: the art or study of effective and persuasive use of language when addressing a public.[44] A style of speaking or writing especially regarding a particular subject is also a feature of rhetoric. The Western description includes the following essential characteristics of rhetoric: (1) It has to accomplish an intended goal; (2) it is geared toward influencing human choices on specific matters that require immediate attention; and (3) it concerns persuasion pursued at public forums. The rhetorically competent communicator consciously uses symbols to create understanding and to form, strengthen, or change an attitude in their audience.

The rules of rhetoric are known as the five canons of rhetoric: (1) invention (how to persuade), (2) arrangement (structure of a coherent argument), (3) style (presentation of the argument to stir the emotions), (4) memory (memorize a speech), and (5) delivery (making effective use of voice, gesture, etc.). In particular, the first three steps can be recognized in much of Western advertising. An example is the French commercial for Freedent (Illustration 7.1). It demonstrates that the boy doesn't dare to kiss because of bad breath and uses a puppet to show his affection. The argument stirs negative emotions that can turn positive.

Illustration 7.1 **Freedent, France**

Five steps in the Buddhist rhetorical model are (1) theme glorification; (2) explain the main idea; (3) allegory; (4) karma, prove the truthfulness of a theme; and (5) summarize and conclude by giving peace of mind.[45] Again, such steps can be recognized in advertising styles, in particular the use of allegory and metaphors. Illustration 7.2 shows pictures from a Chinese TV commercial for Shangri-La hotels. A hiker gets lost in deep snow and falls down. The wolves come and cover him, so he doesn't freeze. The tagline is "Embrace a stranger as one's own."

Illustration 7.2 **Shangri-La hotels, China**

Three of the steps in the Hindu rhetorical model are (1) simplification, (2) reach commonness of experience, and (3) aesthetic delight.[46] *Aesthetic delight,* as one of the communication effects, can be recognized in Hindu cultural products, their temples, art, TV programs, and in advertising. An example of a television program reflecting this was the Indian soap opera *Ramayana.*[47] An advertising example is the ad for Happydent in India (illustration 7.3). It shows examples of humans serving as lamps which don't shine: as head lights of a car, as lamp posts, as chandeliers, and so on. A wise old man is not able to read a book. The protagonist takes a piece of Happydent, and all lamps start to shine.

These different rhetorical styles are part of mass communication style and forms of advertising used in the various parts of the world. Other elements are appeals and motives as well as specific forms and executional aspects, which will be elaborated in the next sections.

Illustration 7.3   Happydent, India

Advertising Styles

Advertising can be viewed as a symbolic artifact or communication product constructed from the conventions of a particular culture. The sender crafts the message in anticipation of the audience's probable response, using shared knowledge of various conventions. Receivers of the message use the same body of cultural knowledge to read the message, infer the sender's intention, evaluate the content, and formulate a response. Cultural knowledge provides the basis for interaction. If advertising crosses cultures, it lacks the shared conventions. Content, form, and style reflect different roles of advertising across cultures.

In order to analyze differences in advertising styles across culture, four elements of advertising style can be distinguished. Each will vary by culture:

1. Appeal (including motives and values)

2. Communication style (e.g., explicit, implicit, direct, indirect)

3. Basic advertising form (e.g., testimonial, drama, entertainment)

4. Execution (e.g., how people are dressed, the look of kitchens, or male-female roles)

An example of a typical appeal for high uncertainty avoidance cultures is purity, as in the German advertisement for Gerolsteiner, a German mineral water brand

(Illustration 7.4). An example of an individualistic appeal is the international advertisement for Vodafone (Illustration 7.5), which focuses on the individual. The Spanish Airtel (acquired by Vodafone) used a collectivistic appeal, an example of group identity (Illustration 7.6). Chapter 9 describes more examples of relationships between culture and advertising appeals. How the basic forms used in advertising reflect culture will be discussed in Chapter 10. The term *execution* refers to the casting and activities of people, as well as the setting. A British kitchen, for example, looks different from a German or a Japanese kitchen. In this chapter, we focus on the cultural aspects of communication styles used in advertising.

Illustration 7.4
Gerolsteiner, Germany

Illustration 7.5
Vodafone International

Illustration 7.6
Airtel, Spain

A major distinction is between direct style of individualistic cultures and indirect style of collectivistic cultures. In advertising, the direct style uses the personal pronoun *(you, we)*, whereas the indirect style doesn't address people directly but uses indirect methods, such as drama or metaphors. There are variations in indirectness among collectivistic cultures that vary with long-/short-term orientation. Cutler et al.[48] examined advertisements from eight different countries (United States, United Kingdom, France, India, Japan, Turkey, Taiwan/Hong Kong, and Korea) and measured the use of a direct, personalized headline, which appeared to be related to individualism.

Examples of the direct style are ads from the United Kingdom for Centrum (Illustration 7.7) and ProViva (Illustration 7.8), and a German ad for Dove shampoo, saying "can your hair cope with the morning hair brush test?" (Illustration 7.9). Examples of the indirect approach are the international advertisement for Thai Airlines (Illustration 7.10), which uses the eye of the needle to symbolize a small world, and a Spanish ad for Heineken (Illustration 7.11), which reflects the collectivist Friday feeling in an indirect way.

An example of the indirect style from Latin America is a Brazilian TV commercial for Sara Lee Pilão coffee. The message is that it is strong coffee. This message is conveyed by showing just a cup of coffee and a continuous squirt of milk that doesn't make the coffee look lighter. This is a purely visual demonstration.

Illustration 7.7
Centrum, United Kingdom

Illustration 7.8
ProViva, United Kingdom

Illustration 7.9
Dove Shampoo, Germany

Illustration 7.10
Thai Airlines, International

Illustration 7.11
Heineken, Spain

Direct style communication also tends to be more verbal whereas indirect style tends to be more visual. Whereas U.S. advertising utilizes more copy, Japanese advertising uses more visual elements. Chinese-speaking consumers tend to judge a brand name based on its visual appeal whereas English speakers judge a brand name based on whether the name sounds appealing. In Asia, visual symbolism is a key aspect of a firm's corporate identity.[49] The differences between cultures with respect to verbal and visual orientation are reflected in all aspects of marketing communications, such as corporate identity, brand name, package design, advertising styles, and website design. Cultures can be mapped according to their advertising styles, similar to communication styles, using power distance and uncertainty avoidance.[50] However, for mass communication, the new long-/short-term orientation data appear to be a better mapping tool, together with individualism-collectivism, because this dimension distinguishes between literate and oral styles. Cultures thus can be mapped as in Figure 7.4.

The advertising style in the two right quadrants, where cultures are individualistic, is direct and explicit, more verbal than visual, and it uses argumentation. Within this direct-explicit distinction, there are also differences, for example, with respect to the degree of self-enhancement and hard sell arguments for short-term effects. Within the quadrants, we find differences with respect to the other dimensions. For example, in cultures of strong uncertainty avoidance, advertising is more serious and structured. The execution of the visuals will be detailed, often including demonstration of how the product works. In the weak uncertainty avoidance cultures, where ambiguity is tolerated, more humor is used in advertising. Many centrally developed television commercials for Anglo-American brands in the household-cleaning-products category and personal products have used the personalized testimonial format. They are carefully directed to focus on the personality of the endorser and not to include any implicit nonverbal behavior. For the U.S. market, the typical person endorser and spokesperson have a positive impact on recall.[51]

The two quadrants at the left where cultures are collectivistic include styles that are implicit and indirect using symbolism and visuals. The cultures in the upper left quadrant use less argumentation and more symbolism, metaphors, and aesthetics. These are also literate cultures, and playing with words and use of taglines in

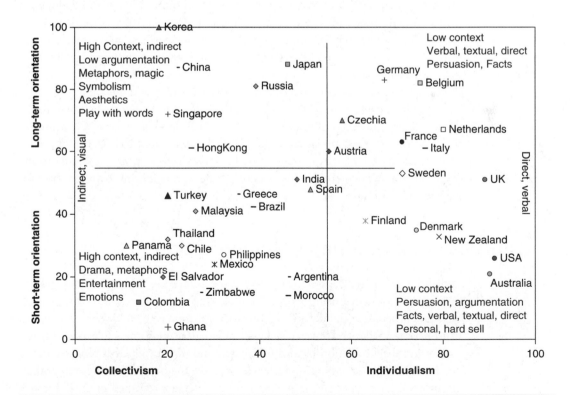

Figure 7.4 Advertising Styles

SOURCE: Data from Hofstede et al. (2010) (see Appendix A).

advertising is popular. But verbal expression is not direct and double entendre is appreciated.[52] An example of indirectness in Japanese advertising is saying "These times exist in life, when someone wants to go somewhere very comfortable" instead of saying "This car offers the most comfortable interior and the smoothest drive."[53] Communication is subdued and works on likeability. The use of aesthetics and entertainment as an advertising form is characteristic of this communication style. Chinese consumers like visual and vivid ads with images. If celebrities are involved, they are not likely to address the audience directly. They play a more symbolic role and associate more with the product rather than endorsing it in a direct way. Visual metaphors and symbols are used to create context and to position the product or brand in its "proper place." They must ensure group norms and help maintain face. Next to the use of drama and metaphor, visuals, play with words (visually), songs, and symbolism are important in advertising in these cultures.

Moving to the lower left quadrant, we see India and Spain in the border area, where communication may be more direct, and a mix of Hispanic, African, and a few Asian cultures that are collectivistic as well as short-term oriented. Advertising style is mostly indirect and uses drama and metaphor although these cultures are more verbal in their communication. For India, a more direct communication style was noticed by Roland,[54] who states, "Indian modes of communication operate more overtly on more levels simultaneously than do the Japanese." In this cluster are mostly oral cultures with intensive interpersonal communication and dialogue as in soaps and other forms of drama. Drama (see Chapter 10) is an indirect style based on dialogue that fits countries such as Spain as well as Latin American cultures. Variations are found between masculine and feminine cultures. In Italy, high on masculinity, show is favored, and the drama form tends to be theatrical and often not based on real life. In Spain, drama style is softer, and metaphorical stories are used to place the product in a context that provides meaning. Although in the United States the drama style is also used, it is even more popular in the countries in the lower left quadrant. Drama in the United States is more "slice-of-life," a form that demonstrates how a product is used in everyday life, whereas drama in the right quadrants is entertainment, meant to build a relationship between the consumer and the brand.

The Purpose of Marketing Communication

The different styles discussed before reflect the differences in the purpose of advertising and how advertising works. In individualistic cultures, advertising must persuade whereas in collectivistic cultures, the purpose is to build relationships and trust between seller and buyer. The desire of Japanese consumers to establish trusting, in-group-like relationships with suppliers and their products is reflected in the tendency of Japanese advertising to focus on inducing positive feelings rather than on providing information.[55] The different purposes are reflected in the difference in timing and frequency of verbal or visual mention of the brand name in television commercials.[56] In a typical Japanese television commercial, the first identification of a brand, company name, or product occurs later than in a typical U.S. television commercial. Japanese advertisers tend to take more of a commercial's time to develop trust, understanding, and dependency. In Japan, the brand name is shown for a longer time than in the United States, where it is more frequently mentioned verbally. In Chinese commercials, brand acknowledgment also appears later than in U.S. commercials.[57] In advertising theory and practice, both the way advertising styles or forms are distinguished and the measurement of advertising effectiveness are based on Western thinking about the purpose of advertising. An example is the distinction between informational and emotional advertising. For the measurement of advertising effectiveness, other models should be developed next to the standard persuasion model.

Informational Versus Emotional

In much Western advertising theory, a distinction is made between informational and emotional advertising. All that is not factual is considered emotional. "Emotional," "transformational," "evaluative," or "feeling" messages are often contrasted with "rational," "informational," "factual," or "thinking" appeals. This suggests that emotions do not carry information. "Logical, objectively verifiable descriptions of tangible product features" and "emotional, subjective impressions of intangible aspects of the product" are viewed as contrasting. This approach to advertising theory varies across Western cultures and is even less applicable to Asian advertising theory. When following this distinction in Asia, most indigenous advertising, being indirect, can be characterized as emotional.

When discussing the role of emotions in advertising, one must distinguish between emotional stimuli (advertising content) and emotional response. Percy, Rossiter, and Elliott[58] view emotion as one of four main processing responses to advertising: attention, learning, accepting or believing what the ad says, and emotion that is stimulated by the ad. An emotional response will mediate what is learned and whether or how a particular point is accepted. Typical emotional responses may be connected to specific motivations. An example is problem removal, portrayed by annoyance with the problem followed by relief, or social approval, and ending with brand usage that flatters the user.

This description of the role of emotions fits the way emotions are exploited in Anglo-American advertising content, which is different from European advertising. Whereas in the United States emotions in advertising tend to be used as part of the argument (dirty goes with disgust and clean with relief or pleasure), in other cultures, in particular in the south of Europe, advertising reflects the pure emotional relationship between consumer and brand without the argumentation. In some cultures, the word *emotion*, in itself, is popular in advertising. An example is the Spanish pay-off *Auto Emoción* for the Seat make of cars. A U.S. example is a TV commercial for Dixie disposable plates (Illustration 7.12). A French example is for Kelloggs (Illustration 7.13) and an Italian for Alfa Romeo (Illustration 7.14). U.S. Dixie uses disgust to debase the competitive brand, which is not strong enough to

Illustration 7.12 Dixie, United States

Illustration 7.13 Kellogg's, France

Illustration 7.14 Alfa Romeo, Italy

use in a microwave oven. The competitor's plate becomes soft; the spaghetti falls and damages the shoes. In the French Kellogg's TV commercial, the actor drops the milk jug and spills the milk. He starts crying because he cannot enjoy the cereal. In the Italian ad for Alfa Romeo, a young man sees the car and gets so excited that he grabs a bottle of champagne and sprays everybody.

As described in Chapter 5, emotions, such as happiness and sadness, are universal only when described abstractly. Rules for emotional displays are culture-specific. Expressive behavior varies by culture, which makes the emotional behavior of people of one culture often not understood by members of another culture. Also, what Americans call emotional can be perceived as sentimental by members of other cultures. Several researchers have tried to classify the emotional content and responses to advertising. A classic example is a study by Holbrook and Batra,[59] who identified dimensions of emotional content in U.S. advertising and linked these to emotional responses. To understand the role of emotions in advertising across cultures, this study should be replicated in other cultures. Typologies of emotional content can be useful to measure the effectiveness of emotional appeals for one culture but not for others.

Because of the strong focus on verbal communication, problem solving, and assumed need for information in low-context cultures, Western advertising people tend to think of the rational elements as the content and the emotional element as execution, seeing them as separate entities. One cannot separate what is said from how it is said. Consumers see the whole picture; they don't see the separate elements.

Advertising theories are also based on the assumption of an active information-gathering and rational consumer who wants to solve problems. To operationalize the distinction between informative and noninformative, the Resnik and Stern[60] typology is usually applied, in which the criterion for considering an advertisement informative is whether the informational cues are relevant enough to assist a typical buyer in making an intelligent choice among alternatives. What is informational for members of one culture may not be informational for members of another culture. As described in Chapter 5, information-gathering behavior varies across cultures, and the degree to which people view themselves as well-informed consumers correlates with individualism. The problem-solving and argumentation approach to advertising will be less effective in cultures where people don't consciously search for information in the buying process and consumers' decision making is emotion based instead of information based. It basically is the cultural configuration of individualism, low power distance, and low uncertainty avoidance, which is Northwest Europe and the Anglo-Saxon world where people consciously search for information. The role of information in advertising is more important in these cultures than it is elsewhere.

Measuring Advertising: Persuasion or Likeability

Because of the different purposes and effects of advertising, measuring effectiveness will need to be different across cultures. Traditional measures of advertising effectiveness are based on persuasiveness of an advertisement. The basic procedure is measurement of purchasing intentions before and after exposure. All elements of advertising—words and pictures—tend to be evaluated on their persuasive role in the sales process. Measures include attitude toward the advertisement (Aad), brand attitude (Abr), purchase intention (PI), memory, and market performance.[61] In Chapter 5, we discussed the varying relationships between attitude and behavior across cultures, as well as how buying intention operates differently, so these measures will not work equally well in all parts of the world. A second limitation is that most effectiveness studies are conducted in laboratory settings, out of context, which may cause bias even more in collectivistic cultures than it does in individualistic cultures.

Also in advertising effectiveness research in the Western world, it has been recognized that persuasion measures do not capture a key element in the link between communication and the thoughts and behavior of consumers. That missing link is the degree to which an advertisement has personal significance for the consumer. When people experience advertising, they do not behave as passive, objective receivers of messages about brands. They interpret the advertisement for themselves, using their own worldview as an interpretative filter.[62] It seems inappropriate to use persuasion tests based on rational, linear processing to test advertising meant for people who process information in a different way. In collectivistic and long-term oriented cultures, using a hard sell or directly addressing consumers turns them off instead of persuading them. Advertising must build trust, and advertising must be liked. Also, Eastern demands such as proper conduct should be a criterion for effective advertising, as in the Buddhist communication model. A Korean study measuring advertising creativity found that advertising should be socially appropriate, sincere, and pleasing, an aspect that has not emerged from past studies among U.S. populations.[63]

Next to persuasion, therefore, likeability has become a measure to predict sales. The following are aspects that contribute to the likeability of advertising:[64]

- Meaningful (worth remembering, effective, believable, true-to-life, not pointless)
- Does not rub the wrong way (not irritating, worn out, phony)
- Warm (gentle, sensitive)
- Pleases the mind (entertaining, aesthetic)
- Be socially appropriate (following the Buddhist demand for proper conduct)

Likeability will be a better effectiveness measurement for cultures where pleasing the consumer is an important objective of advertising. In most cultures where the purpose of communication is to raise trust between the company and the consumer or to build an emotional relationship between consumer and brand, likeability will be a better purpose and measurement criterion than persuasion. Generally, it would be advisable to develop measurement criteria that are appropriate for the advertising styles, purposes, and desired effects for specific countries or clusters of cultures.

A new area for developing effectiveness measurement systems is advertising on the Internet. Next to simple click-through measurement (see Chapter 8), several other aspects play a role. One example is a study of advertising responses in Korea, which found that Korean youngsters respond more positively to advertising on a website after they have revealed personal information on that site.[65] Also, for Internet advertising in Asia, trust may be an important criterion.

How Advertising Works

Most models of how advertising works are based on an assumed hierarchy of effects and on sequential thinking. Although academics worldwide have modified this hierarchy-of-effects model, the sequential way of thinking remains the basis of much of the thinking about how advertising works.

The Hierarchy of Effects

The underlying assumption of how advertising works is that advertising takes people from one stage to another. These linear or sequential or "transportation" models are based on a logical and rational process.[66] This hierarchy-of-effects model has strongly influenced American advertising style and the style used by U.S. advertisers elsewhere. Also, later models, such as the FCB matrix,[67] which categorizes products according to the degree of involvement and cognitive-affective attitude components, are derived from the concept of multiple hierarchies.

High and Low Involvement

One of the early sequences in theory of how advertising works was that people would first learn something about a product or brand, then form an attitude or feeling, and consequently take action, which meant purchasing the product or at least going to the shop with the intention of buying. This sequence is summarized as "learn-feel-do." It was later seen as mainly applicable to products of "high involvement," such as cars, for which the decision-making process was assumed to be highly rational. This so-called high-involvement model assumes that consumers are active participants in the process of gathering information and making a decision.

In contrast, there are low-involvement products, such as detergents or other fast-moving consumer goods, with related low-involvement behavior when there is little interest in the product. The concept of low involvement is based on Herbert Krugman's[68] theory that television is a low-involvement medium that can generate brand awareness but has little impact on people's attitudes. The low-involvement sequence was assumed to be "learn-do-feel." Again, knowledge comes first, after that purchase, and only after using the product would one form an attitude.

The FCB planning model suggests four sequences in the process by which advertising influences consumers: (a) learn-feel-do, (b) feel-learn-do, (c) do-learn-feel, and (d) do-feel-learn. The first two sequences are related to high involvement; the third and fourth sequences are low involvement. International advertising scholar Gordon E. Miracle[69] argued that for the Japanese consumer, another sequence is valid: "feel-do-learn." Japanese advertising is based on building trust, a relationship between the company and the consumer. The purpose of Japanese advertising is to please the consumer and to build *amae* (dependency),[70] and this is done by the indirect approach. As a result, "feel" is the initial response of the Japanese consumer, after which action is taken: a visit to the shop to purchase the product. Only after this comes knowledge. Miracle suggests that this sequence also applies to Korean and Chinese consumer responses. It may well apply to other collectivistic cultures.

Miracle summarized the logic of advertising in two distinct ways. The logic of advertising in Western societies is basically to tell the audience the following:

a. How you or your product is different.
b. Why your product is best, using clearly stated information and benefits.
c. Consumers then will want to buy, because they have a clear reason or justification for the purchase.
d. If they are satisfied, consumers will like and trust the company and the product and make repeat purchases.

The logic of advertising in Japan, which is probably valid for most Asian collectivistic cultures, is essentially the reverse:

a. Make friends with the target audience.
b. Prove that you understand their feelings.
c. Show that you are nice.
d. Consumers will then want to buy because they trust you and feel familiar with you (i.e., the brand and the company).
e. After the purchase, consumers find out if the product is good or what the benefits are.

Later models continue to follow the assumption that the advertising concept is what classical rhetoricians call an "argument from consequence," following the cause-effect way of thinking. Petty and Cacioppo's[71] elaboration likelihood model (ELM) is one of the most advanced U.S. models of how advertising works. Taking into account the role of involvement, it states that persuasion follows a central route, peripheral route, or both. Within the central route, a person engages in thoughtful consideration (elaboration) of the issue-relevant information (arguments) within a message, so actively thinking about the arguments in the message is the central route. When the person is not motivated to think about the arguments, the peripheral route is followed. In the theory, the peripheral route generally includes visual cues like the package, pictures, or the context of the message.

The theory is embedded in Western advertising practice, which uses pictures as illustration of words. Various studies have been conducted to find the influence of pictures, in both the central route and the peripheral route, reviewing affective responses as determinants of persuasion. In collectivistic cultures, where people process advertising holistically and pictures provide the context, the theory may not apply.

Visuals in Advertising

Little is known about how consumers from different cultures process visual images in print advertisements. There are significant cross-cultural differences in pictorial perception. People from different cultural backgrounds are likely to interpret the imagery included in advertising in different ways. Imagery is an important element of advertising, yet it is undervalued in research because of the historical focus on verbal communication. The phrases "copy research" and "copy testing," which are used for testing effectiveness of advertising, including visuals, demonstrate the bias toward thinking in verbal stimuli.

Visuals have been used for standardizing print advertisements worldwide with the underlying assumption that consumers from all around the world can "read" a picture whereas the copy of the advertisement often needs to be translated. These highly standardized visual campaigns, however, do not always convey a uniform meaning among audiences. For example, Benetton's ad showing a black woman nursing a white baby won awards for its message of unity and equality in Europe. At the same time, the ad stirred up controversy in the United States because many believed it depicted a black nanny in the subordinate role as a slave.[72] It is a misconception that visuals are universally understood across cultures. Pictures fit into schemata people have, and schemata vary by culture. A picture, meant in one culture to be associated with freedom (e.g., a lion), may be known in another culture to represent strength.[73] Volkswagen showed a black sheep in a flock in Italy in order to portray the VW Golf owner as an independent self-assured person, but the black sheep doesn't carry the same symbolism in many other cultures. Whereas a black sheep in Italy is the symbol of independence and going one's own way, in other cultures, it is a symbol of the outcast.[74] People can derive different meanings from the same message because contextual people will "see" more in the message than is intended by the producer of the message. Because in high-context cultures people are used to contextual messages, they will read more in pictures and derive "hidden" meaning from a visual image. Even for simple visual images with highly explicit information, the high-context audience may try to construct metaphorical meaning that is not intended by the sender of the message.

Differences in perception and visual processing result in a range of differences in the use of pictures in advertising. A multi-country comparison of visual components of print advertising in the United States, United Kingdom, France, Korea, and India[75] found variations with respect to the size of the visual, frequency of usage of photographs and product portrayals, the size of the product, usage of metaphors, and frequency of persons in general and, specifically, women and children, depicted in advertising.

Also, music used in advertising needs careful consideration. Although music in advertising that is culturally incongruent may enhance memory, it doesn't improve attitude toward the advertisement.[76]

The eternal dilemma of advertising is whether to follow the conventions of advertising for a particular product category in a particular culture or to be distinctive in order to raise awareness and find a place in people's memories. Within countries, the danger of using distinctive, unusual information in advertising to attract attention is that it will not fit in consumers' schemata and will be discarded. This risk is even greater across cultures than within cultures because people's schemata vary.

Appreciation of Advertising in General

In the discussion of how advertising works, another aspect of advertising plays a role: appreciation of advertising in general. In the United States, consumers' attitudes toward advertising in general have been found to influence attitudes toward individual advertisements and brand attitude. Across countries, several factors influence perceptions of advertising in general: the political climate, culture, and the advertising landscape of a country. In small markets, where international advertisers dominate with messages that do not fit the culture of the consumer, people tend to dislike advertising more than in large markets with much homegrown advertising. U.S. students, for example, have been found to have a significantly greater number of affective responses to advertising than Danish and Greek students.[77]

A universal finding is that advertising in general is praised for its economic effects, whereas it is criticized for its social effects.[78] In developing economies, expectations of the economic effects tend to be higher than in developed economies. A 1994 study found that Russians at that time viewed advertising very positively. They saw it as an "engine of trade."[79] Studies comparing people's attitudes toward advertising in the United States and Asian countries found more favorable attitudes toward advertising in Asia than in the United States, which was attributed to economic development and the development of the advertising industry: the more developed, the less favorable the attitude.[80] Data from TGI[81] for 12 countries worldwide of mixed economic development confirm this relationship. The percentages of respondents who agree with the statement, "I find TV advertising interesting and quite often it gives me something to talk about," correlate significantly with low GNI per capita ($r = -.79***$) and with low individualism ($r = -.62*$). An explanation may be that in collectivistic cultures, where advertising is indirect and entertaining, it doesn't offend consumers the way it does in individualistic cultures, in particular when combined with masculinity as in the United States, where conflicts are not viewed as threatening and where consumers can be approached in a somewhat aggressive, direct way. For example, in the United States, comparative advertising is viewed as informative whereas the people of Taiwan view it as distasteful.[82]

Appreciation of advertising is also related to media usage. Across countries, reading the news in newspapers every day goes together with viewing advertising in newspapers as a source of new product information.[83] For television, we see similar relationships. Heavy TV viewing is related to a positive attitude toward advertising on TV. The percentages of heavy viewers correlate positively with the percentage of respondents saying that advertising on TV is a useful source of product information ($r = .66***$).[84]

Thus, certain value patterns make some people generally more receptive to advertising as a phenomenon than others, which must be taken into account when comparing advertising effectiveness across borders.

Website Design

The Internet has become one of the most important means of communication. International companies have to go beyond allowing for only foreign names, zip codes, and countries; currency formats; units of measurement; international telephone numbers; and translation and adapt their websites to the culture of the user. People appear to perform information-seeking tasks faster when using the web content created by designers from their own culture.[85] Cultural adaptation not only enhances ease of use on the website but also leads to more favorable attitudes toward the website, which in turn affects the intention to buy.[86]

For website design, the same laws operate as for other communications. Across cultures, people vary in the ways they want to be addressed. Values and motives vary as well as communication styles. For example, university websites in feminine cultures have a softer approach and are more people oriented than websites of universities of masculine cultures, which are more focused on achievement.[87] Local websites of India, China, Japan, and the United States not only reflect cultural values of the country of their origin but also seem to differ significantly from each other on cultural dimensions. A striking feature of Chinese websites is the recurrent image of the family theme. Japanese websites exhibit clear gender roles and are rich in colors and esthetics with pictures of butterflies, cherry blossoms, or other nature scenes. Indian websites prominently depict the titles of the employees to demonstrate hierarchy. U.S. websites are low-context, direct, informative, logical, and success-oriented with prominent independence themes.[88] Also, local websites for global brands distinguish between low- and high-context communication with more literal visuals in countries such as the United States, United Kingdom, and Germany and more symbolic visuals in countries such as Japan, Korea, and China.[89] McDonald's uses culturally relevant approaches in their websites to profess its slogan "I'm lovin' it": people alone or together, images of individuals separate or together with the product, more text, or more pictures. High-context cultures use more animation and images of moving people than low-context cultures, and the images promote values characteristic of collectivistic cultures.[90] The United Kingdom leads both in text-heavy layout and shorter pages, whereas South Korea leads both in visual layout and in longer pages. South Korea utilizes much more multimedia presentation than the United States and the United Kingdom, where presentation more often is based on text only.[91] There are significant differences between East and West in terms of interactive communication styles used by corporate websites. High-context Eastern websites employ less consumer-message and consumer-marketer interactivity than low-context Western websites. High power distance explains less consumer-marketer interactivity because of a larger gap between marketers and consumers. Collectivism explains more group activities among consumers.[92] So in high-context cultures where people are more motivated by social interaction, online marketers should generate more consumer interaction, such as discussion forums and chat rooms, whereas in low-context cultures where people search for information, online marketers should emphasize information features, such as keyword search and virtual product display.[93]

In short, along with culture, there is variation in the way information is presented; the amount of data used; the use of extreme claims; rhetorical style; the use of visuals or animation; the degree to which information is explicit, precise, and direct; and the option to contact people.[94] Companies reaching their local customers through the traditional media do not have international customers to worry about, but the Internet is available for the world to see. Therefore, it is critical for companies to develop culturally designed international websites.[95] The more the design of a website conforms to culturally familiar communication styles and cultural habits, the more trust is established.[96] Also, designers of web banners tend to follow their own cultural values. They take the same mental approach to their creative activity as do advertising copywriters for traditional media.[97]

Based on content analysis of a large number of business-to-business websites, Usunier & Roulin[98] argue that for global business-to-business communication, high-context cultures are at a relative disadvantage, as the Internet doesn't provide the context that high-context communication needs to be processed, and as a result, these websites are easier to read by people of the same culture but not by people of other cultures, which restricts the usefulness. High-context communication styles may be detrimental to the design of business-to-business websites, making them less readable, less effective in the use of colors and graphics, and less interactive for the global audience. Thus, the advice is to design business-to-business websites following low-context communication rules and/or employ low-context communication designers. On the other hand, Pollach[99] found that for Asian visitors to corporate websites, online game-animated intros are important factors, more than for European visitors, who view animated flash intros as a web design error because of their lack of usability. This is an argument in favor of adapting corporate websites targeting global audiences. Apart from such practical aspects, most of the differences in communication styles discussed in the previous chapters play a role when designing websites.

Design

Design is a means of communication. Color communicates corporate position. Whereas blue is the corporate color in the United States, red is the winning business color in East Asia.[100] Taglines and brand logos in Korea are more symbolic than those in the United States.[101] There is one logo design rule that seems universal: the divine proportion (a ratio of 1:1.618). Many successful global logos follow this rule.[102]

Yet across cultures, corporate identity design follows different rules as can be discovered from manuals for corporate identity design. For the purpose of shaping and maintaining corporate identity, companies develop an "identity standards manual," which is a guide to managing the application of the corporate identity visual system, or how an organization uses logotypes, typography styles, names, and architecture to communicate its corporate philosophy. In high-context cultures, these manuals include more nonverbal features (logo and symbol), traditions and customs (history, values), features defining the context of the communication, accessories or decorative elements, and people (uniforms). In low-context cultures, these manuals include more textual features (name and publications) and direct messages (e.g., incorrect applications); manuals are more prescriptive and simpler than in high-context cultures where manuals use more indirect language and are more complex because of use of indirect language and also have more sections. [103]

Unlike American cartoons, which tend to be bold and full of aggressive colors, the characters by Japanese Sanrio, the owner of Hello Kitty, are more subtle, with rounder features, more pastel colors, and a kind of coziness that strikes a chord in Japan. Sanrio also gives more freedom to designers to adapt to the context than consistency-loving American companies would.[104] The Dutch Dick Bruna sets strict guidelines for the Miffy character. Designers who want to design for other cultures should be aware of the fact that cultural variations may result in different product designs. Designers usually have a deeper knowledge about their own culture than about others and therefore are better able to design products for them.[105] Chapter 11 offers more information in product and packaging design and culture.

Summary

Human communication follows age-old patterns that are still relevant today. Knowing cross-cultural differences in both interpersonal and mass communication is necessary to understand how advertising works and how the media function. How communication works is culture-bound. Also, the roles and function of advertising varies. In one culture, advertising is persuasive by nature; in another, it must be liked in order to build trust between companies and consumers. Thus, models of one culture cannot be projected to other cultures. Different verbal and nonverbal communication styles can be recognized in both interpersonal and mass communication, and culture clusters can be defined where one or the other style prevails. People process information in different ways. For some, pictures contain more information than words; for others, the only way to convey meaning is verbal. These differences are also relevant for e-communications. Academics and researchers across cultures have disputes about the different theories of how advertising works. Maybe no one is right, or, maybe all are right. People look at how advertising works from the perspective of their own culture, which may indeed be very different from the perspective of their counterparts in other cultures. The consequence of the different roles of advertising across cultures is that international advertisers cannot use one standard for measuring effectiveness worldwide. Other communication-related differences are website design and design in general. Design is a communication tool and a few examples are given of how culture influences design.

Notes

1. In particular, authors like Yoshitaka Miike, Guo-Ming Chen, and Wimal Dissanayake have worked on development of Asiacentric communication theory counter to the dominance of Eurocentric communication theory.

2. Schramm, W. (1974). The nature of communication between humans. In W. Schramm & D. F. Roberts (Eds.), *The process and effects of mass communication* (p. 17). Urbana: University of Illinois Press.

3. Holquist, M. (1990). *Dialogism: Bakhtin and his world*. London: Routledge.

4. Singelis, T. M., & Brown, W. J. (1995). Culture, self, and collectivist communication. *Human Communication Research, 21*, 354–389.

5. Miike, Y. (2010). Enryo-Sasshi Theory. In R. L. Jackson II & M. A. Hogg (Eds.), *Encyclopedia of identity* (Vol. 1, pp. 250–252). Thousand Oaks, CA: Sage; The model was developed by Ishii, S. (1984). Enryo-Sasshi Communication: A key to understanding Japanese interpersonal relations. *Cross Currents, 11*(1), 49–58.

6. Kosaka, T. (2010). Listening to the Buddha's own words: Participation as a principle of the teachings of the Buddha. *China Media Research, 6*(3), 94–102.

7. Dissanayake, W. (2010). Development and communication in Sri Lanka: A Buddhist approach. *China Media Research, 6*(3), 85–93.

8. Adhikary, N. M. (2010b). *Sancharyoga*: Approaching communication as a *Vidya* in Hindu Orthodoxy. *China Media Research, 6*(3), 76–84.

9. Ishii, S., & Bruneau, T. (1994). Silence and silences in cross-cultural perspective: Japan and the United States. In L. A. Samovar, R. E. Porter, & E. R. McDaniel (Eds.), *Intercultural communication: A reader* (7th ed., pp. 246–251). Belmont, CA: Wadsworth.

10. Ansu-Kyeremeh, K. (2005). Communication in an Akan political system. In K. Ansu-Kyeremeh (Ed.), *Indigenous communication in Africa: Concept, applications and prospects* (pp. 177–193). Accra: Ghana Universities Press.

11. In Jahn, J. (1961). *Muntu: The new African culture.* New York: Grove Press, p. 164.

12. Morrison, J. (2005). Forum theatre: A cultural form of communication. In K. Ansu-Kyeremeh (Ed.), *Indigenous communication in Africa. Concept, applications and prospects* (pp. 130–140). Accra: Ghana Universities Press.

13. Beier, C., Michael, L., & Sherzer, J. (2002). Discourse forms and processes in indigenous Lowland South America: An areal-typological perspective. *Annual Review of Anthropology, 31*, 121–145.

14. Smith, P. B. (2011). Communication styles as dimensions of national culture. *Journal of Cross-Cultural Psychology, 42*(2), 216–233.

15. Fortner, R. S. (2007). *Communication, media, and identity. A Christian theory of communication.* Lanham, MD: Rowman & Littlefield.

16. Ong, W. J. (1982). *Orality and literacy: The technologizing of the world.* London: Routledge.

17. Lyons, M. (2010). *A history of reading and writing in the Western world.* Basingstoke, UK: Palgrave Macmillan.

18. Yum, J. O. (1987). Korean Philosophy and Communication. In D. L. Kincaid (Ed.), *Communication theory: Eastern and Western perspectives* (pp. 71–86). San Diego, CA: Academic Press.

19. UNESCO Institute for Statistics. http://www.uis.unesco.org/literacy/

20. Tannen, D. (1984). Spoken and written narrative in English and Greek. In D. Tannen (Ed.), *Coherence in spoken and written discourse* (pp. 21–40). Norwood, NY: Ablex.

21. Tannen, D. (1983). Oral and literate strategies in spoken and written discourse. In R. W. Bailey & R. M. Fosheim (Eds.), *Literacy for life: The demand for reading and writing* (pp. 79–96). NY: Modern Language Association.

22. Ong, 1982, p. 29.

23. Ong, 1982.

24. Goodrich, K., & De Mooij, M. (2013). How "social" are social media? A cross-cultural comparison of online and offline purchase decision influences. *Journal of Marketing Communications.* In press.

25. Oyserman, D., Coon, H., & Kemmelmeier, M. (2002). Rethinking individualism and collectivism: Evaluation of theoretical assumptions and meta-analyses. *Psychological Bulletin, 128*, 3–72.

26. Gudykunst, W., & Ting-Toomey, S. (1988). *Culture and interpersonal communication*. Newbury Park, CA: Sage, pp. 99–116.

27. Although the configuration of dimensions chosen by Gudykunst & Ting-Toomey explains much of the differences in interpersonal communication, adding the new data for the long-/short-term orientation dimension might add to the explanation. It would, for example, place Japan together with the other East Asian cultures. We will use this dimension for explaining the differences in styles of mass communication.

28. Kobayashi, Y., & Noguchi, Y. (2001). Consumer insight, brand insight, and implicit communication: Successful communication planning cases in Japan. In M. S. Roberts & R. J. King (Eds.), *The proceedings of the 2001 special Asia Pacific conference of the American Academy of Advertising*.

29. Miyahara, A. (2004). Toward theorizing Japanese interpersonal communication competence from a non-Western perspective. In F. E. Jandt (Ed.), *Intercultural communication* (p. 283). Thousand Oaks, CA: Sage.

30. Sanchez-Burks, J., Lee, F., Choi, I., Nisbett, R., Zhao, S., & Koo, J. (2003). Conversing across cultures: East-West communication styles in work and non-work contexts. *Journal of Personality and Social Psychology, 85*(2), 363–372.

31. Rosenstreich, D., & Wooliscroft, B. (2006). How international are the top academic journals? The case of marketing. *European Business Review, 18*(6), 422–436.

32. Miyamoto, Y., & Schwarz, N. (2006). When conveying a message may hurt the relationship: Cultural differences in the difficulty of using an answering machine. *Journal of Experimental Social Psychology, 42*, 540–547.

33. Kim, H., Kim, G. J., Park, H. W., & Rice, R. E. (2007). Configurations of relationships in different media: FtF, e-mail, Instant Messenger, mobile phone, and SMS. *Journal of Computer-Mediated Communication, 12*(4), article 3.

34. Liu, M., & Zoninsein, M. (2007, December 24). New data suggest China isn't lagging on Internet social networking: It's just innovating differently. *Newsweek*, pp. 48–49.

35. Van Belleghem, S. (2010). Social media around the world. InSites Consulting. Retrieved February 22, 2012, from http://www.slideshare.net/stevenvanbelleghem/social-networks-around-the-world-2010

36. Moerland, R. (2006, August 20). Frans weblog is een café (French weblog is a café). *NRC Handelsblad*, p. 18.

37. Chen, G. M. (1995). Differences in self-disclosure patterns among Americans versus Chinese. *Journal of Cross-Cultural Psychology, 26*, 84–91.

38. Ma, R. (1996). Computer-mediated conversations as a new dimension of intercultural communication between East Asian and North American college students. In S. C. Herring (Ed.), *Computer-mediated communication: Linguistic, social, and cross-cultural perspectives* (pp. 173–185). Amsterdam & New York: John Benjamins.

39. Yum, Y. O., & Hara, K. (2005). Computer-mediated relationship development: A cross-cultural comparison. *Journal of Computer-Mediated Communication, 11*(1). Retrieved from http://jcmc.indiana.edu/vol11/issue1/yum.html

40. Lexander, K. V. (2011). Texting and African language literature. *New Media & Society, 13*(3), 427–443.

41. Levo-Henriksson, R. (1994, January). *Eyes upon wings: Culture in Finnish and US television news* (Unpublished doctoral dissertation, Oy. Yleisradio Ab., Helsinki), p. 84.

42. Perspectives. (1996, September 9). *Newsweek*, p. 11.

43. Li, Z. (2001). *Cultural impact on international branding: A case of marketing Finnish mobile phones in China* (Academic dissertation, University of Jyväskylä, Finland).

44. Ong, 1982.

45. Ishii, S. (1992). Buddhist preaching: The persistent main undercurrent of Japanese traditional rhetorical communication. *Communication Quarterly, 40*(4), 391–397.

46. Dissanayake, W. (2009). The desire to excavate Asian theories of communication: One strand of the history. *Journal of Multicultural Discourses, 4*(1), 7–27.

47. Burch, E. (2002). Media literacy, cultural proximity and TV aesthetics: Why Indian soap operas work in Nepal and the Hindu diaspora. *Media, Culture & Society, 24*(4), 571–579.

48. Cutler, B. D., Erdem, S. A., & Javalgi, R. G. (1997). Advertiser's relative reliance on collectivism-individualism appeals: A cross-cultural study. *Journal of International Consumer Marketing, 9,* 43–55.

49. Schmitt, B. H. (1995). Language and visual imagery: Issues of corporate identity in East Asia. *Columbia Journal of World Business, 3,* 28–37.

50. In previous editions of this book for advertising styles, we followed the interpersonal communication model. However the new long-/short-term orientation data seem to be more appropriate for understanding differences in styles of mass communication as they cover the oral-literal difference which is of more importance to mass communication.

51. Laskey, H. A., Fox, R. J., & Crask, M. R. (1994, November/December). Investigating the impact of executional style on television commercial effectiveness. *Journal of Advertising Research,* pp. 9–16.

52. Wang, J. (2008). *Brand new China. Advertising, Media, and Commercial Culture.* Cambridge, MA: Harvard University Press, p. 63.

53. Kobayashi & Noguchi, 2001.

54. Roland, A. (1988). *In search of self in India and Japan.* Princeton, NJ: Princeton University Press.

55. Watkins, H. S., & Liu, R. (1996). Collectivism, individualism, and in-group membership: Implications for consumer complaining behaviors in multicultural contexts. In L. A. Manrai & A. K. Manrai (Eds.), *Global perspectives in cross-cultural and cross-national consumer research.* New York: International Business Press/Haworth Press.

56. Miracle, G. E., Taylor, C. R., & Chang, K. Y. (1992). Culture and advertising executions: A comparison of selected characteristics of Japanese and U.S. television commercials. *Journal of International Consumer Marketing, 4,* 89–113.

57. Zhou, S., Zhou, P., & Xue, F. (2005). Visual differences in U.S. and Chinese television commercials. *Journal of Advertising, 34*(1), 111–119.

58. Percy, L., Rossiter, J. R., & Elliott, R. (2001). *Strategic advertising management.* Oxford, UK: Oxford University Press, pp. 167–180.

59. Holbrook, M., & Batra, R. (1987). Assessing the role of emotions as mediators of consumer responses to advertising. *Journal of Consumer Research, 14.*

60. Resnik, A., & Stern, B. L. (1977). An analysis of information content in television advertising. *Journal of Marketing, 41,* 50–53; Stern, B. L., & Resnik, A. J. (1991, June/July). Information content in television advertising: A replication and extension. *Journal of Advertising Research, 31*(3), 36–46.

61. Poels, K., & Dewitte, S. (2006, March). How to capture the heart? Reviewing 20 years of emotion measurement in advertising. *Journal of Advertising Research,* pp. 18–37.

62. Blackston, M. (1996). Can advertising pre-tests predict the longevity of advertising effects? *Marketing and Research Today, 24,* 11–17.

63. Kim, B. H., Han, S., & Yoon, S. (2010). Advertising creativity in Korea: Scale development and validation. *Journal of Advertising, 39*(2), 93–108.

64. Biel, A. L. (1990, September). Love the ad. Buy the product? *Admap.*

65. Im, S., Lee, D-H, Taylore, C. R., & D'Orazio, C. (2008). The influence of consumer self-disclosure on web sites on advertising response. *Journal of Interactive Advertising, 9*(1). Retrieved from http://jiad.org/

66. Lannon, J. (1992, March). Asking the right questions: What do people do with advertising? *Admap,* pp. 11–16.

67. Vaughn, R. (1980, June 9). The consumer mind: How to tailor ad strategies. *Advertising Age.*

68. Krugman, H. E. (1965). The impact of television advertising: Learning without involvement. *Public Opinion Quarterly, 29,* 349–356.

69. Miracle, G. E. (1987). Feel-do-learn: An alternative sequence underlying Japanese consumer response to television commercials. In F. Feasley (Ed.), *The Proceedings of the 1987 Conference of the American Academy of Advertising, USA,* pp. R73–R78.

70. Doi, T. (1973). *Amae No Kouzou* [The anatomy of dependence]. Tokyo: Kodansha. *Amae* can be explained as follows: The Japanese divide their lives into inner and outer sectors, each with its own different standards of behavior. In the inner circle, the individual is automatically accepted. There is interdependence and automatic warmth, love, or *amae,* the best translation of which is "passive love" or dependency. Members of the inner circle experience *amae* between each other, but it does not exist in the outer circle. You lose *amae* when you enter the outer circle. You don't expect *amae* in the outer circle.

71. Petty, R. E., & Cacioppo, J. T. (1986). The elaboration likelihood model of persuasion. In L. Berkowitz (Ed.), *Advances in experimental social psychology.* New York: Academic Press. Also in Petty, R. E., & Cacioppo, J. T. (1986). *Communication and persuasion: Central and peripheral routes to attitude change.* New York: Springer.

72. Callow, M., & Schiffman, L. (2002). Implicit meaning in visual print advertisements: A cross-cultural examination of the contextual communication effect. *International Journal of Advertising, 21,* 259–277.

73. Müller, W. (1998). Verlust von Werbewirkung durch Standardisierung [Loss of advertising effectiveness through standardization]. *Absatzwirtschaft, 9,* 80–88.

74. Aslam, M. M. (2006). Are you selling the right colour? A cross-cultural review of colour as a marketing cue. *Journal of Marketing Communications, 12*(1), 15–30.

75. Cutler, B. D., Javalgi, R. G., & Erramilli, M. K. (1992). The visual components of print advertising: A five-country cross-cultural analysis. *European Journal of Marketing, 26,* 7–20.

76. Shen, Y. C., & Chen, T. C. (2006). When East meets West: The effect of cultural tone congruity in ad music and message on consumer ad memory and attitude. *International Journal of Advertising, 25*(1), 51–70.

77. Andrews, J. C., Lysonski, S., & Durvusala, S. (1991). Understanding cross-cultural student perceptions of advertising in general: Implications for advertising educators and practitioners. *Journal of Advertising, 20,* 15–28.

78. Ramaprasad, J. (2001). South Asian students' beliefs about and attitude toward advertising. *Journal of Current Issues and Research in Advertising, 23,* 55–70.

79. Andrews, J. C., Durvasula, S., & Netemeyer, R. G. (1994). Testing the cross-national applicability of U.S. and Russian advertising belief and attitude measures. *Journal of Advertising, 23,* 71–82.

80. La Ferle, C., & Lee, W. N. (2003). Attitudes toward advertising: A comparative study of consumers in China, Taiwan, South Korea and the United States. *Journal of International Consumer Marketing, 15*(2), 5–23.

81. *The global view of TV advertising.* (2007). Global TGI barometer Issue 30. www.tgisurveys.com. Countries are Brazil, Mexico, Colombia, South Africa, Chile, Bulgaria, United States, Germany, United Kingdom, France, Australia, Spain.

82. Chang, C. (2006, September). Cultural masculinity/femininity influences on advertising appeals. *Journal of Advertising Research,* 315–323.

83. Data from Eurobarometer, 1997–1999 (see Appendix B).

84. European Media and Marketing Survey, 1999 (see Appendix B).

85. Faiola, A., & Matei, S. A. (2005). Cultural cognitive style and web design: Beyond a behavioral inquiry into computer-mediated communication. *Journal of Computer-Mediated Communication, 11*(1), article 18.

86. Singh, N., Fassott, G., Chao, M. C. H., & Hoffmann, J. A. (2006). Understanding international web site usage. A cross-national study of German, Brazilian, and Taiwanese online consumers. *International Marketing Review, 23*(1), 83–97.

87. Dormann, C., & Chisalita, C. (2002, September 8–11). *Cultural values in web site design.* Paper presented at the 11th European Conference on Cognitive Ergonomics, ECCEII Catania, Italy.

88. Singh, N. (2005). Analyzing the cultural content of web sites: A cross-national comparison of China, India, Japan, and US. *International Marketing Review, 22*(2), 129–146.

89. Daechun An. (2007). Advertising visuals in global brands' local websites: A six-country comparison. *International Journal of Advertising, 26*(3), 303–332.

90. Würtz, E. (2005). A cross-cultural analysis of websites from high-context cultures and low-context cultures. *Journal of Computer-Mediated Communication, 11*(1), article 13.

91. Hermeking, M. (2005). Culture and Internet consumption: Contributions from cross-cultural marketing and advertising research. *Journal of Computer-Mediated Communication, 11*(1), article 10.

92. Cho, C. H., & Cheon, H. J. (2005). Cross-cultural comparisons of interactivity on corporate websites. *Journal of Advertising, 34*(2), 99–115.

93. Ko, H., Roberts, M. S., & Cho, C. H. (2006). Cross-cultural differences in motivation and perceived interactivity: A comparative study of American and Korean Internet users. *Journal of Current Issues and Research in Advertising, 28*(2), 94–104.

94. Husmann, Y. (2001). Localization of website interfaces. Cross-cultural differences in home page design. Wissenschaftliche Arbeit zure Erlangung des Diplomgrades im Studiengang Sprachen-, Wirtschafts- und Kulturraumstudien (Diplom-Kulturwirt). Universität Passau, Germany.

95. Singh, N., Kumar, V., & Baack, D. (2005). Adaptation of cultural content: Evidence from B2C e-commerce firms. *European Journal of Marketing, 39*(1/2), 71–86.

96. Hermeking, 2005.

97. Fourquet-Courbet, M-P., Courbet, D., & Vanhuele, M. (2007, June). How web banner designers work: The role of internal dialogues, self-evaluations, and implicit communication theories. *Journal of Advertising Research,* 183–192.

98. Usunier, J-C., & Roulin, N. (2010). The influence of high- and low-context communication styles on the design, content, and language of business-to-business web sites. *Journal of Business Communication, 47*(2), 189–227.

99. Pollach, I. (2011). The readership of corporate websites: A cross-cultural study. *Journal of Business Communication, 48*(1), 27–53.

100. Aslam, M. M. (2006). Are you selling the right colour? A cross-cultural review of colour as a marketing cue. *Journal of Marketing Communications, 12*(1), 15–30.

101. Jun, J. W., & Lee. H. S. (2007). Cultural differences in brand designs and tagline appeals. *International Marketing Review, 24*(4), 474–491.

102. Pittard, N., Ewing, M., & Jevons, C. (2007). Aesthetic theory and logo design: Examining consumer response to proportion across cultures. *International Marketing Review, 24*(4), 457–473.

103. Jordá-Albiñana, B., Ampuero-Canellas, O., Vila, N., & Rojas-Sola, J. I. (2009). Brand identity documentation: A cross-national examination of identity standards manuals. *International Marketing Review, 26*(2), 172–197.

104. Belsen, K., & Bremner, B. (2004). *Hello Kitty: The remarkable story of Sanrio and the billion dollar feline phenomenon.* Singapore: John Wiley & Sons Asia, pp. 63–75.

105. De Leur, K. R., Drukker, J. W., Christiaans, H. H. C. M., & De Rijk, T. R. A. (2006). Cultural differences in product design: A study of differences between South Korean and the Dutch kitchen environment. *Journal of Design Research, 5*(1), 16–33.

CHAPTER 8

Culture and the Media

The number and variety of media that are available to reach people are continuously increasing. Worldwide, we find similar traditional media like television, press, and radio and the new media like the Internet and the mobile phone, but how people use these varies. Although the Internet at the start seemed to be a universal global medium, soon usage differences across countries became apparent.

Media usage is an integral part of daily activities. Because people communicate differently across cultures, they also use the media in a different way. In particular, understanding the function of new interactive channels, such as the Internet and the mobile phone, requires cultural knowledge as these are used by individuals with specific communication behaviors in many different cultures. So knowledge of how, when, in which situation, and for which activity the new media are used is as important as it is for the traditional media. The traditional mass media have been around a long time and differences in usage across cultures have been reported for some time. Also, studies of usage of the new media are increasing. Because of the enormous variety of new media that must be integrated in a media planning campaign, media planning has become very complicated within countries and even more complicated across countries. We cannot judge or exploit the new media that have become ingrained in people's lives if we don't understand how they work. They are a type of mediated communication that is different from the classic mass media as they are hybrid communication tools, used both for writing, reading, speaking, and dialogue. This chapter points at the differences in usage of both the traditional mass media and electronic media as well as alternative media that are relevant for emerging markets.

An Ever-Changing Media Landscape

Just think of it, there were ten viewers at the resurrection of Jesus, 460 at the opening of *Hamlet*, thousands at the first performance of Beethoven's *Missa*

Solemnis, and there will be 1.5 billion people simultaneously looking and screaming at the world championship football in Italy.[1]

This is what the German philosopher George Steiner said to poet and author Hans Magnus Enzensberger in 1990. The Olympic Games in Athens in 2004 had 3.9 billion watchers, and the opening ceremony of the Beijing Olympic Games in 2008 attracted 4.4 billion viewers. The estimates for the London games of 2012 were 4.8 billion viewers worldwide. Those who saw and heard *Hamlet* and Beethoven's *Missa Solemnis* saw it live. The majority of watchers of past football championships or Olympic Games have seen them on television. This has changed. Not all people use the television set anymore. They can see the same thing on their TV set, on the screen of their computer, or on their mobile phone. People are also using these different media at the same time, what in the Western world is called multitasking, parallel processing, or perpetual partial attention: watching television, working on the computer, and using the mobile phone at the same time. In particular, young people are using a wide variety of media and spending a good part of their time doing so. The biggest media junkies (15–24 years old) can be found in the Philippines (31.3 hrs a day) and Hong Kong China (26.6).[2]

The Internet has played a pivotal role in changing the way marketers and advertisers reach consumers. It has led to cross-media synergy, it pushed the development of research systems to measure cross-media advertising, and it has redefined integrated marketing communications. Consumers are linked to a network of brand information by way of many different media. In the West, where consistency in messages is expected, marketers have to work hard to get a consistent message through, to speak with one voice. In the East and likely in other collectivistic cultures, messages may vary with the situation, but appropriateness to the context is important.

In modern media planning, the consumer and the brand are central, and differences in how consumers use the variety of means of communication that can connect them with brands make planning and managing media across cultures a real challenge. Media planning, also called *channel planning* nowadays, is defined as the organization of a great variety of contact points between people and brands that the marketer can influence, sometimes directly and sometimes indirectly. People shop while surrounded by a vast array of brand experiences that influence their association networks of brands. These are the branded products themselves and an enormous variety of communication messages, such as in-store promotions, e-mails, (electronic) word-of-mouth, weblogs, social media, direct mail, books, directories, and conversations with friends and family; previous experience with the brands; and advertising seen on television, the Internet, cinema, and posters, as well as in newspapers and magazines and heard on radio. All these exposures leave some trace in consumers' minds, which may play a part in influencing brand choice at the point of purchase.

Marketers' promotional activities can be planned so as to affect (directly or indirectly) any of these contact points between people and brands. To do this with a maximum effect requires insight into consumer lifestyles, attitudes, and behavior, as well as into the role the various channels play in consumers' lives.

In previous chapters, we have learned that in different cultures, people's shopping behavior, people's motives, and their communication behavior vary. As a result, the various media will play different roles in the lives of consumers. The following sections will describe differences in consumer usage of the main media: the traditional media, other media, the mobile phone, and online media.

Media Usage Across Cultures

The major traditional media discussed here are television, radio, and press media. These media vary considerably with respect to usage by consumers.

Television

Television viewing varies by country, but everywhere broadcasting plays a significant role in the leisure activities of people. Although penetration of television sets has converged across countries, differences in viewing time between countries are considerable, and these differences are more or less stable over time. Of all countries reported by Ofcom,[3] North Americans spend the most time watching television with 280 minutes per day. Also across Europe, differences in television viewing are large, even for countries that are close to each other. Whereas Austrians spend 153 minutes per week watching TV, Serbians spend double: 316 minutes per week.[4] In most countries in the past years, the time spent on watching TV has increased, but the relative differences have remained the same. Figure 8.1 shows how many minutes per day people watched television across 11 European countries between 1991 and 2010. Between 1991 and 1993, countries converged with respect to TV viewing time, which can be explained by the advent of commercial channels, such as RTL and SBS, but after that year, the differences remained the same.

For a mix of poor and wealthy countries, TV viewing is negatively correlated with wealth, that is, in the poorer countries, people watch more TV than in the richer countries. In the wealthy countries of the developed world, masculinity explains variance. In 1998, heavy viewing across 19 countries worldwide[5] was related to high masculinity and high power distance. In 2001, similar relationships were found for 24 countries in Western and Eastern Europe.[6] High masculinity explained 37% of the variance, and high power distance explained an additional 14%. In 2006, across 11 wealthy European countries, Japan, and the United States, 56% of variance of viewing time was explained by masculinity.[7] In the Western world, violence in television programs has increased; people in masculine cultures are more attracted to violent programs than people in feminine cultures. An advertisement by CNN illustrates this (see Illustration 8.1).

Several factors influence how much television people watch, including available television services and the quantity of homegrown content. Yet analysis of worldwide data shows a strong negative correlation with wealth, that is, in the poorer

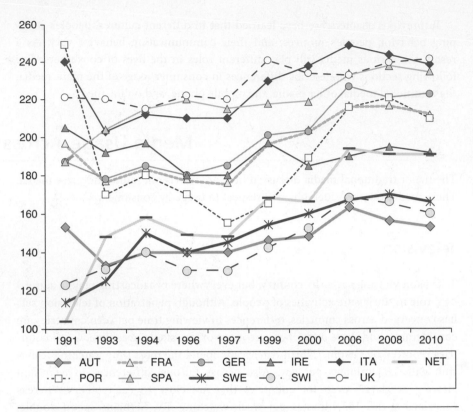

Figure 8.1   **TV Viewing Time: Stable Differences**

SOURCE: IP, TV daily viewing minutes.

Illustration 8.1   **CNN, International**

countries, people watch more TV than in the richer countries. The Organisation for Economic Co-operation and Development's (OECD's) time-spending studies, asking how people spend their leisure time, show that in the high power distance and collectivistic cultures, the percentage of leisure time spent on watching TV and listening to radio at home is highest. By comparison, in the individualistic and low power distance cultures, people spend more leisure time in more active activities such as participating in events. Interestingly, the percentage of total leisure time spent online—also a passive way of spending leisure time—is also higher in collectivistic than in individualistic cultures.[8] Measuring differences is not easy, as in collectivistic, polychronic cultures, the TV set tends to be on the whole day, and the definition of "watching TV" may be different from the definition in individualistic cultures. In Latin America, television is even more integrated into daily life, and people like having the TV set on while doing other things in the house. On average, across eight countries in Latin America, 74% of those aged 18 and older watch television while eating and 34% while talking on the phone.[9]

How people watch TV—alone, with friends, or with family—is also related to culture. Although in all countries children increasingly have television sets in their bedroom, French children watch it there less often than young Swedish children do. This can be explained by greater independence of children in Sweden than in France. Also, the degree to which parents give freedom to their children with respect to what they watch varies.[10]

Across Europe, people hardly watch the programs of other countries, mainly because they do not understand the language. Even within countries, different language groups will watch different programs. Analysis of people-meter data from Germany and the three cultural regions of Switzerland showed substantial differences in television viewing.[11] In most Latin American countries, people are more interested in programs from their own country than from the United States. Although the soap opera was invented in the United States, in Latin America, people even more frequently watch their version of the soap or *telenovela*. Among young people, serials are by far the most preferred TV program across Latin America.[12] However, across the Latin American countries, distinct styles have evolved, so they cannot all be transplanted to the other countries.[13] As a result of local preferences, many international TV channels have localized language and content. CNN International and MTV started as global channels but have localized content and language. As a result, pan-regional television channels have not been successful media for advertising. In particular, pan-European channels have been ill suited for advertisements of fast moving consumer goods (FMCGs). They are most used for advertising luxury goods to business audiences and corporate advertising.[14]

Worldwide, there is an enormous variety in ways to receive television programs, and several are used more in some countries than in others: analogue terrestrial is most used in Brazil; digital terrestrial in Spain; analogue by satellite in Germany; digital by satellite in Poland; analogue by cable in India; digital cable in the United States and Canada; and Internet protocol TV (IPTV) in France.[15] Whether analogue or digital, television still is an important medium, although there are substantial variations by country, reflecting the relative efficiency of television as an advertising medium.

IPTV

Next to watching television programs on the TV set, people can watch them on their computer monitors (*TV over broadband*) or on their mobile phone (*TV over mobile*) via IPTV, where television service is delivered using Internet Protocol over a broadband network. Sending TV signals via Internet is called *netcasting* as compared to traditional *broadcasting*. IPTV provides higher quality TV viewing, which is attractive to art-loving cultures like France, Spain, and Italy, which were the early adopters in Europe.

The degree to which people watch TV on their PCs is related to PC ownership, available TV services, available channels, and general TV watching. If people are heavy TV viewers they will also use new access facilities more. Almost one third of

U.S. broadband households use the Internet to watch video on their TV sets.[16] In countries with limited TV channels, the Internet offers a great deal more. In China in 2006, 70% of adults with broadband at home had watched or downloaded clips from TV programs or whole programs via their PC; 60% of the Japanese and British had done so and 39% of the French.[17] In 2010 in the United Kingdom, 24% did so on a weekly basis, in the United States, it was 22%, but in Germany, it was much lower: only 10%.[18] For watching TV over mobile, users typically subscribe to a package of TV programming (which increasingly includes live scheduled programming) for a monthly charge.

Internet users generally use television as their primary source for sports news, but the Internet tends to be the most common main source of celebrity news and gossip, although this is less so in the United Kingdom than in France, Italy, the United States, and Japan. The Japanese score highest with respect to using Internet TV as a source of celebrity news.[19]

Generally, people watch mobile TV when they are bored, waiting, or using public transport, but this depends on national habits. Japanese people spend a lot of time riding trains to their work. In individualistic cultures like the United States, United Kingdom, or the Netherlands, people are not used to doing much in the public domain, and many people drive to their work by car. Both habits were not fertile ground for fast adoption of mobile TV. In Asia, mobile TV developed faster. One reason for young people was to be able to watch one's own programs when other family members were watching other programs on the main home television. In an exploratory study in Seoul by Do et al.,[20] the Korean authors describe TV watching as group behavior; thus, preferences of others influence program selection, whereas mobile broadcasting is geared to individual watching. Korea was one of the first countries with Direct Multimedia Broadcasting (DMB) by satellite for the mobile phone. Users had it on when commuting and when at work, and they used it most when alone. Mobile TV seems to be complementary to home TV watching. Programs favored tend to be similar to what people are used to seeing on regular television, such as network dramas.

Radio

Radio sets are widely available in most homes. Ownership of radios per 1,000 persons has been correlated with individualism for the last decades.[21] In individualistic cultures, everybody has his or her own radio or even more than one, whereas in collectivistic cultures, one per family may be enough. Even across Latin cultures (Spain, Portugal, and nine Latin American countries)—all scoring more or less collectivistic—radio receivers per 1,000 people correlated with individualism $(r = .64^*)$.[22] These data have become less useful as so many people nowadays listen to radio and music on their mp3 players, mobile phones, or any other mobile hardware. Time spent on listening also varies. For example, the Russians spend the most time listening to radio with 39 hours per person per week; the Japanese and Spanish spend the least with 12.6 hours.[23] The data don't say what people listen to. Internet use does not appear to have had a substantial impact on offline radio consumption habits when compared with its impact on other media platforms. This may be connected to the nature of radio, which for many is on while doing other things.

The Press

The press is a written medium, the medium for literate cultures. Worldwide, the numbers of daily newspapers per 1,000 people correlate significantly with adult literacy rates.[24] Where literacy has been high for centuries, people still read more than in countries where literacy has been lagging, even when they have become literate. Across Europe, the influence of the historical development of literacy on current differences in newspaper readership is shown by Hallin and Mancini[25] for 13 countries in Europe with the relationship between the literacy rates of 1890 and newspaper circulation of 2000.

National wealth, low power distance, and long-term orientation are the variables that explain newspaper readership across countries worldwide. Across Europe, power distance is the strongest explaining variable. Cultures of low power distance are also more participative democracies where people want to be informed about politics and current affairs. The percentages agreement with the statement "I feel well informed about what is going on in politics and current affairs" is also correlated with low power distance.[26]

Several data confirm the relationship with power distance. In 1996, of the measurement "read a newspaper yesterday," for 31 countries worldwide as published by the advertising agency McCann Erickson,[27] 26% of variance was explained by low power distance and an additional 15% by low uncertainty avoidance. Answers to the statement "I read the news in daily newspapers every day," regularly measured by Eurobarometer, consistently correlate with low power distance.

Elvestad and Blekesaune[28] report differences in time spent reading newspapers across Europe and find not only a North-South difference but also differences within the group of countries in the North. Greece has the lowest population of readers of all countries in Europe. In Norway, almost 96% of the population read newspapers on an average day, but the Irish spend *more time* reading a newspaper. Several other databases show the relationship with power distance, for example, for average time spent reading a newspaper and frequency of newspaper readership.[29] The differences appear to be stable over time, as illustrated by Figure 8.2 for 14 countries in Europe.

The data of 1991 represent the percentages of respondents who answered "read any newspaper yesterday," a more general question than the Eurobarometer question that asks whether people read the *news* in the newspaper *every day*. So the percentages are lower for 2006, but the lines run parallel.

A logical result of newspaper reading differences is differences in newspaper advertising expenditures. In 2004, for nine European countries, Japan, and the United States, 72% of variance of newspaper advertising expenditures was explained by low power distance.

In particular, newspapers reach different audiences across cultures. Hallin and Mancini[30] point at differences in relation to newspaper audiences and the roles of

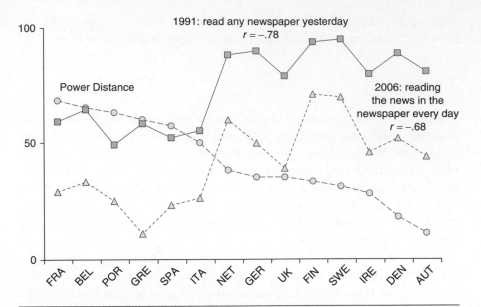

Figure 8.2 Newspaper Reading and Power Distance

SOURCE: Data from Hofstede et al. (2010) (see Appendix A); Reader's Digest 1991 and Eurobarometer 65, 2007 (see Appendix B).

newspapers in social and political communication. Whereas the newspapers of southern Europe address small numbers of well-educated, politically active elites, the newspapers of Northern Europe address a mass public, not necessarily engaged in the political world. These differences are the core characteristics of high- and low power distance cultures. Both literacy and the press developed faster in egalitarian cultures of low power distance than they did in hierarchical cultures. Even in regions where all countries score above average on the power distance index, such as in Latin America, the differences are partly explained by power distance. In 2007, for 15 Latin countries (Latin America plus Spain and Portugal), most of the differences of press circulation were explained by national wealth and partly by power distance.[31]

In many countries, newspaper readership has been decreasing. However, in the developing world, it is increasing. In Africa, newspaper readership has been growing with increased literacy. In India, the newspaper is viewed as something to aspire to; once people have learned to read, they are proud to read a newspaper. But in Japan, young people are moving their readership to the Internet.[32]

As the differences in newspaper readership between countries have existed for more than half a century, they are not likely to disappear. Television will remain a more important medium in the collectivistic and high power distance cultures than newspapers.

Other Media

In most countries, several other media are available for advertising, such as outdoor and cinema. Rules and regulations for outdoor advertising vary across countries.

Cinema visiting is culture-bound. Across Europe, frequency of visits to the cinema or theater is highest in high power distance and collectivistic cultures.[33] Visiting the cinema obviously is a type of communal activity that is found more in collectivistic cultures than in individualistic cultures.

In fast growing emerging economies, such as Brazil, India, and China, there are large rural populations who as yet do not have access to the traditional mass media, such as television or the Internet. In order to reach these rural markets, a mix of conventional and non-conventional media can be used. Examples for India are Video Van advertising and wall (outdoor) advertising. Among others, hoarding (billboards), wall painting, film, song/dance/drama, kiosk, and bus-panel advertising are effective. In particular, hoarding, kiosk advertising, and wall paintings that combine visuals and text rank high in terms of recall.[34]

Several other alternative media that generally are not covered in media planning books can be important for reaching rural populations in emerging markets. The most basic to mention are called *oramedia*—informal media made up of dialogue and verbal exchange provided by the almost constant presence of surrounding listeners. In particular in developing economies, they are strong means of communication for spreading messages. In Africa, oramedia are made up of all sorts of people, instruments, or places that spread messages. Included are the village crier, the gong man, the drums, and the marketplace which is a veritable communication forum. In Java in Indonesia, we find folk puppetry opera, in Brazil singing poets (*cantadores*), and in Thailand cowhide characters (*nong taloogn*). Urban areas are constantly abuzz with rumor. Lively news circulates through non-official oral channels. The sources of these stories are both everywhere and nowhere. In various African countries, specific terms are used for such oral media that are spreading news, for example, *Radio Mall*, *Radio Trottoir* (radio sidewalk), or *Radio Kankan*; in North Africa, they call the rumor mill *le telephone arabe*. These names have been used in particular places to designate rumors interesting enough to be listened to and repeated. Such media are known in many other oral cultures, such as *mofokoranti* (translated into *mouth newspaper*) that is used in Surinam for the semi-official spread of word. Traditional oramedia have merged with new technology. The video film culture of Nigeria, also called *Nollywood*, is a development of the Yoruba traveling theater that next to entertainment included moral instructions. These media might well be used for spreading the word about new products or services.[35]

Hybrid Media

Online communication is a hybrid form of interpersonal and mass communication, as well as of oral and literate communication. The Internet can be used as one-way mass communication, but it also is a medium for interpersonal written communication, when people are e-mailing, blogging, or tweeting. The mobile phone with Internet connection is the most hybrid as it can serve as a medium for oral and written interpersonal communication as well as for unidirectional mass communication.

Whereas the traditional mass media target an anonymous mass audience with top-down communication, mostly by organizations, the newly emerging media, such as the mobile phone, use modes of communication that can be personalized, whether the target of communication is individuals or the masses, what Castells[36] calls mass self-communication. It is the potential for active participative communication that particularly makes the mobile phone with Internet so attractive to Asians.[37] It is said that the combination of classic and new media have created a so-called hyper media space, created through interactions between multiple media, from mobile phones to television. A most obvious example is what happens with reality TV when people not only vote for contestants, conjoining mobile phones, e-mail, and TV, but also mobilize support in interactive communication processes. These effects have led marketers to adopt these new media for supporting their brands. However, several studies show that the degree to which consumers want to interact with brands is limited.

The Mobile Phone

In many countries, the number of fixed lines has been declining slowly while the number of mobile subscriptions has been increasing. By 2007 in 48 countries, there were more mobile cellular phones than inhabitants. In Hong Kong, China, in 2010, there were 190 mobile phone subscriptions per 100 people, more than in the United States with only 90 per 100 people, and Ecuador had more mobile phone subscriptions per 100 people than France.[38] The International Telecommunication Union (ITU)[39] regularly publishes data on mobile phone usage. Recent data show that of percentages of individuals aged 15 to 74 using a mobile phone, Finland is at the top with 97.3%, after which comes Morocco with 94.4% and South Korea with 94.1%, and at the bottom Indonesia with 34.5%. Worldwide, the number of mobile phone subscriptions still correlates with income (GNI per capita at purchasing power parity). This is not the case across Europe,[40] where income has become a weaker variable for explaining differences in mobile phone ownership. In particular for mobile subscriptions with Internet, the main explanatory variable is low uncertainty avoidance, which generally explains differences in adoption of innovations (as discussed in Chapter 5).

Although countries have converged with respect to mobile phone penetration, how people use the mobile phone, for which purpose, and how they pay for it varies with technological development and with culture. In some countries, people prefer postpay subscriptions by contract, while in others, they prefer prepay. Prepay is preferred more in the poorer countries, whereas postpay subscriptions are found more in the wealthy countries.[41]

Mobile phone technology facilitates access to anyone, anywhere, at any time. Within and across societies, differences in usage of this technology are found. Just as with any new form of communication, people use it as an extension of themselves. If people like to talk a lot and communicate extensively with other people, including messaging, they will use the mobile phone to talk more or send more messages. Worldwide, the average mobile messages sent correlates with short-term orientation ($r = -.79{***}$).[42] If people like writing better than talking, they may prefer to use texting via any sort of texting application. The difference also depends on local infrastructure. Where the cost per minute is high, people who may prefer talking are still forced to use a texting application because sending takes less time and thus is cheaper. However, with overall rates going down, this effect may change.

More than the personal computer, the mobile phone is not mainly a technology accessible just to people in the developed world, but also one enabling people in developing economies to get access to information. However, most studies find that both in the developed and the developing world, the mobile phone is mostly used privately, to connect with already existing relationships, not to search for information. Questions about the main benefits of the mobile phone by Eurobarometer[43] show that in Europe, members of collectivistic cultures more than of individualistic cultures view as the main benefit of the mobile phone the possibility to be contacted at any place, any time. Figure 8.3 illustrates this relationship.

The role of the mobile phone in collectivistic cultures also seems to be more integrated within the self than it is in individualistic cultures. Mizuko Ito[44] says, "To not have a *keitai* (mobile phone) is to be walking blind, disconnected from just-in-time information on where and when you are in the social networks of time and place." Among young Latinos from five Latin American countries and the United States, "keeping in touch" was also viewed as the main benefit of the mobile phone. Access to news or information and e-mailing were viewed as the least important benefit.[45] Where people are not active information gatherers, they will use the mobile phone less for this purpose than in cultures where people feel a greater need for information to make buying decisions.

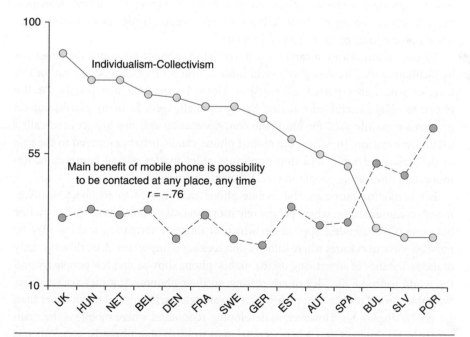

Figure 8.3 Benefit Mobile Phone and Individualism/Collectivism

SOURCE: Data from Hofstede et al. (2010) (see Appendix A); Eurobarometer, E-communications household survey, 2008 (see Appendix B).

The information application was facilitated with the advent of 3G technology to access the Internet, but this also facilitated oral communication when people could use the mobile phone for calling over the Internet (VoIP = voice over IP), which in the end is much cheaper.

NTT DoCoMo in Japan was the first provider to launch a large-scale commercial offering of 3G mobile service through which one could access the Internet and watch TV on the mobile phone. In particular, the Internet service was popular because of low PC penetration. Ishii[46] expected the Japanese to access mobile Internet mostly outside the home but didn't find evidence of this, as nearly half of the mobile Internet access occurred in the home. Even if people had PC Internet as well as mobile Internet, they used these for different activities. PC Internet was used more for obtaining information, news, and viewing videos while mobile phones were used more for social connections. An explanation is the difference in size of the screen. It is easier to perform complicated tasks such as information gathering on a PC keyboard and screen than on the mobile phone. The latter also is more a personal instrument, whereas PCs are often shared, as is the TV set. So young people watch mobile TV mostly at home in their own room, when other family members are watching other programs on the main home TV set.[47] In China, the more people used the mobile phone to text and connect to the Internet, the more they fancied mobile TV. Mobile TV viewers were also heavy TV viewers in general.[48] However, in 2010, the majority of mobile phone users still used it for text messaging, gaming on pre-installed games, and on mobile Internet.[49] A study in 2009 of two major cities in China found that when people accessed mobile Internet, the majority browsed websites or chatted online. E-mailing and downloading music or pictures or playing games was done less.[50] In Korea when mobile television became popular, texting or phone calls decreased, as people tend to postpone messages when in the middle of an interesting program.[51]

Mobile communication carries the potential to enhance economic development by facilitating the circulation of useful information for business, education, health care, or governance-related information. However, the idea that people use the phone to obtain useful information has been challenged. In many places, mobile phones are mainly used for mundane communication and not to access so-called useful information. In Africa, the mobile phone can be better compared to the role of the "talking drum"[52] and thus continues older modes of oral communication more than motivating people to search for information.

For marketing purposes, the mobile phone can be used to reinforce word-of-mouth communication where people rely more on oral communication. The mobile bar code (QR barcodes) application which facilitates information seeking may be most effective in cultures where information seeking is important. A worldwide study of the acceptance of advertising on the mobile phone showed that few people around the world welcome the idea of advertising on their phones. Attitudes are even less favorable toward mobile advertising than toward telemarketing and much lower than for online display ads. However, in developing economies where mobile is the main access to the Internet and where people want to learn about brands, acceptance is higher. Whereas acceptance of mobile advertising is only 11% in the United States, it is 48% in Nigeria.[53] In particular in individualistic cultures where privacy needs are high, people don't want to be disturbed by commercial interruptions.

The World Wide Web

The Internet by its very nature is a global communications channel, with the potential to reach consumers anywhere in the world. However, access to the Internet is still concentrated in the developed world, although developing economies have been catching up fast, with China, Brazil, India, and Nigeria leading in growth. Wealth and individualism are the primary determinants of the structure of international hyperlink flows.[54] With converging incomes, Internet penetration is also converging, but the remaining differences are related to culture. Until 2010, across Europe, the numbers of households with an Internet connection had been mainly correlated with income, but in 2011 with countries converging with respect to wealth, the correlations of these data with cultural variables were stronger than with income.[55] The main explaining cultural variables were cultural femininity and individualism.

Within the developed world, in the low uncertainty avoidance cultures people have adopted the Internet fastest. In 2002, differences in the percentage of population without access to Internet, neither at home nor at work, were related to high uncertainty avoidance, which across 20 countries explained 46% of variance.[56] The relationship is illustrated in Figure 8.4 for 12 countries ($r = .91$***). The same chart illustrates data of 2007: the percentage of people who never use the Internet apart from professional activity.[57] For 24 European countries, uncertainty avoidance explains 59% of variance ($r = .77$***). The relationship is illustrated in Figure 8.4 for 12 countries ($r = .94$***).

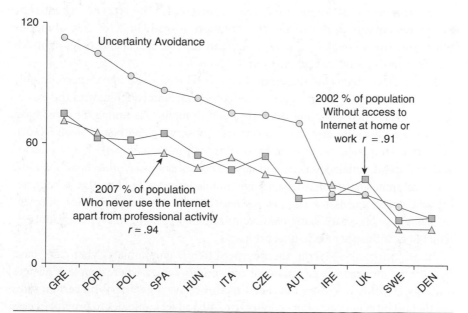

Figure 8.4   Internet and Uncertainty Avoidance

SOURCE: Data from Hofstede et al. (2010) (see Appendix A); European Social Survey, 2002, and Eurobarometer, European cultural values, 2007 (see Appendix B).

Worldwide Internet usage varies with level of education and with urban and rural areas. The largest differences with respect to urban-rural usage are in Brazil, Peru, Chile, Colombia, Ecuador, and Morocco. In most African countries, the majority of people access the Internet from an Internet café as it is difficult to get access in the home because of low incomes and bureaucratic obstacles; an infinite number of documents is required to get access in the home.[58]

Adoption of the Internet developed in different ways. Whereas in the United States Internet usage rose with increased income, that relationship was not so clear in Japan, where people accessed the Internet mostly at work.[59] In Japan, ownership of personal computers has been relatively low for several reasons. Whereas in many Western countries people have embraced the personal computer not only for personal reasons but also to be able to carry on working in the home, in Japan, as in other countries, for example, Italy, there is a stronger separation between home and work life; people do not take work home, so for that purpose, they don't need home computers. Also, in many Asian countries, the school has principal responsibility for education, and parents do fewer educational activities with their children than parents in the West. A study by Roper Starch Worldwide[60] confirmed this difference in computer usage. Whereas Americans use their computers for lots of things related to children and education, in developed Asian countries, parents are less likely to use computers to help their children with school work. Also, Italians rarely used computers on children's behalf. In such an environment, there was no incentive to buy a PC. Also, in individualistic cultures people preferred to access the Internet in the home, whereas in collectivistic cultures where people do more things in the public domain, they accessed the Internet more in cyber café's. With the advent of Internet by mobile phone, Internet usage in Japan increased enormously. The Japanese are now the major users of mobile broadband consumption. Already in 2009, 96% of mobile phones in Japan could receive Internet, and mobile broadband usage is much higher than usage of fixed broadband.[61]

If we look at what people do online in the developed world, the most commonly cited activities on the Internet are e-mail, shopping, and banking, with the exception of Japan, where watching video clips and shopping are among the three most popular weekly online activities.[62] Schroeder[63] observes a contrast between Sweden and the United States on the one hand with high use of computer based Internet and low use of mobile Internet, and Japan and Korea on the other hand with low use of computer-based Internet and high mobile Internet, and he suggests continuing divergence. Asians, but also Latin Americans and Africans, have conceptions of behavior in public space that are different from people living in Western countries, which may influence mobile Internet use.

In a country like Nigeria, the Internet often is communal. Cyber cafés have become the modern village square, or community center, where people of all ages and classes gather to use the Internet directly or have others perform certain tasks for them. The cyber café offers wireless broadband technologies to provide access to the Internet for paying members of the public and thus provides surrogate ownership to people who would otherwise not have access. In a society where ownership is usually defined in communal terms and where private and public domains are blurred, this public access to ICT is synonymous with personal ownership. Thus, when researching Internet behavior, even if people don't own a computer, they will say they have personal access because for them the public and the personal merge.[64]

The Internet takes time from the old media or other activities. These tend to be the activities on which people already spent relatively little time. An example is Internet usage replacing book reading in collectivistic cultures, where people already read fewer books than in individualistic cultures. In collectivistic cultures, where people generally participate less in active sports, people expected that the Internet would reduce time spent on sport or physical activity. In the United States and in the United Kingdom, there are indications that time spent on the Internet primarily comes from time otherwise spent watching television rather than from reading newspapers or magazines.[65] In Hong Kong, China, Internet users spend significantly less time on traditional media than nonusers, but time spent on the Internet doesn't take time from the amount of time spent on sociability. Generally, online relationships are weaker than those formed and maintained offline. People keep spending time on real-world social activities to enhance or maintain their social relationships.[66] In Latin American, mostly collectivistic and polychronic cultures, where people are used to doing more things at the same time, Internet usage and TV viewing are not mutually exclusive activities. In the home, the TV is placed next to the computer monitor so that people can watch the two things at the same time.[67]

For Internet users, privacy is a worldwide concern, but the importance people attribute to it varies. Whereas in the United States privacy is seen as a basic human right, entrenched in the constitution, the constitutions of Asian countries indicate little or no recognition of privacy. A survey among Internet users in Seoul, Singapore, Bangalore, Sydney, and New York found that in individualistic cultures Internet users were more concerned about privacy than those in collectivistic cultures. In individualistic and low uncertainty avoidance cultures, people will be more pro-active in self-protection behaviors than in high uncertainty avoidance cultures where people appear to be more inclined to avoid privacy threatening situations by using other media to gather information or shop.[68]

The Internet supports a wide variety of uses: from simple communications, such as e-mail, chat, or twitter, to sophisticated real-time video and audio communications; from access to digital newspapers or information sources, to blogging, wikis, and other user-generated content; from educational and research purposes to online gaming or downloading music and videos; from accessing local government services to checking the bank account. ITU data on Internet activities across 25 countries plus an average for 27 countries of the European Union show great differences in usage of the various Internet possibilities: For example, the highest usage of the internet for e-mail is in Chile; the highest usage for education is in Brazil; most use of Internet for reading and/or downloading newspapers, magazines, or books is in Hong Kong, China; and the highest use for interaction with the government is in the average EU countries. [69]

Levels of interactivity vary across cultures. In low-context cultures, people search more for information and facts, clicking into deeper links and using search engines, whereas in high-context cultures, people are more interested in social interaction, interacting with other people and participating in customer discussions. In high-context communication cultures, people trust the information they obtain from their online interpersonal communication more than members of low-context communication cultures do.[70]

At the start, the Internet was all-English, but soon countries started portals in their own languages. At the start, the dot-com, or commercial, domain was mostly used by international companies. Increasingly, global companies register their name in multiple global and local domains but tend to promote their global website at just one domain. Companies of individualistic cultures use more dot-com domains whereas those from collectivistic cultures tend to adopt country domains.[71] This difference may be due to universalism of individualistic cultures.

The Internet has become part of everyday life. People routinely integrate it into the ways in which they communicate with each other. E-mail and social network services are used for contacting distant friends and relatives, but even more frequently, they are used to contact those who live nearby. The way the various Internet functions are used fit people's communication styles, as described in Chapter 7 (Interpersonal Communication Styles section and Digital Communication section). Communication via the Internet is also called cyber communication, or viral communication. The term *viral* is used as a metaphor for how messages travel through the Internet from brain to brain the way viruses travel from person to person. For such messages, Richard Dawkins[72] coined the term *memes,* or ideas, that are passed from person to person and are either adopted for their usefulness or abandoned.

For describing the different functions of the Internet, we distinguish between *information* (search for, compare, and buy products), *entertainment* (games, online video) and *social* (e-mail, social networks, and chat rooms).

The Information Function of the Internet

The differences in the need for information are reflected in information searches on the Internet. Whereas in individualistic cultures people first try to find information via search engines, in collectivistic cultures, they will go to a discussion forum where people comment on and recommend various activities. Where upholding face is important, people can take part in discussion forums anonymously. Vuylsteke et al.[73] compared differences between Belgian and Chinese students with regard to their search for information on the Internet before making a buying decision. They found that Chinese search more frequently, but fewer base their final decision on information found online, as they rely more on recommendations from peers. Chinese often go directly to a forum or consumer website without doing other searching, and if they search, they do so in a more holistic way than Belgians do. Belgians tend to look at fewer results before they click on one, whereas Chinese may scroll down longer, to see the whole, before clicking for the first time. One measurement of the effectiveness of Internet advertising is by the number of online clicks. This search difference may influence comparison of effectiveness across cultures if based on numbers of clicks.

A wider approach is looking more generally at what people search for on the Internet. Understanding differences in search behavior will aid proper application to marketing. Jeong and Mahmood[74] analyzed search terms of 11 countries and categorized them according to three country characteristics: political freedom, wealth, and culture. A notable difference with respect to a political search was that political issues were least searched in the United Kingdom where political freedom is guaranteed. Russians searched more for politically historic memorial days or events, and the Chinese searched for international political issues. In the wealthy countries, more searches were found for recreation, news, education, airline, and luxury items. Education was of greater interest in the lower income countries.

Instead of the expected globalization effects of the Internet there is a trend of "hyperlocalism" or "ultralocalism," the trend of focusing on the immediate neighborhood. This applies to information retrieval as well as to online social networking. What people actually read on the Internet can be found by the number of clicks on stories, and such analysis shows that most clicked-on stories are local.[75] Also, social media increasingly have become local. Nigel Hollis[76] argues that what Facebook calls *global pages* is a misnomer as people get to see local content since Facebook automated the ability to serve a localized view of the site. Local versions of a brand's page are translated and marketers can customize content.

E-Commerce

Searching, comparing, and buying on the Internet are part of the information function of the Internet. Differences in e-commerce expenditures will be related not only to Internet penetration but also to the retail history of a country. In some countries, historically, people have bought more by mail order than in others. A local effect of the Internet is that ordering by Internet replaces mail order. But there are more differences in the degree to which people use e-commerce and what they order.

Although online sales have been most pervasive in the United States, Chinese consumers also are very active online shoppers and buyers. In particular, social networking helps them to make better comparisons.[77] Chinese websites show collectivistic community activities like group buying that you wouldn't find on U.S. websites.[78]

Several problems such as insecurity and privacy concerns are associated with online buying. A study among respondents from the United States, Canada, Germany, and Japan showed differences between countries with respect to concerns about payment security, company legitimacy, and assurance. The Japanese in particular note telephone follow-up as desirable because it is more personal than e-mail. In general, people prefer local website design features.[79] A comparison between U.S. and Korean shoppers found that the perceived risk of online shopping was higher among Korean consumers than U.S. consumers.[80]

Differences in what people buy online across cultures reflect the same differences in products or services people buy in regular stores. For example, more event tickets or video games are bought online in individualistic than in collectivistic cultures.[81] The Internet offers the opportunity to compare products. Across Europe, in the individualistic, low uncertainty avoidance, and low power distance cultures where decision making is more information based, more people tend to search for information and compare products on the Internet even when they do not buy online or buy in the shop. Collectivists prefer shopping to compare products, and they visit different shops.[82]

The prospect of an emerging global Internet consumer has enticed many international organizations as it would enable standardization of Internet strategies on a worldwide basis. Instead, with more companies of different countries selling on the Internet, Internet strategies have increasingly localized. Misunderstanding consumer preferences can cause a strategy that is successful in one country to fail elsewhere. Companies that have an understanding of and an ability to mirror the culture of their target country will have a competitive global advantage. Whereas, in the past, selling across countries was facilitated by agents and local distributors who knew their customers, global e-commerce marketers need to understand their customers from a global perspective. This means being able not only to manage logistical requirements to ensure products are available and deliverable to a global market but also improving online features for communicating and interacting directly with consumers. Webpage design, language, and content must take into account cultural relevancy for consumers positioned around the globe.[83] In particular, website design must be culture relevant, as discussed in Chapter 7.

The Social Function of the Internet

The creation of social networking and entertainment sites builds on the interactive power of the Internet. This has caused a shift in control of the media from publishers to the people. User-generated content has a huge impact on the traditional media. In this respect, two formats are discussed in more detail: social networks and blogging. The entertainment function, except TV or video watching, mostly merges with the social function. Gaming can be a carrier of advertising for specific target groups, mostly young males, but this may vary across countries. McDonald's uses in-game advertising to target young people for special offers. In-game advertising can be integrated into the game through a display in the background, such as an in-game billboard or a commercial, or be highly integrated within the game, for example, if the advertised product is necessary to complete part of the game. Highest expectations for advertising are for social network services.

Social Network Services

A *social network service* (SNS) builds online social networks for communities of people who share interests and activities or who are interested in exploring the interests and activities of others. Most services provide various ways for users to interact, such as chat, messaging, e-mail, file sharing, blog, micro-blogs, forums, and discussion groups.

Social network services got their name because they facilitate the maintenance and investigating of existing social connections among others by creating content (*social searching*) and seeking new contacts or connections (*social browsing*). The main types of social networking services are those which contain directories of some categories (such as former classmates), means to connect with friends (usually with self-description pages), and recommender systems. Across cultures, people use social networks for different purposes, and because of that, network formats vary across cultures. For Brazilians, the main functions are communicating with friends and entertainment. For the Chinese, conversation, video content, and online gaming are most important. Russians are most drawn by file sharing of music and movies and online gaming, and in India, because of language differences, use is less textual and more directed at entertainment, watching videos, and listening to music.[84]

Several comparative studies have found that everywhere the main usage of social media concerns contacts with friends and family. Chatting does not necessarily make global communities. It often is a group of existing relations that intensify their communication. Young people of the same city or even in the same street form closed groups that even block out strangers with the argument that it is easier to talk to people one knows than to strangers.[85] In collectivistic cultures, people prefer sharing experiences with known others and they make fewer contacts with strangers than in individualistic cultures, but fear of the unknown in high uncertainty avoidance cultures may have the same effect. A comparison of Hispanic students in Argentina, Chile, Colombia, the United States, and Urugay showed that the main use of social media was to maintain contact with friends and family members. Most liked activities were sharing photos, reconnecting with old friends, and keeping in touch with others.[86] A comparison of such behavior across five other countries (United States, United Kingdom, Italy, Greece, and France) found that social browsing was more important for French and Italian users than for U.S. users. For the French users, status updates and photographs were less important than for U.S. users. In general, the largest differences were between U.S. users on the one hand and UK, French, and Italian users on the other hand.[87] In Russia, different social media attract different classes. What distinguishes Facebook from its Russian competitors is cachet; it provides status. Facebook is the network of choice for the urbane, wealthier, well-traveled, cosmopolitan Russian with foreign friends who is living in large cities like Moscow and St. Petersburg.[88]

The greatest difference in usage of social media is between individualistic and collectivistic cultures, in particular with respect to social media use by mobile phone. In collectivistic cultures, people use more social media by phone than in individualistic cultures.[89] In individualistic cultures, social networks are viewed more as providing a path to resources, such as access to people who may have the right information to help deal with a health or medical issue.[90] In collectivistic cultures, Internet networks reinforce the sharing of feelings and ideas. Although collectivistic cultures are most motivated to use social networks, the ways they are used varies with long-/short-term orientation. Across developed countries the time spent on social networking is highest in short-term oriented cultures.[91]

To much of the English speaking world, it may appear that Facebook has become ubiquitous, but in many countries, local social networking sites generate more traffic than Facebook, for example, orkut.com in Brazil; weibo, kaixin, and renren in China; Mixi in Japan; CyWorld in South Korea; and vkontakte.ru in Russia. Africa's biggest social network is MXit. It sells itself as a community network and includes a digital wallet that works via the mobile phone service provider. Local SNSs were developed because the purpose of using social media varies with culture; consequently, the designs of local social network sites will also vary. Users of different social network services display different online practices, and even users of the same social media may use them in different ways and for different purposes. For example, users of Korean-based SNSs (e.g., Cyworld) have fewer but more intimate friends, keep their public profile anonymous, and use more nonverbal communication means, such as graphics or icons, as compared with users of American-based SNSs (e.g., Facebook). Users of French SNSs like to carry out discussions that are not personal. And users of Chinese SNSs like to play more games. SNSs appear to be cultural systems in themselves.[92]

In Chapter 5, we described how in short-term oriented cultures, self-enhancement is important. One should show the best of oneself without much critical self-reflection, whereas in long-term oriented cultures, people are more modest, showing competence indirectly, and are more inclined to self-improvement which includes self-criticism. Facebook is the typical platform for self-enhancement. Morozov[93] cites U.S. psychologist Jean Twenge who says, "Facebook rewards the skills of the narcissist, such as self-promotion, selecting flattering photographs of oneself and having most friends." This aspect of Facebook makes it less popular in East Asia. Whereas the percentage of online Facebook users in the United States in 2010 was 70% as it was in the United Kingdom, it was only 3% in Japan and 10% in Korea.[94] In Japan, social media users prefer Japanese social media, such as Mixi. In contrast to Facebook, Mixi allows anonymity. Whereas Facebook is all about the people behind the profile seeking self-enhancement, the Japanese like to be anonymous. They use all sorts of mechanisms to disguise their true identity, such as pseudonyms and nicknames. Mixi is also less about interacting with friends and more about interacting on popular community pages where personal identity is not important, and it offers greater control of which friends get to see your personal information.[95] For East Asian collectivists, strong private in-group bonds may conflict with the public function of social networks. Korean CyWorld solved that problem by designing mini homepages where mainly existing personal relationships are consolidated.[96] In other Asian countries that are more short-term oriented, such as Thailand and the Philippines, Facebook is very popular. Unlike social media critics who cite it as intrusive, many Thais feel the opposite. They view Facebook and other platforms as an extension of their normal life.

A related phenomenon in long-term and individualistic cultures, as in Germany, is the need for privacy. Online and offline privacy is a key concern to Germans, who have shown frustration with frequent privacy changes on Facebook.[97] Culturally, Germans tend to be very private and do not freely share personal information. Many still feel that their data are not safe online.[98] The differences in the degree of self-disclosure, as discussed in Chapters 5 and 7, can be recognized in social media behavior across countries. The Chinese say they are more open online than in real life. Being more easily open online refers to personal feelings, such as a happy things or personal events, but also to unpleasant, embarrassing things. Although young Chinese often are hesitant to reveal deep emotions, especially sad feelings, in their blogs they do so, be it in a restricted way.[99] In Western eyes, they are not telling the "truth."

The numbers of friends users report vary greatly. In East Asia, social network users have fewer friends than in South Asia and in Latin America. Social network users in Malaysia have, on average, 233 friends whereas in Japan, social network users have only 29 friends. China is similarly low with 63 friends on social networks. The United States and United Kingdom show similar average numbers of friends with respectively 200 and 173 friends. Across Europe, the differences are large, with Russians having 89 friends, the French 95, the Germans 113, the Dutch 115, the Spanish 100, and Italians 152. Latin American users score high, with Brazilians having 360 friends. These differences are similar to those for professional membership networks.[100] The numbers of friends people have across cultures correlate with short-term orientation. It is a manifestation of self enhancement. In other cultures, needs for prestige are leading. In Brazil Google's Orkut has been very popular from the start. Orkut, being invite-only, implied you were "well-connected," which added prestige. Friends could rate you, based on how sexy you were, how cool, and how trustworthy. Also, one could amass "fans." Brazilians are very image-conscious, and carefully craft their online persona. Image and reputation are important parts of status, and guide online behavior.[101]

The degree to which social networkers post information on products, brands, and companies is higher in China, India, Brazil, and Argentina than it is in Europe. Whereas in China more social networkers follow brands, in the United States on average, more brands are followed. In the United States, Canada, and Argentina, brand followers are most interactive.[102]

Because individualism/collectivism and long-/short-term orientation differentiate usage and design of social media, we can map countries according to these differences, as in Figure 8.5. It shows how the different countries can be mapped according to their social media behavior. In collectivistic culture, people use more social media than in individualistic cultures, and in the short-term oriented cultures, impression management is stronger.

Figure 8.5 shows four different quadrants that can be taken into account when differentiating electronic communication strategies. Whereas in short-term oriented collectivistic cultures, people identify and present themselves in a self-enhancing way and are more interactive, in long-term oriented collectivistic cultures, people want to be anonymous and feel part of the larger community in a more passive way. Culture-related motives for social media such as self-enhancement and status are stronger in South America than in East Asia. Marketers therefore should consider using brand messages which emphasize self-expression to these short-term

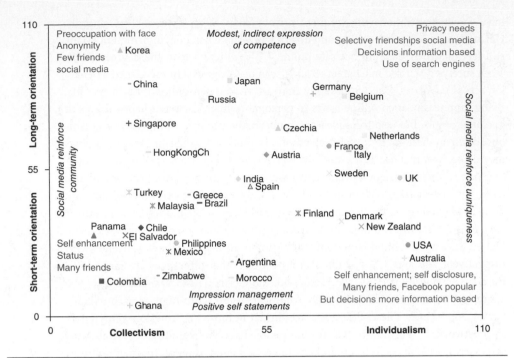

Figure 8.5 Social Media Culture Map

SOURCE: Data from Hofstede et al. (2010) (see Appendix A)

orientation cultures but emphasize group orientation and anonymity to long-term orientation countries with additional presence on social media sites other than Facebook. Across individualistic cultures in the two right-hand quadrants, long-/ short term orientation also explains differences with respect to the degree of privacy needs and self-enhancement, for example, as expressed by the difference in numbers of friends. In individualistic cultures, people search for information more by seeking facts than by discussion with others as decision making is more information and fact based, and they are also more interactive. In view of the different usages in collectivistic and individualistic cultures, marketers should consider using social media more in collectivistic cultures and using search engine marketing more in individualistic cultures, thereby, further differentiating between short- and long-term oriented cultures.

Advertising on social networks can range from large-scale profile pages to banner ads bought from the social network site. Chat programs like MSN Messenger can be used for advertising to reach specific target groups. Because social networks are rather personal, unsolicited ads may be viewed as spam, in particular in cultures where privacy is important.

Because social media have different functions across cultures, their function in the consumer decision-making process will vary. An important question is whether social media are viewed as sources of information, similar to the traditional media, or as influences in opinion formation, similar to interpersonal or word-of-mouth communication.

The Weblog or Blog

A *weblog* or *blog* is an online space regularly updated, presenting the opinions or activities of one or a group of individuals and displayed in reverse chronological order. As for social media, the degree to which people blog, their motives, and topics vary by culture. In terms of blog posts by language, in 2007, Japanese was the most used blogging language followed closely by English. There are more bloggers in collectivistic cultures than in individualistic cultures. Worldwide, the percentage who say they are involved in blogging correlates negatively with individualism ($r = -.83***$).[103] Although blogging is often part of social media usage, there are several comparative studies that found differences in blogging.

Results from a study across 22 countries[104] comprising Southeast Asia, Japan, North America, and Europe suggest differences in topics covered as well as blogging motivations. Japanese blogs, for example, are dominated by hobby and recreational blogs, whereas personal blogs dominate in most other cultures. Australia has a large proportion of political blogs. Although more than half of North American blogs are personal, a large percentage can be categorized as political, hobby, and religious blogs. There is a notable lack of religious blogs across Asian cultures.

Companies use blogs for various purposes and in various business areas, for example, as a public relations instrument. It may increase a company's reputation for being open and concerned with its customers and environment or may help in rebuilding a damaged reputation by entering the market debate with a different side of the story.

Companies use different types of blogs; for example, a company leader may talk about his or her vision and the strategy of the company, or an expert may present new products.[105] Whereas American CEOs will disclose information about events in their personal lives, Japanese CEOs will be reluctant to do so. Too much self-disclosure and revelation of personal feelings and private life will not result in trust and may even suggest incompetence.

Varying Internet Use for Consumer Decision Making

Both the search function of the Internet and social media are exploited by consumers to help make buying decisions. Both are more active means than classic display advertising and thus marketers are eager to use them. Yet the different Internet applications have different appeals to consumers across cultures.

In low power distance and individualistic cultures where individuals search for information to maximize their personal utility, people depend less on other people and base decision-making more on facts and data, consciously gathering information throughout the decision-making process. Consumers' online research into brands is stronger in cultures of low power distance.[106] Personal contacts serve more as a source of information, whereas in collectivistic and high power distance cultures, personal contacts tend to serve to form opinions, and people rely more on online forums and social media. In collectivistic and high power distance cultures, individual utility is less important than sharing with others, so new electronic media are used more for sharing ideas and opinions than for personal information search. People rely more on personal sources of recommendation, are more active opinion seekers, and are less active in information seeking via impersonal sources.[107] By 2006, La Ferle and Kim[108] had found that U.S. citizens are more likely to be motivated to shop and look for information online than Korean consumers. In contrast, Korean consumers are more motivated than U.S. consumers to head online to fulfill social goals, such as making friends, meeting people, and participating in newsgroups.

Low power distance Western cultures also are more likely to use websites emphasizing marketer-to-consumer interactivity than high power distance Eastern cultures, where individuals favor consumer-to-consumer interactivity, due to a larger distance between marketers and consumers.[109]

In collectivistic cultures, social media reinforce word-of-mouth communication about products and brands. In China, the major influence on purchase decisions is word-of-mouth.[110] This is intensified by the various discussion opportunities offered by the Internet.

In low uncertainty avoidance cultures, more opinion seekers are found,[111] and consumers base their decisions on more information sources than do consumers in high uncertainty avoidance cultures, where feelings of trust dominate decision making. Analysis of data from a survey on the Internet's influence on decision making across 55 countries worldwide shows that uncertainty avoidance together with long-term orientation explain 37% of variance in trust in search engines.[112] Also, data from a Eurobarometer study on consumer empowerment[113] show a significant correlation between low uncertainty avoidance and the use of the Internet to compare prices or services ($r = -.71^{***}$).

Consumers from short-term oriented cultures rely more on the human factor and prefer to get their information from people, whereas in long-term oriented cultures, consumers rely more on facts and data. Significant correlations were found between long-term orientation and both trust in search engines ($r = .50^{***}$) and trust in on-line product reviews ($r = .41^{***}$). Short-term orientation uniquely explains 36% of variance in trust in family. These cultural differences might also apply to various other online purchase decision sources.[114]

These findings are of importance to companies that want to use the Internet to sell their products or brands. Many Western company websites are text heavy and rational, with an explicit and informational communication style, reflecting low-context culture. This is caused by the Western focus on information in the sales process. The British change their mind about which brand to buy following research on the web more than the Italians do.[115] The differences are correlated with low uncertainty avoidance ($r = -.68^*$) and low power distance ($r = -.57^*$), the configuration of low-context cultures, and also confirm the findings that people in low uncertainty avoidance cultures tend to search from more information sources.

An important aspect is that search engine spiders search for specific keywords, and websites should be optimized for such keywords. Spiders crawl through text, looking for keyword placement, keyword density, the use of titles, alt tags for images, and useful anchor text. The spider will also "want to see" a logical link structure aiding movement from one page of the site to another. This is the logic of low-context cultures. A search engine cannot crawl through the information contained in a picture, so websites of high-context culture companies should also contain enough keywords for a search engine to find the relevant information. Search engine optimization (SEO) companies are specializing in this.[116]

Internet Marketing and Advertising

An important aspect of online advertising is its ability to offer targeted, personalized, measurable campaigns. Internet advertising can serve several purposes, such as to provide a brand reminder message to people visiting a website; it can also be used like a display advertisement in traditional media or as a way to entice people to visit the advertiser's site by clicking on a banner or button to the website.

The different roles of the Internet require different approaches. Those who access the Internet to seek information must be approached through different formats from those who seek entertainment or social communication. Several studies have classified World Wide Web motives. The Web Motivation Inventory (WMI), a categorization of such motives, distinguishes between the following motives:[117]

- Research (information acquisition, goal directed, or exploratory)
- Communicate (connect, e-mail, communicate with friends, family, others)
- Surf (entertainment, online gaming)
- Shop

A host of research findings show that the first function is more useful to people of individualistic cultures whereas in collectivistic cultures, people will focus more on conversation and communication. Thus, when selecting Internet channels, an important choice is between search and social media. The various advertising formats can be used for both functions, although social media logically can be used in a more interactive way than search engines. Formats that can be used for Internet marketing and advertising are e-mail, banner ads, and viral marketing for which the various Internet applications can be used. Expectations of social media have been high, but knowledge of the effects is still limited.

One of the attractive features of e-mail advertising is that it is inexpensive. However, the blasting of millions of unsolicited e-mail messages to e-mail boxes has become highly irritating.

The banner ad is the oldest form of advertising on the Worldwide Web. Web banners function the same way as traditional advertisements. They can raise brand awareness, but they can also serve as a direct marketing device because of the click-through function. Banner ads can include streaming video or even be complete mini-sites. The *Interactive Advertising Bureau (IAB)*[118] continuously releases guidelines for display Internet advertising with sets of sizes for various formats to make ad sizing more predictable and better for both consumer and producer. Unit names for which standards are published are Billboards, Filmstrip, Portrait, Pushdown, Sidekick, and Slider, including initial and maximum expanded dimensions, various load sizes, maximum frame rates, lengths, and CPU usage. They provide criteria for

Universal ad packages, specifically for the Medium Rectangle, Rectangle, Wide Skyscraper, (Super) Leaderboard, Half Page, Button, and Micro Bar. Next, they provide Rich Media Guidance with standards for InBanner Video, Pop Ups, and various other formats. Also, guidelines are available for mobile advertising.

Different countries prefer different banner formats, and preferences are changing rapidly. By 2007, the traditional banner had already become less popular, and rich media advertisements using interactive and audiovisual elements, such as streaming video, were increasingly used.[119] Acceptability of ad formats varies across countries. A study by telecom company Orange[120] in 2006 found that in the United Kingdom in general, all formats were acceptable, whereas in Italy, larger formats were more readily accepted. The Spanish scored rich media, such as flash or video, very high on impact and don't mind the intrusion. In Germany, people accept little intrusion. In the Dutch view, the less intrusive and smaller the better, and ads that are too bold and flashy are regarded as less appealing. Such findings reflect the differences in low- and high-context communication as well as differences between masculine and feminine cultures. Low-context cultures accept less intrusion than high-context cultures. Italians like big ads and the Dutch small ads.

Several studies have tried to compare effectiveness of formats. A UK study among Internet users in the context of online gaming found that the largest banner ads are more effective in generating click-through than the smaller sized banners.[121] Although cross-country studies are still rare, it has become clear that standard formats do not produce standard responses.

Social Media Marketing

An important aspect of social media is that they are not like the classic *lean back* media like TV. Television has traditionally been a medium associated with relaxation. On TV, content is presented to viewers who are looking to be entertained or informed. The Internet and, in particular, social media are different. When people are actively seeking information or entertainment online, they are leaning forward as they interact with what is on the screen. In the Western model of how advertising works, such advertising must be relevant to the user's activity because advertising that is not immediately relevant to the task at hand may be regarded as annoying. Relevance must be established quickly, and the ad should fulfill the same need as the context.[122] Because of lesser consistency needs in the collectivistic model of how advertising works, many different formats and messages that a company sends to develop a relationship with consumers may be acceptable as it is clear the message is from the company one knows.

In the social media, people are actively looking at what friends are doing and their specific interests.[123] If used for increasing brand equity, the brand must be present in personal conversations, and people should recommend the brand, being part of the buzz. In order to be part of conversations, companies must search for content that is personally relevant.[124] This asks for more than just display advertising as in the classic media. It also asks for a different advertising specialization than the classic sender-oriented communication, and companies increasingly engage journalists for writing relevant or personalized stories. When clicking on a "like" on Facebook without getting any or only a standard response, a potential consumer is lost.

Yet many advertisers use the Internet mainly in an integrated way in addition to their media campaign. An example of tying in to a wider marketing communication campaign was the Kit Kat "Crane" campaign, that ran a TV ad featuring crane operators "taking a break" across both digital and terrestrial channels. The crane motif was carried through into the online display campaign which incorporated an interactive game housed within the ad unit itself. The game was also supported through Facebook display advertising. Another, more interactive approach for Kit Kat was making people choose between different flavors, asking people to vote for their flavor of choice.[125] Another example of using the Internet in an interactive way is using coupons as a means of communication between advertisers and consumers, for example, clicking on a coupon for McDonald's fried chicken legs which a consumer can redeem but which also accesses rich media content linked to the product. The opportunities are unlimited, but the question is how long a time span will people accept being approached by advertisers when they are socially active. Having to wait for a commercial to end before being able to see your friend's video posted on a social network may not be acceptable to the same degree in all cultures.

Another use of social media is for customer care. One characteristic of social media in collectivistic cultures is that people may complain or ventilate discontent with companies more online than they will do in person, because digital display of negative feelings is easier than in personal communication. This offers an opportunity to companies in collectivistic cultures to get feedback. In Brazil, for example, social media usage related to brands is focused on customer care. Also, in China, people express complaints via social media which they wouldn't do in person.[126]

Many brands that are successful on social media are strong brands in their own right, and fan pages tend to serve as small communities for loyal fans. Social media should be more than a pursuit of fans and followers. In many countries, just buying "likes" or paying followers for recommending the brand is not accepted. Yet many advertisers prefer to go online because of the possibility of short-term measurement of response. Paying for advertising based on clicks or any other immediate action works well for search, but for longer term brand building, exposure is also important. For this, the industry keeps searching for comparable measurement systems.

The revenues of much of social media advertising, just like mobile advertising, tend to be overstated.[127] Advertisers have to be aware of the fact that not all people are active on social media, and of those, only small percentages are engaged with brands or other commercial activities. Increasingly, measurement systems are being developed to measure the effects of social media marketing. For example, FanIndex by Millward Brown[128] measures page performance as a composite score of fans' opinions, attention to brand posts, and likelihood to recommend and revisit.

Viral Marketing

The terms *viral marketing, guerilla marketing,* or *buzz marketing* refer to the idea that people will pass on and share striking and entertaining content, also called user generated content (UGC); this is often sponsored by a brand that is looking to build awareness. These viral commercials often take the form of funny video clips, or interactive Flash games, images, or text. Viral marketing can use e-mail to circulate a message among family and friends, but it mostly uses social networks. In order to go viral, content must be funny and entertaining, otherwise it is not shareable. One example is the Diet Coke/Mentos experiment, which resulted in a geyser and exploded again and again in films on the Internet. That viral advertising was watched worldwide. Other viewers concocted their own versions and uploaded them on YouTube. Mentos mint sales rose 15%.[129] Another example is the *Axe effect* campaign. Axe is a deodorant body spray from Unilever that is famous for its attention-grabbing advertisements with the phrase, The Axe Effect, which proposes that all women are attracted to a guy who has used the Axe body spray. A series of commercials were produced, some being very naughty. Bloggers download the Axe commercials and spread them on the web via YouTube. Consumers have also made Axe commercials themselves and published them on YouTube. Banner ads on websites tie into the commercials. Illustration 8.2 shows an example from Germany, in which women fight for T-shirts tested by a man using Axe. Illustration 8.3 shows

Illustration 8.2　**Axe Girl fight, Germany**

Illustration 8.3　**Axe Clix Nick Lachey film**

a commercial in which American singer and actor Nick Lachey clicks for every woman whose attention he gets, but another man who uses Axe Clix has collected many more clicks. A webpage from Venezuela tying into this commercial is shown as Illustration 8.4.

In different countries, people have selected the ads they like best and circulated them. Commercials are also discussed on weblogs, such as Americans asking Japanese to explain what the action is about. Unilever also tied into local events, for example, with ads showing Hillary Clinton wearing an Obama button with the pay-off "Imagine the power of Axe." Two examples in Illustrations 8.5 and 8.6 are a Japanese Axe YouTube film and a print ad of Hillary Clinton with Obama button.

Illustration 8.4　**Axe Click banner, Venezuela**

Illustration 8.5　**Axe Japan**

Illustration 8.6　**Axe: Hillary Clinton with Obama button**

Mobile Marketing and Advertising

Mobile marketing or *m-commerce* includes instant messaging, video messaging, and downloading banner ads on mobile websites. The simplest way to use the mobile phone for advertising is text messaging. The mobile operator offers free text messages and/or free minutes of voice calls per month as long as the subscriber agrees to receive a number of advertisements by text message per day. To sign up for the service, customers must fill out a questionnaire about their hobbies and habits. Thus, if marketers use a mobile firm's profiles of its customers cleverly, they can tailor their advertisements to match each subscriber's habits. Members of collectivistic cultures may be more open to SMS ads via their mobile phones than members of individualistic cultures. A comparison between Korean and American youngsters found that young Korean consumers' intentions to opt in to SMS ads via their mobile phones were stronger than those of their American counterparts.[130] Being polychromic, collectivists also have fewer objections to being interrupted.

Beyond the branding opportunity of banner ad messaging, marketers can employ a variety of response mechanisms: drive traffic to branded mobile website, click to call, campaign-specific page information, or send a text (SMS), picture, audio, or video message (MMS) to the user directly from the phone.[131] The Mobile Marketing Association (MMA), a global organization, has set standards for mobile advertising formats, following the way standards for online advertising are set.

For understanding the effect of culture on m-commerce, two types of mobile communication can be distinguished: *interpersonal* or *synchronous communication* (voice and video call) and *impersonal* or *asynchronous communication* (SMS, e-mail, mobile payment, and news). Collectivists are more in favor of the former and individualists more in favor of the latter. A study comparing m-commerce in the United Kingdom and Hong Kong found that voice services were more used in Hong Kong than in the United Kingdom and video calls were viewed as more useful and satisfactory in Hong Kong than in the United Kingdom.[132] Although this is still very relevant to the situation in emerging markets, the 3G and 4G smart phones offer similar opportunities as described for the Internet in general: the search and social media functions but mostly opportunities to connect with people when they are on the road.

Media and Globalization

Many still assume that global media will mold consumers into one global consumer culture. This has been the discourse about the classic media, and it is repeated with respect to the Internet. However, although the technology may be universal, the content and people's interpretation is not.

Analysis of the content of classic media shows large differences. Hardly any universal newspaper stories, formats, or television soaps exist. Usually when media content is distributed across countries, the way it is interpreted varies. The process through which media present and transmit information follows specific formats which consist among others of how material is organized and the style in which it is presented. As most publishers are also part of their culture, media may reflect the values of the publisher. We find, for example, more tabloids in Britain and the United States than in Germany. Particularly in oral cultures with more human interest than interest in abstract societal developments, the tabloid is popular. We find them in many African countries as well as in Latin America.

There may be global television formats, but the type and content varies. If one program, for example, a soap opera, is exported from one country to another, people do not perceive the same meaning, may reject the values and behavior of the characters, or just not understand what is happening. Japanese viewers of *Dallas* asked themselves why, if the family is so rich, they set the table by themselves? Why, if they are so rich, they have their own helicopter but the bride carries her own suitcase? When in their study of *Dallas* across cultures Liebes and Katz[133] asked for the meaning derived from the soap opera, North American respondents protested that *Dallas* cannot have a special meaning as it is just entertainment, not reality. Respondents from other cultures reproduced all sorts of different meanings from the soap. Arabs, accepting *Dallas* as reality, rejected the values of the characters, and Russians were anxious about the morality of the producers. The communication style was not viewed as compatible with Japanese communication style: Characters are not subtle enough, showing no restraint in their passions, and the soap was too explicit about what was good and bad. Overall, the program was viewed as violating Japanese sensibilities about how people should interact publicly and privately in order to achieve and maintain harmonious relationships. Whereas German viewers expressed great admiration for J.R., they also declared allegiance to Miss Ellie, the virtuous mother. For Algerians, *Dallas* was a reminder of the reality they were fast losing: the traditional values of a world where one's basic allegiance is to the extended family, with three generations living under the same roof and where the pater familias is king. The *Gbagyi* of Nigeria perceived J.R., the oil magnate in *Dallas* as *Gbagwulu*, a trickster worm from Gbagyi mythology.[134]

Soap operas developed in Europe are different from American soaps, and they also vary across countries within Europe, as to form and content. Across Latin America, several TV products easily cross borders, but also these are often adapted to national or regional particularities. Even producers of formats that cross borders, such as *Big Brother* or *Idols,* say it isn't easy to make culture fit local adaptations.[135] Chapters 9 and 10 of this book will also show how advertising formats do not easily travel across cultures.

Just as global marketers had too high expectations of the potential of global television to reach global markets, so many marketers are still excited about the Internet and the potential online ability to reach a global consumer market with one message and strategy because of its potential for global reach. However, the examples in this section show that culture influences online behavior. Diverse expectations regarding website design, layout, language, content, products, quality, and trust are all a product of cultural orientation. Therefore, having presence via a global medium does not necessarily mean companies are ready for global consumers or sales. Increasingly, interactive advertising is local, and not every company with a website is ready for global consumer interactions.[136]

Many Internet global commercial services originally initiated in the United States and later were exported to other countries, continents, and cultures. It appears this has not led to cultural homogeneity in cyberspace. Several studies have found more divergence than convergence on the Internet. For example, Segev et al.[137] found growing diversity of content in MSN local homepages. Local homepages in MSN tended to differ from the U.S. homepage over time in terms of both content and form.

The Organization of International Media Planning

Countries vary with respect to their media landscapes, so media plans of the home country cannot be used in another country. Availability, cost, and effectiveness of media vary. For example, for the classic media, the cost per gross rating point (GRP) will differ across countries. As a result, each country may need a different number of GRPs to reach the same target groups. A German washing powder manufacturer might typically buy around 80 housewife GRPs a week to support an autumn launch, but the same brand might need more than 300 GRPs a week to meet the same objectives in Italy. In another country, air time may have to be placed mainly in peak segments to achieve reasonable coverage. For television, countries can differ according to the number of channels available, viewing time, the degree of advertising clutter, and differences in television measurement techniques. Also, for the press, readership data vary by country, with the result that countries cannot easily be compared. Internet advertising has promoted development of new research systems to capture the effects, interactions, and synergies of different media in a media mix. Tying in to consumer Internet searches makes companies become more aware of what consumers want and allows them to respond to consumer wants in a more sophisticated way. The Internet allows for better consumer insight to tie into different behavioral profiles.[138] Finding the most effective media mix for each different country requires experts who know the national media landscapes.

With respect to international media planning, the choice between centralizing and decentralizing media planning is clear. Centralizing planning and implementation is possible only when media conditions are similar across markets, which is hypothetical. Foreign subsidiaries and their agencies comprehend the conditions and culture of their country best, so they are best equipped to select and plan media.

International media planning needs specialists, and most of the large international media agencies have proprietary media effectiveness tools in place to measure a variety of means of communication per product category. These tools are based on quantitative and qualitative consumer research to evaluate consumers' interaction with specific media. The outcome provides insights in consumer preferences with regard to what extent they value media, from TV advertising to point-of-purchase materials. Continuous surveys (tracking) allow benchmarking for numerous product categories and target groups.

Within advertising agencies, international media planning is still frequently relegated to specialty teams. These specialists know the media owners and how to negotiate the best value/price of each channel. For effective international media planning, such specialists are of great value. When selecting media for foreign markets, U.S. firms tend to emphasize criteria supported by American advertising research (target market, reach and frequency, and budget size), but one cannot take a successful media configuration from domestic operations and apply it abroad because the same media types are often not available.[139] If they are available, consumers don't use them in the same way. This applies even more to the Internet and mobile advertising than it does to the traditional mass media.

Summary

Marketers' promotional activities must be planned so as to affect contact points between people and brands. An increasing variety of media is available to contact consumers, in the developed world and in emerging economies. Both traditional and electronic media like the Internet and the mobile phone are available worldwide but are used by consumers in different ways. This chapter has provided many examples. Marketers have high expectations of the electronic media but at the time of writing this book, little research on effectiveness was available. Yet they cannot be ignored as consumers worldwide are increasingly using these new media.

Media have to be analyzed in the different countries in view of the communication objectives for a company's brand. Raising brand awareness will require a different choice of media than an immediate sales objective. Proper media selection and planning identify the most relevant means of communication to connect the brand and its audience. A proper media plan has to be designed and executed either locally or with the help of local experts. In order to reach the right people in the right place, at the right time, and at the right cost in different countries, first of all, consumer insight is needed in how the various media are used. The enormous variety of available media as well as the differences across cultures makes choice of media and an effective combination of media a challenge. Knowledge of how culture influences media usage across countries is of great importance.

Notes

1. George Steiner to Hans Magnus Enzensberger in an interview with *Haagse Post*, March 3, 1990.

2. *Young Asians Survey.* (2010). Ipsos Hong Kong (see Appendix B).

3. *Ofcom International Communications Market Report.* (2010, December 2), Retrieved February 20, 2012, from http://stakeholders.ofcom.org.uk/binaries/research/cmr/753567/icmr/ICMR_2010.pdf

4. IP Television. (2011). *Daily viewing minutes for Europe 2010* (36 countries). Retrieved from http://www.ip-network.com/rd/assets/file_asset/Viewing_Time_Individual.pdf

5. Austria, Belgium, Denmark, Finland, France, Germany, Greece, Ireland, Italy, Japan, Netherlands, Norway, Portugal, Spain, Sweden, Switzerland, Turkey, United Kingdom, United States. See Initiative Media (1998). Retrieved from http://www.initiative.com/

6. *Cinema, TV, and radio in the EU.* (2002). Eurostat Statistics on audiovisual services. Data Sources 1980–2002 (see Appendix B).

7. *Ofcom International Communications Market Report.* (2006). Minutes per day TV viewing per person for nine European countries (United Kingdom, France, Germany, Italy, Poland, Spain, Netherlands, Sweden, Ireland) plus Japan and the United States. Masculinity explained 56% of variance. Several other data, e.g., by Eurostat (2002), result in correlations with masculinity and power distance.

8. *TNS digital world, digital life.* (2008). http://tns-global.com (see Appendix B).

9. Bringué, X., Sádaba, C., & Tolsá, J. (2010). *La Generación Interactiva en Iberoamérica 2010: Niños y adolescentes ante las pantallas.* Fundación Telefónica: Colección Generaciones Interactivas.

10. Pasquier, D., Buzzi, C., d'Haenens, L., & Sjöberg, U. (1998). Family lifestyles and media use patterns: An analysis of domestic media among Flemish, French, Italian, and Swedish children and teenagers. *European Journal of Communication, 13,* 503–519.

11. Krotz, F., & Hasebrink, U. (1998). The analysis of people-meter data: Individual patterns of viewing behavior and viewers' cultural backgrounds. *The European Journal of Communication Research, 23,* 151–174.

12. Bringué et al., 2010.

13. Soong, R. (1999, November 8). Telenovelas in Latin America. Retrieved from http://www.zonalatina.com

14. Chalaby, J. K. (2008). Advertising in the global age: Transnational campaigns and pan-European television channels. *Global Media and Communication, 4*(2), 139–156.

15. *Ofcom International Communications Market Report,* 2010.

16. Media Literacy Clearinghouse. (2012). *Media use statistics.* Retrieved March 6, 2012, from http://www.frankbaker.com

17. *Ofcom International Telecommunications Market Report* (2006). United Kingdom, France, Germany, Italy, United States, Japan, China.

18. *Ofcom International Communications Market Report,* 2010.

19. *Ofcom International Communications Market Report,* 2010.

20. Do, J., Kim, D., Kim, D. Y., & Kim, E-m. (2009). When mobile phones meet television . . . : An FGI analysis of mobile broadcasting users in Korea. *Media, Culture & Society, 31*(4): 669–679.

21. From 1980 onward, for 44 countries worldwide and for 15 developed countries in Europe, individualism explained between 40% and 72% of variance. Data Sources, UN Statistical Yearbooks (see Appendix B).

22. Medios de comunicacion Annuario de Medios: El escenario Iberoamericano. (2007). Madrid. Fundacion Telefonica.

23. *Ofcom International Communications Market Report,* 2010.

24. UNESCO Institute for Statistics. See http://www.uis.unesco.org/literacy/

25. Hallin, D. C., & Mancini, P. (2004). *Comparing media systems.* Cambridge, MA: Cambridge University Press, p. 64.

26. *Social values, science, and technology.* (2005, June). Eurobarometer Report (EBS 225), 27 countries (see Appendix B).

27. Coen, R. J. (1997). *The insider's report.* New York: McCann Erickson. Retrieved from http://www.McCann.com

28. Elvestad, E., & Blekesaune, A. (2008). Newspaper readers in Europe: A multilevel study of individual and national differences. *European Journal of Communication, 23*(4), 425–447.

29. Data Sources, *European Social Survey* 2004/2005 (see Appendix B) and *European Media and Marketing Survey* 2012 (see Appendix B) (r = −.66***).

30. Hallin & Mancini, 2004.

31. Medios de comunicacion Annuario de Medios: El escenario Iberoamericano. (2007). Madrid. Fundacion Telefonica.

32. Houston Santhanam, L., & Rosenstiel, T. (2011). The state of the news media 2011. Pew Research Center's Project for Excellence in Journalism. Retrieved March 7, 2012, from http://stateofthemedia.org/2011/mobile-survey/international-newspaper-economics/

33. *European Media and Marketing Survey* 2012 (see Appendix B).

34. Bhatia, T. K., & Bhargava, M. (2008). Reaching the unreachable: Resolving globalization vs. localization paradox. *Journal of Creative Communications, 3*(2), 209–230.

35. De Mooij, M. (2014). *Human and mediated communication around the world*: A *comprehensive review and analysis.* Cham: Springer International.

36. Castells, M. (2009). *Communication power.* Oxford, UK: Oxford University Press.

37. Jinghua, H., & Xuerui, Y. (2009). Influences on use of the mobile phone for Internet connectivity in China. *Media Asia, 36*(4), 210–215.

38. Data World Bank, 2010 (see Appendix B).

39. The International Telecommunication Union (ITU), originally founded as the International Telegraph Union, is a specialized agency of the United Nations which is responsible for information and communication technologies (see Appendix B).

40. *E-Communications household survey.* (2011). Special Eurobarometer Report (EBS 362) (see Appendix B).

41. *Ofcom International Communications Market Report,* 2010.

42. *Ofcom International Communications Market Report,* 2010.

43. *E-Communication household survey.* (2008). Special Eurobarometer Report (EBS 293). (See Appendix B.)

44. Ito, Y. (1993). The future of political communication research: A Japanese perspective. *Journal of Communication, 43*(4), 69–79.

45. Albarran, A. B., & Hutton, B. (2009). Young Latinos use of mobile phones: A cross-cultural study. Retrieved December 10, 2011, from http://connection.ebscohost .com/c/articles/45615662/young-latinos-use-mobile-phones-cross-cultural-study

46. Ishii, K. (2009). Mobile Internet use in Japan: Social consequences of technology convergence. *Media Asia, 36*(4), 201–209.

47. Korenaga, R., & Komuro, H. (2009). Going out of tune? Use of mobile phone TV among Japanese youth. *Media Asia, 36*(4), 194–200.

48. Wei, R., & Jinhua, H. (2009). Mobile phone as third screen? An adoption study of mobile TV in China. *Media Asia, 36*(4), 187–193.

49. Phillips, S. (2010, August 4). Mobile Internet more popular in China than in U.S. *Nielsenwire.* Retrieved February 25, 2012, from http://www.nielsen.com/us/en/newswire/ 2010/mobile-internet-more-popular-in-china-than-in-u-s.html

50. Jinghua & Xuerui, 2009.

51. Do et al., 2009.

52. Archambault, J. S. (2011). Breaking up "because of the phone" and the transformative potential of information in Southern Mozambique. *New Media & Society, 13*(3), 444–456.

53. AdReaction 2012–Global report. *Millward Brown.* Retrieved January 10, 2013, from http://www.millwardbrown.com/ChangingChannels/2012/Docs/AdReaction/Millward Brown_AdReaction2012_Global.pdf

54. Barnett, G. A., & Sung, E. (2005). Culture and the structure of the international hyperlink network. *Journal of Computer-Mediated Communication, 11*(1), article 11. Retrieved from http://jcmc.indiana.edu/v0111/issue1/barnett.html

55. *E-communications household survey,* 2008.

56. *European Social Survey,* 2003. (See Appendix B.)

57. *European cultural values.* (2007). Special Eurobarometer Report (EBS 278). (See Appendix B.)

58. ITU, 2011.

59. La Ferle, C., Edwards, S. M., & Mizuno, Y. (2002, April). Internet diffusion in Japan: Cultural considerations. *Journal of Advertising Research,* pp. 65–79.

60. *The Public Pulse.* (1997, October/November). *Roper Starch Worldwide, 12,* 5.

61. *Ofcom International Communications Market Report,* 2010.

62. *Ofcom International Communications Market Report,* 2010.

63. Schroeder, R. (2010). Mobile phones and the inexorable advance of multimodal connectedness. *New Media & Society, 12*(1), 75–90.

64. Akpan-Obong, P. (2010). Unintended outcomes in information and communication technology adoption: A micro-level analysis of usage in context. *Journal of Asian and African Studies, 45*(2), 181–195.

65. Mareck, M. (1999, December). Research watch. *M&M Europe,* 47.

66. Peng, T-Q., & Zhu, J. J. H. (2010). A game of win-win or win-lose? Revisiting the Internet's influence on sociability and use of traditional media. *New Media & Society, 13*(4), 568–586.

67. *Los Medios y Mercados de Latinoamérica.* (1998). In Zonalatina.com, posted by Roland Soong, September 4, 1999.

68. Cho, H., Rivera-Sánchez, M., & Lim, S. S. (2009). A multinational study on online privacy: Global concerns and local responses. *New Media & Society, 11*(3), 395–416.

69. ITU, 2011.

70. Ko, H., Roberts, M. S., & Cho, C. H. (2006). Cross-cultural differences in motivations and perceived interactivity: A comparative study of American and Korean Internet users. *Journal of Current Issues and Research in Advertising, 28*(2), 93–104.

71. Murphy, J., & Scharl, A. (2007). An investigation of global versus local online branding. *International Marketing Review, 24*(3), 297–312.

72. Dawkins, R. (1989). *The selfish gene.* Oxford, UK: Oxford University Press.

73. Vuylsteke, A., Wen, Z., Baesens, B., & Poelmans, J. (2010). Consumers' online information search: A cross-cultural study between China and Western Europe. *Journal of Interactive Marketing, 24*(4), 209–331.

74. Jeong, Y., & Mahmood, R. (2011). Reading the world's mind: Political, socioeconomic and cultural approaches to understanding worldwide Internet search queries. *The International Communication Gazette, 73*(3), 233–251.

75. Berger, G. (2009). How the Internet impacts on international news: Exploring paradoxes of the most global medium in a time of "hyperlocalism." *The International Communication Gazette, 71*(5), 355–371.

76. Hollis, N. (2012). The new Facebook global pages are really local pages [Blog]. *Straight Talk.* Retrieved January 10, 2013, from http://www.millwardbrown.com/Global/Blog/Post/2012-11-05/The-new-Facebook-global-pages-are-really-local-pages.aspx

77. Maddox, L. M., & Gong, W. (2009). Online buying decisions in China. In H. Li, S. Huang, & D. Jin (Eds.), *Proceedings of the 2009 American Academy of Advertising Asia-Pacific Conference* (p. 261). American Academy of Advertising, in conjunction with China Association of Advertising of Commerce, and Communication University of China.

78. Ahn, H., Kwon, M. W., & Yuan, L. (2009). When talking about global brands in cyberspace, culturalfree or cultural-bound? A cross-cultural study of the U.S. and Chinese brand community web sites. In H. Li, S. Huang, & D. Jin (Eds.), *The Proceedings of the 2009 American Academy of Advertising Asia-Pacific Conference* (p. 117). American Academy of Advertising, in conjunction with China Association of Advertising of Commerce, and Communication University of China.

79. Cyr, D., Bonanni, C., Ilsever, J., & Bowes, J. (2003). *Trust and design: A cross-cultural comparison*. ACM Conference on Universal Usability. Vancouver, BC.

80. Krishna, R., & Guru, S. (2010). Online shopping: Motivators and barriers. *Media Asia, 37*(3), 157–162.

81. Goodrich, K., & De Mooij, M. (2011). New technology mirrors old habits: Online buying mirrors cross-national variance of conventional buying. *Journal of International Consumer Marketing, 23*(3–4), 246–259.

82. *Consumer empowerment.* (2011, April). Special Eurobarometer Report (EBS 342). (See Appendix B.)

83. La Ferle, C. (2007). Global issues in online advertising. In D. W. Schumann & E. Thorson (Eds.), *Internet theory and research* (p. 295). Philadelphia: Lawrence Erlbaum.

84. Hollis, N. (2012). *Straight Talk* [Blog]. Blogs about how social media helps brand building: October 1: China; October 15: Brazil; November 8: Russia; November 26: India. All retrieved on January 10, 2013, from http://www.millwardbrown.com/Global/Blog/Post/2012

85. Veilbrief, A. (2007, January). Chattend de puberteit door (Chatting through adolescence). *NRC Handelsblad Maandblad,* pp. 20–25.

86. Albarran, A. B., Dyer, C., Hutton, B., & Valentine, A. (2010, August 4–7). *Social media and young Latinos: A cross-cultural examination.* Paper presented to the Media Management and Economics Division at the 2010 AEJMC Conference, Denver, Colorado. Retrieved February 25, 2012, from http://www.allacademic.com/meta/p433602_index.html

87. Vasalou, A., Joinson, A. N., & Courvoisier, D. (2010). Cultural differences, experience with social networks and the nature of "true commitment" in Facebook. *International Journal of Human-Computer Studies, 68,* 719–728.

88. Ioffe, J. (2010, December 29). Facebook's Russian campaign. *Business Week.* Retrieved from http://www.businessweek.com/magazine/content/11_02/b4210032487137.htm

89. Social media use per country as a percentage of overall mobile web traffic. In Von Tetzchner, J. (2011). *State of the mobile web, April 2011.* Retrieved November 12, 2011, from http://www.opera.com/smw/2011/04/

90. Boase, J., Horrigan, J. B., Wellman, B., & Rainie, L. (2006). The strength of Internet ties. *Pew Internet & American Life Project,* Washington, DC. Retrieved from http://www.pewinternet.org/Reports/2006/The-Strength-of-Internet-Ties.aspx

91. Goodrich, K., & De Mooij, M. (2013). How "social" are social media? A cross-cultural comparison of online and offline purchase decision influences. *Journal of Marketing Communications* [Special Issue: Word of Mouth and Social Media].

92. Qiu, L., Lin, H., & Leung, A. K.-Y. (2013). Cultural differences and switching of in-group sharing behavior between and American (Facebook) and a Chinese (Renren) Social Networking Site. *Journal of Cross-Cultural Psychology, 44*(1), 106–121.

93. Morozov, E. (2011). *The net delusion: The dark side of Internet freedom.* New York: PublicAffairs.

94. See http://www.checkfacebook.com/

95. Sawers, P. (2011). Why Twitter outguns Facebook in Japan. *TNW Conference 2011.* Retrieved April 25, 2011, from http://thenextweb.com/socialmedia/2011/02/02/why-twitter-outguns-facebook-in-japan/

96. Kim, K-H., & Yun, H. (2007). Cying for me, Cying for us: Relational dialectics in a Korean social network site. *Journal of Computer-Mediated Communication, 13*(1), article 15. Retrieved from http://jcmc.indiana.edu/vol13/issue1/kim.yun.html

97. Moore, T., (2010, April 13). Facebook under attack in Germany over privacy. *Time.com.* Retrieved from http://www.time.com/time/world/article/0,8599,1981524,00 .html

98. Williams, J., (2011, February 11). The growing popularity of social networking in Indonesia. Pronet Advertising. Retrieved from http://www.pronetadvertising.com/articles/ the-growing-popularity-of-social-networking-in-indonesia.html

99. Sima, Y., & Pugsley, P. C. (2010). The rise of a "me culture" in postsocialist China: Youth, individualism and identity creation in the blogosphere. *The International Communication Gazette, 72*(3), 287–306.

100. Van Belleghem, S. (2010). Social media around the world. InSites Consulting. Retrieved February 22, 2012, from http://www.slideshare.net/stevenvanbelleghem/social-networks-around-the-world-2010

101. Specht, N. (2010). How social media is used in Germany, China and Brazil. Retrieved from   http://blog.hubspot.com/blog/tabid/6307/bid/5948/3-Social-Media-Lessons-For -Global-Marketers.aspx

102. Van Belleghem, S., Thijs, D., & De Ruijck, T. (2012). Social media around the world. InSites Consulting. Retrieved April 16, 2013, from http://www.slideshare.net/ InSitesConsulting/social-media-around-the-world-2012-by-insites-consulting

103. *TNS digital world*, 16 countries.

104. Su, M. N., Wang, Y., Mark, G., Aiyelokun, G., & Nakano, T. (2005). A bosom buddy afar brings a distant land near: Are bloggers a global community? *Proceedings of the Second International Conference on Communities and Technologies* (C&T, 2005).

105. Lewis Global Public Relations. (2007, March). *Blogs and business value.* Retrieved from http://www.lewis360.com/2007/03/blogs_and_busin.html

106. *EIAA Online Shoppers 2008, Executive summary* (2008), Data Mediascope.

107. Dawar, N., Parker, P. M., & Price, L. J., (1996). A cross-cultural study of interpersonal information exchange. *Journal of International Business Studies, 27*(3), 497–516; Pornpitakpan, C. (2004). Factors associated with opinion seeking: A cross-national study. *Journal of Global Marketing 17*(2/3), 91–113.

108. La Ferle, C., & Kim, H. J. (2006). Cultural influences on Internet motivations and communication styles: A comparison of Korean and U.S. consumers. *International Journal of Internet Marketing and Advertising, 2*(3), 142–157.

109. Cho, C. H., & Cheon, H. J. (2005). Cross-cultural comparisons of interactivity on corporate web sites: The United States, the United Kingdom, Japan, and South Korea. *Journal of Advertising, 34*(2), 99–116.

110. Schultz, D. E., & Block, M. P. (2009). Understanding Chinese media audiences: An exploratory study of Chinese consumers media consumption and a comparison with the U.S.A. H. Li, S. Huang, & D. Jin (Eds.), *Proceedings of the 2009 American Academy of Advertising Asia-Pacific Conference.* American Academy of Advertising, in conjunction with China Association of Advertising of Commerce, and Communication University of China.

111. Pornpitakpan, 2004.

112. Goodrich & De Mooij, 2013.

113. *Consumer empowerment.* (2011). Special Eurobarometer Report (EBS 342).

114. Goodrich & De Mooij, 2013.

115. *EIAA Online Shoppers 2008, Executive summary.* (2008). Mediascope Europe. Retrieved from http://www.eiaa.net

116. Appleton, R. (2008, September 29). Writing SEO copy that sells. Retrieved from http://www.searchmarketingstandard.com/articles/2008/09/writing-seo-copy-that-sells.html

117. Rodgers, S., Chen, O., Wang, Y., Rettie, R., & Alpert, F. (2007). The Web Motivation Inventory: Replication and application to Internet advertising. *International Journal of Advertising, 26*(4), 447–476.

118. IAB display advertising guidelines: The new 2012 portfolio. IAB (Interactive Advertising Bureau). Retrieved November 27, 2012, from http://www.iab.net/guidelines/508676/508767/displayguidelines

119. OPA (Online Publishers Association) Europe. See http://www.opa-europe.org

120. *Reconnect Europe.* (2006, July). Research conducted by Orange Home UK plc and OMD Insight. Over 12,500 respondents were surveyed in six countries: United Kingdom, France, Germany, Italy, Spain, Netherlands.

121. Robinson, H., Wysocka, A., & Hand, C. (2007). Internet advertising effectiveness— the effect of design on click-through rates for banner ads. *International Journal of Advertising, 26*(4), 527–542.

122. Moorey-Denham, S., & Green, A. (2007, March). The effectiveness of online video advertising. *Admap,* pp. 45–47.

123. Hollis, N. (2012, June 18). Why I think the best advertising on Facebook is not actually advertising [Blog]. *Straight Talk with Nigel Hollis.* Retrieved January 11, 2013, from http://www.millwardbrown.com/Global/Blog/Post/2012-06-18/Why-I-think-the-best-advertising-on-Facebook-is-not-actually-advertising.aspx

124. Hollis, N. (2012, May 8 & December 10). How does social media affect brand equity? [Blog] *Straight Talk with Nigel Hollis.* Retrieved July 20, 2012, from http://www.millwardbrown.com/Global/Blog/Post/2012-05-08/How-does-social-media-affect-brand-equity.aspx; Beyond the mindless pursuit of fans and followers. [Blog] *Straight Talk with Nigel Hollis.* Retrieved January 10, 2013, from http://www.millwardbrown.com/Global/Blog/Post/2012-12-10/Beyond-the-mindless-pursuit-of-fans-and-followers.aspx

125. Millward Brown. (2011). Nestlé KitKat 2011. Retrieved July 20, 2012, from http://www.millwardbrown.com/Files/SABR%20-%20Nestle%20Kit%20Kat.pdf; Kit Kat "Choose a Chunky Champion" campaign [The Trump Card Blog]. Retrieved January 13, 2013, from http://thetrumpcard.tumblr.com/post/16183489588/kit-kat-social-media-campaign

126. Hollis, 2012, October 1 and 15.

127. Hollis, N. (2012, June 20). Is mobile advertising ever going to live up to expectation [Blog]. *Straight Talk with Nigel Hollis.* Retrieved January 13, 2013, from http://www.millwardbrown.com/Global/Blog/Post/2012-06-20/Is-mobile-advertising-ever-going-to-live-up-to-expectation.aspx

128. Millward Brown & DynamicLogic. (2012). FanIndex–Measuring the brand value of your Facebook fan page. Retrieved January 13, 2013, from http://www.millwardbrown.com/Solutions/ProprietaryTools/FanIndex.aspx

129. Moriarty, S., Mitchell, N., & Wells, W. (2009). *Advertising principles & practice.* Upper Saddle River, NJ: Pearson, p. 293.

130. Muk, A. (2007). Consumers' intentions to opt in to SMS advertising: A cross-national study of young Americans and Koreans. *International Journal of Advertising, 26*(2), 177–198.

131. Mobile advertising guidelines. (2007, December). Mobile Marketing Association, p. 2.

132. Harris, P., Rettie, R., & Kwan, C. C. (2005). Adoption and usage of m-commerce: A cross-cultural comparison of Hong Kong and the United Kingdom. *Journal of Electronic Commerce Research, 6*(3), 210–224.

133.   Liebes, T., & Katz, E. (1993). *The export of meaning: Cross-cultural readings of Dallas*. Cambridge, MA: Polity Press.

134.   Rogers, E. M., Singhal, A., & Thombre, A. (2004). Indian audience interpretations of health-related content in the bold and the beautiful. *Gazette: The International Journal for Communication Studies, 66*(5), 437–458.

135.   De Mooij, M. (2014). *Human and mediated communication around the world: A comprehensive review and analysis*. Cham: Springer International.

136.   La Ferle, C. (2007). Global issues in online advertising. In D. W. Schumann & E. Thorson (Eds.), *Advertising and the World Wide Web*. Philadelphia: Lawrence Erlbaum Associates.

137.   Segev, E., Ahituv, N., & Barzilai-Nahon, K. (2007). Mapping diversities and tracing trends of cultural homogeneity/heterogeneity in cyberspace. *Journal of Computer-Mediated Communication, 12*(4), article 7. Retrieved from http://jcmc.indiana.edu/vol12/issue4/segev.html

138.   Briggs, R. (2005, April). How the Internet is reshaping advertising. *Admap,* pp. 59–61.

139.   Kanso, A. M., & Nelson, R. A. (2007). Multinational corporations and the challenge of global advertising: What do U.S. headquarters consider important in making media-selection decisions? *International Marketing Review, 24*(5), 563–590.

CHAPTER 9

Culture and Advertising Appeals

Three aspects of advertising style were pointed out that are each prone to influence by culture: (a) the values and motives included in the appeal, the central message; (b) the basic advertising form; and (c) the execution: the casting and activities of people, the setting, and the interrelationship. Consumers do not distinguish these elements the way advertising academics or professionals do. For consumers, it is the total picture that is important. The total picture reflects communication style and enables people to connect. Yet, for professional purposes, we have to understand the role of all elements of an advertisement to be able to analyze whether an advertisement is culture-fit. This chapter will focus on the appeals in advertising. It will discuss the *value paradox* in advertising and give examples of how cultural dimensions can be recognized in advertising appeals. A few specific appeals will be discussed, like the country-of-origin appeal and the use of humor in advertising.

Appeals in Advertising

The appeal in advertising is a comprehensive concept. The appeal includes values and motives that define the central message. Moriarty, Mitchell, and Wells[1] state that an appeal "connects with some emotion that makes the product particularly attractive or interesting, such as security, esteem, fear, sex, and sensory pleasure." The appeal is also used to describe a general creative strategy. Emphasis on the price is an economy appeal. A status appeal is used for presenting quality, expensive products. The combination of the appeal (including motives), basic advertising form, and execution makes up advertising style.

Advertising is shaped by the culture in which it is practiced, so logically, appeals reflect the values of that culture. When the values of consumers are congruent with the values reflected in advertising, the link to liking the ad, the brand, or the company increases, and advertising will be more effective.[2]

Many studies have pointed at cultural values reflected in advertising, and particularly, content analysis based studies have revealed culture-specific appeals in advertising that can be explained by the Hofstede dimensions. Although most research conducted to analyze values in advertising appeals is comparative content analysis of advertising,[3] content analysis has been criticized for providing description without prescription.[4] However, we argue that if in a country certain style elements are more common than in others, these style elements are used because they appear to be more effective.[5]

A problem of cross-cultural content analysis is the organization and logistics of a large-scale cross-country study. In particular, when using cultural variables like the Hofstede dimensions, comparison should be across more than two countries.[6] Unfortunately, there are few large-scale cross-cultural studies, and most compare the United States with one other country. Some regions are clearly understudied, such as Africa and Latin America. Out of 36 studies found by Chang et al.,[7] 25 studies compared only two countries, and culture as a key concept was seldom explicitly defined. In 33 studies, the United States was the point of reference, and the most used cultural dimension was Hofstede's individualism/collectivism. In none of the studies was cultural paradox taken into account. It is not easy to recognize values in advertising as advertising appeals do not necessarily follow the norms of a culture. They may even go against them. To understand this, we first have to return to the value paradox.

The Value Paradox as an Effective Advertising Instrument

In advertising, some values can easily be recognized as a reflection of culture. Self-actualization, self-interest, and self-esteem are examples of such values. They fit individualistic cultures. Also, doing it your own way and going it alone are expressions of an individualistic culture. But belonging is also a strong value of individualistic cultures. This seems paradoxical. That is because there are often opposing elements in one value. Thus, advertising appeals or claims may represent two opposing statements about values. This is related to the desirable and the desired, the distinction between what people think ought to be desired and what people actually desire, or how people think the world ought to be versus what people want for themselves, as discussed in Chapter 3.

In advertising, the opposing values of a culture, although often paradoxical, appear to be effective because they relate to the important aspects of people's lives. Belonging is a ubiquitous value in American advertising, particularly in the sentimental, emotional form. It is included in the concept of "homecoming." It is not a value to use in an appeal in Japanese advertising. In individualistic cultures, the need to belong may be a reaction to extreme individualism and can be reflected in showing more family life than there may actually be. Not understanding this paradox causes researchers to formulate wrong hypotheses or express feelings of surprise about the results of comparative studies, as Okazaki & Mueller[8] do, writing "surprisingly, the data revealed that Japanese ads made less use of group/consensus appeals than did U.S. ads. Also unexpectedly, Japanese ads were found to make greater use of the typically Western individual independence appeal than US ads."

The desired and the desirable are reflected in people's behavior and in how they relate to each other. Both the desired and the desirable are recognized in advertising appeals or claims, but they may be expressed in opposing ways. This makes it even more difficult to understand words and concepts that are labels of values of a culture other than one's own. An example is the concept of sharing in the English language. Superficially, this may imply a non-individualistic and/or feminine caring concept, meaning "not keeping things for oneself." Yet in a masculine and individualistic culture, it reflects more. It reflects winning and communicating one's success and achievement to others. One shares only the positive things of oneself. One does not share failure. Facebook uses the concept of sharing in this sense, but translations into other languages do not necessarily refer to the same concept.

Generally, one has to be very cautious with such concepts as they are ambiguous, and when translated into other languages, half of the meaning may be lost. If translated, a positive meaning may also change into a negative one.

Paradoxical value statements can be recognized in three ways:

1. Statements contrary to common belief, for example, that the Japanese are individualizing whereas they actually are collectivistic. As in all increasingly wealthy societies, the Japanese are focusing more on individuality, but their behavior is collectivistic compared with Western societies. What is perceived as individualizing is changing competitive behavior.

2. Statements that seem contradictory but that may in fact be true. Seemingly opposing values of one dimension, such as "belonging" and "going it alone" coexist in an individualistic culture.

3. As paradox type 2: Values that seem to be paradoxical within one dimension but can be explained by the configuration with other dimensions. An example is simultaneous "equality" and "large wage differences," a paradox of the configuration low power distance and masculinity.

The next sections will present some examples of paradoxes.

Equality Paradox

Equality is a strong desirable value of U.S. culture, but the actual behavior of Americans does not show so much equality. American behavior is related to fairness: the belief that people should get what they deserve if they have the capabilities and work hard. This value results in inequality: If you have worked hard, you have earned the right to be different, to earn more—sometimes excessively more—money than others. CEOs of U.S. companies can earn 40 times as much as an ordinary production worker. The biggest increases in income inequalities have occurred in America, Britain, and New Zealand. Wage differences in most of continental Europe also changed, but to a lesser degree. In continental Europe, increased wages of top managers of large companies have caused protests, and CEOs have even been asked to lower their salaries. So equality in the United States means the poor have equal rights to become rich, and equality in a large part of Europe means the rich should be equally "poor."

Dependence and Freedom Paradoxes

Another paradox can be found in dependence versus independence, the opposing values related to power distance and individualism. In high power distance and collectivistic cultures, children remain dependent on their parents much longer than in low power distance and individualistic cultures, where children are supposed to go their own way, be self-reliant, and make their own decisions at an early age. This is extreme in the United States. An example is an event in 1996, when a 7-year-old girl who wanted to set the record as the youngest pilot in the world crashed and died. Her mother was quoted as saying, "It was her own decision." Independence is a widely used concept or cue in Western advertising but also in Japan. There, an appeal in advertising is independence as opposed to dependency, which is such a strong part of Japanese culture. Also, a study comparing advertising appeals in the United States and Russia found independence as an appeal both in the United States and Russia.[9]

Related to dependency are the opposing values and paradoxes of freedom. In low power distance cultures, freedom means independence. In a collectivistic culture, the opposing values are freedom and harmony. Freedom can mean disharmony, as one ought to conform to the group. Freedom versus belonging can be opposing values for feminine cultures. Because of affiliation needs in feminine cultures, belonging is an implicit value and is related to conformance, consensus. Yet in order to succeed, one wants to express oneself, be different. This goes against the norm, the desirable. Freedom reflects the desired. The freedom-belonging paradox is typical of the Scandinavian cultures and the Netherlands. The Dutch, for example, are notorious for searching for freedom in their holidays by traveling to France or Spain, but they take their own mobile homes (caravan or trailer) with them and go to a camping area where they are sure they will find their compatriots.

In a strong uncertainty avoidance culture, too much freedom may lead toward undesired chaos, which cannot be tolerated, so the opposing value is order. In strong uncertainty avoidance cultures, freedom breeds uncertainty, whereas in weak uncertainty avoidance cultures, freedom breeds success. People in strong uncertainty avoidance cultures take calculated risks to avoid failure; in weak uncertainty avoidance cultures, people take risks to succeed.

In sum, freedom paradoxes vary by culture. For a high power distance culture like France, it is freedom versus dependence. For a collectivistic culture like Japan, it is freedom versus harmony. For a feminine culture like the Netherlands, it is freedom versus belonging, and for a high uncertainty avoidance culture, it is freedom versus order.

Success Paradoxes

The norm, the desirable, in short-term oriented cultures, in particular when combined with high masculinity, is that one wants to shine, to show one's success. Success is communicated, shared, and displayed because it is natural to show off. This is less the norm in long-term oriented cultures, in particular when combined with femininity. Although a universal desire is to be recognized when one achieves something, success cannot be demonstrated directly. Because showing off is against the norm, demonstrating success must be done indirectly. Whereas the British (masculine culture) can say straightforwardly that they are the best, as British Telecom does: "We have the best connections," the Dutch, Danes, and Swedes (feminine) are not likely to do so. The paradox is frequently found in appeals such as, "There is more to it than meets the eye" or "True refinement comes from within" (Volvo, Sweden). Advertising in a masculine culture says, "Show your neighbors," whereas in a feminine culture advertising will say, "Don't show your neighbors." The paradox is in an advertising claim like "Brilliant in its simpleness" (Omega watches, the Netherlands): On the one hand, one should not show off (the desirable), yet if successful, one wants to be recognized (the desired).

The Innovation and Global Paradox

Although low uncertainty avoidance cultures tend to be more innovative, appeals like new, modern, and innovative are also attractive to members of high uncertainty avoidance cultures. This is similar for international or global appeals. Members of high uncertainty avoidance cultures like to be international, global, cosmopolitan, although in reality, the local is more important. Characteristic of strong uncertainty avoidance is resistance to change, yet words like *new* are also found in high uncertainty avoidance cultures like France and Germany.[10] Although the cue word *new* is much seen in advertising, actual buying behavior may not be so innovative. For individualists, new and modern means adventure; for collectivists, being modern and international reflects belonging to a greater world. Although local is the norm, global is an attractive appeal. On the one hand, the Chinese are driven by the desire for global cosmopolitanism and derive face from global brands; on the other hand, they have a countervailing desire for local goods that use Chinese appeals.

In particular in Spain, the innovation and global paradoxes are strong. The Spanish way of life as reflected in advertising is warm, caring about others, different and original, even if full of unpredictable factors. On the one hand, the Spanish feel the desire to be modern and innovative; on the other hand, the desirable is stability because of the difficulty of coping with ambiguity.

Examples of Appeals by Dimension

In this section, examples of appeals found in advertising will be described by dimension, as well as activities and interactions between people in television commercials that are often deemed to be "only executional" but that reflect basic cultural values. In this chapter, as in most of the book, the Hofstede dimensions are used because these have been applied most to advertising across cultures.

Power Distance

Status symbols are less frequently used in low power distance cultures than in high power distance cultures where prestige is an important appeal. An example is the use of certain status sports such as golf. Power claims can be verbal and direct: "Save your power for the work place" (from an advertisement for the Lexus in Singapore) or as a verbal or visual metaphor: blue blood or yachts, referring to royalty (found in advertising in Portugal, see Illustration 9.1). In the execution, power distance can be shown in the way people interrelate or by the type of people shown (older vs.

younger). In high power distance cultures, the elder (grandmother, mother, or aunt) advises the younger (daughter or niece). Procter & Gamble has carefully differentiated its advertising for this cultural difference, as found in commercials for the brand ACE and washing liquid brands Dreft and Yes. In low power distance cultures, the younger advises the elder (daughter advises mother), as in P&G commercials for Yes in Sweden and Dreft in the Netherlands. A typical Japanese example of high power distance behavior is in a commercial for Shinko Sangyo, "Saideria Home," which reflects the custom that when a group of people share a car, the boss or any higher placed person must always be brought home first, even if others live closer to the road taken. In this commercial, this custom allows the whole group to admire the nice home of the boss.

Another example is a TV commercial (see Illustration 9.2) for Boss canned coffee, which reflects the *senpai-kohai* (elder-younger in work) relationship. A famous Japanese rock singer (Eikichi

Illustration 9.1 Alfa 33, Portugal

Illustration 9.2 Boss, Japan

Yazawa) plays the role of an elder (*senpai*) Japanese salaryman. It is raining when he leaves the office, and a younger colleague (*kohai*) offers to get his older colleague's car, so he will not get wet. This is a situation not found in low power distance cultures where equality values are strong.

In high power distance cultures, where elders are respected, ads also tend to refer to generations, for example, to fathers and grandfathers who also used the product or brand. This reference to generations is reflected in the advertisement for Azzaro, showing three generations (Illustration 9.3). In high power distance cultures, elder people who dress up as young ones are viewed as "not grown-up." A global advertisement for Carrera sunglasses shows what is perceived as an older man (known to Americans as the professional wrestler Terry Bollea, nicknamed "Hulk Hogan") dressed up as a young hippie. This is not a particularly attractive picture to people in high power distance cultures (Illustration 9.4). People will judge such a person as not grown up.

Independence is an appeal reflecting the desirable in low power distance cultures. In high power distance cultures, it reflects the desired. A Japanese ad for Honda uses the words in the copy, "I'm independent," in English. In high power distance cultures, children are more protected and are independent at a later age than in low power distance cultures. Showing a young child alone, struggling to enter a building with his bicycle, as in a Dutch commercial for Blue Band margarine (Illustration 9.5), is not accepted in high power distance cultures. The Dutch will see the boy as an enterprising, independent child, whereas in other cultures, he will be pitied because he is left on his own. In contrast, an Italian TV commercial for Granarolo milk shows a young (spoiled) boy in a high-status setting (country manor, servants). He doesn't want to drink milk, although the servants offer him all sorts of cookies, but when Granarolo is offered, he accepts, and everybody applauds (Illustration 9.6).

Illustration 9.3 Azzaro, International

Illustration 9.4 Carrera, International

Illustration 9.5 Blue Band, Netherlands

Illustration 9.6   Granarolo, Italy

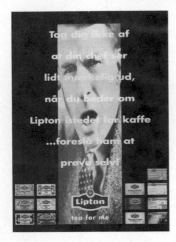

Illustration 9.7   Lipton, Denmark

Respect or disrespect for teachers or bosses in advertising is a reflection of high or low power distance. A Danish advertisement for Lipton tea saying, "Drive your boss mad by making him drink your tea" (Illustration 9.7), should not be used in France, Spain, or Italy. Low power distance is reflected in the antiauthoritarian elements of parody and humorous advertising.

The concept of an "empowered consumer" included in a company's claim, "Judge for yourself"—or more implicitly when a company stresses its role as a facilitator instead of imposing ideas or creating a dependency relationship with the consumer—is part of low power distance cultures.

Individualism/Collectivism

As described in earlier chapters, an important difference between individualistic and collectivistic cultures is between low-context and high-context communication. In individualistic cultures, the public tends to be addressed in a direct and personalized way. Words like *you*, *we*, and *I* are frequently used. So are imperatives. U.S. examples are "You flip a switch and . . ." (Detroit Edison), "Treat yourself right" (Crystal Light), "You have a dream, make a wish . . ." (Reebok). Whereas presenters in individualistic cultures address the public directly, the purpose of using well-known presenters or endorsers in collectivistic cultures is that the audience can associate with them. In individualistic cultures, the personal pronoun *I* is frequently used, as in the global advertisement for Nike (Illustration 9.8) and in the advertisement for Lucky Strike (Illustration 9.9). The latter was used in Spain, where this approach is not very attractive. A better approach is in the advertisement for the cigarette brand L&M (Illustration 9.10), which says, "Better in companionship." A Chinese commercial for Adidas (see illustration 9.11) at the Olympics of 2008 shows a Chinese swim champion who wins being carried by the group. It says "Together in 2008. Impossible is nothing."

Low-context communication is more textual and high-context communication more visual. However, new technology has made it easier for art directors worldwide to make more visual integrated ads. Also, in a low-context culture like the United States, this has led to less copy.[11]

Illustration 9.8 Nike, Spain

Illustration 9.9 Lucky Strike, Spain

Illustration 9.10 L&M, Spain

Illustration 9.11 Adidas, China

Context also plays a role in the sense that in collectivistic cultures like China, local appeals fit in advertising for local brands, whereas foreign appeals fit in advertising for global brands. To the Chinese, global brands reflect modernity, sophistication, and technology. They expect global, Western-type advertising and appeals for global brands, but advertising for their own Chinese brands must reflect Chinese values. Global brands are not supposed to use Chinese values as appeals, and non-Chinese spokespersons should not invoke Chinese values in advertising.[12]

The difference between the independent and interdependent self has an important impact on advertising appeals. Members of individualistic and collectivistic societies will respond differently to advertisements emphasizing individualistic or collectivistic appeals. In collectivistic cultures, such as China and Korea, appeals focusing on in-group benefits, harmony, and family are more effective, whereas in individualistic cultures like the United States, advertising is more effective when it appeals to individual benefits and preferences, personal success, and independence.[13] A commercial where a man breaks out from a group and starts doing something on his own that the group hasn't thought of would be seen as positive in the individualistic cultures of the West but negative in collectivistic Asian cultures.[14]

Yet, paradoxically, the appeal of deviating from the group has been found in collectivistic cultures. Although the Chinese are not known for deviating from the collective norm, this may not apply to choice of commodities. The beer brand Beck's used the deviation idea by showing a field of sunflowers facing the sun. One turns to the west where a bottle of Beck's stands. Another version shows a family of crabs moving sideways in a single, tight row. One of them spots a bottle of Beck's beer in the sand and breaks ranks.[15] This demonstrates the paradoxical aspect of individualism-collectivism. In individualistic cultures, there is no point in a message saying you can deviate since there is no collective norm, but in collectivistic cultures it has meaning, unless it concerns more important issues than buying commodities.

Yet sharing remains an important element of collectivism. Whereas in collectivistic cultures people like to share things, in individualistic cultures, people may keep the nice things for themselves. The ice cream brand Magnum has used this approach, as illustrated in the German advertisement that says, "I share many things, but not everything" (Illustration 9.12).

Other examples are the two following appeals: "It is so good, you want to share it with others" (Hermesetas, Portugal) versus "It is so good, you want to keep it for yourself" (Evers, confectionery, Denmark).

With respect to time, individualistic cultures are monochronic and collectivistic cultures are polychronic. The clock as a symbol of efficiency will not be understood in polychronic cultures.

In collectivistic societies, people do not like being alone or eating alone whereas in individualistic societies, people may cherish their privacy. In collectivistic cultures, being alone means you have no friends, no identity. If alone, one is outside the group to which one belongs. In the United States, Levi's changed their advertising for the Hispanic market and downplayed individualism. Although in the United States the independent hipsters in Levi's TV ads had been drawing young customers, they didn't work for Levi's Hispanic customers. "Why is that guy walking down the street alone?" they asked. "Doesn't he have any friends?"[16] Whereas in individualistic cultures people can enjoy a beer alone and being alone can even have a relaxing function, this is not the case in collectivistic cultures where one enjoys beer together. Images from a German TV commercial for Jever beer (Illustration 9.13) and for the Spanish Mahou (Illustration 9.14) illustrate the difference.

Illustration 9.12   Magnum, Germany

Illustration 9.13 **Jever, Germany**

Illustration 9.14 **Mahou, Spain**

Both in individualistic and collectivistic cultures, families are depicted in advertising, but advertising in individualistic cultures rarely shows multiple generations including grandparents, as in a Spanish commercial for sugar (Azucarera, Illustration 9.15). The most paradoxical phenomenon of the individualism-collectivism dimension is that showing families is as much or even more found in individualistic than in collectivistic cultures. In collectivistic cultures, advertisers may feel little need to depict families because the family is part of one's identity; it is not the desirable.

Appeals in individualistic cultures can refer explicitly to the independent self, for example, the

Illustration 9.15 **Azucarera, Spain**

text of a Tampax commercial: "Free yourself, to be yourself. Do what you want, wear what you want any day you want." Examples of individualistic claims are "Designed for the individual" (Mitsubishi), "Privat concert" for Privat cigarettes (Denmark), Tchibo Privat Kaffee (Germany), "In a world of conformity some things are still made for the individual" (Herblein watch), "Go your own way" (Ford

Human Circle

Over the past 45 years, Chiyoda has accumulated extensive experience as an integrated engineering firm serving a broad spectrum of industries worldwide. We have achieved an impressive track record with over 600 major completed projects including more than 300 overseas, in the execution of projects, we work together with people around the world and extensively utilize

Prospering Together

resources such as equipment and materials from many different countries. Chiyoda also makes full use of global resources by entering into partnerships with overseas companies such as manufacturers, subcontractors and engineering firms. We are fully committed to carrying out projects in cooperation with people around the world for the greater prosperity of mankind.

▼ **CHIYODA** CORPORATION

Main areas of operation:
• Petroleum • Gas • Petrochemicals and chemicals • Power plants, • Environmental preservation, • Automotive plants • Pharmaceutical and food processing • Industrial facilities • Integrated development • Communications and information systems • Optical/atomic works

Illustration 9.16 Chiyoda, International

Probe), and "It's my crazy life. Be yourself, king of your craziness" (Chrysler PT Cruiser, United Kingdom). Examples of collectivistic claims are "Prospering together" (International ad for Japanese Chiyoda Bank, Illustration 9.16), "Be part of the group" (J&B whiskey, Portugal), or showing a group of happy people with the tagline, "the best moments" (Ballentines, Spain).

Members of collectivistic cultures have a different perception of hospitality than members of individualistic cultures. In collectivistic cultures, an unexpected guest will always be served food, so there is always enough food available. A claim like the Dutch one for party snacks, saying "Duyvis, for when there is a party," is not effective for collectivistic cultures, where this sort of product should always be available, not just for a party.

As mentioned in the section on the innovation and global paradox, popular appeals in collectivistic cultures are "modern" and "international" because they appeal to the need to conform, belonging to a new and greater world. Reader's Digest[17] publishes data on personal traits found in readership surveys. One of the traits is measured by the scale modern-traditional. The percentages of answers by people who considered themselves modern correlate with collectivism.

The importance of both context and the relationship orientation of the self in collectivistic cultures can explain how the use of celebrities in advertising varies across cultures. The configuration individualism and masculinity makes people have respect for those who stand out and are successful, which may explain why in the United States the cult of personality and obsession with celebrity and stardom is pronounced. In collectivistic cultures, however, in particular in Asia, celebrities are even more frequently used in advertising than in the United States, with South Korea leading. In his description of the celebrity phenomenon, Carolus Praet,[18] a Dutch professor who teaches international marketing in Japan, provides explanations that refer to two collectivistic aspects: the relational self and context. In Japan, celebrity appearances are not limited to famous actors, singers, sports stars, or comedians. Advertising is a stage for established celebrities to capitalize on their fame, but it also is the steppingstone for models and aspiring actors toward fame.[19] In Japan, the word *talent* (*tarento*) is used to describe most celebrities in the entertainment world, and *star* is reserved for those who are seen to have long-lasting popularity. Many of the talents are selected on the basis of their cute looks. In the context of entertainment and advertising, this phenomenon seems not to pose problems of distinctiveness, or standing out. Whereas most Western stars are popular because of their salient physical or personal attributes, the appearances of Japanese idols are only a bit above average, so as not to alienate or offend the audience, but just enough to give their fans the sense that they too can become stars if they try hard enough. The function of such *tarento* is also to give the brand "face" in the world of brands with similar product attributes. Instead of adding abstract personal characteristics to the product, it is linked to concrete persons. This is also explained as part of the creative process in which a creative team in the advertising agency prefers to explain a proposed campaign by showing the client a popular talent around whom the campaign is to be built rather than talking about an abstract creative concept. An important difference is that in individualistic cultures, a celebrity can be linked with only one brand or company to be credible as the celebrity's unique and desirable characteristics are supposed to transfer into the brand, and brands must differentiate from other brands. In collectivistic cultures, this uniqueness is not relevant. In China, a celebrity may be associated with over 20 brands.[20]

Considering the fact that approximately 70% of the world population is more or less collectivistic and many global advertising campaigns reflect individualistic values, it is fair to assume that much global advertising is effective only for a small part of the target. Most global ads address people in a direct way, show people alone, and refer to all sorts of individualistic claims.

Masculinity/Femininity

Winning and achievement, characteristics of masculine cultures, are frequently reflected in U.S. advertising. In particular, the combination of individualism and masculinity (the configuration of Anglo-German cultures) leads to the strong need to win, to be successful and show it, combined with the wish to dominate. Examples are "Being first," "The one and only in the world," and "Be the best." Hyperbole, persuasiveness, and comparative advertising are reflections of masculinity. A claim like "We'd like to set the record straight on who finished first in Client/Server Applications" (SAP integrated software) is typical for a masculine culture and reflects competitiveness. An advertisement for Nikon cameras says, "More winners per second" (Illustration 9.17), and a German ad for Skiny underwear says, "Simply the Best" (Illustration 9.18).

Aggressive typology and layout are another reflection of competitiveness. Dreams and great expectations are expressions of masculine cultures. Statements like "A dream come true" or "A world without limits" reflect the value "mastery," the idea that anyone can do anything as long as they try hard. This is opposed to feminine cultures, where dreams are said to be delusions. In masculine cultures, status is important for demonstrating one's success. To become Man (Woman) of the Year is the ideal for people in masculine cultures because mediocrity is the proof of failure. In Chapter 4, we showed how this was used in a commercial for Tylenol in the United States. Another reflection of masculinity, typical of American culture, is "bigness." America is a land of big egos, big cars, the Big Mac, the Quarter Pounder (or even a half pounder), and the big idea.[21] Illustration 9.19 shows an image from a TV commercial for Taco Bell.

The configuration of individualism and masculinity explains the frequent hyperbole in American advertising with statements like "All the cosmetics in the world can't do what we can," "The only plastic

Illustration 9.17 Nikon, International

Illustration 9.18 Skiny, Germany

Illustration 9.19 Taco Bell, United States

wrap with Reynolds strength behind it," "The greatest of ease" (for a white plastic garden chair), "You'll never find a softer toilet paper than new Northern Ultra," "The pain reliever that hospitals use most," or "The world's number one contact lens" (Acuvue).

Although both the United States and the United Kingdom score high on the masculinity index, there is a difference. The United States scores higher on uncertainty avoidance, which also influences the difference between overstatement and understatement. In the United Kingdom, one also wants to state that one has success, but this is often done "tongue in cheek."

Feminine cultures are characterized by favoring caring, softness, and the small. An international business advertisement for Russian Norilsk Nickel expresses love for the weak, showing a child in its advertising (Illustration 9.20). Instead of hyperbole, feminine cultures like understatement, as in the international advertising campaign for Carlsberg, with the tagline "Probably the best beer in the world" (Illustration 9.21). Much of Volvo advertising (Volvo is from Sweden, the most feminine culture in the world) tends to focus on safety, protecting the family. In feminine cultures, showing off is negative. The Volvo advertisement in Illustration 9.22 says, "True refinement comes from within," meaning to say you don't have to show off.

Another example of understatement was in an advertisement for the Audi 100 in the Netherlands: "You have a small house (the visual is a mansion), and a small car, but your neighbors live far enough away, they cannot see it. Moreover, the most important part cannot be seen, it is under the hood." An opposing claim was by Seat, Italy, showing the car in a garage with a glass door: "It can always be shown, it can always be seen."

Illustration 9.20 Norilsk, International

Illustration 9.21 Carlsberg, International

Illustration 9.22 Volvo, International

Understatement is also recognized in a Spanish print advertisement for the Audi A4 Avant, an expensive top model of Audi, which reads as follows:

> Deceive all of them, saying it's a family car. The new Audi A4 Avant. Never speak about power in public. If, one day, someone mentions something about the 5 valves per cylinder, change the topic, tell him it seems like it's going to rain. 150 hp?—You don't know anything.—Quattro-traction?—What's that? Use the interior space and the variability as a pretext. So that no one thinks that you actually love its design. While traveling with friends make them think that you are bored. Even yawn. Do it and everybody will think that the Audi A4 Avant is only a family car. After all, there are a lot who want to deceive you, saying that they drive a sports car.

This text reflects the configuration of collectivism, high power distance, femininity, and strong uncertainty avoidance. You are not allowed to talk about power in public. You just have it. To avoid confrontations, things should not be said directly. Indirectly, a number of important details are communicated about the technical aspects. It reflects modesty and harmony.

If celebrity endorsement is used in feminine cultures, well-known people and presenters tend to downplay the fact that they are well known or they are belittled or even ridiculed. In more extreme cases, the parody style will be utilized. In the Netherlands, a look-alike of Pamela Anderson was used for an optician retail chain called Hans Anders, belittling her body shape and suggesting that this is as much a prosthesis as eyeglasses are. In Spain, a retail optician chain used another "hero" of the soap *Baywatch,* running fast and bumping into a shack, for the audience to conclude that he should have worn glasses.

Strong and weak role differentiation are both reflected in advertising. An example of strong role differentiation is the claim in a Mexican ad for Jethro jeans: "Be his pin up girl" (Illustration 9.23). In Danish advertisements, men can be seen wearing aprons, as in the advertisement for Matas (Illustration 9.24).

Illustration 9.23   Jethro, Mexico

Illustration 9.24   Matas, Denmark

The Slovak Republic scores very high on the masculinity scale. In that country, a successful brand name by Danone is *Dobrá Máma* (good mother) which typically points at the importance of the mother role. Such a brand name would not work well in cultures that score low on the scale.

Men wearing aprons and playing an active role in family life, shopping, cooking, or caring for children are seen in Spanish advertising, as illustrated in an image from a TV commercial for Gallina Blanca (Illustration 9.25) and for La Piara, showing a father shopping with his children (Illustration 9.26). Also, in France, fathers are seen in ads with their children, as in an image from a TV commercial for Maggi (Illustration 9.27). An image from a TV commercial for Ajax in Sweden (Illustration 9.28) shows a man wiping the floor with pleasure. He swings the mop as if it is a golf club.

When in masculine cultures men play a role in the household in TV commercials, they often are depicted as the stupid guy, and the woman knows better. She will play the role of the expert and advises how to use the product. Women want to be the competent housewife and be in control of their men. In the advertisement for Triumph underwear, it is called the "control thing" (Illustration 9.29).

Illustration 9.25   Gallina Blanca, Spain

Illustration 9.26   La Piara, Spain

Illustration 9.27   Maggi, France

Illustration 9.28   Ajax, Sweden

Illustration 9.29   Triumph, United Kingdom

The women serve the family, as in the image from an Italian TV commercial for Casa Modena (Illustration 9.30). If men do something with babies, it likely serves their own purposes. A U.S. TV commercial for Honda shows a man with a baby approaching his car. He sees a spot on it and uses the baby's nappy to clean the car (Illustration 9.31). In masculine cultures, women can be shown to be tough; in feminine cultures, men can be shown to be tender. Illustration 9.32 shows three images from a classic award-winning Japanese TV commercial for a Hitachi vacuum cleaner in which a woman fights the flies. Illustration 9.33 shows three images of a Thai award-winning TV commercial for Asia Telecom in which in an airport a father tells a bedtime story to his daughter by video phone.

Appeals of masculine cultures are more task or success oriented whereas appeals of feminine cultures will be more affiliation and relationship oriented.

Illustration 9.30 **Casa Modena, Italy**

Illustration 9.31 **Honda, United States**

Illustration 9.32 **Hitachi, Japan**

Illustration 9.33 **Asia Telecom, Thailand**

German commercials for detergents tend to argue the effectiveness of the detergent by showing large piles of dirty clothes or many dirty children and the result: large piles of clean clothes or many clean children in brilliant white clothes. Women are cast in the role of effective housewives. In feminine cultures, a more affiliation-oriented approach will be more successful, casting the woman in her role of effective mother who has a happy relationship with her children. Clean children are part of her relationship with them. The two are very different approaches.

In particular in business-to-business advertising in English-language business magazines, women tend to be used as decoration, resulting from the fact that much international advertising is from U.S. companies.

Uncertainty Avoidance

Strong uncertainty avoidance translates not only into the need for explanations, structure, testing, test reports, scientific proof and advice, and testimonials by experts but also into high regard for technology and design, the latter even more in the configuration with high power distance. An example is an advertisement for the Italian car brand Lancia (Illustration 9.34). Advertisements tend to be structured and detailed. An example of detailed advertisement is a Russian one for a facial cream, the name of which means something like "Purity Line" (Illustration 9.35). It includes a lot of information plus a picture of a laboratory, thus illustrating scientific proof.

An appeal frequently found in high uncertainty avoidance cultures is fear of bacteria, used for advertising detergents, household cleaning products, and hand soap, as in illustration 9.36 for Protex Brazil. The woman repeats all sorts of

Illustration 9.34 Lancia, Italy

Illustration 9.35 Purity Line, Russia

Illustration 9.36   **Protex, Brazil**

activities like locking doors, opening drawers, and picking up the phone, but she needs anti-bacterial Protex hand soap only once to properly clean her hands.

Purity and freshness are important appeals for food products in high uncertainty avoidance cultures. Examples of mineral water were presented in Chapter 4. In a Spanish ad for packaged gazpacho, the freshness is demonstrated by tomato pickers who enter the kitchen through the door of the refrigerator (Illustration 9.37).

Illustration 9.37   **Alvalle gazpacho, Spain**

In high uncertainty avoidance advertising, the competence of the manufacturer must be demonstrated. Showing how a product works, with all the technical details, is important. This is in contrast with weak uncertainty avoidance cultures, where the result is more important. Two advertisements and TV commercials for toothpaste illustrate the difference. In the advertisement for elmex and aronal (Illustration 9.38), the brands are called experts for tooth health, and the details of how the product works are illustrated. In contrast, an English advertisement for Crest focuses on the results of using the product: beauty (Illustration 9.39).

The TV commercials in illustrations 9.40 and 9.41, for Odol Med 3 (Austria) and Crest (U.S.), show a similar difference. Odol Med 3 demonstrates how the toothbrush and toothpaste work in the mouth. The Crest commercial is one of a campaign saying that you can say the most awful things if your smile is OK. The ad is about a couple that is going to be married; her husband-to-be and his lawyer, with a smile, tell her that they don't trust her.

Illustration 9.38   **elmex and aronal, Germany**

Illustration 9.39   **Crest, United Kingdom**

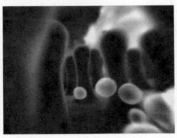

Illustration 9.40   **Odol Med 3, Austria**

Illustration 9.41   **Crest, United States**

Testing and test reports are favored in strong uncertainty avoidance cultures, although the execution tends to be different. Favorite German expressions are "*Die Besten im Testen*" (The best in the test) and "*Testsieger*" (Test winner). The

Odol Med 3 commercial of Illustration 9.40 ends with a package shot adding that the product had very good test results. Technical explanations about the product can be very detailed for all sorts of products, be they cars, toothpaste, or shampoo.

Fear appeals are more effective in high uncertainty avoidance cultures than in low uncertainty avoidance cultures, where people are more responsive to benefits than to threats. This is of particular importance for nonprofit, health-related communication.[22]

Design is a strong element of German and Italian advertising, although German advertisements also tend to focus on the technological aspect, whereas the Italians focus more on the outer appearance. The French and the Spanish are more art and fashion oriented.

In high uncertainty avoidance cultures, people tend to be better groomed than in weak uncertainty avoidance cultures. In advertisements from the southern European and Germanic countries, people are significantly better dressed than in advertising from the northern European cultures. Being well groomed means matching the right colors and picking the right accessories. A Spanish advertisement for Honda illustrates this (Illustration 9.42). It suggests that people match the color of their car with their shoes, bag, sunglasses, mobile phone, and so forth. The ultimate understatement of sophistication is an Australian advertisement for Stella Artois beer (Illustration 9.43). Other examples are two breakfast situations, an Italian one for Saccottino (Illustration 9.44) where mother and father are well groomed and, in contrast, a Dutch one for Blue Band Goede Start—Good Start (of the day)—showing a father in his underwear (Illustration 9.45).

In high uncertainty avoidance cultures, presenters tend to be experts, the competent professional or the competent boss—the professor or physician type—preferably wearing a white coat. In low power distance, weak uncertainty avoidance cultures, a parody of the expert is favored.

Illustration 9.42   Honda, Spain

Stella Artois. About as sophisticated as a beer can get.

Illustration 9.43   Stella Artois, Australia

In high uncertainty avoidance cultures, emotions can be shown, and the word *emotion* as such is attractive. An example is the payoff used for the Spanish Seat brand, "*Auto emoción*."

An appeal recognized in advertising in strong uncertainty avoidance cultures is relaxation in the sense of relief from anxiety and tension. This may be expressed explicitly, whereas relief from tension is more implicit in weak uncertainty avoidance cultures.

Illustration 9.44   Saccottino, Italy

Illustration 9.45   Blue Band Goede Start, Netherlands

Long-/Short-Term Orientation

The opposing values of long-term orientation are "save for tomorrow" versus "buy now, pay later." Short-term orientation is reflected in the sense of urgency so frequently encountered in U.S. advertising. Examples are "Hurry," "Don't wait," or "Now 50% off, no money down, two full years' free credit, it's on now!" Another expression of short-term thinking is "instant pleasure," as in an advertisement for Häagen-Dazs ice cream (Illustration 9.46) or living in the now and not thinking about the future, as in the advertisement for CK: "Be good, be bad, just be" (Illustration 9.47). The new data for this dimension point at an important additional aspect

Illustration 9.46   Häagen-Dazs, United Kingdom

Illustration 9.47   CK, Spain

of short-term orientation: service to others, including generosity. This can be recognized in "the big man" in African countries that score low on this dimension, who spreads resources to his family members, extended family members, and networks outside his family. This is what Oyedele and Minor[23] have observed in Nigeria and South Africa as an important theme in advertising.

Symbols of long-term orientation are thick trees or explicit referral to future generations, as depicted by the Japanese telecom company NTT DoCoMo in its international advertisement shown in Illustration 9.48. An international campaign by Korean LG also used long-term orientation symbolism, as in Illustration 9.49 that symbolizes continuity: What the old man cannot finish in his life, the baby will. The advertisement also symbolizes man in harmony with nature.

Harmony, with both nature and fellow humans, is a popular appeal in Asian advertising. It is part of an indirect approach that helps to build trust in the company. Much advertising is pure entertainment, and visuals and objects are used that please the eye, many of which relate to nature: bamboo trees, flowers, autumn leaves, or other representations of the seasons, which often have a symbolic meaning unknown to foreigners. Many Westerners do not understand the butterflies in ads for computers or other nature elements in Asian advertising. The combination of collectivism and long-term orientation demands harmony of man with nature and thus explains this advertising style, the objective of which is to please the customer, not to intrude.

Illustration 9.48   NTT DoCoMo, International

Illustration 9.49   LG, International

Consequences for Advertising Concepts

Certain configurations of dimensions have significant consequences for the effectiveness of advertising appeals. Appeals or concepts can be presented in two-dimensional maps showing culture clusters where the appeal will be more or less effective. An example is the use of status, an appeal that varies with power distance and masculinity. Status is used to demonstrate one's social position and uphold face in high power distance cultures and to show success in masculine cultures. In feminine cultures, particularly those of low power distance (Scandinavia and the Netherlands), status needs are low. Feminine cultures are characterized by modesty and jealousy, and so the use of status will be counterproductive. Cultures that score high on both masculinity and power distance will be particularly sensitive to the status motive, and luxury brands fulfill that need. Advertising for these brands logically uses status appeals. In particular for Chinese consumers, achievement satisfies the social need for admiration from their communities; it is socially directed, and luxury brands can meet the needs of Chinese consumers to be respected by others through the actions of buying, possessing, and consuming those brands.[24]

Figure 9.1 shows a two-dimensional map of 30 countries, with culture clusters that will be more or less sensitive to status as an appeal in advertising. In the lower left quadrant are the Scandinavian countries and the Netherlands, cultures in which the status appeal will not work very well or mostly in small segments of society. In the upper left quadrant is the Anglo-German cluster, where status will be most appealing if connected with success. The two right quadrants show a mixture of European, Latin American, and Asian cultures. In the lower right quadrant, status is mostly linked with social position and face. The extremes are in the upper right quadrant, where both social position and success are drivers for status brands and appeals in advertising: Mexico, Venezuela, Japan, and China are high-status cultures.

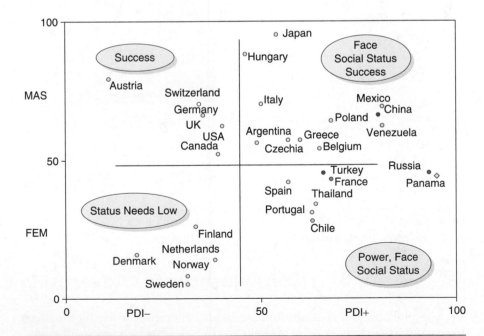

Figure 9.1   Status Needs

SOURCE: Data from Hofstede et al. (2010) (see Appendix A).

Do Great Ideas Travel?

Great ideas or concepts, if they are based on values, are ideas that touch the heart of the consumer. That type of concept tends to reflect the core values of the home country and can travel only to a limited number of other countries. The international advertising world is full of concepts that cannot travel. An example of a concept that is particularly attractive to the British is freedom of choice, a concept that is irrelevant to many other Europeans. Why wouldn't consumers in a free country have freedom of choice?

A concept that is frequently used for wireless technology, "Work where you want," is typical of individualistic cultures, where people mix work and home life more easily than in collectivistic cultures. In Chapter 8, we discussed the influence of individualism on penetration of home computers and mobile Internet. Whereas in individualistic cultures people like to move their work from the office to the home, the park, or even the beach, in collectivistic cultures, the workplace is part of one's "family," and people like to stay there with their colleagues to finish the job. So an advertisement like the one for Orange, showing individuals working in the park (Illustration 9.50) is culture-specific and cannot travel farther than northwest Europe and the Anglo-Saxon world. It shows individuals with laptops in a park saying "Business knows no bounds."

A campaign that has been described as a successful global idea as mentioned in Chapter 2 was the "Dirt is Good" campaign for the detergent brand OMO. The idea was based on the belief that when children are developing and learning, they will sometimes get dirty. Some parents worry about this. The idea is to encourage

Illustration 9.50 Orange, International

parents to leave their children free to get dirty and develop as OMO takes care of the dirt.[25] Yet, according to Hollis, the brand promise may need to be interpreted differently according to culture and context. OMO in Asia delivers the "Dirt is Good" message in a different way than Persil in the United Kingdom does because attitudes to dirt differ. In Asia, dirt is dangerous and threatening, to be avoided. In the United Kingdom it is more an unsightly nuisance.[26]

Sometimes a company has a great idea with a central message worldwide, but consumers decide it isn't congruent with their values, and the way they read the message changes according to their own values. For quite some time, L'Oréal has run a global advertising campaign with the central theme "Because I am worth it." But consumers in Asia read it as "Because you are worth it" because they are not willing to say "I am worth it." So the company changed it accordingly, but it became the authority of the company that speaks, not the consumer herself. So the central message had been changed.[27]

Some great ideas that do travel are not based on values but on product attributes or benefits (see also Chapter 11). These are pieces of art that relate to the product and give a positive feeling about the product. This type of advertising is not persuasive communication, provides no information, and follows the likeability model. An example is a TV commercial for Honda, in which a 60-person choir vocalizes the experience of driving the new Honda Civic (Illustration 9.51).

Illustration 9.51   Honda, International

Such concepts can be used for well-known brands in addition to other messages or for corporate advertising. The purpose can be no more than awareness and/or building trust (see also Chapter 11).

Hollis[28] mentions two key measures for the ability of great ideas or exceptional ads to travel: the ability to engage the audience and establish long-term memories that are linked to the advertised brand, and, the persuasion measure that captures the immediate motivational power of the ad. However, of ads measured to be exceptional in one country, 27% performed below what is viewed as an acceptable standard in other countries. International advertisers who have found a great idea for their own country and think they can extend it to others are advised to test their ads before running it in a new location. They shouldn't assume it is going to work the same way as it did in its country of origin.

The Country-of-Origin Appeal

An appeal that travels to a certain extent is the country-of-origin appeal (COO). The appeal is based on the combination of the product category and country of origin. Consumers are sensitive to the country of origin of products and brands. Country of origin of products or brands or foreign-sounding brand names influence consumer perceptions.[29] Consumers use country of origin as stereotypical information in making evaluations of products.[30] Consumers who have positive or negative attitudes toward a particular country will show favorable or unfavorable responses to country-related advertisements.[31] Attitudes toward foreign products vary by country of origin of the product. *Fashionable* for clothes will relate to French origin, whereas *quality* for cars will relate to Germany or Japan. The German automobile brand Volkswagen uses this appeal in a very simple way by using the tagline *Das Auto* in German. A clear combination like *French perfume* can be used worldwide. However, country images can change over time, and consumer attitudes can vary. The great luxury brands use Western appeals as most have a Western cultural origin which makes them particularly attractive to cultures where status appeals are important, such as in Asia. This explains why advertising for such brands in other countries is rarely adapted. This also applies to their websites.[32]

Preference for products from one's own country is called *consumer nationalism* or *consumer ethnocentrism*. Consumer nationalism may be related to patriotism which is stronger in cultures that are short-term oriented.

As discussed in Chapter 2, a positive product-country match exists when a country is perceived as very strong in an area (e.g., design or technology), which is also an important feature for a product category (e.g., furniture, cars). Such product-country match is called *prototypicality*. Views of what product categories are prototypical for which countries may vary.[33]

Why Humor Doesn't Travel

In some cultures, humor is a much used device in advertising, and in others it is scarce. The statement that humor doesn't travel is frequently heard. Why? Because humor is a subversive play with conventions and established ideas; it is based on breaking taboos. Comedy plays with ways of breaking the rules of convention, going against what ought to be. Because it uses cultural conventions, it can be understood only by those who share the culture. An example is a fragment in Gogol's play *The Revisor,* where the Revisor's servant is seen lying on a bed. To the Russians of Gogol's time (1836), this was very funny because servants used to sleep on the floor, and being on a bed meant being on one's master's bed, which was seen as an unheard-of liberty.[34] This fits Russian culture, which was and still is a country that has one of the highest scores on power distance in the world. The servant's act would have been impossible to understand by members of low power distance cultures and thus not be viewed as funny.

Culture also influences the type of humor used. Parody, for example, fits low power distance cultures because it disguises the voice of authority. Much of British humor is based on antiauthoritarianism. Weak uncertainty avoidance cultures, being able to cope with ambiguity, will use the more subtle types of humor, parody, and understatement. In strong uncertainty avoidance cultures, the more straightforward type of slapstick humor tends to be used. The admonishing humor of the

Germans has to do with their need for perfectionism, which explains their infrequent use of irony.[35] Much of Belgian humor is straightforward. Comparison of differences in the liking of humorous television commercials between the Netherlands and Belgium shows that explicit jokes are liked better in Belgium than in the Netherlands, which can be explained by the difference in level of uncertainty avoidance. Puns and word games are liked better in the Netherlands than in Belgium. Absurdism, parody, and satire, in particular commercials that do not take experts seriously, are less appreciated by Belgians than by the Dutch.[36]

In studies of the use of humor in advertising, a number of different humorous devices are usually distinguished: puns or word games, understatements, jokes, the ludicrous, the "comic" (as in comic strips), comedy, slapstick, satire, parody, irony, and black humor. In contrast to the stereotype of the German lack of humor, German studies (see Hillebrand[37] and Merz[38]) distinguished a similar number of types of humor with only one difference: In English/American studies, *understatement* is mentioned as a humorous device. This was not specified as a humorous device in the two German studies, which mentioned *Schadenfreude* (malicious pleasure) as a humorous device, one not mentioned in the Anglo-Saxon studies.

Weinberger and Spotts[39] distinguished six categories of humor in the United States and the United Kingdom: pun, understatement, joke, the ludicrous, satire, and irony. The U.S. advertising style included more of the ludicrous and the United Kingdom's more satire. This can be explained by the different scores on the uncertainty avoidance dimension. Alden, Hoyer, and Lee[40] examined the content of humorous television advertising from Korea, Germany, Thailand, and the United States and found one type of humor that worked across all compared countries: incongruity. Incongruity is the unexpected turn in a story that makes people laugh. Almost 60% of the humorous ads in all four nations contained incongruent contrasts, but there were some cultural differences. In the collectivistic cultures of Thailand and Korea, humorous appeals involved groups—three or more central characters were included—whereas in the United States and Germany, both individualistic cultures, substantially fewer ads with three or more characters were found. In the high power distance cultures (Thailand and Korea), more humorous ads featured unequal status between main characters than in the two low power distance cultures (Germany and the United States).

Using humor in advertising is a management decision. The reason it is used more in some countries than in others has to do with the cultural values of management; it does not reflect the sense of humor of advertising audiences. Humor in advertising is found particularly in cultures of low power distance and weak-to-medium uncertainty avoidance, such as the United Kingdom, Denmark, Sweden, Norway, and the Netherlands. Obviously, this configuration of dimensions makes managers willing to use humor in advertising whereas in strong uncertainty avoidance cultures, management is less likely to do so.

Consumers from culturally diverse countries prefer ad appeals that fit their culture to ad appeals that don't. When crossing borders, a humorous commercial may not be understood. Failed humor is counterproductive. It not only confuses the audience but may also give offense.[41]

Summary

Within each culture, there are opposing, seemingly paradoxical, values. The contrast is between the desirable and the desired values of each culture. Those who do not understand the cultural value paradoxes may be tempted to think that the world's values are converging, which is not the case. Each culture has its value paradoxes, and they are different from the value paradoxes of other cultures. They can be understood through the five dimensions.

A culture's opposing values appear to be important for advertising because they are recognized as the most meaningful elements of a culture. Both the desirable and the desired values are used for developing meaningful appeals in advertising. Sometimes a desired value of one culture may seem to be similar to a desirable value of another culture.

Showing people alone in advertising in collectivistic cultures is interpreted as having no friends. It may go deeper than that: It may mean they have no identity because their identity is in the group. As more than 70% of the world's population is more or less collectivistic, advertisers would be wise to show more people in their advertisements. It doesn't hurt the members of individualistic cultures to see more people in advertising, but it is negative to show solitary people in collectivistic cultures.

Because of the domination of North American advertising, there is much more hype in international advertising than members of less masculine or collectivistic cultures appreciate. Taking into account that a large number of cultures of the European continent are more or less feminine, international advertisers focusing on Europe might consider using less hype or competitive advertising.

Finally, understanding the values of culture helps explain why humor doesn't travel: Humor uses the conventions of culture that cannot be understood by those who do not share the culture.

Notes

1. Moriarty, S., Mitchell, N., & Wells, W. (2009). *Advertising: Principles and practice* (8th ed.). Upper Saddle River, NJ: Pearson Prentice Hall, p. 364.

2. Polegato, R., & Bjerke, R. (2006, September). The link between cross-cultural value associations and liking: The case of Benetton and its advertising. *Journal of Advertising, 46*(3), 263–273.

3. Okazaki, S., & Mueller, B. (2007). Cross-cultural advertising research: Where we have been and where we need to go. *International Marketing Review, 24*(5), 499–518.

4. Samiee, S., & Jeong. I. (1994). Cross-cultural research in advertising: An assessment of methodologies. *Journal of the Academy of Marketing Science, 22*(3), 205–217.

5. McQuarrie, E. F., & Phillips, B. J. (2008). It's not your father's magazine ad: Magnitude and direction of recent changes in advertising style. *Journal of Advertising, 37*(3), 95–106.

6. De Mooij, M., & Hofstede, G. (2010). The Hofstede model. Applications to global branding and advertising strategy and research. *International Journal of Advertising, 29*(1), 85–110.

7. Chang, T.-K., Huh, J., McKinney, K., Sar, S., Wei, W., & Schneeweis, A. (2009). Culture and its influence on advertising: Misguided framework, inadequate comparative design and dubious knowledge claim. *The International Communication Gazette, 71*(8), 671–692.

8. Okazaki, S., & Mueller, B. (2007). Evolution in the usage of localized appeals in Japanese and American print advertising. *International Journal of Advertising, 27*(5), 771–798.

9. Rhodes, D. L., & Emery, C. R. (2003). The effect of cultural differences on effective advertising: A comparison between Russia and the U.S. *Academy of Marketing Studies Journal, 7*(2), 89–105.

10. Maleville, M. (1993). How boringly respectable can you get? A study of business slogans in three countries. *Toegepaste Taalwetenschap, 2.*

11. McQuarrie, E. F., & Phillips, B. J. (2008). It's not your father's magazine ad: Magnitude and direction of recent changes in advertising style. *Journal of Advertising, 37*(3), 95–106.

12. Zhou, N., & Belk, R. W. (2004). Chinese consumer readings of global and local advertising appeals. *Journal of Advertising, 33*(3), 63–76.

13. Han, S.-P., & Shavitt, S. (1994). Persuasion and culture: Advertising appeals in individualistic and collectivistic societies. *Journal of Experimental Social Psychology, 30,* 326–350; Zhang, Y., & Gelb, B. D. (1996). Matching advertising appeals to culture: The influence of products' use condition. *Journal of Advertising, 25,* 29–46.

14. Bowman, J. (2002). Commercials rise in the East. *M&M Europe: Pocket Guide on Asian TV.* London: Emap Media, p. 8.

15. Wang, J. (2008). *Brand new China. Advertising, media and commercial culture.* Cambridge, MA: Harvard University Press, p. 70.

16. Mitchell, R., & Oneal, M. (1994, September 12). Managing by values. *Business Week,* pp. 38–43.

17. These surveys are conducted each year. (www.rdtrustedbrands.com) (See Appendix B.)

18. Praet, C. L. C. (2001). Japanese advertising, the world's number one celebrity showcase? A cross-cultural comparison of the frequency of celebrity appearances in TV advertising. In M. Roberts & R. L. King (Eds.), *Proceedings of the 2001 Special Asia-Pacific Conference of the American Academy of Advertising.* Kisarazu, Japan, pp. 6–13.

19. Praet, C. L. C. (2008). The influence of national culture on the use of celebrity endorsement in television advertising: A multi-country study. *Proceedings of the 7th International Conference on Research in Advertising (ICORIA),* Antwerp, Belgium, s.1. [CD-ROM]; Praet, C. L. C. (2009). National wealth or national culture? A multi-country study of the factors underlying the use of celebrity endorsement in television advertising. In P. De Pelsmacker & N. Dens (Eds.), *Research in advertising: The medium, the message, and the context.* Antwerpen: Garant.

20. Ma, R., Hung, K., Belk, R., Choi, S. M., Chan, K., & Tse, D. K. (2009). Special topics session: New perspectives in endorsement effects. *The proceedings of the 2009 American Academy of Advertising Asia-Pacific Conference and international symposium of advertising development and education.* Retrieved from http://www.aaasite.org/Proceedings.html

21. Land of the big. (1996, December 21). *Economist,* p. 68.

22. Reardon, J., Miller, C., Foubert, B., Vida, I., & Rybina, L. (2006). Antismoking messages for the international teenage segment: The effectiveness of message valence and intensity across different cultures. *Journal of International Marketing, 14*(3), 115–138.

23. Oyedele, A., & Minor, M. (2012). Consumer culture plots in television advertising from Nigeria and South Africa. *Journal of Advertising, 41*(1), 91–107.

24. Lu, P. X. (2008). *Elite China: Luxury consumer behavior in China.* Singapore: John Wiley & Sons, p. 57.

25. De Swaan Arons, M., & Van den Driest, F. (2010). *The Global Brand CEO: Building the ultimate marketing machine.* New York: Airstream, p. 114.

26. Hollis, N. (2010). *The Global Brand: How to create and develop lasting brand value in the world market.* New York: Palgrave Macmillan, pp. 183–184.

27. Sulaini, K. E. (2006). *Blink: Tackling the communication flux within the Asia-Pacific region.* A research project submitted in fulfillment of the requirements for the degree of bachelor of communication, RMIT University, Melbourne, Australia and MARA University of Technology, Malaysia.

28. Hollis, 2010.

29. Diamantopoulos, A., Schlegelmilch, B. B., & Du Preez, J. P. (1995), Lessons for pan-European marketing? The role of consumer preferences in fine-tuning the product-market fit. *International Marketing Review, 12,* 38–52; Keillor, B. D., & Hult, G. T. (1999). A five-country study of national identity: Implications for international research and practice. *International Marketing Review, 16,* 65–82.

30. Maheswaran, D. (1994). Country of origin as a stereotype: Effects of consumer expertise and attribute strength on product evaluations. *Journal of Consumer Research, 21,* 354–365.

31. Moon, B. J., & Jain, S. C. (2002). Consumer processing of foreign advertisements: Roles of country-of origin perceptions, consumer ethnocentrism, and country attitude. *International Business Review, 11,* 117–138.

32. Lin, E.-Y. (2011). Luxury branding on the Internet: Website characteristics, country-of-origin, and cultural context. In C. La Ferle & G. Kerr (Eds.), *Proceedings of the American Academy of Advertising Asia Pacific Conference.* Published in cooperation with the Queensland University of Technology and the Australian and New Zealand Academy of Advertising. Retrieved from http://www.aaasite.org/Proceedings.html

33. Lee, C. W., Suh, Y. G., & Moon, B.-J. (2001). Product-country images: The roles of country-of-origin and country-of-target in consumers' prototype product evaluations. *Journal of International Consumer Marketing, 13,* 47–62.

34. Van den Bergh, H. (1996, November 14). Lachen als bevrediging. *NRC Handelsblad,* 33.

35. Bik, J. M. (1996, November 14). Variant op ernst. *NRC Handelsblad,* 35.

36. Scheijgrond, L., & Volker, J. (1995). *Zo dichtbij, maar toch ver weg* [So close yet so far away]. Unpublished study for the Hogeschool Eindhoven, studierichting Communicatie.

37. Hillebrand, K. (1992). *Erfolgsvoraussetzungen und Erscheinungsformen des Humors in der Werbung—Dargestellt am Beispiel von Low-Involvement-Produkten* [Effect hypotheses and manifestations of humor in advertising: Described for low involvement products]. Prüfungsamt für wirtschaftswissenschaftliche Prüfungen der Westfälischen Wilhelms-Universität Münster. Unpublished.

38. Merz, G. (1989). *Humor in der Werbung* [Humor in advertising]. Freie Wissenschaftliche Arbeit zur Erlangung des akademischen Grades Diplomkaufmann und der Wirtschaftsend Sozialwissenschaftlichen Fakultät der Friedrich-Alexander-Universität Erlangen-Nürnberg, Nürnberg. Unpublished.

39. Weinberger, M. C., & Spotts, H. E. (1989). Humor in U.S. versus U.K. TV commercials: A comparison. *Journal of Advertising, 18,* 39–44.

40. Alden, D. L., Hoyer, W. D., & Lee, C. (1993). Identifying global and culture-specific dimensions of humor in advertising: A multinational analysis. *Journal of Marketing, 57,* 64–75.

41. Lee, Y. H., & Lim, E. A. C. (2008). What's funny and what's not: The moderating role of cultural orientation in ad humor. *Journal of Advertising, 37*(2), 71–84.

CHAPTER 10

Culture and Executional Style

E xecutional styles or basic forms used in advertising represent contexts for the advertising message.[1] A number of basic advertising forms, which are used in different variations, can be distinguished. Major international advertisers have used a single form indiscriminately across cultures. An example is the testimonial form used worldwide by Procter & Gamble. That does not mean that these formats are a first choice of all cultures. The "comparison" form, for example, is controversial. Certain forms have proved to be effective in one culture but not in others, like entertainment, which is effective in Japan but less in the United States. For international advertising, it is necessary to determine which basic forms are universal and which are not. There is little knowledge of the relative effectiveness of forms of one culture in others. The purpose of this chapter is to review basic advertising forms—how they reflect culture and serve different advertising purposes. Classifications of advertising forms are reviewed, and one will be described comprehensively.

Classifications of Advertising Forms

As pointed out in previous chapters, advertising style consists of appeal and execution. We noticed that appeals may differ across cultures. So does the execution. Even if a common motive or appeal can be found for different countries, it often needs different expressions. Executional style reflects interpersonal communication style, so it is very much culturally relevant, and understanding execution differences is important. An essential aspect of execution is the basic advertising form, of which there are many different types. For the purpose of comparing advertising across cultures, all sorts of classification systems have been developed. Some are very comprehensive, covering all aspects of advertising style; others cover only a few aspects. This section reviews the systems that tend to be used for classifying the various aspects of a print advertisement or a television commercial.

Classifications found in literature tend to mix two elements of advertising: strategy (level of communication) and form. The most used classification of advertising, *message strategy,* is based on the distinction *informational-transformational.*[2] Moriarty[3] mentions it as two main message strategies. Informational advertising covers explicit messages; transformational advertising covers images. German professor Kroeber-Riel[4] uses the terms *functional* and *emotional.* Another term used for the same classification is *soft sell* versus *hard sell,* as used by Mueller,[5] for example, to distinguish comparative advertising from mood or atmosphere. Yet another similar distinction is between *product information* and *product image,* which includes symbolic information.[6] This type of classification originates in the United States where the dichotomy *information-emotion* is pronounced, as described in Chapter 7. In particular, the distinction hard sell–soft sell is a U.S. driven approach. It is mostly used for comparing U.S. advertising with advertising in an Asian country, usually Japan, but there are hardly any generally accepted definitions. Descriptions in comparative studies tend to mention—as a main element of hard sell—clear-cut product related appeals and product recommendation with emphasis on sales orientation. In soft sell ads, human sentiments are emphasized over clear-cut product related appeals. Attempts to measure soft-sell and hard-sell appeals have typically been unsophisticated, often relying on a single item. Basically, the hard-sell/soft-sell distinction is between direct and indirect. The latter is also viewed as "vague" by those who are used to the direct approach. Also, attention to the product in advertising is not necessarily hard sell as in Chinese advertising much attention normally is paid to the product.[7] Although a categorization system covers all aspects of culture, this chapter describes a compilation of different categorizations that may help to understand differences. Rarely will an advertisement fit only one category, often two or more.

The most basic categorization of advertising forms is by Moriarty, Mitchell, and Wells,[8] who distinguish between drama and lecture. According to Moriarty and colleagues, *drama* is a form of indirect address, like a movie or a play, because in a drama, the characters speak to each other, not to the audience. It relies on the viewer to make inferences. A *lecture* is a form of direct address; the speaker delivers a lecture about the product and addresses the audience from the television screen or the written page. In a lecture, the speaker presents evidence (data) and employs techniques such as arguments to persuade the audience.

Several other authors have distinguished basic forms, such as slice-of-life; little story around the product; testimonial (from experts, stars, or "average" people); talking heads; characters associated with the product; demonstration; product in action; cartoon; lifestyle (connection between product, person, and usage); personalization (people talking about the product); product image (symbolic information on product and context); description (what the brand looks like); comparative (naming competitors); association (lifestyle or situation); and symbolic (metaphor, story telling, and aesthetics).[9] These classifications cover most of American advertising forms.

French advertising professionals have provided a classification of descriptors[10] *la Séduction,* or temptation (French advertising tempts the consumer with its offering);

le Spectacle (French advertising is theater, drama, show); *l'Amour* or romance (eroticism, desire, display of affection); and *l'Humour* (amusing associations, playful use of words, humor). This classification reflects a totally different advertising style than the classifications developed by American researchers.

The most comprehensive classification of advertising forms is by Moriarty,[11] who lists 14 types of commonly used execution forms in the United States: (a) news announcement; (b) problem-solution; (c) product as hero; (d) demonstration; (e) torture test; (f) song-and-dance spectacular; (g) special effect; (h) before-and-after and side-by-side comparison; (i) competitive comparison; (j) announcer; (k) dialogue/interview/conversation; (l) slice-of-life; (m) spokesperson; and (n) vignette. Six of these seem to cover most of U.S. advertising forms: comparative advertising, announcer, dialogue/conversation, slice-of-life, testimonials, and vignettes.

Seven Basic Advertising Forms Worldwide

The classification system for comparing advertising forms across cultures that is presented in this chapter is an adaptation of a classification model by Franzen,[12] who used this model to analyze the characteristics of advertising that influence effectiveness and found that a limited number of basic forms and executions accounted for differences in effectiveness. Franzen's categorization of eight forms was based on literature and a lifelong advertising experience in Europe. It was tested by content analysis of Dutch advertising, using a comprehensive code list of 112 variables and by statistical analysis. My adaptation is based on analysis of television commercials of more than 11 different cultures. The model consists of seven groups and a number of subgroups. The seven main groups are announcement, association transfer, lesson, drama, pure entertainment, imagination, and special effects.

Analysis of advertising across cultures demonstrates that Franzen's basic forms exist in most cultures, although the distribution and the way they are executed vary. An adapted version of Franzen's model is presented in this section (see Table 10.1). Each basic form is described and related to culture. There are seven groups, and each group has subdivisions. The basic forms are not mutually exclusive, so a commercial or print advertisement may represent more than one main form or subcategory. The forms can be recognized in layers: There may be a dominant form, but the underlying tone of the advertisement may represent another form. Some combinations are found more often than others.

1. Announcement

Announcements are presentations of facts with no use of people. The facts or visuals are assumed to speak for themselves. This is the most basic type of advertisement: the product and information about the product.

Table 10.1   Seven Basic Advertising Forms

Basic Form	Subcategories
1. Announcement	1.1 Pure display
	1.2 Product message
	1.3 Corporate presentation, documentary
2. Association transfer	2.1 Lifestyle
	2.2 Metaphor
	2.3 Metonymy
	2.4 Celebrity transfer
3. Lesson	3.1 Presenter
	3.2 Testimonial/endorsement
	3.3 Demonstration
	3.4 Comparison
	3.5 "How to"
4. Drama	4.1 Slice of life
	4.2 Problem-solution
	4.3 Vignettes
	4.4 Theatre
5. Entertainment	5.1 Humor
	5.2 Play or act around product
6. Imagination	6.1 Cartoons
	6.2 Film properties in action
	6.3 Other, unrealistic acts
7. Special effects	7.1 Product in action, animation
	7.2 Film, video techniques, artistic stimuli

Illustration 10.1   Clinique, International

1.1 Pure display. Pure displays include all forms that are based primarily on a product's appearance, rather like a product in a shop window or showroom. The product is the hero. This is a relatively culture-free form and may be useful for international advertising. It is found in advertising for fashion items, jewelry, and perfume. An example is an international advertisement for Clinique (Illustration 10.1).

1.2 Product message. This form is based on presentation of product attributes. It can include visual presentation or explanation of facts about the product or brand. It is found most often in low-context cultures because factual, logical explanation is a characteristic of individualistic, low-context cultures. This form is typical for new products or services, cameras, business-to-business products, printers, copiers, computers, and innovations. Messages can be about ingredients or availability of the product, news about products and services, discounts, sales, locations, films, and more. Examples of this form are also found in retail advertising. When used internationally, translations (voice-over and text) of instructional text are used.

An example is an international TV commercial for Dremel (the German version) illustrated by three TV images (Illustration 10.2).

Illustration 10.2   **Dremel, Germany**

1.3 Corporate presentation. This is the typical form used for corporate advertising. It can be compared with a documentary and concerns the presentation of the company and its products or services verbally and visually, sometimes including people in relation to the company or product to illustrate its activities. In an international commercial, people from all parts of the world may be shown. The visuals, products, or people should be of interest to the company's stakeholders. The company's message may be presented in a voice-over or a song. This is a form that can easily be internationalized by translating the voice-over, which can present facts. The amount of facts used is culture-bound: more in low-context cultures and less in high-context cultures. The style used for corporate presentation tends to be related to the culture of the company. Thus, American corporate advertising will be more direct and personalized and will include facts, whereas Asian corporate advertising will be more indirect and will include Asian values. This is recognized in corporate advertising by Asian companies, for example, by Korean LG, of which we showed examples in Chapters 3 (Illustration 3.5) and 9 (Illustration 9.49), visuals that were also used in corporate TV advertising by LG. Different styles are illustrated by images of an international TV commercial for Shell (Illustration 10.3) and for the French construction company Vinci (Illustration 10.4). The Shell commercial shows a young female Shell employee

Illustration 10.3   **Shell, International**

Illustration 10.4   Vinci, France

who studies the environmental effects of oil drilling. The French commercial for Vinci demonstrates the Vinci products in an indirect way, reflecting the art orientation of the French. The viewer is led into the famous Mona Lisa painting. The camera zooms into details of the picture where the viewer sees bridges and roads. The commercial ends with a person using his mobile phone while watching a picture of the Mona Lisa.

2. Association Transfer

In association transfers, the product is combined with another object, a person or situation, or an environment. Associations with the objects or persons are meant to be transferred to the brand. Subforms include lifestyle, metaphor, metonymy, and celebrity transfer. Most of these represent an indirect style.

2.1 Lifestyle. The lifestyle concept is meant to transfer an association with people (young, successful, etc.). The type of lifestyle is culture-bound. Masculine cultures prefer to associate with the successful, the rich; feminine cultures will want to associate with nice, friendly people. High power distance cultures will associate with people

Illustration 10.5   Tio Pepe, Spain

Illustration 10.6   **McDonald's, International**

Illustration 10.7   **Beck's, Germany**

who have the right social status. As people are often depicted interacting with other people, the execution of the form is culture-bound. The type of lifestyle depicted will vary by product category. Illustration 10.5 shows images of a Spanish commercial for Tio Pepe, which reflects high society. Illustration 10.6 shows images of an international commercial for McDonald's, showing "young lifestyle." Illustration 10.7 shows images of a commercial for the German Beck's beer, the sporty lifestyle of young people aged twenty plus.

2.2 Metaphor. A metaphor can be used to transfer the characteristics of an object or an animal (concrete) or an idea (abstract) to the brand by drawing a parallel. Metaphors are used in advertising for all product categories. They can be verbal or visual, concrete or abstract. Visual metaphors are used more in high-context cultures, verbal metaphors more in low-context cultures.

Illustration 10.8 shows a Spanish advertisement for the Peugeot 206 using the horns of the bull to symbolize safety.

Illustration 10.8   **Peugeot, Spain**

2.3 Metonymy. Metonymy transfers the meaning of the original object to the brand, for example, a flower turning into a perfume, a piece of fruit turning into syrup, or a strawberry turning into jam. Because it is an indirect and visual way of explaining, it will be more appealing to high-context than low-context cultures. In a Spanish TV commercial for the railway Renfe, the zipper of the girl's dress turns into a railway track (Illustration 10.9).

Illustration 10.9   Renfe, Spain

2.4 Celebrity transfer. This subform covers advertising in which a celebrity is shown or in which a celebrity acts with other persons without demonstrating, endorsing, or giving a testimonial. The only objective of showing the celebrity is for the target group to associate the product with the celebrity. Examples are showing Michael Jordan with Nike or Gatorade or showing an elegant actress who puts on a fashionable watch and engages happily in a party. The image of the sports star is transferred to the sports shoes or the sports drink; the image of the actress, or "elegance," is transferred to the watch. An actress playing the role of a housewife and referring to a refrigerator is viewed as an endorsement, not as pure association, because there is no transfer of elegance to a fridge. If in a commercial for Martini in Italy the model Naomi Campbell appears at the end and says no more than "Martini, it's a party," it is an association with a celebrity or celebrity transfer rather than an endorsement by a celebrity. In a collectivistic culture, such as Japan, segments or age groups have their own stars. The many famous people who appear in commercials usually support the brand indirectly so that people can associate with the stars or *tarento* (see Chapter 9). They may say only a few words, such as "tastes good." Countries vary with respect to the use of domestic or international celebrities. In a study comparing the use of celebrities in Korea and the United States, all of the celebrities were domestic stars except a Hong Kong actor (Jackie Chan) and the Dutch coach of the Korean football team.[13]

Individualistic, low-context cultures need more facts and thus will use more endorsements than association transfers, which are a more indirect form fit for collectivistic cultures. Illustration 10.10 shows the Spanish actress Judith Mascó,

Illustration 10.10   Norit, Spain

Illustration 10.11   Epson, Japan

who is pregnant and looks at the baby clothes of her first child, which still look like new because she washed them with Norit. Illustration 10.11 shows images of a Japanese TV commercial for Epson color printers. People in the office discuss the need for color printing and the cost. At the end, a famous actor (Tamura) just says "Epson."

3. Lesson

Lessons are direct communications—presentations of facts and arguments— meant to lecture the audience. They state, explain, show, or try to convince or persuade. This is the form that is typical of low-context, individualistic cultures. There may be presenters or voice-overs telling or explaining something to the audience, demonstrating, or comparing, often with the help of visuals. The audience is addressed in the "we-style" or the "you-style," and imperatives can be used. Examples from the United States are "Meet the all-new Ford 150," "Take control with Nicotrol," "The only good wrinkle is the wrinkle you never get" (Oil of Olay), "Any time you need us, anywhere you need us" (Wells Fargo), "You are over 50 and have not lost your edge..." (Centrum Silver nutritional supplements). There is little or no interaction or dialogue. The lesson form is typical of low-context cultures, and it particularly fits the American preoccupation with facts. Advantages of the lecture form are that it costs little to produce and is compact and efficient. A lecture can deliver a dozen selling points in seconds, if need be. There are several variations.

3.1 Presenter. Presenters are persons with a dominant presence, speaking into the camera and conveying the main message. They can give a demonstration, make a comment only, and interview or be interviewed, with or without the interviewer being shown. The role of the presenter and the way he or she behaves will vary by culture. A single dominant presenter is characteristic of individualistic cultures. More than one presenter may be used in collectivistic cultures, and they may be less persuasive in style. In cultures scoring high on masculinity, the presenter will be a "personality" or play a dominant role. In cultures of the configuration masculinity-individualism, presenters use a persuasive style that is perceived as "pushy" and irritating by members of feminine cultures. Feminine cultures do not like dominant people, so the presenter and the approach will be more soft-spoken. Presenters in cultures of strong uncertainty avoidance must convey competence related to the product or service. In low uncertainty avoidance cultures, a presenter's expertise will be understated because people don't like experts.

Illustration 10.12 shows images from a TV commercial for Ariel in the Ukraine. At the time, not all people were used to modern washing machines and detergent. The presenter shows the product and compares it with old-fashioned hand soap. A laboratory situation is added to add credibility. Illustration 10.13 shows images of a Spanish commercial for Leche Asturiana (milk). Two experts (a beekeeper and a cattle farmer) are discussing the quality of the ingredients. Illustration 10.14 shows images of a Dutch TV commercial for milk. The presenter treats the cow as a dog. In the final shot, the cow wants to bury the bone. The only message is that milk contains calcium, which is good for your bones.

3.2 Endorsement and testimonial. In this subform, a presenter or spokesperson suggests that he or she is a user of the product (testimonial) or has an opinion about it and therefore endorses the product (endorsement). Pure user testimonials are used in low-context cultures and particularly by American companies. Procter & Gamble has used this form worldwide for a number of brands in the category of disposable products (diapers, sanitary napkins/towels). Unilever has

Illustration 10.12   Ariel, Ukraine

Illustration 10.13   Leche Asturiana, Spain

Illustration 10.14   **Melkunie, Netherlands**

used the form successfully for the international introduction of Dove. In several countries, local users—not celebrities—testified about the effectiveness of soap and deodorant. Illustration 10.15 shows images of such testimonials. People have tried the product for 7 days and testify about the effects. Dutch Linda Schelvis-Bijl testifies and so does Italian Dariella Camuniti. Other examples are for Dove deodorant. Polish Sylwia Broda tells how effective it is, raising her arms to demonstrate her shirt is clean, and so does Iratxe Martín from the Spanish Basque area. For Dove, Unilever focuses on women with normal body shapes, not celebrities (see also Chapter 5).

Endorsements may include celebrities or experts who, because of their role in society or expertise, are supposed to have an opinion, are credible, and can convince. Credibility is an important element for cultures occupied with seeking the truth where testimonials must be credible. The celebrity must actually use the product. Football shoes, for example, should be endorsed by a football player. Models must use the shampoo they endorse. Credibility is less of a requirement for Asian cultures. Whereas a celebrity endorsing a Western brand generally has some

Illustration 10.15   **Dove soap, Netherlands and Italy (*top*); Dove deodorant, Poland and Spain (*bottom*)**

association with the product category (e.g., Michael Jordan for Nike's shoes), Asian celebrities can be associated with a range of different product categories. Examples are Chinese basketball star Yao Ming endorsing consumer electronics, clothing, and fast food chains in China, and Bollywood Superstar Shah Rukh Khan endorsing many different brands in India.[14] Even more than Americans, Indian consumers are more likely to be affected by celebrity endorsement than by ordinary users of the product because of the celebrity's perceived status and glamor.[15] Another important difference is that in India the personality of the celebrity doesn't have to fit well with the brand personality.[16]

The French company L'Oréal uses celebrity endorsement for selling their shampoos and facial care products. All sorts of international film and TV celebrities endorse the various shampoo brands. The universal payoff used is "because I am worth it," which is subtitled, used in voice-over, or translated depending on what various countries are used to. Next to international celebrities, L'Oréal uses local celebrities, like Indian actress Aishwarya Rai and German soprano and actress Maria Furtwängler. Illustration 10.16 shows examples from the United States, France (with model Claudia Schiffer), and Germany (with Maria Furtwängler). In Chapter 9, we mentioned that in Asia, the payoff was changed to "because you are worth it."

Illustration 10.16   L'Oréal, United States, France, Germany

For low-context cultures, another effective type of testimonial is the expert testimonial, for example, used in comarketing communications by Procter & Gamble. Two examples are in Illustration 10.17. Horst Kett of Bosch (washing machines) endorses Ariel Futur in Germany, and Stewart Nowell of Puma endorses Ariel Futur in the United Kingdom, demonstrating that the product doesn't damage the Puma sports shirts.

The testimonial form is used in various cultures, but the roles of the presenters in both endorsements and testimonials vary. In masculine cultures, presenters tend to be high profile—celebrities, stars, or known people. In individualistic cultures, if ordinary people give testimonials, they are identified, their name is mentioned, and sometimes their signature is added. In collectivistic cultures, celebrities are less identified in the commercials as compared to United States commercials, where celebrities tend to provide their name and/or profession.[17] In feminine cultures, ordinary people testifying tend to be anonymous and celebrities downplay their

Illustration 10.17 **Ariel Germany with Busch and United Kingdom with Puma**

stardom. In a high-context society like Japan, things are said indirectly and implicitly, for example, "They say it is good" (instead of saying, "It is good for you"), without the explicit argumentation and product merit found in U.S. testimonials. A typical Japanese testimonial, therefore, is an implicit recommendation by a familiar talent.

Western cultures combining masculinity and strong uncertainty avoidance use high-profile presenters who are also experts: competent experts who must provide credibility. This is the type found in countries like Germany and Italy. Feminine cultures don't take their heroes seriously or else downplay their importance. Big egos are not appreciated. Well-known people do not present themselves in a serious way, sometimes resulting in a parody on the testimonial. The roles of presenters can be summarized according to four culture clusters, as illustrated in Figure 10.1.

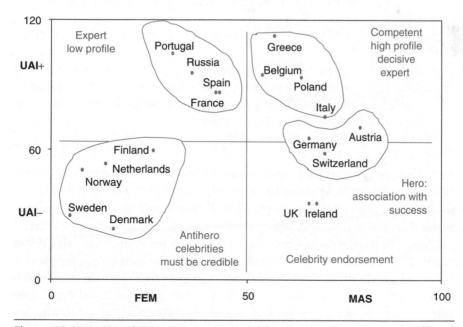

Figure 10.1 **Roles of Presenters**

SOURCE: Data from Hofstede et al. (2010) (see Appendix A).

3.3 Demonstration. The advertisement shows how (well) the product works. Product attributes and benefits may be shown or the situation before and after use. A presenter may demonstrate how the product works. The amount of information, details, and instruction will vary with the degree of uncertainty avoidance. Strong uncertainty avoidance cultures will need more detailed information than weak uncertainty avoidance cultures. Focus can be on the attributes and benefits of the product—before and after using the product—and testing. An example is an international TV commercial for Listerine, shown in Spain. The presenter is walking on human teeth and tells how the product works. Pictures show how Listerine removes the bacteria in the mouth. It is the direct approach of a low-context culture but used in a high-context culture (Illustration 10.18).

Illustration 10.18   Listerine, Spain

3.4 Comparison. Three types of comparative advertising can be distinguished:

- Competitive comparison: the brand is compared with another, identified brand
- The brand is compared with an unidentified product, not named, called "Brand X," "the other brand leader," or a "conventional" product, often presented in the form of side-by-side comparison, or the brand is said to be better than "other products in the category"
- "The best" or "the best in the world"

Examples of competitive comparison are Electrasol (United States) and Halifax (United Kingdom) (Illustrations 10.19 and 10.20). The TV commercial for Electrasol Powerball shows how the product works, then a package of the competitive brand, Cascade, and a hand that covers the Cascade package with an Electrasol package. The Halifax commercial shows a singing bank employee who shows boards with the interest rates of Halifax and competing banks. An example of a brand compared with an unidentified competitive brand is Illustration 10.21, which shows images of a TV commercial for the German detergent brand Persil. Two sisters meet, and one gets a dress of one of the children of her sister, who has washed the dress in Persil. The good quality is compared with clothes that are washed with another, not named detergent.

Illustration 10.19   Electrasol, United States

Illustration 10.20   Halifax, United Kingdom

Illustration 10.21   Persil, Germany

The appreciation of comparative advertising is culture-bound. It is a typical form of the United States. It fits best in cultures of the configuration individualism-masculinity and weak-to-medium uncertainty avoidance. It is not appreciated in most other cultures. Acceptance and nonacceptance can best be explained by the varying configurations of individualism-collectivism and masculinity. Figure 10.2 shows four culture clusters. In three of them, the form is not acceptable.

The lower left quadrant shows the combination collectivism-femininity, with Portugal and Spain. Feminine Asian and Latin American cultures would also fit in this quadrant. This is no-go area for competitive comparative advertising. In collectivistic cultures, comparison with the competition is not acceptable because it makes the other party lose face. It will backfire: You are the one who loses face, as it is not proper. More than two thirds of the world population is more or less collectivistic, which may explain the relatively low use of comparative advertising. It is not perceived as an attractive form in feminine cultures

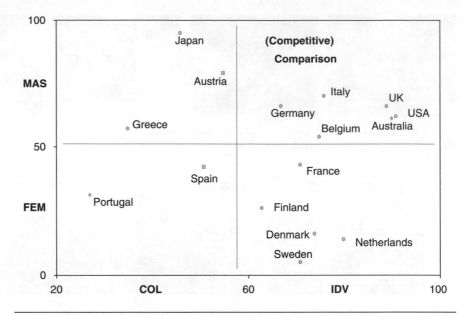

Figure 10.2 Comparative Advertising

SOURCE: Data from Hofstede et al. (2010) (see Appendix A).

either because it is considered too aggressive. Also, modesty makes people feel that it is not proper to demonstrate how good you are.

The upper left quadrant shows the combination collectivism-masculinity. Masculine cultures, characterized by their interest in winning and fighting, are basically in favor of competitive comparative advertising. Although these cultures may want to express the fact that they are good, the combination with collectivism makes avoiding loss of face for others overriding. If comparison is used, the comparison is with another product of the same company to show, for example, that an innovative new product is better than an old product from that company. Japan is the typical example of such a culture, but a number of Latin American cultures are also in this cluster.

The lower right quadrant shows cultures of the configuration individualistic-feminine. This is the Scandinavian-Dutch cluster. Feminine cultures, because of affiliation needs, are more in favor of the soft approach. They do not like the confrontation included in direct comparison. Being the best is OK, but saying so is not: "Probably the best beer in the world" (Carlsberg, Denmark).

The upper right quadrant shows the combination masculinity-individualism. In cultures of this combination, people tend to focus on their rights. As a result, Anglo-Saxon cultures, and in particular U.S. culture, tend to see comparative advertising as informational, offering the consumer "the right to choose." Only the Anglo-Saxon cultures like the hard confrontation as represented by the "cola wars." Germany, Austria, and Switzerland may also like it but are inhibited by their strong uncertainty avoidance, which makes it difficult to cope with the related ambiguities—such as having to prove the correctness of the claim. Various types of competitive comparison are used in the United States. Examples include side-by-side comparisons, demonstrations with competitor's name mentioned, or pictures of packages of competitors' brands with a cross through them.

3.5 "How to." Use of the product and the result achieved are explained or demonstrated. All recipe advertising is covered by this form. Another example is demonstrating how to use technical products. This basic form can be used internationally, but differences in design (kitchens, living rooms), how people look, and the like must be taken into account. Illustration 10.22 gives an example of how to use the Moulinex mixer in a Spanish commercial.

Illustration 10.22   **Moulinex, Spain**

4. Drama

Drama entails the interplay between two or more people. There is a continuity of action, a beginning, middle, and "happy ending." The performers deliver the message. Although drama is intended to convey a product message, it is a more indirect form than a lesson. It originated in the United States and was blown across the ocean with the soap operas. Small stories and plots are included; people experience things, interact and react to situations, and relate to each other. Unlike in the lesson forms, viewers are not addressed directly; they are observers. It is assumed they will watch how other people interact and draw their own conclusions. Subforms are slice-of-life, problem-solution, and vignettes. The indirectness of the form makes it useful for high-context cultures, yet we should keep in mind that the form is based on the typical "solution" or "happy ending" orientation of the United States.

4.1 Slice-of-life. Slice-of-life advertisements have dramatized dialogue dealing with everyday events and "true-to-life" situations. The product is pivotal to the story. There is usually an emotional reward for using the product. A slice of life from one culture cannot be implanted in another culture without adaptation. The adaptation will concern not only how people look but also how they relate to each other. For example, in Italy, France, and Spain, the elder will advise the younger whereas in the Netherlands, Germany, the United Kingdom, and Scandinavia, the younger person will advise the elder. Related to this is the choice of depicting people alone or in groups—a family consisting only of parents and two children or an extended family showing older and younger people including grandparents. Also, the degree of role-differentiation is reflected. Another important choice is whether to show people inside or outside the home. In southern Europe, the social context of many products is outside the home whereas in northern Europe the social context is inside the home.

There also are differences in how products deliver emotional rewards to consumers. A first distinction is between two types of emotional reward: task orientation or relationship orientation. Individualistic cultures are task oriented; collectivistic cultures are relationship oriented. A second distinction is between ego needs and affiliation needs. Masculine societies are characterized by ego needs whereas feminine societies are characterized by affiliation needs. These characteristics can be recognized in commercials. The role of the housewife in German commercials is task- and ego-oriented. The results shown can be lots of dirty clothes and then lots of clean, white clothes. In feminine cultures, the emotional reward will be the relationship between mother and children.

An example of slice-of-life is a German TV commercial for the disposable kitchen towel Bounty. At a barbecue party, all sorts of people are shown who need to wipe something (Illustration 10.23).

Illustration 10.23   **Bounty, Germany**

4.2 Problem-solution. This is an easily recognized advertising form in Western society. It is related to cause-effect thinking. The problem is dirt—the detergent cleans. The problem is dandruff—the solution is Head & Shoulders.

The form is frequently used for detergents. An example is a TV commercial for Clorox (Illustration 10.24). A boy catches a frog in a brook, wipes his hands on his shirt. The best detergent is Clorox (in comparison with a regular one). The shirt is clean—mother and son look happily at the frog. Another example is a Polish TV commercial for the antidandruff shampoo Denorex (Illustration 10.25). A boy points at dandruff on his father's shoulder. A scientist in a laboratory gives evidence of the effectiveness of Denorex, including a detailed picture of how it works on the hair. The happy ending is the boy who touches his father's hair and there is no dandruff. The variations in these examples are comparison in the U.S. Clorox commercial and scientific evidence in the Denorex commercial in Poland, which scores high on uncertainty avoidance.

 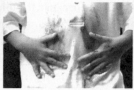  

Illustration 10.24 **Clorox, United States**

Illustration 10.25 **Denorex, Poland**

4.3 Vignettes. Vignettes are a series of independent sketches or visual situations with no continuity in the action. The product plays a part in each vignette. Vignettes are characterized by interaction between people. There may not always be a dialogue but instead a voice-over or song suggesting the relationship between the product and visualized activities. An example is a German TV commercial for Merci chocolates, which shows vignettes of a girl preparing a present for Mother's Day and all sorts of happy people (Illustration 10.26).

Illustration 10.26 **Merci, Germany**

5. Entertainment

A characteristic of entertainment is that it is an indirect form of communication. Entertainment can be in the form of theatrical drama, musicals, shows, comedies, slapstick, humor, horror, or satire. It is meant to please the audience rather than to sell. The form outshines the content of the advertising. Pure entertainment does not fit in the persuasive communication model. It is, however, a typical form for collectivistic cultures where it is effective because it builds relationships and trust between consumers and companies. According to the Japanese advertising agency Dentsu, Japanese people don't want to be lectured, they want to be entertained.

What makes advertising entertaining can be best judged by the people of the culture in which it is meant to entertain. Entertainment is also relative: In countries where advertising generally uses much direct selling, even the slightest deviation from the direct address may be perceived as entertaining. Much of Japanese advertising may be perceived by the Japanese as a clear message to the consumer whereas to Western eyes, it may seem to be purely entertaining. To low-context cultures, all high-context advertising may seem to be meant to entertain. Subforms are humor and plays or acts around the product, which includes a theatrical form of drama.

5.1 Humor. Humor is anything that makes an audience laugh. There are various types of humor, which were described in Chapter 9 under the Why Humor Doesn't Travel section. Humor doesn't travel because humor reflects culture: One often laughs about the most characteristic aspects of one's own culture. The type of humor that is said to travel is incongruity, the unexpected thing happening. Humor in advertising is most often encountered in cultures of weak uncertainty avoidance. England, Denmark, Norway, the Netherlands, South Africa, and Australia have produced award-winning humorous television commercials. One of the forms mentioned before can also be presented in a funny way. An example is a commercial for Electrolux vacuum cleaners from Hong Kong, China (illustration 10.27). A man threatens to commit suicide by jumping from a roof. He jumps but doesn't reach the ground as he gets stuck to a window where a woman is cleaning.

Illustration 10.27 **Electrolux, Hong Kong, China**

5.2 Play or act around the product. All non-humorous entertaining commercials fit this subform. An example is an Italian TV commercial for Lavazza coffee (Illustration 10.28). In a surreal world in the clouds with flying horses (Pegasus), people are drinking coffee and discussing an accident with the Pegasus. In the end, two men have to apologize to the Pegasus. A Japanese award-winning TV commercial for Nissin Cup Noodle (Illustration 10.29) shows rock people throwing rocks at a dinosaur. There is no relationship with the product. It only says, "Hungry? Cup Noodle."

Illustration 10.28   **Lavazza, Italy**

Illustration 10.29   **Cup Noodle, Japan**

6. Imagination

The imagination format covers cartoons or film and video techniques that depict events experienced as nonrealistic—presentations of a make-believe world. The form is often used for children's products or to avoid a too literal interpretation when conveying messages for sensitive products such as sanitary products. An international application is the promotion of film properties, such as characters in Disney films. Advertisements in this format can cross borders. Subforms include cartoons, film properties in action, or other unrealistic acts. Often personality symbols are used or icons that are associated with the brand or product attributes, like softness for fabric softeners. Examples of film properties are the monkeys used for detergent OMO in France and the little men used for the household cleaning brand Cif. A fabric softener that carries different brand names in different countries uses a teddy bear to convey softness. The illustration shows images of TV commercials with the bear in four different countries in Europe: Bamseline in Denmark, Coccolino in Italy, Cajoline in Greece, and Kuschelweich in Germany (Illustration 10.30). The bear is the unifying international factor.

Illustration 10.30   **Bamseline, Denmark; Coccolino, Italy; Cajoline, Greece; Kuschelweich, Germany**

7. Special Effects

The special effects format covers all sorts of artistic elements, animation, cartoons, camera effects, recording and video techniques, music, and tunes. It may overlap with the imagination form as it may also use film properties. Modern techniques offer a new range of artistic resources for developing creative advertising that can be adapted to the stimuli of particular target groups. This is a popular form for advertising on channels for the young, like MTV. The use of artistic stimuli is found more in some cultures than in others (e.g., more in art-oriented Spain or India than in Germany). Showing the "product in action" through animation is a visual that can cross borders, provided there is no value included. Illustration 10.31 shows an example of a product in action, two images of a TV commercial for M&Ms in Poland. Recent technology makes it possible to produce pieces of art, based mainly on video techniques, which can be viewed as pure entertainment. This style appeals to the art-oriented cultures of southern Europe.

In various countries, the telecom company Vodafone has used this form. One example is a commercial by Vodafone in the Czech Republic (illustration 10.32) in which chameleons discuss the degree to which they want to adapt. This is a combination of product message and special effects.

Another Vodafone campaign, originating in India, is a campaign that packages product messages in imagined beings, the so-called ZooZoos, which are advertisement characters promoted by Vodafone since the Indian Premier League Season 2. ZooZoos are white creatures with ballooned bodies and egg heads who are used to promote various value added services of Vodafone. Although these characters look animated, they are actually humans in ZooZoo

Illustration 10.31 **M&Ms, Poland**

Illustration 10.32 **Vodafone, Czech Republic**

costumes. They have become a rage and also got a large fan following on social media.[18] Illustration 10.33 shows three different Vodafone services: easy backup of phone books (instead of having to copy your friends' faces), sending musical greetings, and listening to prayers.

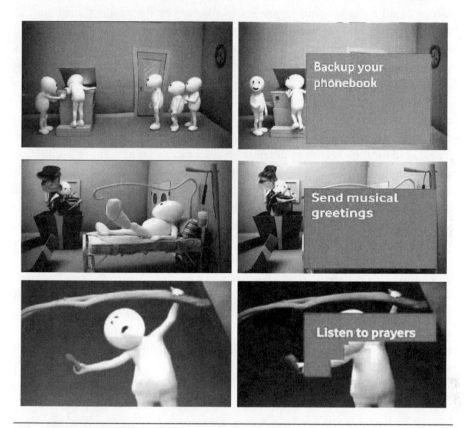

Illustration 10.33 **Vodafone, India**

Relationship Among Basic Form, Culture, and Product Category

A few observations can be made with respect to the relationship between basic forms, product category, and culture. Although the use of some basic forms seems to be related to specific product categories, an observation is that basic forms are more related to the market leader's culture than to the product category. The problem-solution form has been a basic form used for detergents in many countries. The likely cause is the fact that the leading company, American Procter & Gamble, has used this style for half a century. Henkel, the German detergent manufacturer, has followed the example and has used a similar form for much of its advertising for detergents and fabric softeners across European countries. British Reckitt Benckiser uses the form for the brand Vanish Crystal White throughout Europe. Nestlé has its own style, as does Beiersdorf, the company selling the global brand Nivea. The French company L'Oréal has exploited the authority of film stars worldwide.

The basic form used in international advertising is decided by the culture of the advertiser but also by the international development stage of a company. New entrants into a market tend to present themselves by the product attributes. In 1996, a number of new Asian entrants into European markets (e.g., Daewoo and Hyundai) used a simple announcement style. More experience in foreign markets has led to a more sophisticated approach, although in many cases East Asian values are recognizable in their advertising. The styles of the country of origin of a company can be recognized in the approaches and basic forms used in their international advertising. P&G markets brands in a number of product categories from perfumes and cosmetics to detergents and sanitary napkins/towels. The basic forms used for their brands of different product categories have more in common with the culture of the company than with the culture of the audience or the product category. For several product categories, a few dominant multinationals like P&G, Unilever, and German Henkel have used the problem-solution form, testimonial, or side-by-side comparison. These are sanitary products (e.g., Always, Evax, Ausonia Seda, Carefree, Tampax), personal care and cosmetics (e.g., Max Factor, Oil of Ulay/Olay/Olaz, Dove), detergents and other cleaning products (e.g., Ariel, Dash, Vizir, Calgon, Dreft, Yes, Fairy, Fleuril, Sunil), diapers (e.g., Pampers, Liberos, Dototis), pet food (e.g., Whiskas, Pedigree Pal), and other brands, such as Head & Shoulders, Clearasil, and American Express. Only slowly are advertising styles and forms being selected that fit the cultures of the target audiences of international companies. An example is Kellogg's, which for some of its subbrands advertises in the style of the country.

Summary

Seven basic advertising forms can be distinguished that are used worldwide. Their distribution varies and appears to be related to culture. The lesson style is part of Anglo-German culture and was exported to many other cultures where one might wonder if it is equally effective. Comparative advertising mainly fits individualistic-masculine, weak uncertainty avoidance cultures—which covers only the Anglo-Saxon world. Pure entertainment will work better in collectivistic cultures than in individualistic cultures because it is an indirect style.

Some basic forms have become representative for product categories because companies from specific cultures have dominated the product category—they have become corporate forms. There are specific P&G and Henkel forms. Although large multinationals like Procter & Gamble have been successful in using one basic form across cultures and adapting it to cultural differences in a meaningful way, they might be even more successful if they were to use the forms that fit the cultures where they want to sell their products or brands.

Notes

1. Laskey, H. A., Fox, R. J., & Crask, M. R. (1994, November/December). Investigating the impact of executional style on television commercial effectiveness. *Journal of Advertising Research*, 9–16.

2. Laskey, H. A. (1988). *Television commercial effectiveness as a function of main messages and commercial structure* (Unpublished doctoral dissertation). University of Georgia, Athens, GA. Cited in Ramaprasad, J., & Hasegawa, K. (1992, January/February). Creative strategies in American and Japanese TV commercials: A comparison. *Journal of Advertising Research*. The classification was also used by Puto, C. P., & Wells, W. D. (1984). Informational and transformational advertising: The differential effects of time. *Advances in Consumer Research, 11*, 638–643.

3. Moriarty, S. E. (1991). *Creative advertising: Theory and practice* (2nd ed.). Englewood Cliffs, NJ: Prentice Hall, p. 82.

4. Kroeber-Riel, W. (1990). *Strategie und Technik der Werbung: Verhaltenswissenschäftliche Ansatze*. Kohlhammer, Edition Marketing, 2. Aflage. Stuttgart. Cited in Appelbaum, U., & Halliburton, C. (1993). How to develop international advertising campaigns that work: The example of the European food and beverage sector. *International Journal of Advertising, 12*, 223–241.

5. Mueller, B. (1992, January/February). Standardization vs. specialization: An examination of Westernization in Japanese advertising. *Journal of Advertising Research*, 15–24.

6. Leiss, W., Kline, S., & Jhally, S. (1986). *Social communication in advertising*. London: Methuen.

7. Wang, N. (2007). Comparison and application in advertising between Western countries and China. *China Media Research, 3*(2), 9–13.

8. Moriarty, S., Mitchell, N., & Wells, W. (2009). *Advertising principles and practice*. Upper Saddle River, NJ: Pearson Prentice Hall, p. 364.

9. Appelbaum, U., & Halliburton, C. (1993). How to develop international advertising campaigns that work: The example of the European food and beverage sector. *International Journal of Advertising, 12*, 223–241; Katz, H., & Lee, W.-N. (1992). Oceans apart: An initial exploration of social communication differences in U.S. and U.K. prime-time television advertising. *International Journal of Advertising, 11*, 69–82; Cutler, B. D., & Javalgi, R. G. (1992, January/February). A cross-cultural analysis of the visual components of print advertising: The United States and the European Community. *Journal of Advertising Research*, 71–80.

10. Taylor, R. E., & Hoy, M. G. (1995). The presence of la séduction, le spectacle, l'amour and l'humour in French commercials. In S. Madden (Ed.), *Proceedings of the 1995 Conference of the American Academy of Advertising*. United States. Retrieved from http://advertising.utexas.edu/AAA/AAA95.html

11. Moriarty, 1991, 89–91.

12. Franzen, G. (1994). *Advertising effectiveness*. Henley-on-Thames, Oxfordshire, UK: NTC Business Publications.

13. Choi, S. M., Lee, W. N., & Kim, H. J. (2005). Lessons from the rich and famous: A cross-cultural comparison of celebrity endorsement in advertising. *Journal of Advertising, 34*(2), 85–98.

14. Roll, M. (2006). *Asian brand strategy: How Asia builds strong brands*. Trowbridge, UK: Cromwell Press Limited, p. 74.

15. Biswas, S., Hussain, M., & O'Donnell, K. (2009). Celebrity endorsements in advertisements and consumer perceptions: A cross-cultural study. *Journal of Global Marketing, 22*, 121–137.

16. Roy, S. (2006). An exploratory study in celebrity endorsements. *Journal of Creative Communications, 1*(2), 139–153.

17. Choi, Lee, & Kim, 2005.

18. Pramanik, A. (2011, July 6). Vodafone's Indian ZooZoos to be introduced in global markets. *India Today*. Retrieved on February 8, 2013, from http://indiatoday.intoday.in/story/zoozoos-of-vodafone-to-be-introduced-in-global-markets/1/143801.html

CHAPTER 11

From Value Paradox to Strategy

The previous chapters have provided tools for understanding how culture influences consumer behavior, branding, and advertising. In contrast to books on global marketing that mostly follow the management approach, the focus of this book has been on the consumer and the influence of culture. Marketing is about consumers, and marketing and advertising will be successful only if the values of consumers match the values of the product or brand, which means that strategies successful in one culture can be extended only to other cultures with similar relevant values. New strategies have to be developed for cultures with different values. This applies to corporate and marketing strategy. Only after understanding the impact of culture on consumers, how they buy, how they communicate and perceive advertising, can we make strategy decisions. This is why the strategic implications are covered in the last chapter of this book.

This final chapter points at a few strategic issues. It reviews corporate strategy, the marketing mix, product/market development, branding strategy, retail and marketing communications strategy. Relatively, much attention is given to branding strategy which nowadays is viewed as fundamental to marketing and communication strategy. Brand value means mindshare: the position the brand has in the mind of the consumer. To reach global mindshare, a brand must fit in the minds of consumers in different cultures. In global brand strategy, the choice is not between global and local but between ineffective global standardization and effective cultural segmentation strategy. We have learned that similar cultures can be clustered with respect to product-relevant values, needs, motives, and communication styles. This also applies to brand strategy.

Common perception is that a strategy can be global, but execution must be local. This is not correct. At the core of strategy is culture. Both mission statements and brand positioning statements appear to be culture-bound because they reflect the philosophy of a company's leaders and brand managers. Any global corporate or brand strategy, to be effective, must incorporate not the values of its leaders but the values of all stakeholders—the shareholders of the company and consumers of the brand in all countries where the company operates. From the first levels of strategy development, a company's mission and vision, culture is involved.

Corporate Global Strategy

One of the basic corporate decisions a global company or a company that wants to internationalize is whether and how to enter which markets in other parts of the world, also referred to as *modes of entry of international markets*. Also at corporate level, decisions are made about the core business of a company and what the company stands for, which tends to be formulated as a mission statement. Other activities at corporate level are deciding on corporate identity and public relations strategy and management. These topics will be discussed in the following sections.

Modes of Entry of International Markets

Companies internationalize in different ways, for which various stages of internationalization can be distinguished:

- Exporting, using international agents, distributors, or export management houses
- Foreign production through licensing or franchising
- Strategic alliance or joint venture, for shared manufacturing, R&D and/or distribution
- Foreign manufacture, also called Greenfield operation
- Skipping these stages, as done by so-called born global companies, mostly in the ICT sector, which develop products for the whole world right from the start

A historical reason for internationalization of U.S. companies has been following customers abroad. The clearest example has been Coca-Cola, which started the internationalization process in 1928 when it traveled to the Amsterdam Olympics with the U.S. team. When the United States entered World War II, Coca-Cola rallied behind the armies and promised that "every man in uniform would get a bottle of Coca-Cola for 5 cents wherever he is." Bottling plants followed, so Coca-Cola could be placed "within arms' reach of desire." In the slipstream of Coca-Cola's internationalization, its advertising agencies did so, in order to serve their clients outside the United States.

Exporting has been more important for company growth for companies with small home markets than for companies with large home markets. Some of the large global companies have originated in small countries. Examples are Nestlé (Switzerland) and Unilever (Netherlands), IKEA (Sweden) or Nokia (Finland). For companies with large home markets, export may deliver mainly some additional revenue. As mentioned in Chapter 1, this is a weak incentive for adaptation. Companies with strong export dependence succeed because of commitment, accumulated experience, product adaptation, and channel support. Poor performance is caused by errors in pricing and product adaptation.[1] Similar to the discussion of standardization versus adaptation of advertising, for most product categories, adaptation to local usage is necessary except for some luxury products and some technology.

When selecting international markets, several criteria must be reviewed. These are market size and growth, economic development, political conditions, competition, distribution system and retail structure, and cultural distance. Whereas some companies invest mostly in culturally close markets, others do so in culturally distant markets, if they view large growth potential in such markets.

Strategic alliances, mergers, and acquisitions involve cooperation with people of different cultures. In some cases, cultural incompatibility can have such negative effects that cooperation in joint ventures or mergers can affect results. An example was the merger between Daimler and Chrysler where the American and German styles of working were so different that the merger failed.

Another culture-bound variable is the level of control and involvement in a foreign operation.[2] Generally, companies originating in high power distance cultures are used to central control, whereas in low power distance cultures, there is more delegation of decision making. Power distance also explains differences in standardization or adaptation choices, as central control often leads to higher standardization, giving less freedom to the locals to implement their own cultural values in marketing and communication.

A Company's Mission and Vision

Worldwide, it is agreed that the *mission statement* is a crucial element in the strategic planning of a business organization. It is an explicit formulation of what the company stands for. In addition, the *vision* of a company states where the company wants to be sometime in the future. Some companies include *strategic intent* in the vision. Vision and mission should give focus to everyone who is involved with the company, be it directly (employees) or indirectly (e.g., shareholders).

The Western origin of the mission statement concept can be recognized in a definition by North American Christopher Bart:[3]

A good mission statement captures an organization's unique and enduring reason for being, and energizes stakeholders to pursue common goals. . . . It compels a firm to address questions like "What is our business? Why do we exist? What are we trying to accomplish?"

Next to the individualistic value of uniqueness, the statement reflects the practice of self-analysis of individualistic cultures.

Although the concept of the mission and vision are Western inventions, the practice has been embraced by companies worldwide. It has become global management practice to provide statements expressing a company's strategic intent, its philosophy, values and ethics, or operational effectiveness. This doesn't imply, however, that form and content are similar. The mission statement of American companies is an abstract statement of what the company stands for, its identity. In collectivistic, high-context cultures where companies function like families, what the company stands for is not necessarily made explicit, and if it is made explicit, it expresses the philosophy and vision of the company's leaders.

Any corporate mission or vision, both in form and content, reflects the worldview of its management, which usually represents the values of the culture of origin of the company.

The most famous examples of Japanese strategic intents were Canon's "Beat Xerox" and Komatsu's "Encircle Caterpillar."[4] Japan is a competitive society; each company pointed its arrows at one (bigger) competitor. An example of Asian *form* and *content* is formulating the company statement as a "Message from Top Management," as on Toyota's website. The subtitle of this message forms the content: "Harmony with people, Society and the Environment."[5] The corporate philosophy of Japanese Canon is *kyosei,* or "All people, regardless of race, religion or culture, harmoniously living and working together into the future."[6] Korean Samsung's management philosophy is "We will devote our human resources and technology to create superior products and services, thereby contributing to a better global society."[7]

American statements reflect the need for performance, leadership, greatness, and growth. General Electric says, "Being a reliable growth company requires consistent execution on strategic principles that drive performance every quarter and every year." This includes building leadership businesses, driving growth, and spreading ideas across great people and teams.[8] Microsoft's mission is "To help people and business throughout the world to realize their full potential."[9] This mission reflects the Anglo-Saxon value of self-actualization. Dutch Philips reflects the feminine value quality of life by stating its mission as a passion to "Improve the quality of people's lives through timely introduction of meaningful innovations."[10] French L'Oréal calls its mission the L'Oréal spirit: "At L'ORÉAL, we believe that everyone aspires to beauty. Our mission is to help men and women around the world realize that aspiration, and express their individual personalities to the full. This is what gives meaning and value to our business, and to the working lives of our employees. We are proud of our work."[11]

Corporate Identity

From the vision and mission, a corporate identity can be distilled, which includes the core values of a company. This practice is also of Western origin. This is reflected in definitions of corporate identity that are based on the Western identity concept. The British communication consultant Nicholas Ind,[12] for example, defines *corporate identity* as "an organization's identity in its *sense of self,* much like our own individual sense of identity. Consequently, it is unique." Uniqueness and consistency of corporate identity in individualistic cultures is opposed to a collectivist's identity, which can change according to varying social positions and situations. When global companies define their corporate identities, they might consider including variations for the different cultural contexts in which they operate.

Usually, the task of creating a corporate identity begins with the selection of an appropriate corporate name. Other factors that contribute to corporate identity include the logo of the organization and marketing communications. All this, including language, lettering, and associations, is logically a reflection of the home country of the organization. Altogether, they reflect the communication style. For example, corporate visual identity of Korean companies is more symbolic and visual than that of North American companies.[13] Many Western organizations prefer worldwide consistency of all these elements without realizing that this can be counterproductive, as not all elements are equally meaningful or understood in all countries. Some American companies in China have learned to adapt. Coca-Cola, for example, has changed its name to adapt to the visual orientation of the Chinese. The company renamed its brand to *Kokou Kole,* which translates into "happiness in the mouth."

The basis of the Western concept of corporate identity is that it should be perceived universally, but in reality, it translates differently in different parts of the world. Perception of a corporate identity is also dependent on the use of the company name as a corporate brand. For example, Unilever (Netherlands) and Procter & Gamble (United States) are very big companies but hardly known to the general public because historically they have mainly marketed product brands. Other companies such as Nestlé (Switzerland); Heineken (Netherlands); Yakult, Sony, and Mitsubishi (Japan); Daewoo (Korea); and BenQ (Taiwan) are world players who use their corporate name on (almost) all of their products. Some Western companies, such as Heineken (Amstel, Tiger) and Nestlé (Nescafé, Perrier, Nestea, KitKat), in addition to the corporate brand name, keep using other brand names of companies that they acquired. East Asian companies tend to stick to one corporate brand name. As discussed in Chapter 7 (The Purpose of Marketing Communication section), the reason for using a company brand in collectivistic cultures is the need for trust in the company. Next to this, many Japanese companies change their product models more frequently than Westerners. Japanese avoid the purchase of unfamiliar brands, so it is easier to accept new products under the corporate umbrella brand. As a result, corporate image has a stronger influence on Japanese than on American consumers.[14]

Until recently, Unilever has chosen not to use its corporate name on its different brands and products. The reason for this was that a scandal (such as the nitrite in their Iglo frozen foods in 1980 in the Netherlands) could easily transfer consumer scare to other Unilever products. Driven by cultural specifics of collectivistic cultures like Russia, Japan, and China, however, Unilever has chosen to include its corporate name on all its brands. The very least that should be added to product brands in Asian advertising is the company's name. For some time, P&G in China has done so by adding a P&G signature, for example, to Head & Shoulders in TV commercials; and Nippon Lever in Japan has done so for its Japanese products. For sweet biscuits (cookies), Danone uses the brand name Lu in Europe, but in Asia, the corporate name Danone is also on this type of product.[15]

Brand values should fit the values in the overall company vision and mission. Brand vision should match corporate vision; they should enhance each other. This is of equal importance in individualistic and collectivistic cultures. If the brand and company vision are aligned and clear, trust in the company will transfer trust to the brand and vice versa. This strategy is more difficult for companies that have many brands, such as Unilever or Procter & Gamble. If a brand portfolio includes brands with contradictory values, protests may arise in the Western world because consistency is expected. An example is the contradictory values of Unilever's brands Axe and Dove. Axe's message is that by using Axe, men can get lots of attractive women, whereas Dove's message is that beauty is inside. A positive connection is between Unilever's mission "to add vitality to life and to do this in a sustainable way" and Unilever's intention to have all its palm oil certified sustainable by 2015.[16]

Another aspect of corporate identity is registering as a global company on the Internet, only using a dot-com domain or registering in country domains for local online identity. Worldwide companies follow quite different strategies. For example, British and Swiss companies are less likely to use a local strategy than Japanese and Brazilian companies.[17]

Public Relations and Culture

A much used definition of PR that originated in the United States says that it involves managing relationships between organizations and publics. This implies, among other things, a communication dialogue.[18] Also European academics tend to point at communication as central to PR, as expressed in the definition "PR is the maintenance of relationships with publics by communication in order to establish mutual understanding."[19]

Central to public relations theory and practice are the concepts *relationship* and *publics*. The idea that *relations* have to be organized and the abstraction of the notion of *publics* are both elements of Western, individualistic worldviews. In collectivistic cultures, relationship orientation is ingrained in one's being and is an essential element of everyday life; where relations are personal, an abstract notion like a public may not be workable. Another important difference is that in the relationship between organizations and publics in individualistic cultures, there is no distinction between in-group and out-group as in collectivistic cultures, where also personal and public relationships may overlap. For Westerners, a public is a group of individuals who may belong to an organization or be unrelated, who can influence the organization and/or who are active stakeholders regarding some issues in an organization. An organization's publics can be identified, such as community, government, media, stockholders, or consumers.

As to professional ethics, Western ones tend to be absolute and universal, as compared to East Asian standards that are situational and informal and vary with the type of ties people have, such as family ties or ties with friends, work ties, or ties with strangers. Theories of public relations are dominated by Western ethical standards, views on the role of governments and media, and a Western perspective on history.[20]

The Anglo-Saxon origin of PR has led to a focus on conveying explicit information, based on the assumption that target groups want to be informed and that information will lead to a positive attitude. In collectivistic cultures, usually also of high power distance, an important goal is developing long-lasting personal relationships. In particular for the Chinese, the meaning of relationship (*guanxi*) is much broader than in the West, including relationships as a resource or a mixture of favors, interests, and privileges, and maintaining "pleasant interpersonal relationships" which is the most important task of a PR manager. It means frequent chatting with secretaries or other intermediaries "at the right time and in a pleasant way."[21] Interviews with Korean PR practitioners show that they view personal relationships as an influence on communication. They believe journalists will select news stories based on journalists' personal relationships with PR practitioners.[22] Because of this important difference between Asian PR and Western PR, Huang[23] suggests adding a fifth Eastern strategy, "social activity strategy," to the four Western types of public relations strategies—mediated communication, interpersonal strategies, bilateral strategies, and symmetrical communication.

Also in public relations practice in India, the personal influence model plays an important role, which manifests itself in a quid pro quo relationship between public relations managers and key individuals in places such as the government and the media. Practitioners engage in various techniques aimed at establishing personal friendships with strategically placed individuals whom they call "contacts." Gifts and hosting dinners are important for public relations officers for laying a foundation for seeking return favors when needed by the organization. Personal relationships are the most important aspects of success, and they extend to private life. Also, contacts with media representatives are in the personal sphere, including taking members of the media for dinner or cocktails regularly. The importance of personal relations can also be found in other collectivistic cultures, such as in Slovenia in Europe, in Latin America, in Japan and Korea.[24]

In Mexico, also a collectivistic culture, shaping interpersonal relationships is a most important element of public relations, and a few other Mexican cultural characteristics play a strong role in this. One of them is *confianza*, or trust, which is a key to developing and maintaining good relationships; another is *palanca*, a concept which is not easily translatable, but can be viewed as providing a person or connection a favor. Mexican personal and organizational roles also overlap, including interest in colleagues' families and discussing personal matters before doing business. The palanca concept is particularly important for public relations. It is part of an act of generosity toward one's fellow man without any explicit demand or suggestion of reciprocity. In public relations practice, it is manifested in philanthropic work that is done by the firm to enhance its reputation, but it is much more than that as it involves more than simple friendship with concrete benefits. It is being part of a social network which provides opportunities that outsiders don't have. Through an exchange of favors, palanca helps facilitate contacts. Outsiders are at a disadvantage. Companies of individualistic cultures may explain the phenomenon as bribery.[25] It can be recognized as an aspect of short-term orientation, which includes "service to others" and self-enhancement as an important cultural value.

Next to the different types of relationships found across individualistic and collectivistic cultures, another, related characteristic of collectivistic cultures, which often also score high on power distance, is the fact that CEOs are the ones who build relationships at the highest level and are not inclined to delegate this to their PR officers, as these do not belong to the decision-making layer in a company. As a result, in these cultures, PR officers tend to be less independent.

In high power distance cultures, where power holders disperse information as they see fit, PR is likely to have a different function from the one in low power distance cultures, more to build relationships to achieve trust than to inform, as in low power distance cultures where information builds trust. In individualistic cultures, when a problem occurs, a company tends to organize a great PR effort, providing information to contain the damage. In collectivistic cultures, companies have problems admitting mistakes and see it as loss of face. Sometimes, companies try to hide mistakes or tragedies because of feelings of shame. In collectivistic and high power distance cultures, a firm's reputation is important because of the need for trust in the company, which is particularly important for online shopping. A firm's good reputation contributes to customer e-loyalty.[26]

Because good communication management is essential for PR, sensitivity to different communication styles is essential. PR officers communicate with publics via the media in all sorts of ways, for example, by issuing press releases or by organizing events that are covered by the media. The Western, individualistic origin of PR is recognized by the importance of the press release. International PR has to take into account differences in media usage across cultures and differences in usage of electronic media like weblogs and other computer-mediated communication, as discussed in Chapter 8.

In international PR, whatever is communicated should be locally relevant, or the message will be thrown into the waste basket. For journalists, what doesn't fit their mental maps will not be used. If you don't have locally relevant messages, it is difficult to maintain an ongoing relationship with journalists of the relevant media. Messages will have to be translated, as not all journalists are fluent enough to understand the essentials of a message—better to do a translation yourself than depend on the journalists' capabilities.

Companies increasingly use corporate websites with virtual press rooms for PR purposes. How content is designed is also culture-bound. Analysis of corporate press rooms of 120 companies in the United States and seven European countries found most of them lacking with respect to resources such as reports, financial data, and histories, as well as in having poor organization and classification of certain sections.[27] As discussed in Chapter 5, people classify information in different ways across cultures, so when people organize information when designing a website, they will do this according to their own cultural practice. The result is that people from other cultures may have difficulties getting information that may not be in the place they expect it to be.

The Global Marketing Mix

The standardization-adaptation debate as summarized in Chapter 1 concerned mostly advertising, but the basics apply to the whole marketing mix. The argument for standardization often is the existence of somewhat similar demographic groups, such as urban young people. These segments have become saturated with the presence of global brands and offer fewer opportunities for growth. Increasingly global marketers view large emerging markets, such as India, China, and Brazil, as an opportunity for growth. Catering for these segments asks for different marketing programs. For example, in India, Hindustan Lever's plan changed the packaging (smaller one-use size), price and distribution as well as advertising, but capitalized on the well-established brand image in the detergent and soap markets, using women to form the distribution, changing the logistics, and using point of purchase displays to reach the smaller urban and rural markets.[28]

Rarely can one and the same product cross borders with the same price, through the same distribution channels. Many marketing failures concern the product, its packaging and its price. Price is more than the cost of manufacturing, shipping, exchange rates, and consumers' disposable income. Price can communicate status or low or high quality. Prices cannot be set regardless of the competition. In China, the Chinese brand Future Cola was 6 cents cheaper than Coke and Pepsi, and to compete, Coca-Cola launched cheaper cola's in returnable bottles, cutting the price down and saying that Coke costs the same as water.[29] Product ownership and usage often have historical roots, and in previous chapters, we have seen how many product categories vary with culture. Both the product and communication is culture-bound. Finally, the retail structure of a country can be very different from that of the home country which can influence success. Many retailers who have entered new markets have failed because of not understanding the local retail environment and needs of shopping consumers.

Product/Market Development Across Cultures

Although some companies view themselves as pure marketing organizations that focus only on branding, the basis of existence of a global company is its product or service and the ability to develop or adapt product concepts for different markets. A most important decision of a company is deciding which products or product variations to market to which markets.

Many products sell better in some markets than in others. The cause of such variations can be wealth or culture. If the cause of low penetration of a specific product in a specific country is culturally defined, products should be adapted to better fit that culture.

New product-market combinations must be developed when entering new markets of different cultural configurations. Life insurance, for example, is a product for individualistic cultures; entering a market with a collectivistic culture demands different products. An example could be offering parent-related pension insurance to the Singapore yuppies whose new mobile lifestyles make it more difficult to fulfill their obligations to look after their parents, a strong element of their collectivistic and Confucian values.

Well-defined cultural differences can help to develop more appropriate products or product adaptations for different cultures. If certain do-it-yourself products do not sell as well in strong as in weak uncertainty avoidance cultures, adapt the product to the need for competence. Add instructions, offer training, whatever argument to make the customer feel competent. Similarly, electronic appliances, such as remote control devices and mobile phones, should be easy to use for weak uncertainty avoidance cultures but may have complicated details for strong uncertainty avoidance cultures where people want to control the process.

Finally, an important part of product development is taking the major steps of brand management: formulate a brand vision, determine brand identity and desired brand image, position the brand and communicate the brand's position including its price.

Predicting Market Development Across Cultures

Understanding the role of culture can lead to better predictions of how markets will develop and how new products and services diffuse and thus help develop marketing strategy. Although in some cultures people adopt a new innovation or habit quickly, people of other cultures may not, as discussed in Chapter 5 (pp. 148–150). Let's take the Internet as an example. At the end of the 20th century, expectations were that the Internet would cause greater productivity everywhere and make all societies more egalitarian. Instead, people have adopted it for their specific culturally defined purposes. For better predictions, countries can be mapped according to cultural similarity. An example is a culture map for the development and effects of the Internet. The Internet first penetrated the economically developed markets of low to medium uncertainty avoidance where people adopt innovations faster than in markets of high uncertainty avoidance. These markets are in the lower two quadrants in Figure 11.1. In the upper two quadrants of Figure 11.1 are the lagging markets, the high uncertainty avoidance cultures. When the Internet became more common in all developed markets, purposes of usage varied. Whereas in the low masculine markets people have adopted the Internet to enhance the quality of life, using it more frequently, and more for leisure and educational purposes, in the high masculine markets, the Internet was initially and most importantly expected to enhance productivity for greater competitiveness.

A third dimension that explains variance of adoption rates is power distance. In the high power distance cultures, governments can exert greater power to influence new developments. In France, the government had an early influence on information technology by backing the Minitel system. In Spain, the government pushed Internet usage by sponsoring its use in schools. In South Korea, the government has pushed broadband communications. As a result, already in 2001, South Koreans spent more time online than the people of any other nation in the world, which also had a beneficial effect on the Korean economy.[30] South Korea is one of the countries with the highest broadband penetration in the world.

When developing such maps for different product categories, next to uncertainty avoidance, another product-relevant dimension must be selected. These can be found from comparative usage and attitudes studies.

As uncertainty avoidance distinguishes markets with respect to adoption of innovation, it also has to be considered when selecting a test market for acceptance of a new product or product variety. Selecting Denmark in Europe or Singapore in Asia as test markets is not wise, as these countries will adopt any innovation fast and are not representative for the rest of the region. It is better to select a country that scores somewhere in the middle on the scale.

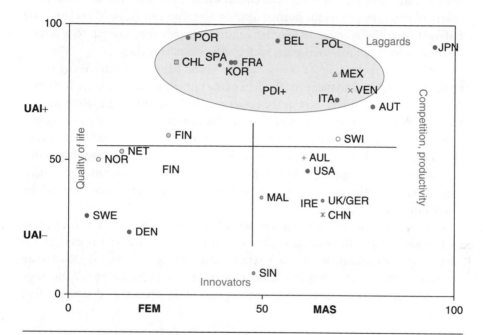

Figure 11.1 Mapping Cultures for the Internet

SOURCE: Data from Hofstede et al. (2010) (see Appendix A).

Product Development and Design

When crossing borders, many products have adapted, to the physical environment, to user habits, or to motives driven by cultural values. Where kitchens are smaller, household appliances have to be smaller. Sizes of people are different, which influences clothing and shoes. Fashion tastes vary. Washing machines adapt to the type of clothes people need to wash, to the available electrical current, to the size of kitchens. American pillowcases are a different size than German ones. Lack of such knowledge added to Wal-Mart's failure in Germany. For years, Western companies have been selling their irons to Japanese and Korean consumers, only to discover at a very late stage that they do not iron standing up but sitting down. This obviously asks for different ergonomic requirements. How designers shape objects is part of their culture. Scandinavian design is sleek and simple, which can be recognized by the design of the Nokia mobile phones. The Chinese like phones with glitter or perfumed phones or anything else that delivers status. The perception of what is nice, beautiful, and necessary in kitchens is different.

Basically, the choice between standardization and adaptation depends on the type of market wanted. If a product is marketed to another culture with different values and not adapted, it may have only a niche market. When adapted, it may be able to attract a mass market. This is illustrated in Figure 11.2. Cultures can overlap with respect to some values and related habits. Some values are found everywhere, but they are more prevalent in some cultures than in others. The distribution of values of a culture follows the normal distribution. The averages of one culture are different from the averages of another culture, but they may overlap to a certain extent. For international marketers, such overlaps can be niches.

A global marketer's choice is to adapt the brand values and advertising to the target culture or stick to the specific values of the home culture. The latter will result in having only a niche market in the target market instead of the mass market at home. An example is the Italian car brand Alfa Romeo. Italians are more aggressive drivers than are the British or the Finns, and the Alfa Romeo caters to aggressive drivers. In Finland, there will be some people who like to drive aggressively, but this is a relatively small segment. Alfa Romeo, which can cater to a mass market in Italy, will, without adapting their product and communication strategy, have only a niche market in Finland.

In Chapter 2, we gave examples of successful product adaptations, such as by McDonald's. Many others do so. In China, Kentucky Fried Chicken serves egg drop soup. Unilever's shampoos add black sesame and ginseng variants. P&G's hair care lines are fortified with strong antidandruff formula.[31] The Chinese manufacturer of household appliances adapted their washing machines when they discovered that

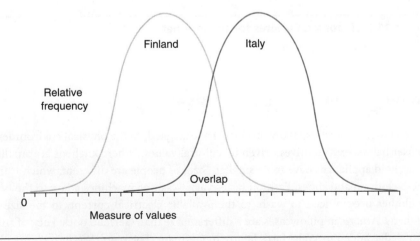

Figure 11.2 **Culture Overlap**

the pipes got blocked because users washed yams (sweet potatoes) in them. Instead of instructing the masses to stick to clothes washing, they designed a new machine with enlarged pipes.[32] In India, the detergent brand Nirma was developed as a response to Hindustan Lever's Surf that was still too expensive for most consumers. Nirma offered a washing powder that was superior to the washing soaps used by many Indian consumers but of lower quality than Surf.[33]

Also, the number of line extensions may vary by country. In the home country, where people know the product and the company who produced it better, consumers may be open to more variations of the product than in foreign markets. In Western Europe, only one type of the Japanese Yakult, a product containing specific live bacteria, which are supposed to be good for your intestinal flora, is sold. In Japan, Yakult has many more products on the market, for example, for soothing the stomach, to control sugar intake, and Yakult for mental relaxation. Each of the Yakult products has some specific ingredient, and Japanese consumers know much about all these different ingredients. Moreover, they trust the Yakult Honsha Company to deliver good and beneficial products. It is Yakult they trust, and they therefore consume their products.

In general, product usage does not change overnight. Because people's behavior is stable, past or current behavior can often explain future behavior. When developing and marketing new products, it is useful to analyze past and current behavior to predict the future. In countries where people are used to entertaining in bars and cafés, they also access the Internet in the cyber café. If you want to sell advanced digital photo printers to people in different cultures, first analyze in which cultures people used the most analog films.

Aspects of product design can be culture-specific. When designing products, some shapes can have undesirable associations. IKEA has standardized most of their product offerings. Chinese furniture stores have a broad range of tables with tabletops made of glass, and these are also available in IKEA in China. The design of a coffee table available at IKEA Shanghai was made up of a circle surrounded by a square through the glass tabletop. To a Western consumer, it looks like a normal small table, but for a traditional Chinese consumer, it is not right. In China, a circle represents the sky, while a square represents the earth. Putting the sky in the earth makes no sense.[34]

Packaging Design

The physical package is important because of differences in transportation, climate, and so on. But more important is the design of a package when it reaches the consumer as the package communicates a message about the product or brand. Package design varies with respect to three-dimensional design as well as graphic design, and it often has local flavor. Packages vary with respect to the use of textual information, contrast, position and size of the brand logo, the quantity of verbal information, aggressiveness of typography, use of colors (soft or bright, harmonious or contrasting), shape, use of symbolism, degree of structure, and detail in the packaging design. For deodorants, for example, Japanese packaging uses relatively abstract symbolism, whereas German packaging uses more concrete symbols. In the feminine cultures, generally softer harmonious colors are used more than in the masculine cultures, but this may vary by product category. The Japanese are particularly fond of meticulously packaged products.

Even for global brands that pretend to appeal to global tastes worldwide packaging strategies have not converged. This is because the package reflects the brand values, and it provides information for which the need varies across cultures. In 2003, McDonald's introduced a single set of brand packaging with a single brand message around the world, but 2 years later, the company announced plans to localize nutritional value charts on the package.[35]

A comparative study of package design across seven countries found that packages differ both in three-dimensional design and in the way they communicate through graphical design and vary in the use of textual information; use of color, shape, and symbolism; and degree of structure and detail in the package design. Culture appears to be of great influence on the noted differences.[36]

The right choice of colors is important for package design. Van den Berg-Weitzel and Van de Laar[37] found that packages for deodorants for women used greater contrast and brighter colors in feminine cultures, whereas they used soft harmonious colors and low contrast in masculine societies to endorse female softness in societies with strong role differentiation. The picture of the Fruitella packages in Chapter 5 (p. 136) showed the influence of mental processes, such as field dependency on design of pictures. Basically, just like advertising, packaging reflects communication styles of cultures by using symbolism or words, by the way people are depicted, by the colors, decorative elements, and shape.

The Japanese are extremely fond of well-packaged products. Mineral water manufacturer Kinki Partners made a package for Hyotan Kara Mizy mineral water in the shape of traditional water gourds to differentiate its product. These gourds used to be scooped and dried and used to carry water or grain. Inside is the water of the famous Yoshino mineral water source in de prefecture of Nara. See Illustration 11.1.

Illustration 11.1   Hyotan Kara Mizy package

Retail

Despite the emergence of supermarkets and large shopping malls worldwide, countries vary with respect to retail infrastructure and shopping behavior. In Chapter 5, differences in shopping behavior were discussed. Retail chains that want to expand to other countries have to adapt to differences in infrastructure and shopping behavior. Important differences between countries are if people go shopping every day because of small space in the home or wish for fresh food every day, if people do bulk weekly shopping, or shop for entertainment. For Indian middle-class consumers, shopping is the chief form of entertainment. It is part of the family outing. In the past it was the bazaar, nowadays the modern malls, with Big Bazaar and McDonald's that are part of a circuit families take.[38] Increasingly, Western retail chains, such as Wal-Mart, Costco, Metro, and Carrefour are penetrating other countries. Failures tend to result from merely replicating a successful model of one culture into another and not acknowledging the differences.

U.S. Wal-Mart operates 8,500 stores in 15 countries but operates under different names, such as Asda in the UK and Seiyu in Japan. It has been successful in some countries but not in others. It was successful in South America and China, but not in Germany and South Korea. It entered Japan by the purchase of a stake in the Seiyu chain, but their human resource strategy, resulting from cost-cutting, has not made the chain very popular in Japan. Originally, it was also the Wal-Mart model of everyday-low-prices that did not work in Japan where shoppers associated low prices with low quality. However, the economic recession has made the Wal-Mart model more appealing to the Japanese.[39] British Tesco, strong in its management of *own brands*, entered Taiwan in 2000 intending to open 22 stores. In 2005, it had opened only six stores and exited the market. One of the reasons was a big gap between identity and image of Tesco. Whereas in the home market, low price and budget were key to perceptions of the Tesco brand, in Taiwan, consumers didn't even know these own brands existed as there was hardly any advertising and promotion for Tesco's own brands. Taiwan consumers had always viewed retail brands as "cheap" or poor quality. Tesco also offered foreign products like cornflakes and macaroni that were not thought suitable for Taiwanese habits.[40]

Because retail is local, most international retailers have entered new markets by merging with local shops. Exceptions are IKEA from Sweden and Toys"R"us from the United States that opted for organic growth by replicating the original format in other cultures.[41] Not all elements of this original format are accepted everywhere. The IKEA formula is based on self-assembly, which is not attractive to high power distance cultures where people want service. However, for other reasons, it can be successful. For example, IKEA offers total concepts—living rooms, bedrooms—which are attractive to collectivistic and high power distance cultures where people think more holistically. Although Russia scores high on power distance, IKEA is very successful in that country. Also across Asia, there are differences. IKEA is very popular in China but it has failed in Japan because the do-it-yourself concept does not fit Japanese culture where well-prepared and compact scaled products are preferred. Other examples are Starbucks which in China has created a typical teahouse atmosphere and Olay which has not presented the brand as a Western product but rather integrated it in the local culture by including ingredients of natural remedies.[42]

Several European fashion retail chains, such as Marks & Spencer (M&S) and C&A, entered other European markets and failed because they offered the home-market fashion to other countries or extended their strategy and philosophy of the home market too consistently to other markets. In continental Europe, their emphasis on the British brand St Michael alone and their refusal to accept credit cards didn't work as it did in the United Kingdom. Also in Asia, it didn't adapt enough. Marks & Spencer opened a shop in Shanghai, which the Chinese considered too British, and the few expat shoppers complained it was too Chinese.[43]

The design of shop interiors, the type of product offered, and how products are presented in retail varies. In supermarkets in feminine cultures, more men do food shopping, even with children. This influences the type of shopping carts. In low power distance cultures where independence of children is important, small shopping carts are available for children so they can shop independently. In high uncertainty avoidance cultures, more product information is provided on the shelves next to the price. Personnel are better dressed, and cleanliness must be demonstrated, for example, by white floors. To symbolize freshness of food products or the offer of the day, handwritten information may be provided instead of well designed, consistent printed information, which cannot be produced instantaneously. A difference related to individualism and power distance is how products are categorized: by sort or by relationships or even by color. Belgian supermarkets tend to present products by relationship, for example, pastas with pasta sauce or wine with meats, whereas in the Netherlands, products are often categorized by sort, for example, pasta with rice. Other differences are visual routing signs versus verbal routing signs.[44]

Also shopping mall designs cannot just be transplanted from one culture into another. Many factors influence success or failure, some of them simply being infrastructure. In South China, the Dongguan Sanyun Yinghui Investment & Development company replicated the suburban shopping/themed leisure environment of the "Mall of America" built 18 years earlier in Minnesota. There were several reasons why this South China Mall failed. The population density in the area was too low and access by road was limited and so was public transportation. The connectivity between the different zones was weak and confusing. The success of the Mall of America was based on the lack of leisure/entertainment/retailing facilities within a large geographical area, whereas in the neighborhood of Dongguan, there were several well-established shopping malls not too far away. Many other shopping malls in China have been successful as consumers do shift away from traditional high street shopping to the modern shopping centers. Failure tends to be caused by lack of planning, omitting the right mix of retail and entertainment, as well as low accessibility.[45]

The vast majority of international retailing research has concluded that standardization of the retail mix across various countries is problematic.

Branding and Culture

In various chapters in this book, the influence of culture on branding was discussed. The brand concept, as such, is a Western, individualistic phenomenon because brands generally are positioned as unique personalities with abstract characteristics in terms of personal traits. Across individualistic cultures, personal traits vary, so one brand personality will not be equally attractive in all cultures. Trust-worthiness is an attractive brand characteristic in high uncertainty avoidance cultures, and prestige is important in high power distance cultures. In collectivistic cultures, consumers will select products from companies that they trust. As a result, *company brands* are more customary in Asia whereas the *product brand* is a more Western, individualistic phenomenon (see also Chapter 5, section on Personality and Identity in Marketing). Product brands are developed for positioning purposes, both against the competition and against other brands of the company's brand portfolio. In collectivistic cultures, an important purpose of marketing is to build relationships and trust between companies and consumers. Developing strong company brands is a better strategy for this purpose than developing a portfolio of competitive product brands.

Because in Asia brands are most successful if they are linked to companies with a successful image, all sorts of products that in the West would not be considered fit for use under one brand name can be linked to a company brand name. Whereas in the West, a diaper by the Japanese cosmetics company Shiseido would be judged primarily in terms of whether cosmetics and diapers go together, in Asia, the image of Shiseido would provide enough justification for giving the product a try.[46] The need for brand extension fit is typical of individualistic cultures as described in Chapter 5 (Categorization subsection).

Also, collectivistic cultures do not relate to brands as persons. They buy products with specific product features, not abstract brands. Illustration 11.2 shows outdoor advertising for the Super Sol retail chain in Barcelona, Spain, which mentions offering the leading products, not the leadership brands, as a North European retailer would.

A company that wants to work globally should consider the cultural specifics of the brand concept. When formulating the brand identity, be aware that Asian consumers are not so interested in an abstract brand identity or personality. They are more interested in what a company stands for,

Illustration 11.2 Super Sol, Barcelona, Spain

how reliable it is. A global company should align its corporate and brand identity in a way that both North Europeans/Americans (brand identity) and Asians (corporate identity) can be addressed.

Global brand companies tend to measure the equity of their brands in the various countries. An important element of brand equity is consumer equity, which is measured in part by brand associations. Many of these associations are abstract and are expressed differently across cultures. In this respect, Western measurement systems are not adequate to measure global brand equity. Hsieh[47] demonstrated that the brand value calculated based on brand associations for 19 car brands in 16 countries varied significantly. In Europe, the average brand value of the 19 brands was higher than in the Asian countries. These differences appear to correlate with individualism ($r = .68$). Other studies confirm that different cultural conditions lead consumers to different brand evaluations.[48]

Brand Positioning Across Cultures

A brand position is the market space a brand is perceived to occupy or what the brand stands for in a world of brands. This position includes the associations it has in the mind of the consumer. It includes all aspects of a brand: the product attributes, benefits, and values. When developing brand strategies, companies tend to formulate the desired brand position in a brand positioning statement.[49]

The *brand positioning statement* links the external aspects of the brand with the internal aspects. With the description of these two aspects, we cover the most used set of terms of Western branding theory. The *internal aspects* of a brand are the brand elements injected into the brand by the company. They include the brand identity and values attached to the brand by which people should be able to recognize its identity. The identity is what the sender (company, organization) wants to convey about the brand, which includes the brand's characteristics in terms of personality.

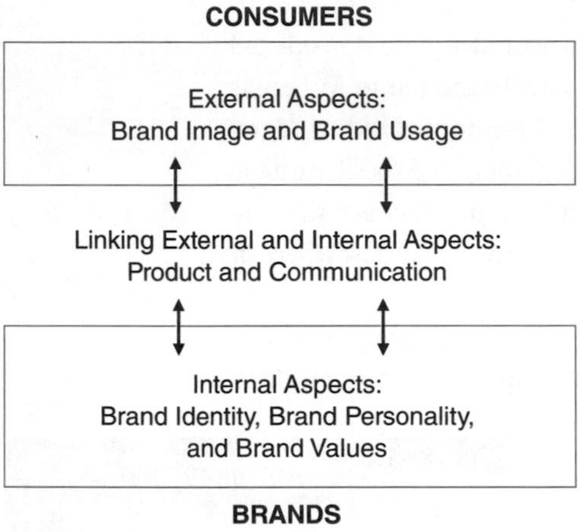

The *external aspects* of a brand include the take-out by the consumer, its image (or how the consumer perceives the brand) and usage (or how the brand's products are used in daily life). The role of the brands and products in daily life can contribute to the desired brand identity.

A brand is well positioned if there is a proper link between the external and internal aspects. This is visualized in Figure 11.3.

Several marketing mix elements contribute to transferring the identity to an image, of which the *product* itself and the *communication* are the most visible and culturally sensitive elements. The other marketing instruments, *price* and *distribution,* are also culturally relevant, in particular if price is used as a positioning strategy.

CONSUMERS

External Aspects:
Brand Image and Brand Usage

Linking External and Internal Aspects:
Product and Communication

Internal Aspects:
Brand Identity, Brand Personality,
and Brand Values

BRANDS

Figure 11.3 **Elements of a Brand Positioning Statement**

External Aspects: Product Usage and Brand Image

To enable the formulation of a brand identity, knowledge of the current brand image is needed, as well as how consumers deal with the brand and its product(s). These are the tools of the marketer. The image is what consumers see of the brand and how they consequently perceive and mentally integrate all messages. It is the association network in the mind of the consumer. Ideally, the image matches the identity, what the sender wants to convey about the brand.

Product Usage

Understanding how a global brand is perceived requires in-depth consumer research in many countries to understand all the situations in which the brand is used. It includes not only talking with consumers but also walking with consumers: Go into their houses and see what they are doing and how the brand fits (or could fit) their needs.

Large global companies like Procter & Gamble and Unilever have accumulated consumer insight by going inside the consumers' homes: P&G makes films of their consumers' toilet and showering behavior; Unilever puts on tape what consumers are doing in kitchens in countries as diverse as Nigeria, Vietnam, Paraguay, New Zealand, and Germany. They have learned that decision making based on assumptions about consumer behavior is one of the worst mistakes a company can make. Knowledge of how a brand is perceived and how the brand's products are used is essential for defining the brand identity. There are many techniques such as "meet the consumer" sessions to develop knowledge and insight in brand/product perception and usage.

Knowledge of existing behavior often can help in understanding future behavior. It is easier to reinforce existing habits embedded in the culture than to introduce new ones. An example of reinforcing existing habits is the introduction of the Senseo coffee machine in a joint venture between Philips and the coffee company Sara Lee/Douwe Egberts. The Senseo was a new type of coffee machine that is a hybrid of the espresso machine and the drip-filter machine. Like the espresso machine, it makes one or two cups of coffee at a time, but it is cheaper. It is more convenient than a drip filter: One pad containing coffee is all you need. It appeals to individualistic cultures by individualizing the coffee experience. Every individual can select a coffee flavor according to his or her own taste because each cup is made separately. If your partner likes decaf while you like strong arabica, you are able to make each cup to your liking. This concept fits the trends of convenience and individualism: a hassle-free cup of coffee to your own liking in the shortest possible time. It reinforces individualistic values. Consumer behavior has slightly changed, but the coffee-drinking ritual in the home is maintained, so the coffee maker is a typical machine for home use. In cultures where coffee consumption takes place more in the public domain, it is likely to be less popular. The reason for the success of Starbucks in Spain is not because it satisfies a need for the variety of coffee offered but because it confirms the existing need of young people to sit together at leisure and chat.

When predicting product usage in developing countries, one should not expect people to copy behavior of the developed world, in particular North American behavior. They may copy some behavior because it delivers social status, but after some time, people will return to behavior that fits their old values. Right after World War II, the Japanese adopted Western clothing. At the start of the 21st century, young Japanese rediscovered the kimono.

Neither globalization nor modernization is the same as Westernization. As discussed in Chapter 1, people may desire to think globally, but as a result of globalization, they actually become more aware of their specific local values. People increasingly identify with their local or regional communities. Most countries in Asia are adopting new technologies but retaining their identity at the same time. Rather than becoming like the West, Asian countries are developing their own form of modernity.[50]

The more money people possess, the easier it is for them to stick to or refine their culturally determined behavior. People will select brands that comply with this cultural behavior. This means that the brand position should be multifaceted because a brand will mean something different to a Portuguese woman than a Vietnamese man.

Brand Image

Brand image is the representation of the brand in the mind of the consumer. It is an outcome of brand identity. In Western cultures, the image can be like a human being with unique characteristics. In collectivistic cultures, it can be quality and the representation of trust in a supplier—the product is part of a trusted family of products.

Ideally, the brand identity should be reflected in the image, which is the out-take of the consumer. Within cultures, discrepancies between identity and image occur, but across cultures, the gap between identity and image is likely to be wider. Many marketing research agencies offer positioning models, which help define brands in terms of human personality traits or values that are suggested to be universal, but the characteristics of their own culture often can be recognized in the descriptions. Consumers will attribute the brand characteristics that fit their own mental maps and from there develop a brand image. This does not necessarily reflect the intended brand identity. To North Americans, the image of McDonald's may be different from what it is to the Chinese as McDonalds has adapted their positioning in the various markets, for example, as a family restaurant or a place for young people to be. In other countries, the original image is mostly attractive to travelers from the United States who expect cleanliness and the type of food they are used to. It enables travelers to cope with the uncertainties of an unfamiliar culture and experience a feeling of being at home while abroad.[51] McDonald's would not be able to survive on only the business of tourists.

Entering a market with the same positioning as existing brands will not work. The launch of the Milka chocolate brand in the United Kingdom failed because Cadbury's Dairy milk already had the full-cream milk positioning that had made Milka successful in Germany.[52]

Many global brands that desire a consistent brand identity and hope this will result in a consistent brand image end up with different brand images across cultures. In Chapter 5 (Personality and Identity in Marketing subsection), we showed that strong global brands have different, culturally relevant brand characteristics in different cultures. Such different, culturally relevant images across cultures are a likely reflection of success of these global brands, although the companies may not have intended their success coming in this way. Success may have been due to product quality, innovativeness, and intensive distribution. Comparison of the image of Red Bull in the United Kingdom, Singapore, Austria, Germany, the Netherlands, and the United States shows differences in perceptions of the Red Bull brand personality. Although the global advertising campaign pushed competence and excitement as brand characteristics, these seem mostly to appeal to the United Kingdom public. A differentiation approach to creating brand personalities for culturally different markets may be more market oriented than a consistent approach.[53]

Asian marketers who don't have the desire to be consistent let brands float from culture to culture, saying different things in different cultures. A brand like Hello Kitty projects different images and meanings in different cultures and lets target groups select themselves: in Japan, teens and even grown-up women; and in the United States, small kids.[54]

Internal Aspects: Brand Identity and Personality and Brand Values

The internal aspects are the brand characteristics that the company inserts into the brand. Western global companies generally want to inject personality characteristics and values that are consistent across target groups and across countries, although in some cases, some marketers also vary these characteristics by target group.

Different brand values can be selected for different cultures. As long as the brand values selected for international exposure are not contradicting the brand values used in specific countries, several may well exist next to each other. In a similar way, it should be possible to develop an international brand identity with local variations that also make it culturally relevant locally. After all, how many consumers notice that a brand is communicating different values in different countries? The only consumers who do are probably the company's own employees.

Brand Identity and Personality

What has been said in this chapter regarding corporate identity also pertains to brand identity. The Western wish to develop a consistent brand identity leads toward connecting symbols to the brand that are thought to be universal, but often are not, or labeling the brand personality with concepts that may mean different things in different languages/cultures. An example of failed consistency was the Kotex campaign that used a red dot as a symbol for menstruation, which was not accepted in Asian markets. It was rejected in Vietnam, and in China, older women disliked the image because of its strong association with blood. In Korea, consumer resistance led to creating a white dot, symbolizing cleanliness, purity, and freshness.[55] Instead, a better option is to find what is meaningful with respect to the brand and its role in people's lives in different culture clusters and to load the brand with different core values, although the product may be the same worldwide.

Because personal traits vary across cultures, personality descriptors for brand positioning across cultures will not be equally understood in all countries. First, there are culture-specific personality dimensions, such as ruggedness in the United States and peacefulness in Japan. Brand personalities fitting in such indigenous dimensions are not likely to be as fitting in other countries as they are in the home country. As discussed in the subsection Brand Image, consumers attribute personalities to strong brands that fit their own culture rather than the identity the marketer has thought of. Second, similar trait labels can have different associations, so the meaning of seemingly similar trait descriptions can be very different. This poses a problem when brand personality traits are used for global brand positioning and particularly when they are used as a basis for marketing communications concepts.

Brand Values

As described in Chapter 2, there are three levels of communication: attributes, benefits, and values. Many international companies want to go beyond presenting product attributes or benefits and add values to the product to position the brand in the mind of the consumer. In particular, Anglo-American companies have propagated this approach to global advertising because of their belief in universal, global values. Thus, happiness is used to sell fast food, success to sell cars or wristwatch brands, unlimited human potential ("just do it") to sell trainers, and freedom to sell jeans.

Many global advertising campaigns of American origin reflect American values. Levi's, for example, focused on freedom (of movement) in international advertising, as in Illustration 11.3, which shows images from an international TV commercial for Levi's in Spain. It shows two people running fast, as if in competition. The takeout of Spanish viewers was competition, not freedom, and personal competitiveness is frowned upon.

Although Asians do not consciously add values to their brands, successful Asian brands do carry values. Brands like Tsing Tao beer in China position themselves as "sons of the soil" that understand local consumers. Pan-regional Asian brands, like Tiger Beer from Singapore, portray an image of Asian-ness. Contemporary Asian symbolism, as well as references to the West as a sort of stamp of approval, add regional appeal.[56]

One of the reasons for desired cross-cultural consistency in global branding strategies is the wish for control. Companies want to be sure that their brand values are consistently similar across countries. Various studies are finding that the

Illustration 11.3   Levi's, Spain

elements the company injects into the brand end up in different images in the minds of consumers in different countries. If consumers elsewhere perceive these global brands as having different values than the company intended, the process is out of control; to keep control, it may be better to define specific brand characteristics (product characteristics, brand values, traits, and company values) for the various cultures where the company operates.

Brand Communication Across Cultures

A key benefit of building a strong brand is increased marketing communication effectiveness.[57] Brands are strong when they have strong sets of associations in the mind of the consumer. Communication is supposed to convey the brand identity and its accompanying values. This should result in a brand image in the mind of the consumer that will make him or her assess the possibility to buy the recommended product.

Applying the Value Concept to International Branding and Advertising

Values are part of a brand's association network and are reflected in the appeal, in the advertising style, in the basic form, and in executional details. Western brand managers select values consciously when formulating their brand strategy, whereas Asian marketers don't do this explicitly, but values are attached to brands by associating them with specific persons. Whether explicit or implicit, all marketing communication carries values. Values offer an opportunity to differentiate brands by going beyond attributes and benefits or the deliverance of higher level consequences to consumers. Adding values creates association networks that distinguish the brand vis-à-vis the competitive brands in the category and thus can help build strong positions for brands.

A tool for developing brand communication strategy is the *value structure map* (VSM), which describes how a particular group of subjects tends to perceive or think about a specific product or brand.[58] A value structure map links the product's attributes and benefits to values.

Attributes can be concrete or abstract; benefits can be functional or psychosocial consequences of the product's attributes. Value structure maps provide a structure of people's associations with a brand at the three levels: attributes, benefits, and values. They show how the types of associations that people make between a specific attribute of a product and its subsequent benefits and values are connected. This connection, developed by Gutman,[59] was presented as the means-end chain model. Gutman formulated the essence as follows: Means are objects (products) or activities in which people engage; ends are valued states of being, such as happiness, security, accomplishment. A *means-end chain* is a model that seeks to explain how the choice of a product or service facilitates the achievement of desired end-states.

Such a model consists of elements that represent the major consumer processes that link values to behavior. Rokeach's distinction of instrumental and terminal values compares with the means and ends.

The technique used to develop means-end chains is *laddering,* an in-depth, one-on-one interviewing technique used to develop an understanding of how consumers translate the attributes of products into meaningful associations with respect to the self.[60] By using this laddering technique, sets of linkages can be determined between perceptual elements, which are then represented at different levels of abstraction. Figure 11.4 shows three levels of associations for toothpaste, and Figure 11.5 shows six levels of (hypothetical) associations for Coca-Cola. An example of a value structure map is one for automobiles in Figure 11.6, including a number of Rokeach's terminal and instrumental values as well as one Asian value, harmony with nature.

Advertisers who want to differentiate a brand can follow different routes via attributes and benefits to reach end values. In this system, the product attributes may be the same worldwide, yet different end values may be connected to the attributes (to be found through research), reflecting different cultures. An example of a route in the VSM for automobiles is selecting, for example, one attribute, a Strong Motor, and one end value, Pleasure, and following the route Fast Acceleration → Imaginative,

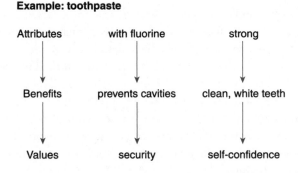

Figure 11.4   **Levels of Communication (VSM, Laddering)**

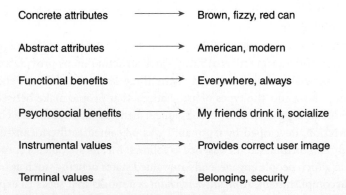

Figure 11.5   **Levels of Communication: Coca-Cola**

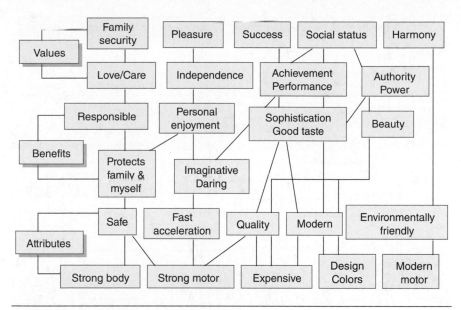

Figure 11.6   Value Structure Map: Automobiles

Daring → Personal Enjoyment → Independence → Pleasure. Another route takes the same attribute as a starting point but continues via Safe → Protects the Family & Myself → Responsible → Love/Care → Family Security. This could be an example of a route for a feminine culture. Volvo has used this route from the attribute Strong Body. A route for cultures of the configuration collectivist/high power distance/high uncertainty avoidance would be Design/Colors → Modern → Sophistication/Good Taste → Authority/Power → Social Status. Different routes can be followed, depending on the target group, the culture, and the competition. In a multinational campaign targeted at countries that are similar with respect to one or more dimensions, it may be possible to select one route with values that the different countries have in common. Two other examples are VSMs in Figures 11.7 and 11.8.

These VSMs were developed by a group of Spanish and German students who, in casework, had to develop a common strategy for Spain and Germany for the beer brand Corona Extra. First, they selected the attributes, and then they tried to find common terminal values. What they found the Spanish and German cultures had in common were Friendship, Distinguished, and Acceptance. The Spanish found Belonging and Stability to be important terminal values with Self-Esteem and Being With Others as instrumental to the terminal values. The Germans found that Self-Esteem was a terminal value for them and that Stability and Being With Others were instrumental to the terminal value Self-Esteem. They concluded that only the two routes leading toward Belonging and Stability for Spain and to Self-Esteem for Germany could not be used for a common strategy, whereas Friendship, Distinguished, and Acceptance, which they formulated as terminal values, could be shared and used for one common strategy.

Both attributes, benefits, and values associated with the brands should be in line with the users' needs and motives. Some product attributes are culture-bound by

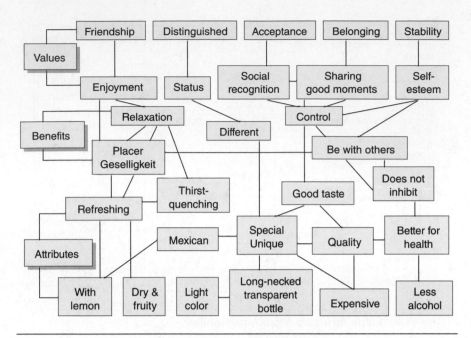

Figure 11.7 **Value Structure Map: Corona Extra, Spain**

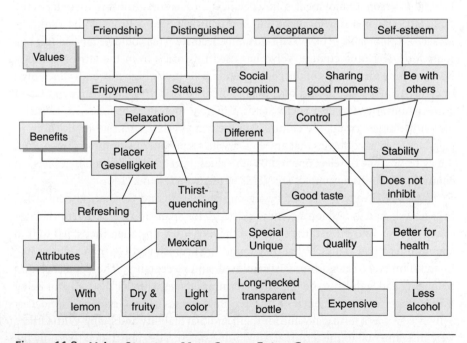

Figure 11.8 **Value Structure Map: Corona Extra, Germany**

definition. Anti-bacterial claims for detergents, household cleaning products, and hand soaps are mainly attractive in high uncertainty avoidance cultures. Several products claiming to kill bacteria were not successful in the Netherlands, but they are attractive to the Germans and Spanish.

Many benefits, what the product does for the consumer, also have to be carefully observed. Brand consultant and professor Larry Percy[61] states that positioning a brand correctly requires careful attention to verifying the specific need, as consumers see it, and the benefits they associate it with. In addition, the communication styles and formats must fit the culture of the consumer.

Next to attributes, benefits, and values, brands are differentiated in contrast to competitive brands by the type of presentation, consisting of advertising style and basic forms, as described in the previous chapters. Some brands have avoided adding values and became successful by just presenting product attributes, only adapting executional details. Others have developed culture-specific basic forms to convey attribute and benefit. Most successful international brands of European origin focus on continuously innovative product attributes or benefits and employ culturally relevant advertising forms and styles. Examples are L'Oréal, Nivea, Actimel (by Danone), and Volkswagen. Illustrations 11.4 and 11.5 show TV images from Volkswagen commercials in Germany and France. The product attribute is "4-Motion." The German commercial (Illustration 11.4) reflects the typical German need for testing and demonstration. The driver by accident gets on a toboggan run and drives down the mountain that way to a coffee bar. When he orders a cup of coffee, he discovers he has lost his wallet, and he returns driving upward. This is the extreme test. The French commercial (Illustration 11.5) uses the metaphorical approach and associates the 4-Motion technique with all sorts of tricks, like cutting a woman in two, boxing tricks, and film tricks.

Formulating a brand position based on cultural analysis early in the process will facilitate effective communication and lay the foundation for building strong international or global brands. Only a few companies have successfully formulated and executed a global brand positioning with a very limited set of brand

Illustration 11.4   **Volkswagen 4-motion, Germany**

Illustration 11.5   **Volkswagen 4-motion, France**

values and benefits. Gillette has built its reputation on the word *close*. With each innovation, its products shaved closer. Communication has remained at the attribute level. Coca-Cola is an example of a brand that has defined its essence in terms of a thirst quencher that is available everywhere. The take-out by consumers in some places in the world has been fun and happiness, in others social status. Gillette and Coca-Cola have defined a worldwide uniform identity, but they allow the message consumers take out, the image they have of the brands, to differ across countries. Because they continuously monitor the take-out by consumers, they are in control. There is no problem with different take-outs as long as companies are aware of these differences, and the take-out by consumers fits their mental maps. If this is not the case, a company should work on obtaining a better fit cross-culturally.

Global Marketing Communication Strategy

In Chapter 2, six global brand strategies were described. Depending on the brand strategy, a configuration of form and style must be decided to communicate the desired brand position. The selected form, as we learned in Chapter 10, can be related to culture or, historically, to the product category. Time and again, marketers need to ask themselves whether they want to stick to one format (as P&G, for example, does for some brands) or to give freedom (as Volkswagen does with completely different styles in different countries). Several brand-communication configurations are possible, which also vary by stage of market development. Each strategy uses a different combination of basic forms and execution. Global advertising eventually boils down to six different strategies.

1. Fully Standardized: One Product or Brand, Display

There is one product or brand that is sold across borders. The product is the message. Advertising focuses only on the product attributes. This basically is export advertising. It will be in one language. This strategy is used in umbrella campaigns additional to local advertising as, for example, for perfumes and alcoholic beverages. Examples are Clinique and Bacardi. It is also recognized in corporate advertising. Be careful not to include any values, or it will run into cultural problems. Focusing on product attributes alone can be a successful strategy when introducing a new product. In a world of growing parity in products and brands, such a strategy is rarely effective in the long term.

2. Semistandardized: One Brand, One Advertising Form, and Standard Execution (Voice-Over and/or Lip Sync)

Innovative product attributes and benefits are central to the advertisement. In some countries, the original language is used (often English); in others, voice-over or subtitles are added. As not all countries are used to lip sync, showing a person's lips while talking is not advisable, as it shows too clearly that the advertising is "imported." In countries where people are not used to voice-overs in television programs, this irritates consumers. This strategy is most used for international personal care brands (e.g., Gillette and L'Oréal). Using only a voice-over and not showing interaction with dialogue between people allows for cross-border usage. It is the strategy for brands that thrive on distinct product attributes or benefits and continuous innovation.

3. One Brand, One Form, Varying Standard Executional Elements

This strategy, also called pattern standardization, uses one advertising form, including a number of executional elements that can be used in different configurations. The executional elements may reflect different values (e.g., expressed by different user benefits). The risk of this strategy is in the combination of opposing values in one advertisement because the concept tends to reflect the values of the country of origin and contrasting values can be added in the execution. An example would be focusing on value for money in the Netherlands and adding a line about testing, which is not culture-fit for the Netherlands. In such cases, the cultural specifics are compromised. The combination of appeals may not be as effective as each separate appeal would have been in the countries where it fits. Such combinations of appeals are found in pan-European campaigns, for example, for shampoo, toothpaste, and household products.

4. One or Different Brand Names, One Advertising Form, Different Executions

This is a strategy used by many Anglo multinationals like P&G, advertising similar products with different brand names using one consistent basic advertising form, such as comparison, testimonial, or drama, but adapting to people, languages, and culture. It is used for sanitary napkins and detergents or cleaning liquids (Dreft, Fairy, Ace). P&G has used this strategy successfully in the Western world. Based on one form, different commercials are made for each country, and the execution reflects appropriate cultural values. An example is how in large power distance cultures, the elder advises the younger and in small power distance cultures, the opposite.

5. One or Different Brand Names, One Concept, Different Executions Based on Culture-Fit Advertising Styles

One abstract platform or idea is the basis for different local executions. Examples are campaigns for Actimel by Danone and for Axe, a male deodorant, by Unilever.

The Actimel concept is that it regenerates people in bad times, such as in winter or in hectic life. The Axe concept is that it attracts women vigorously. Many different executions are used to express the concepts. There will be recognizable elements such as the brand name and package, the payoff, music, a symbol. Different executions based on the concept can be developed in different countries and adopted by others of similar cultural configurations. The advantage of this strategy is a centrally recognizable idea that can be expressed using local values. Actual ads may be used globally, regionally, or locally depending on the need for cultural adaptation.

6. Cultural Segmentation: Act Global, Think Local

This is the opposite of the "think global—act local" paradigm. It means reaping all the benefits of globalization in production, sourcing, distribution, marketing, and the connected benefits of economies of scale in production and organization but with the exception that mental images cannot be standardized. Advertising is mostly local but endorsed by the company. This is the global strategy of companies which have learned to exploit local cultural values or communication styles. These companies build relationships with local consumers. The company's name is used as endorsement. This is Nestlé's strategy; it can be recognized in Volkswagen's strategy and in strategies of many Japanese companies. The product is central, so focus is on product attributes, but the advertising style varies by culture cluster (Volkswagen 4-Motion).

Communication Strategy by Stage of Market Development

Different stages of market development ask for different communication strategies. In global marketing for new products in all sorts of durable goods and technology categories, but also for advanced food products, worldwide income will be the main driver of penetration across national markets. In economically homogeneous areas, acceptance of new products will vary with the degree of uncertainty avoidance. After introduction, further penetration will depend on needs and motives of different cultural configurations. Thus, at the time of introduction of a new product, when it still is more or less generic, for some product categories, advertising can focus on product attributes, and both product and advertising can be standardized. With increased competition, products are differentiated, and advertising must differentiate by focusing on benefits or values. Customer demand becomes more heterogeneous, and because of varying consumer needs across cultures, the benefits and values used in communications can better be adapted to varying needs. We suggest three stages of international market development with different consequences for international marketing communications in each stage.

Stage 1: Global Products, Global Marketing Communications

Market penetration of the generic product will depend on national wealth in economically heterogeneous areas and on cultural factors in economically homogeneous areas. An example was the penetration of the television set when it was introduced. A more recent example is penetration of mobile phones. In this first stage, marketing communications can be based on product attributes and can be relatively standard. The success of Coca-Cola in foreign markets was in this first stage, when there was relatively little competition in the category and their global advertising was effective. Nokia introduced mobile phones with standardized international advertising. Nokia claimed the generic attribute for mobile communications by saying "Connecting people," a statement that also reflects the basic value of human communications. The mobile phone producers piggybacked on the mobile phone service providers, who were the national telecom companies and who penetrated their own markets by offering locally meaningful services with culturally meaningful local advertising. The messages of the mobile phone producers in this stage remained generic, introducing new product attributes, for example, small or well-designed phones.

Stage 2: Global Products, Adapted Marketing Communications

When markets become saturated, differentiation takes place within and across markets, which is likely to follow different patterns across markets. Although the same differentiated products are sold everywhere, some are sold better in some cultures than in others. Following the example of the television set, all producers developed wide-screen TV and teletext reception features; but in the high uncertainty avoidance cultures, more wide-screen televisions were sold, and in the individualistic cultures, teletext was more used. In this stage, the mobile phone service providers differentiated their services. SMS messaging was first adopted in the individualistic cultures. In a collectivistic culture, like Spain, special services were offered to mothers to communicate with their children. In high power distance Belgium, school children were offered special after-school rates in order not to conflict with the authority of school teachers who wouldn't want children to use the phone during school hours. In the feminine cultures, electronic banking services by phone were introduced. New services followed existing habits and preferences. In this stage, because markets are not saturated for the generic product, products can still be standardized; but marketing communications must be adapted, and this can be done by defining culture clusters. The mobile phone producers adapted their products and advertising only with respect to language. Advertising went a level higher, to the benefit level, with messages like Nokia's, "You have information under control." When Coca-Cola entered this stage, they continued their strategy of Stage 1, which became less effective. They thereby created room for local brands such as Mecca-Cola (France), Raak (Netherlands), and Virgin (UK).

Stage 3: Local Products, Local Marketing Communications

This is a stage when markets become saturated for the generic product, and strong competition forces companies to differentiate both products and marketing communications. It will be profitable to develop product extensions for specific applications to comply with cultural differences in usage and motives across national markets. These can be single markets or clusters of markets following the product-relevant cultural values. In the television category, the example is interactive television or broadcasting by computer and Internet. The VCD (video CD) player—a system that can play compressed video on a TV, offering the possibility of random access playback—penetrated much faster in Asia than in the United States because it was used for karaoke. In 2002, the mobile phone had entered Stage 3, but in Europe, mobile phone producers kept standardizing their products and advertising as if they were still in Stage 1. Only in large developing markets, like China, did Nokia market its cellular phones with features that appealed to local tastes, such as greeting cards with popular Chinese astrological symbols.[62] Nokia did not, however, develop specific handset designs to specific markets. Via a subsidiary, Nokia did offer an expensive luxury subbrand (Vertu) in gold or platinum that should appeal to the rich and famous of this world, and Siemens offered "fashion accessory phones" under the name Xelibri.[63] In China, a taste for faux diamond-studded handsets developed that was considered kitschy and thus bad taste in the West. As a result, in China, handset brands, such as TCL, Ningbo Bird, and Amoisonic, quickly gained market share, and Nokia and Motorola were losing. Too late, Motorola started copying the diamond-studded phone designs so popular in China.[64] Coca-Cola, which had entered Stage 3 long ago, changed its strategy only at the end of the 20th century into one of local product development.

In Stage 3, marketing communications should be multilocal or differentiate by culture cluster. In this stage, both Nokia and Ericsson used pan-European advertising based on the "You can work where you want" appeal, which fits the cultural configuration of the Scandinavian countries of origin of the brands, not the south of Europe.

Of the three development stages, Stage 2 is the most important for international marketing because in that stage, markets start to differentiate, while the company still reaps the benefits of their successful Stage 1. If a company understands local consumer behavior in this stage, it is an investment that will pay off in Stage 3.

Summary

For global marketing and advertising, the choice is between global and local. In this book, we have argued that the real choice is between failure and success. One standard strategy has been assumed to reduce costs because of economies of scale. What is gained by cost reduction, however, is lost by loss of effectiveness. Consistency in presentation is another frequently heard argument for standardization.

This reflects a Western frame of mind that is not shared globally. If you want to reach consumers in different parts of the world, speak to them in a way they understand. How to speak in such a way can be learned not only by studying the minds and behavior of consumers across cultures but also by understanding how the worldview of managers is reflected in their strategies. At the highest level, corporate missions, visions, and identities are formulated that reflect the worldviews of top management. So do brand strategies and brand positioning statements reflect the worldview of brand managers. They tend to forget that markets are people.

Although several studies have pointed at greater effectiveness of local sensitivity, others point at an emerging more-or-less global consumer culture. By now, most marketers have understood that not all Asians are the same. Yet, for Europe, expectations are found that with greater economic integration, advertising will increasingly be standardized.[65] This is wishful thinking. This book has given plenty of examples of the lasting cultural differences across Europe.

In fact, the past years have seen increased cultural sensitivity of marketing managers and more research establishing insight in how culture influences consumer behavior. The new paradigm is cultural segmentation—defining markets based on their cultural specifics and developing culture-fit strategies. A strong global corporate identity can go together with cultural sensitivity. Instead of being consistent, brands should be pragmatic and adapt to the cultural mind-sets of consumers. This will be the future of global marketing, branding, and advertising.

Notes

1. Cavusgil, S. T., & Zou, S. (1994). Marketing strategy performance relationship: An investigation of the empirical link in export market ventures. *Journal of Marketing, 58*, 1–21.

2. Malhotra, S., & Sivakumar, K. (2011). Simultaneous determination of optimal cultural distance and market potential in international market entry. *International Marketing Review, 28*(6), 601–626.

3. Bart, C. (1998). Mission matters. *CPA Journal 8*, 56–57.

4. Murphy, J. J. (2004, August 8). The concepts of vision and mission revisited. Negotiation Academy. Retrieved November 21, 2004, from http://www.calumcoburn.co.uk/articles/articles-vision-mission/

5. Retrieved November 5, 2008, from http://www.toyota.co.jp

6. Retrieved November 5, 2008, from http://www.canon.com

7. Retrieved November 5, 2008, from http://www.samsung.com

8. Retrieved November 5, 2008, from http://www.ge.com/investors/investing/faqs.html

9. Retrieved November 5, 2008, from http://www.microsoft.com

10. Retrieved November 5, 2008, from http://www.philips.com/about/company/missionandvisionvaluesandstrategy/index.page

11. Retrieved November 5, 2008, from http://www.loreal.com/_en/_ww/html/our-company/the-1-oreal-spirit.aspx

12. Ind, N. (1992). *The corporate image: Strategies for effective identity programmes.* London: Kogan Page, p. 19.

13. Jun, J. W., & Lee, H.-S. (2007). Cultural differences in brand designs and tagline appeals. *International Marketing Review, 24*(4), 474–491.

14. Souiden, N., Kassim, N. M., & Hong, H. J. (2006). The effect of corporate branding dimensions on consumers' product evaluation, a cross-cultural analysis. *European Journal of Marketing, 40*(7/8), 825–845.

15. ACNielsen. (n.d.). *Global mega brand franchise: Extending brands within a global marketplace.* Retrieved June 25, 2004, from http://hu.nielsen.com/pubs/2003_q1_ci_mega .shtml

16. Retrieved November 6, 2008, from http://www.unilever.com/ourcompany/newsand- media/pressreleases/2008/

17. Murphy, J., & Scharl, A. (2007). An investigation of global versus local online branding. *International Marketing Review, 24*(3), 1265–1335.

18. Elements of the definition by the Public Relations Society of America, 1988.

19. Ruler, B. van, & Verçiç, D. (2002). *The* Bled Manifesto *on public relations.* Paper presented at the 9th International Public Relations Research Symposium, Bled, Slovenia, July 4–7.

20. Creedon, P., & Al-Khaja, M. (2005). Public relations and globalization: Building a case for cultural competency in public relations education. *Public Relations Review, 31*, 344–354.

21. Liu, X. (2006). Beauty is in the eye of the beholder: Public relations and multinational corporations. *International Journal of Advertising, 25*(4), 447–470.

22. Kim, Y., & Bae, J. (2006). Korean practitioners and journalists: Relational influences in news selection. *Public Relations Review, 32*, 241–245.

23. Huang, Y. H. (2003). A Chinese perspective of intercultural organization-public relationship. *Communication Studies 12*(4), 251–276.

24. Bardhan, N., & Sriramesh, K. (2006). Public relations in India. *Journal of Creative Communications, 1*(1), 39–60.

25. Hackley, C. A., Dong, Q., & Howard, T. L. (2009, March 11–14). Koichi Yamamura (Ed.). *International public relations faces challenges: The impact of palanca in shaping Mexico's public relations.* Paper presented at the 12th Annual International Public Relations Research Conference, March 11–14, Coral Gables, Florida (pp. 163–173). Retrieved February 5, 2012, from http://www.instituteforpr.org/wp-content/uploads/IPRRC_12_Proceedings.pdf

26. Jin, B., Park, J. Y., & Kim, J. (2008). Cross-cultural examination of the relationships among firm reputation, e-satisfaction, e-trust, and e-loyalty. *International Marketing Review, 25*(3), 324–337.

27. González-Herrero, A., & Ruiz de Valbuena, M. (2006). Trends in online media relations: Web-based corporate press rooms in leading international companies. *Public Relations Review, 32*, 267–275.

28. Bhatia, T. K., & Bhargava, M. (2008). Reaching the unreachable: Resolving globalization vs. localization paradox. *Journal of Creative Communications, 3*(2), 209–230.

29. Wang, J. (2008). *Brand new China: Advertising, media and commercial culture.* Cambridge, MA: Harvard University Press, p. 131.

30. Drewitt, N. (2001, June). Korea opportunities. *M&M Europe,* 15–22.

31. Wang, 2008, p. 131.

32. Wang, 2008, p. 151.

33. Sinha, D. (2011). *Consumer India: Inside the Indian mind and wallet.* Singapore: John Wiley & Sons (Asia), p. 98.

34. Grønlien, L. (2005). *Understanding the challenges of entering the Chinese market.* Trondheim: Norwegian University of Science and Technology, Department of Product Design.

35. *Businessweek.* (2006, January 23). Global packaging: The reality. Retrieved February 15, 2013, from http://userwww.sfsu.edu/hussain/mktg680/bw%20012306%20global%20 packaging%20reality.pdf

36. Choi, I., Nisbett, R. E., & Smith, E. E. (1997). Culture, category salience, and inductive reasoning. *Cognition, 65*, 15–32.

37. Van den Berg-Weitzel, L., & Van de Laar, G. (2001). Relation between culture and communication in packaging design. *Brand Management, 8*, 171–184.

38. Sinha, 2011, p. 91.

39. Banjo, S. (2012, September 27). Wal-Mart says time is right for Japan. *The Wall Street Journal*, retrieved February 15, 2013, from http://online.wsj.com/article/SB10000872396390 4435893045776356834903344436.html

40. Ho, C.-W., & Temperley, J. (2009). Consumers' reaction to Tesco's market entry in Taiwan: A comparison with the UK experience. *Proceedings of the Fifth Asia Pacific Retail Conference*, Hong Kong, August 25–27, 2009.

41. Suh, J. G. (2007, September 4–6). Entry and growth strategy of multinational retailers in Korea: A case of Samsung-Tesco. *Proceedings of the Fourth Asia Pacific Retail Conference*, College of Management, Mahidol University, Bangkok, Thailand.

42. Zhang, Y. (2009, July 26). *Design for global markets. Balancing unilateral global brands with local cultural values* (Master's thesis). University of Cincinati, Ohio.

43. Parry, S. (2009, January 5). Shoppers shun flagship M&S store in China for being "too British and too expensive." *Daily Mail, MailOnline*. Retrieved January 5, 2009, from http://www.dailymail.co.uk/news/article-1104775/Shoppers-shun-flagship-M-S-China-British-expensive.html

44. These are examples of findings by students of the master of retail design at the Willem de Kooning Academy at Rotterdam, 2006, 2007, and 2008. They compared the Dutch supermarket Albert Heijn with the Belgian supermarket Delhaize, using stores of the same size in similar neighborhoods.

45. Ness, A., Choi, A., & Kuo, Y. (2009, August 25–27). Success and failure in southern China shopping mall development. In *Proceedings of the Fifth Conference on Retailing in Asia Pacific*. Oxford Institute of Retail Management and The Hong Kong Polytechnic University, Institute for Enterprise.

46. Schmitt, B. H., & Pan, Y. (1994). Managing corporate and brand identities in the Asia-Pacific region. *California Management Review, 36*, 32–48.

47. Hsieh, M. H. (2004). Measuring global brand equity using cross-national survey data. *Journal of International Marketing, 12*(2), 28–57.

48. Koçak, A., Abimbola, T., & Özer, A. (2007). Consumer brand equity in a cross-cultural replication: An evaluation of a scale. *Journal of Marketing Management, 23*(1–2), 157–173; Yoo, B., & Donthu, N. (2002). Testing cross-cultural invariance of the brand equity creation process. *Journal of Product and Brand Management, 11*(6), 380–398.

49. The basis of the text on brand positioning is by Dr. Arne Maas, president of Ameuse consultancy, who co-authored this chapter for the third edition.

50. Roll, M. (2006). *Asian brand strategy: How Asia builds strong brands*. Trowbridge, UK: Cromwell Press Limited, p. 40.

51. Bengtsson, A., Bardhi, F., & Venkatraman, M. (2010). How global brands travel with consumers: An examination of the relationship between brand consistency and meaning across national boundaries. *International Marketing Review, 27*(5), 519–540.

52. Hollis, N. (2010). *The global brand*. Palgrave MacMillan, p. 127.

53. Foscht, T., Maloles, III, C., Swoboda, B., Morschett, D., & Sinha, I. (2008). The impact of culture on brand perception: A six-nation study. *Journal of Product and Brand Management, 17*(3), 131–142.

54. Belson, K., & Bremmer, B. (2004). *Hello Kitty. The remarkable story of Sanrio and the billion dollar feline phenomenon*. Singapore: John Wiley and Sons, p. 166.

55. Wang, 2008, pp. 91–92.

56. Cayla, J., & Eckhardt, G. M. (2007). Asian brands without borders: Regional opportunities and challenges. *International Marketing Review, 24*(4), 444–456.

57. Keller, K. L. (2009). Building strong brands in a modern marketing communications environment. *Journal of Marketing Communications, 15*(2–3), 139–155.

58. Olson, J. C., & Reynolds, T. J. (1983). Understanding consumers' cognitive structures: Implications for advertising strategy. In L. Perry & A. G. Woodside (Eds.), *Advertising and consumer psychology*. Lexington, MA: Lexington Books.

59. Gutman, J. A. (1982). Means-end chain model based on consumer categorization processes. *Journal of Marketing, 46*, 60–72.

60. Reynolds, T. J., & Gutman, J. (1988, February-March). Laddering theory, method, analysis, and interpretation. *Journal of Advertising Research*, 29–37.

61. Percy, L. (n.d.). *Tools for building strong brands*. Retrieved December 2003 from http://www.larrypercy.com/tools.html

62. Cai, Y. (2001, Fall). Design strategies for global products. *Design Management Journal*, pp. 59–64.

63. The origins of Vertu. (2003, February 22). *Economist*, pp. 66–67.

64. The local touch. (2003, March 8). *Economist*, p. 62.

65. Jiang, J., & Wei, R. (2012). Influences of culture and market convergence on the international advertising strategies of multinational corporations in North America, Europe and Asia. *International Marketing Review, 29*(6), 597–622.

Appendix A

Hofstede Country Scores and Gross National Income (GNI)/Capita at Purchase Power Parity 2011, for 66 Countries

Country	Abbreviation	GNI/cap at PPP 2011, US$	IDV-COL	PDI	LTO	MAS	UAI	IVR
Argentina	ARG	17,250	46	49	20	56	86	61
Australia	AUL	36,410	90	36	21	61	51	71
Austria	AUT	42,080	55	11	60	79	70	62
Bangladesh	BAN	1,940	20	80	47	55	55	19
Belgium	BEL	39,270	75	65	81	54	94	56
Brazil	BRA	11,500	38	69	43	49	76	59
Bulgaria	BUL	13,980	30	70	69	40	85	15
Canada	CAN	39,730	80	39	36	52	48	68
China	CHI	8,450	20	80	87	66	30	23
Chile	CHL	16,330	23	63	30	28	86	68
Colombia	COL	9,640	13	67	13	64	80	83
Croatia	CRO	19,330	33	73	58	40	80	33
Czech Republic	CZE	24,280	58	57	70	57	74	29
Denmark	DEN	42,300	74	18	34	16	23	69
Ecuador	ECA	8,310	8	78		63	67	
Estonia	EST	20,830	60	40	82	30	60	16
Finland	FIN	38,500	63	33	38	26	59	57

(Continued)

(Continued)

Country	Abbreviation	GNI/cap at PPP 2011, US$	IDV-COL	PDI	LTO	MAS	UAI	IVR
France	FRA	35,650	71	68	63	43	86	47
Great Britain	GBR	35,940	89	35	51	66	35	69
Germany	GER	39,970	67	35	82	66	65	40
Ghana	GHA	1,820	20	77	4	46	54	72
Greece	GRE	26,090	35	60	45	57	112	49
Guatemala	GUA	4,800	6	95		37	101	
Hong Kong, China	HOK	51,490	25	68	60	57	29	16
Hungary	HUN	20,260	80	46	58	88	82	31
Indonesia	IDO	4,530	14	78	61	46	48	37
India	IND	3,620	48	77	50	56	40	26
Iran	IRA	11,400	41	58	13	43	59	40
Ireland	IRE	33,230	70	28	24	68	35	64
Israel	ISR	27,120	54	13	37	47	81	
Italy	ITA	32,710	76	50	61	70	75	29
Japan	JPN	35,530	46	54	87	95	92	41
Korea Rep.	KOR	30,340	18	60	100	39	85	29
Latvia	LAT	17,820	70	44	68	9	63	12
Lithuania	LIT	19,690	60	42	81	19	65	15
Malaysia	MAL	15,190	26	104	40	50	36	57
Mexico	MEX	15,060	30	81	24	69	82	97
Malta	MLT	24,170	59	56	47	47	96	65
Morocco	MOR	4,910	46	70	14	53	68	25
Netherlands	NET	43,260	80	38	67	14	53	68
Nigeria	NIG	2,300	20	77	13	46	54	84
Norway	NOR	62,970	69	31	34	8	50	55
New Zealand	NZL	28,970	79	22	32	58	49	74
Pakistan	PAK	2,880	14	55	49	50	70	0
Panama	PAN	14,740	11	95		44	86	
Peru	PER	10,160	16	64	25	42	87	46

Country	Abbreviation	GNI/cap at PPP 2011, US$	IDV-COL	PDI	LTO	MAS	UAI	IVR
Philippines	PHI	4,160	32	94	27	64	44	41
Poland	POL	20,480	60	68	37	64	93	29
Portugal	POR	24,480	27	63	28	31	104	33
Romania	ROM	15,140	30	90	51	42	90	19
Russia	RUS	19,940	39	93	81	36	95	19
(El) Salvador	SAL	6,690	19	66	19	40	94	88
Serbia	SER	11,640	25	86	52	43	92	28
Singapore	SIN	59,790	20	74	71	48	8	45
Slovak Republic	SLK	22,230	52	104	76	110	51	28
Slovenia	SLV	26,960	27	71	48	19	88	47
Spain	SPA	31,660	51	57	47	42	86	43
Sweden	SWE	42,200	71	31	52	5	29	77
Switzerland	SWI	52,320	68	34	73	70	58	66
Taiwan	TAI	38,200	17	58	92	45	69	49
Thailand	THA	8,390	20	64	31	34	64	45
Turkey	TUR	17,340	37	66	45	45	85	49
Uruguay	URU	14,740	36	61	26	38	100	53
U.S.A.	USA	48,890	91	40	25	62	46	68
Venezuela	VEN	12,620	12	81	15	73	76	99
Vietnam	VIE	3,260	20	70	57	40	30	35

SOURCES: Hofstede et al. (2010); Latvia and Lithuania: Huettinger, M. (2006). Cultural Dimensions in Business Life: Hofstede's Indices for Latvia and Lithuania. *Journal of Baltic Management*. Data for Ghana and Nigeria for four dimensions are Hofstede's scores for West Africa, LTO and IVR are from Minkov, in Hofstede et al. 2010. GNI/capita 2011 (at Purchasing Power Parity): World Development Indicators database, World Bank national accounts data, http://data.worldbank.org/indicator/NY.GNP.PCAP.CD. GNI/capita Taiwan from CIA World Factbook.

Appendix B

Data Sources

Many secondary data sources were used for the cultural analysis in this book. Databases are of several types.

1. Consumer surveys sponsored by the media that ask questions about consumption of products and media usage. The surveys used are the *Reader's Digest* Surveys, *A Survey of Europe Today 1970* and *Eurodata 1991,* and the *European Media and Marketing Surveys (EMS)* of 1995, 1997, 1999, 2007, and 2012.

2. Statistical data on sales of various products measured in value and liters or kilograms per capita from commercial sources like *Euromonitor*. Several global market research companies publish data on the Internet. Examples are TNS, Ipsos, and TGI.

3. Economic statistics published by governmental or nongovernmental organizations: World Bank, United Nations, OECD, and Eurostat.

4. Surveys of opinions and habits of citizens of countries published by governmental organizations. The major studies used are the Eurobarometer reports published by the European Commission Directorate.

5. Academically driven value studies. Examples are the *World Values Survey* and the *European Value Study.*

6. Industry-driven studies, for example, by the tourism trade, car industry, or telecommunications industry. Examples are International Telecommunications Union (ITU), which offers data on telephones, Hotrec on tourism, and the Beverage Marketing Corporation of New York.

7. Studies on specific areas of consumer behavior conducted and published by market research agencies, media, or companies. Examples are studies by Roper Starch, Nielsen, Synovate, or TGI, and the "Trusted Brands" study by *Reader's Digest.*

This appendix describes the studies in Categories 1 through 6. In addition to these, the notes at the end of each chapter mention various other studies from which data were drawn.

1. Media-Sponsored Consumer Surveys

The Reader's Digest Surveys. Studies of the lifestyles, consumer spending habits, and attitudes of people in 17 European countries, published in 1970 and 1991. The data of the 1970 survey were the results of a probability sample representative of the national population aged 18 and over. Comparable sample surveys were conducted in 16 Western European countries in early 1969. Approximately 24,000 personal interviews were involved. *Eurodata 1991* was based on comparable sample surveys conducted in the early summer (May/June) of 1990. Approximately 22,500 personal interviews were involved. The study was commissioned by the Reader's Digest Association, Inc., in cooperation with its editions and offices in Europe. With the exception of Sweden, it was conducted by the Gallup-affiliated companies and institutes in Europe and was coordinated by Gallup, London. Probability samples were employed in each of the 17 countries, representative of the population aged 18 and over, living in private households. Reader's Digest Association Limited, London.

Countries surveyed were Austria, Belgium, Denmark, Finland, France, Germany, Greece, Ireland, Italy, Luxembourg, the Netherlands, Norway, Portugal, Spain, Sweden, Switzerland, and the United Kingdom.

The European Media and Marketing Survey (EMS) (originally conducted by Inter/View-NSS [http://www.interview-nss.com], Amsterdam, the Netherlands. Data used from surveys of 1995, 1997, 1999, 2007, and 2012). Originally, the study was conducted by Inter/View-NSS, which was later owned by Synovate, and in 2013 by Ipsos, which continues conducting the surveys (www.ipsos.com). EMS is a European "industry" survey (later extended to other world regions), which measures national and international media usage as well as ownership of some products and services. EMS covers the main income earners living in the top 20% of households in the survey countries, an estimated population of almost 44 million affluent Europeans. Data are based on interviews and self-completion questionnaires. Reports are available to subscribers only. In 2012, 21 countries were surveyed: Austria, Belgium, Czech Republic, Denmark, Finland, France, Germany, Greece, Hungary, Ireland, Italy, Luxembourg, the Netherlands, Norway, Poland, Portugal, Spain, Sweden, Switzerland, Turkey and the United Kingdom. EMS is expanding to Africa and the Middle East.

Synovate PAX is the Asia-Pacific Cross-Media Survey that offers continuous tracking data on media, product, and brand consumption from a sample of over 20,000 high-end consumers. It covers large cities in Asia: Bangkok, Hong Kong, Jakarta, Kuala Lumpur, Manila, Singapore, Taipei, Seoul, and Tokyo; in India: Mumbai,

New Delhi, and Bangalore; in Australia: Sydney and Melbourne. *PAX Digital Life* provides data on digital media usage.

Ipsos Young Asians Survey (2010) provides data on digital media consumption of young people aged 15–24 in Asia. It is based on a sample of 13,708 in China, Hong Kong China, India, Indonesia, Korea, Myanmar, Philippines, Singapore, Taiwan, Thailand, and Vietnam.

2. Commercial Statistical Databases and Market Research

Euromonitor. Consumer Europe 1997 is a compendium of pan-European market information on sales, in value and volume, of a large number of products; and *Consumer International 1997,* by Euromonitor PLC, London. Euromonitor publishes databases on consumption and ownership of products worldwide (*Consumer World*) and category-specific data reports (www.euromonitor.com).

Countries included in *Consumer Europe 1997* were Austria, Belgium, Denmark, Finland, France, Germany, Greece, Ireland, Italy, Luxembourg, the Netherlands, Norway, Portugal, Spain, Sweden, Switzerland, and the United Kingdom.

TNS Digital World (2008) and *Digital Life* (2011) are global reports by tns-global, published on the website http://www.tnsdigitallife.com. TNS is a research company that is part of a consultancy firm (Kantar). In 2008, the company interviewed 27,522 people aged 18–55 in 16 countries around the world about online behavior, trust in online sources, or preferences for recommendations by friends; and in 2011 in 60 countries, 72,000 people were asked about what they do online and why they do it.

TGI (www.globaltgi.com) annually publishes its TGI product book with data on product consumption; in 2012, data were published for 62 countries worldwide.

Nielsen is a global market research company, which publishes global trends—with excerpts from their findings, but usually for a limited number of countries.

3. Economic Statistics

World Bank. Annual World Development Reports include economic data and data on infrastructure; separate reports on world development indicators; data on most countries in the world (World Bank, New York (www.worldbank.org). Income data from Table 1. *Key Indicators of Development* include data on daily newspapers, Internet, PCs, and so on in Table 5.11. *The Information Age.*

United Nations. UN Statistical Yearbooks include economic data and data on product ownership and media, with data on most countries in the world. New York: United Nations (http://unstats.un.org/unsd/syb/).

OECD is the Organisation for Economic Co-operation and Development. They publish several statistics on social indicators, such as income, population developments, labor, and so on, but also some special reports such as on risky behavior, leisure time, and time spent eating. For example, *Society at a Glance* (2009) includes data on health care, leisure time, and eating time. Data on literacy are provided by the OECD Programme for International Student Assessment (PISA).

Eurostat. (a) Annual Reports include demographic data and data on consumption. Data cover the member states of the European Union. (b) Social Indicators Reports. (c) Family Budgets Surveys. The report *Consumers in Europe: Facts and Figures* (2001) covers data from 1996 to 2000, and it is published by the Office for Official Publications of the European Communities, Luxembourg. Data are on European Union member countries Austria, Belgium, Denmark, Finland, France, Germany, Greece, Ireland, Italy, Luxembourg, the Netherlands, Portugal, Spain, Sweden, the United Kingdom, and some data for candidate member countries Bulgaria, Cyprus, Czech Republic, Estonia, Hungary, Lithuania, Latvia, Malta, Poland, Romania, Slovenia, Slovakia, and Turkey. The report *How Consumers Spend Their Time* (2002) covers data from 1998–2002. The report *Cinema, TV and Radio in the EU*, with data 1980–2002, covers statistics on audiovisual services.

4. Governmental Opinion Surveys

Eurobarometer. The standard Eurobarometer reports cover the resident populations (aged 15 years and over) of the European Union member states. The basic sample design applied in all member states is a multistage, random (probability) one. The number of interviews for Report 53 (October 2000) was 16,078. The results of Eurobarometer studies are reported in the form of tables, data files, and analyses that are published by the European Commission Directorate, Brussels. Until 2004, separate surveys were conducted for the EU member states and for the EU candidate countries. After the EU enlargements in 2004 and 2007, the candidate countries were included in the standard Eurobarometer. Since 2007, surveys cover 24 or 27 countries. Some go beyond the EU and add countries like Switzerland, Turkey, and Israel.

The results are published on the Internet server of the European Commission: http://europa.eu.int/comm/dg10/epo. Each year standard reports are published including specific questions that are repeated every year, such as the degree of satisfaction with life in general.

Several special reports are published, and some are repeated in the years after, which makes comparison possible. Examples are *Measuring the Information Society* (1997 and 2000); *The Young Europeans* (1997, 2001, and 2007); and *Trend Variables 1974–1994* (November 1994); One series of surveys is called Special Eurobarometer (EBS), another Flash Eurobarometer. Data from the following flash and Special Eurobarometer surveys were used for this book.

Eurobarometer. (1997). *Standard Eurobarometer Report* (47)

Eurobarometer. (2000). *How Europeans See Themselves*

Eurobarometer. (2000). *Measuring Information Society* (53)

Eurobarometer. (2001). *Standard Eurobarometer Report* (55)

Eurobarometer. (2002). *Standard Eurobarometer Report* (57.1)

Eurobarometer. (2002). *Consumer Survey.* Flash Eurobarometer (117)

Eurobarometer. (2003). *Globalisation.* Flash Eurobarometer (151b)

Eurobarometer. (2004). *Citizens of the European Union and Sport* (EBS 213)

Eurobarometer. (2005). *Social Values, Science and Technology* (EBS 225)

Eurobarometer (2006, 2008, 2011). *E-Communications Household Survey* (EBS 249, 293, and 362)

Eurobarometer. (2007). *European Social Reality* (EBS 273)

Eurobarometer. (2007). *European Cultural Values* (EBS 278)

Eurobarometer. (2007). *Young Europeans: A Survey Among Young People Aged Between 15–30 in the European Union.* Flash Eurobarometer Report (202)

Eurobarometer. (2008). *E-Communications Household Survey* (EBS 293)

Eurobarometer. (2008). *Information Society as Seen by EU Citizens.* Flash Eurobarometer (241)

Eurobarometer. (2008). *Attitudes of European Citizens Towards the Environment* (EBS 295)

Eurobarometer. (2008). *Towards a Safer Use of the Internet for Children in the EU—A Parents' Perspective.* Flash Eurobarometer (248)

Eurobarometer. (2009). *Confidence in the Information Society.* Flash Eurobarometer (250)

Eurobarometer. (2010). *Science and Technology* (EBS 340)

Eurobarometer. (2011). *Consumer Empowerment* (EBS 342)

Eurobarometer. (2011). *Youth on the Move.* Flash Eurobarometer (319)

5. Academically Driven Value Studies

World Values Survey. A study of values via public opinion surveys was started in the early 1980s as the European Values Study. In 1981, it was carried out in 10 EU member states. In 1990, a second round was started, and 16 countries were added.

It was renamed the *World Values Survey (WVS)*. Four waves have been conducted: in 1981–1984, 1990–1993, 1995–1997, and 1999–2004. It eventually covered 53 countries, representing about 70% of the world's population, with a questionnaire including more than 360 forced-choice questions. Examples of areas covered are ecology, economy, education, emotion, family, health, happiness, religion, leisure, and friends.

The 1990 data are published in the following:

Inglehart, R., Basañez, M., & Moreno, A. (1998). *Human Values and Beliefs: A Cross-Cultural Sourcebook.* Ann Arbor: University of Michigan Press.

Data for Europe of 1999/2000 are published in the following:

European Values Study: A Third Wave. Source Book of the 1999/2000 European Values Study Surveys. Loek Halman, Tilburg University. PO Box 90153, 5000 LE Tilburg, The Netherlands (evs@uvt.nl). The complete data files 1998–2004 can now be downloaded from http://www.worldvaluessurvey.org

European Social Survey. Another survey is *The European Social Survey* (R. Jowell and the Central Co-ordinating Team, Centre for Comparative Social Surveys, City University, London). The European Social Survey (the ESS) is a biennial multi-country survey covering over 30 nations. The first round was fielded in 2002/2003, the second in 2004/2005, and the third in 2006/2007. The latest data are of 2012. The project is funded jointly by the European Commission, the European Science Foundation and academic funding bodies in each participating country. The project is directed by a Central Co-ordinating Team led by Roger Jowell at the Centre for Comparative Social Surveys, City University, London. http://www.europeansocial-survey.org. For information contact ess@city.ac.uk.

The questionnaire includes two main sections, each consisting of approximately 120 items; a "core" module, which will remain relatively constant from round to round, plus two or more "rotating" modules, repeated at intervals. The core module aims to monitor change and continuity in a wide range of social variables, including media use, social and public trust; political interest and participation; sociopolitical orientations, governance, and efficacy; moral, political, and social values; social exclusion, national, ethnic, and religious allegiances; well-being, health, and security; demographics and socioeconomics. In addition, a supplementary questionnaire is presented to respondents at the end of the main interview. The first part of this questionnaire is a human values scale (part of the core), while the second is devoted to measures to help evaluate the reliability and validity of items in the main questionnaire. The full data file (in SPSS) can be downloaded from http://ess.nsd.uib.no.

6. Industry-Driven Organizations

International Telecommunications Union (ITU) offers data on telephony worldwide (www.itu.int).

The Beverage Marketing Corporation of New York sells worldwide data on soft drinks (www.beveragemarketing.com).

Hotrec publishes data for the tourism trade: hotels, restaurants, and cafés in Europe (www.hotrec.org).

ComScore, Inc. is a Global Internet Information Provider. It maintains proprietary databases that provide a continuous, real-time measurement of the myriad ways in which the Internet is used and the wide variety of activities that are occurring online (www.comscore.com).

Ofcom—Office of Communication, is an independent organization that regulates the UK's broadcasting, telecommunications, and wireless communications sectors. Publications are communication market reports providing data on television, radio, and telecommunications for several countries (www.ofcom.org.uk). Especially relevant is the *Ofcom International Telecommunications Market Report* (2010).

Index

About the Author

Marieke de Mooij, PhD (Netherlands), is an independent researcher and consultant in cross-cultural communications and has wide experience in teaching about culture, marketing, and advertising around the world. She is a retired *profesora asociada* at the University of Navarra, Spain. She is the author of several academic publications on the influence of culture on marketing, advertising, and consumer behavior. Her other book published by SAGE is titled *Consumer Behavior and Culture: Consequences for Global Marketing and Advertising* (2nd edition). A book on communication theory and culture is titled *Human and Mediated Communication Around the World: A Comprehensive Review and Analysis* (Springer International).